THE ROMAN DE LA ROSE

GARLAND MEDIEVAL BIBLIOGRAPHIES
(VOL. 8)

GARLAND REFERENCE LIBRARY
OF THE HUMANITIES
(VOL. 1358)

GARLAND MEDIEVAL BIBLIOGRAPHIES

Europe in Transition: A Select, Annotated Bibliography of the Twelfth-Century Renaissance
Chris D. Ferguson

François Villon: A Bibliography
Robert D. Peckham

Medieval Sexuality: A Research Guide
Joyce E. Salisbury

War in the Middle Ages: A Bibliographic Guide
Everett U. Crosby

The Medieval Consolation of Philosophy: An Annotated Bibliography
Noel Harold Kaylor, Jr.

The Roman de la rose: An Annotated Bibliography
Heather M. Arden

Giovanni Boccaccio: An Annotated Bibliography
Joseph P. Consoli

Roger Bacon: An Annotated Bibliography
Jeremiah Hackett

Medieval Visions of Heaven and Hell: A Sourcebook
Eileen Gardiner

Sports and Games of the Middle Ages
John Marshall Carter

Sir Gawain and the Green Knight: *An Annotated Bibliography, 1978–1989*
Meg Stainsby

Beowulf *Scholarship: An Annotated Bibliography, 1979-1990*
Robert J. Hasenfratz

The Medieval Charlemagne Legend: An Annotated Bibliography
Susan E. Farrier. Dutch materials treated by Geert H. M. Claassens

Pilgrimage in the Middle Ages: A Research Guide
Linda Kay Davidson and Maryjane Dunn-Wood

THE ROMAN DE LA ROSE
An Annotated Bibliography

Heather M. Arden

GARLAND PUBLISHING, INC. • NEW YORK & LONDON
1993

© 1993 Heather M. Arden
All rights reserved

Library of Congress Cataloging-in-Publication Data

Arden, Heather, 1943–
    The Roman de la rose : an annotated bibliography / by Heather M. Arden.
        p.   cm. — (Garland medieval bibliographies ; vol. 8) (Garland reference library of the humanities ; vol. 1358)
    ISBN 0-8240-5799-6 (alk. paper)
    1. Guillaume, de Lorris, fl. 1230. Roman de la rose—Bibliography. 2. Love poetry, French—History and criticism—Bibliography. 3. Jean, de Meun, d. 1305—Bibliography. 4. Love poetry, French—Bibliography. I. Title. II. Series. III. Series: Garland reference library of the humanities ; vol. 1358.
Z8374.6478.A73   1993
[PQ1528]
841'.1—dc20   93-15492
                                                                CIP

Printed on acid-free, 250-year-life paper
Manufactured in the United States of America

For my mother, Catherine Schwartz

> C'est cele qui tant a de pris
> et tant est digne d'estre amee
> qu'el doit estre Rose clamee
>
> *Roman de la rose* 42-44

TABLE OF CONTENTS

Preface	ix
Introduction	xiii
Chapter 1 - The Text of the *Roman de la rose*	1
I. Complete editions	1
II. Partial editions	6
III. Translations	7
IV. Studies of manuscripts and editions; concordances	20
Chapter 2 - Other works by or attributed to Jean de Meun	33
Chapter 3 - Critical studies of the *Roman de la rose*	61
Chapter 4 - The Influence of the *Roman de la rose*	265
Chapter 5 - Miscellaneous	361
Index	365

> La corruption de ce siecle où l'on empesche que la verité soit ouvertement divulguée me contraint à... cacher mes principales reprehensions, soubs des songes qui sembleront sans doute pleins de niaiseries à des ignorans, qui ne pourront pas penetrer jusques au fond.
>
> Sorel, *Francion*

PREFACE

Scholars have long recognized the importance of the thirteenth-century French romance, the *Roman de la rose*. It has been described as "medieval France's greatest poem, a work without which Dante's *Comedy* would have been inconceivable" (Karl Uitti); "un éblouissant chef-d'oeuvre" (Paul Zumthor); "the most important (in the sense of being the most widely read and most influential) vernacular poem of the Middle Ages" (John Fleming). It has been said to rival "the Bible, the *Aeneid*, and the *Metamorphoses* as the most influential works of Western literature" (Stephen Barney). In addition to the many literary works influenced by the *Rose*, critical works have, in the last hundred years, become more numerous and more sophisticated. More than 300 scholarly works on the *Rose* have been published in the past twenty-five years--almost half the total bibliography on the poem. Therefore, it seemed to the editors at Garland Publishing and to me that the time was right for an annotated bibliography of scholarship on the *Rose*. This book provides an overview of research not only on the romance itself but on related areas, such as the Middle English *Romaunt*.

The principal focus of the bibliography is twentieth-century criticism; virtually all modern critical discussions of the *Rose*, both in books and articles, are included. In addition, the bibliography contains chapters on editions and translations of the *Rose*, Jean de Meun's translations, manuscript studies, and the influence of the *Rose* on later writers. The chapter on the *Rose*'s influence also includes works on the fifteenth-century debate called the Querelle de la Rose and on Chaucer. While these chapters do not attempt to be as complete as the one on critical studies, the titles included give scholars the necessary basis for further study. More details about the principles and structure of the bibliography are given in the Introduction.

The task of putting together a bibliography of this size and complexity was greatly helped by a number of people. I thank my assistant, Kathryn M. Lorenz, who wrote some of the entries and helped locate materials. In addition, other scholars wrote some of the foreign language entries: Keith Busby, Maria Romagnoli Brackett, Anita Suess-Kaushik, and Judith S. Zollinger. Their willingness to help and their careful annotations have made this bibliography more complete. Special thanks go to my "foreign correspondent," Leslie C. Brook of the University of Birmingham, England, who generously helped with bibliographical information on European publications and Jean de Meun's translation of the letters of Abelard and Heloise, on which he is a specialist. I also want to thank the other scholars who helped with information and suggestions: Paul Burrell, Richard K. Emmerson, Kathryn Gutzwiller, Sylvia Huot, Kornel Huvos, Douglas Kelly, Betty Kooris, Jeanne Nightingale, Jonathan Riess, Armando Romero, Connie Scarborough, and my department chair, Judith Muyskens, who contributed funds and encouragement throughout--to borrow a phrase from Christine de Pizan--"le long procès."

Many libraries helped make possible the research for this bibliography. The librarians of the University of Cincinnati Inter Library Loan Service were unfailingly patient and persistent; special thanks to Christine Brunkala and Linda Gromen. Thanks also to Daniel D. Gottlieb, Don Tolzmann, and above all Leslie V. Vuylsteke, a genius at resolving bibliographical problems. I also express my appreciation for the help of the librarians of the Bibliothèque Nationale in Paris, the Library of Congress, the Widener Library at Harvard, and the Inter Library Loan departments of the hundreds of other libraries who made this bibliography possible. The University of Cincinnati contributed funds for travel and research expenses; I thank the Taft Fund and the University Research Council for their support.

Phyllis Oberacker, who designed and produced the final camera-ready copy, deserves special acknowledgement and thanks. Finally, to the man who not only tolerated my obsession with the *Rose* for five years and even encouraged me during moments of discouragement but also helped edit the text of the bibliography, my husband, Bruce Craddock: thank you.

It has been challenging, frustrating, and enlightening to spend five years in the realm of *Rose* scholarship. I hope that the synopses offered here will stimulate and facilitate the long dialogue on the *Rose* that began over seven centuries ago, when Jean de Meun picked up a pen and wrote the first lines of his continuation, "Et si l'ai je perdue, espoir, / a poi que ne m'en desespoir" (ll. 4029-30).

INTRODUCTION

ce est li Romanz de la Rose
ou l'art d'Amors est tote enclose

In the century since Ernest Langlois's *Origines et sources du "Roman de la rose"* showed the way to a more contextual approach to the *Roman de la rose*, this most popular and influential of medieval French romances has moved from the periphery of scholarly attention to near the center. Scholarship on the *Rose*, which today shows increased respect for the romance and a more nuanced appreciation of its poetic principles, has discussed such varied topics as manuscript marginalia, the *Rose*'s influence on Rabelais and Voltaire, and Jean de Meun's house in Paris. The *Roman de la rose* touches on many aspects of medieval and Renaissance thought and literature; in the words of Charles Muscatine, "There are very few paths through medieval life and thought that do not cross here" (*Chaucer and the French Tradition* 72). Since space limitations prevent the discussion here of all the topics related to the *Rose* and covered in the works annotated in this bibliography, this introduction will outline the principal critical questions that scholars have raised. The organization of the bibliography itself is described at the end of the introduction.

THE HISTORY OF *ROSE* SCHOLARSHIP

Scholarship on the *Rose* can be divided into five general kinds of studies: literary history, sources, allegorical meaning, literary techniques, and influence.

Literary History

> *car quant Guillaumes cessera,*
> *Jehans le continuera,*
> *enprés sa mort, que je ne mante,*
> *anz trespassez plus de xl..*

There has been much progress in this century in establishing the literary history of the *Rose* and its authors. Until the mid-nineteenth century scholars had few facts but much hearsay and speculation. The work is attributed to two authors, Guillaume de Lorris and Jean de Meun (also spelled Meung or Mehun), both from the province of Orleans, because this is what le Dieu d'Amour tells us at the midpoint of the *Rose* (but see Dragonetti's contradictory view).[1] While some information has been gathered about Jean, we have no facts about Guillaume. Scholars have disputed the town of his birth (see Guillon, Jarry), and the possibility has even been suggested that he is the fictional creation of Jean de Meun (see Hult, Dragonetti). Based on the social values expressed in his poem, most scholars accept the hypothesis that Guillaume was noble, but Ott argues for a bourgeois origin. Guillaume's narrator, whom scholars often identify with the poet himself, tells us that he is twenty-five at the time of composing the *Rose*, which is the account of a dream he had five years earlier. Guillaume may have died before completing his poem (again based on the remarks of le Dieu d'Amour, ll. 10531-34 [see discussion of edition used p. xxvii]), although some scholars have suggested that the first part may be complete as it stands (Hult, Strohm) and others have reconstructed what the ending might have been (Kelly). It has been observed that it would have been indiscreet for Guillaume to complete the dream since he claims to be talking about a real-life experience with a real lady who might take offense. One early scholar even hypothesized that Jean destroyed Guillaume's ending in order to substitute his own (Paul Huot). Thus Guillaume remains a mysterious figure.

While we know almost nothing about Guillaume, we appear to know too much about Jean: over the centuries there have been many speculations, mistaken beliefs, and apocryphal stories about Jean--that he wrote the romance in the early fourteenth century, that he limped, that he had a personal grudge against women, that he played a trick on the mendicant orders at his death--until scholars such as Quicherat and Thomas began to uncover facts about Jean de Meun's life and the dating of the romance. Documentary evidence places Jean in the early fourteenth century in Paris (the site of his house is today marked by a plaque), where he evidently earned a master of arts degree. He died before November 1305. Manuscripts of the *Rose* give his family name as Chopinel or Clopinel and his birthplace as Meun-sur-Loire (Lecoy ll. 10535-37). Jean tells us in the preface to his translation of Boethius's *De consolatione Philosophiae* that he translated a number of Latin works: "je Jehan de Meun qui jadis ou Rommant de la Rose, puis que Jalousie ot mis en prison Bel Acueil, enseignai la maniere du chastel prendre et de la rose cueillir et translatay de latin en françois le livre Vegece de Chevalerie et le livre des Merveilles de Hyrlande et la Vie et les Epistres Pierres Abaelart et Heloys sa fame et le livre Aelred de Esperituelle Amitié, envoie ore Boece de Consolacion que j'ai translaté de latin en françois" (see Dedeck-Héry's edition). Only his translations of the letters of Abelard and Heloise, the *Consolation* (which Chaucer probably used for his translation), and the *Art de chevalerie* still exist. A number of manuscripts attribute a *Testament* and a *Codicile* to Jean, but scholars have not established their authenticity. Many other works have been attributed to him over the years (see Langlois edition, 1:24-25), primarily alchemical works, but the continuation of the *Rose* is the only work of fiction universally accepted as authentic.

----

[1] Representative works will be referred to in the Introduction by the author's last name (or first and last names, if needed to distinguish between two authors). For more information on the topic, the reader should consult the entries for each author.

The dates attributed to the *Rose* varied considerably until scholars realized the implications of Jean's discussion of Charles d'Anjou and Manfred (Lecoy ll. 6601-58). These remarks suggest that the second part of the *Rose* was composed in 1270-1276 or earlier. Again turning to le Dieu d'Amour (ll. 10557-60), we learn that Jean continued the poem more than forty years after Guillaume ceased writing, which would place the composition of the first part about 1225-1230. Thus the two parts of the *Rose* span the reign of Saint Louis, fifty years marked by great intellectual, literary, and social change in France.

Another aspect of the literary history of the *Rose* that has begun to receive serious study are its many manuscripts--more than 300 are still in existence, dating from the late thirteenth to the sixteenth centuries. Again it was Langlois who first undertook a systematic study of this important aspect of the *Rose*'s history: in preparation for his edition of the *Rose* he examined 215 manuscripts and classified them into families. Although flawed, Langlois's study has not yet been replaced. In addition, a number of manuscripts and fragments have since been discovered. Many *Rose* manuscripts contain beautiful miniatures; many also have marginal notes and glosses. After Fleming first used the miniatures to help interpret the romance, other scholars have looked at what the miniatures, glosses, and other aspects of the manuscripts can tell us about medieval views of the *Rose* (see Braet, Huot, Walters).

All manuscripts but one contain both parts of the *Rose*; in addition some contain an anonymous 76-line continuation. There is disagreement among scholars over the popularity of the first part, since it appears independently in only one manuscript: would it have survived without Jean's continuation? In any case, the manuscript tradition is remarkably stable, especially for the continuation, despite numerous variants and added or omitted lines. That is, the *Rose* appears to have been accepted as a book in the modern sense and was not revised or adapted to the same extent as, for example, the Arthurian romances. There was one important early adapter, however, a thirteenth-century cleric named Gui de Mori, who edited and revised the *Rose*; his revisions have attracted the attention of several scholars (see Hult, Huot, Jung, Langlois). At the end of the Middle Ages, the poet Jean Molinet translated the *Rose* into prose and moralized it, finding Christian symbols and allusions for every aspect. For example, Guillaume de Lorris, giver of the first part, figures Moses, and Jean de Meun, giver of the second part, becomes Jean the Baptist. (Molinet's version has no modern edition; see Tuve for an analysis of this kind of imposed allegorization). In addition, it is believed that the author of a modernization of the *Rose* first published in 1526 is the poet, Clément Marot, who wanted to make the work accessible to a public who could no longer read thirteenth-century French (see Baridon). The *Rose* was edited many times during the Renaissance (see Bourdillon), but after 1533 it was not edited again until 1735. Since then the principal editions are those of Méon (1814), Langlois (1914-24), and Lecoy (1965-75). The most recent edition is an Old French edition with facing Modern French translation by Armand Strubel (1992) in an inexpensive format that makes the *Rose* readily available for classroom use.

Sources

> *Gallus, Catillus et Ovides,*
> *qui bien sorent d'amors trestier,*
> *nous reüssent or bien mestier;*
> *mes chascuns d'aus gist morz porriz.*

The *Roman de la rose*, which begins as a dream vision about love and ends as a satiric exploration of sexuality, is the culmination of the major literary, moral, and philosophical traditions of the Middle Ages. Langlois was the first scholar to examine the many preceding works which contributed to the *Rose*. His approach, which was followed by several generations of scholars, consisted principally of simply identifying the works that are either referred to by the authors of the *Rose* or that he believed may have influenced them. For Guillaume, who mentions only Macrobius, Langlois points to the clear but unacknowledged presence of Ovid's *Ars amatoria* and *Metamorphoses* (for the story of Narcissus). Langlois also outlined a number of medieval allegorical and erotic works that he believed were known to the author of the first part of the *Rose*. The difficulty of dating many medieval works led him later to revise some of these observations.

The situation for Jean is very different: Langlois identified more than forty authors and works that are reflected in the second part, either directly or indirectly. He further claimed that two-thirds of the lines in the second part are lifted or imitated from earlier authors. The most important sources for Jean are Boethius, *De consolatione Philosophiae*, especially for Raison's discussion of Fortune; Alain de Lille, *De planctu Naturae*, for Nature's complaint and for the characterization of her priest, Genius; and Ovid, *Ars amatoria*, for the discourses of l'Ami and la Vieille, and the *Metamorphoses*, for the myth of Pygmalion.

Langlois and other scholars, both before and after his study of sources, tended to interpret this wealth of "borrowed" material as a literary weakness. Jean's continuation was described as "un recueil de *Origines* 93); as a hodge-podge of digressions designed to show off Jean's erudition; as an encyclopedic outpouring of everything he knew for the benefit of the uneducated. In effect, Jean's use of materials from other sources (standard medieval literary practice) was seen as the reason for the disorganization of his poem and as another of its major differences from the first part.

Since Langlois's early study, our understanding of medieval intertextuality has become more sophisticated and sympathetic to medieval models. Consequently, studies have appeared that are not content to point out a source but also attempt to understand how Jean adapted his sources in an original manner: Jean's Genius, for example, is not Alain de Lille's, nor is his Pygmalion Ovid's. (Some of the more perceptive source studies are those of Baumgartner, Fritz, and Regalado.) Furthermore, a striking change in scholarly perceptions of the use of mythographic material can be seen in critical views of the *Rose*'s retelling of the myths of Narcissus and Pygmalion. While many early summaries and discussions of the romance simply omitted mention of these episodes or dismissed them as digressions, scholarly attention now recognizes that they embody the kernel of the poets' thought, and they have been singled out for thorough study: in addition to many articles, monographs have been published on each of these myths in the past few years (see, for example, Cortes Vazquez, Dornbush, and Knoespel), while others have been devoted to Jean de Meun's use of Ovid in general (Pelen). This is perhaps the clearest indication of significant scholarly progress in understanding the *Rose* and medieval literature generally. Finally, some scholars have pointed to a new kind of "source," which Fleming calls the "supertext" (*Reason and the Lover* 69): an authority that shapes the *Rose* without being acknowledged. Thus another dimension has been added to the discussion of the *Rose*'s sources.

Allegorical Meaning

> *La verité, qui est coverte,*
> *vos sera lores toute overte*
> *quant espondre m'oroiz le songe,*
> *car il n'i a mot de mençonge.*

Both poets promise to explain the meaning of the dream, but they never actually do so. The question of the allegorical meaning or "verité coverte" of the *Rose*, more than of any other medieval work, has tantalized readers virtually since its creation. The first critical exchange about a literary work was provoked by the *Rose* (see the discussion of the Querelle de la Rose in Chapter 4), and scholars are still debating some of the same questions raised by Christine de Pizan in the early fifteenth century. The widely varying interpretations of the *Rose* that have been offered can seem bewildering: it has been seen as pagan, pious, or pagan and pious at the same time; as celebrating rationality or sexuality; as a work of popular science or subtle theology. By inciting readers to define their critical assumptions, the *Rose* leads us to focus on the act of reading itself.

The major division among critics of the *Rose*, one which reflects our approach to medieval literature as a whole, is between those who see it as religious and those who see it as secular. Robertson and Fleming, who are recognized as the leading proponents of a Christian interpretation of the *Rose*, argue that the most popular literary work of the Middle Ages must be Christian; specifically, that the *Rose* reenacts man's Fall from Eden through the portrayal of a foolish lover who forsakes charity for concupiscence. This Augustinian conception of love sees physical desire as inherently sinful, and consequently the elements in the *Rose* which appear on the surface to be positive are interpreted by the patristic approach as negative: the God of Love is an avatar of the devil; the rose is simply the female genitalia.

Other scholars, however, point to the diversity of medieval culture and to the coexistence of a wide range of viewpoints, including heterodox religious beliefs. To the fundamental question which the Robertsonians pose, "Can any work of medieval literature not be Christian?," many scholars implicitly answer that it can. Thus the overwhelming majority of *Rose* scholars, and virtually all the French, see the first part of the romance as a largely admiring exploration of purely courtly values. Specifically, Guillaume's *Rose* portrays the initiation of a young nobleman into that form of love called *fin'amors* in the Middle Ages and "courtly love" today. According to this approach Guillaume is sincere in his celebration of the beauty and refinement, despite the pain, of the amorous experience that the dreamer undergoes. Some scholars do see a certain distance between the protagonist of the dream and the narrator, who is five years older and able to comment on the dream events from a different viewpoint. But few if any scholars of the "courtly" approach believe that Guillaume or his narrator repudiates the dreamer's experience as sinful.

Two interpretations of the first part that are subcategories of the major approaches (the religious and the social) have been offered. Some scholars see the poem as a positive religious experience that expresses a mystical but not necessarily Christian view of love (Kamenetz, Le Merrer, Ribard). A variant of the social approach has been formulated by Ott, who argues against scholars' view of an aristocratic Guillaume and his dreamer, suggesting instead that certain details in the poem point to the poet's bourgeois origins. Nonetheless, the interpretation of the first *Rose* as a document reflecting courtly values and ideals remains the dominant one.

One approach to interpreting the first part looks at the poem's structure as a key to the allegorical meaning. Scholars have seen Guillaume's part as a succession of lyric, romance, and didactic elements: a lyric beginning, followed by the lecture on love by le Dieu d'amour, followed by l'Amant's quest for the rose after the episode at the Fountain of Narcissus, and concluded by a return to the structure of the lyric (Accarie, Hult, Gertrude Meyer). It is possible that le Dieu d'Amour's description of the pains and joys of love, which l'Amant enacts in the second half of the first part, is the "verité coverte" referred to by the narrator.

In addition to exploring the *Rose*'s structure, scholars have analyzed key episodes or characters that suggest the possible hidden meaning of Guillaume's romance. For example, the apparently minor character, Oiseuse, may be a key to understanding Guillaume's conception of love: nine articles have appeared in the past fifteen years proposing a variety of interpretations of her meaning and function. She has been seen in a favorable light, that is, as an expression of the leisure necessary for courtly love or for an aristocratic or contemplative life (Alvar, Richards), or as unfavorable--a symbol of sloth or worse, lust (Fleming). The difficulty scholars have in understanding this one character is a reflection of the complexity, the irony, and perhaps the fundamental ambiguity of Guillaume's dream of love.

Above all, it is Guillaume's version of the story of Narcissus--centered on the Fountain of Love and its two enigmatic crystals--that has incited more critical ink to flow than any other topic in the first part (see for example Frappier, Harley, Hillman, Hult, Knoespel, Köhler, Poirion, and Rychner). It is crucial to understand this turning point in the romance: does Guillaume become another Narcissus (is the episode emblematic?) or does he turn away from the trap of narcissism to search for an external love object (is the episode exemplary)? Furthermore, critical attention has been focused on one particular aspect of the Narcissus episode: the meaning of the crystals in the fountain. C. S. Lewis was the first to suggest that they represented the beloved's eyes, the sight of which causes the dreamer to fall in love. At this point in the allegory, however, the dreamer has not yet seen the rosebud (several scholars, including Zumthor, have mistakenly claimed that l'Amant sees the rosebud in the fountain; in reality the text says that he sees rosebushes, not the bud with which he later falls in love). Others have suggested that the crystals are the dreamer's eyes or an allegory of human sight, either negative (Fleming) or positive (Knoespel). Thus the major interpretative problems confronting scholars in the first part concern the significance of certain of Guillaume's allegorical and symbolic entities.

The problems of interpretation posed by the second part are different from those of the first for a number of reasons (in addition to length). The first critical stumbling block to understanding the continuation was the question of whether Jean's poem could be said to have a unifying structure, message, or point of view. Nearly all early scholars and a few contemporary ones assume that the continuation is simply a chaos of disparate pieces, that Jean wrote whatever came into his head, or that he was simply offering his erudition. Even scholars of the caliber of C. S. Lewis--one of the first modern scholars to admire medieval allegory--refused to grant Jean a plan or unifying purpose. It was Gunn's *Mirror of Love* that effectively changed the terms of the discussion and convinced most scholars that Jean's poem is a unified work of art. Although many scholars do not accept Gunn's particular definition of that unity, few accuse Jean any longer of being digressive or incoherent.

One of the principal difficulties in interpreting the second part is the fact that Jean puts so much of the romance into the mouths of his major characters. The principal structural difference between the two parts is the development in the continuation of long discourses both by characters who had appeared in the first part and by new ones. Thus, while the first part is structured by the lyric model or the quest, the second is composed of a series of lectures by authorities or teachers. All have their say: speaking in turn are Raison, Ami, le Dieu d'Amour, Faux Semblant, la Vieille, Nature, Genius, and the narrator. One of the thorniest questions raised by the disputants in the Querelle de la Rose, one that is still argued today, is which if any of these characters can be seen as speaking the author's views. Early scholars, and some contemporary ones, often ignore the principal of "decorum" (a character speaks in an appropriate way), which was already discussed as early as the fifteenth century. Consequently, scholars have attributed statements from any or all characters to Jean de Meun. Since Jean's characters hold widely divergent views, he too can be made to hold a surprising variety of opinions. Contemporary scholars, however, are generally more conscious of the methodological assumptions they are making when they choose one character or another as the keynote speaker for the entire romance.

Although Gunn believed that Faux Semblant is the one character who does not fit into the *Rose*'s teachings on love, some scholars have seen Faux Semblant as the key to understanding Jean's literary conception (Emmerson and Herzman, Stakel); others have focused on l'Ami, or la Vieille. The major split in critical opinion occurs between those scholars who see Raison as the privileged speaker and those who focus on the couple Nature and Genius. Scholars who choose Raison create an orthodox Jean who follows the traditional Christian rejection of passionate love as not only irrational but sinful; following l'Amant's rejection of Raison, the romance becomes an acting out of *fol amour*. Other scholars, represented most forcefully by Payen, point to Nature and Genius as conveying Jean's message, thus creating a heterodox view of Jean as a believer in the primordial value of natural sexuality and procreation. Accordingly, the *Rose* becomes a celebration of Nature's bounty and plenitude.

Rather than privileging one of the many speakers, some scholars have argued for an epistemological approach (Arden, Hult, Regalado) that steps back from the debate and looks at how we can know which speaker to believe. Instead of conveying a position in the words of one of the lover's teachers, Jean is asking his readers to become conscious of their sources of knowledge and belief: authority, experience, and reason. In Hult's words, "Jean's brilliance resides in his submission of ideas to the broader question of epistemological inquiry, which becomes the central aspect of the fictional frame. Ultimately, he calls into question rigid systems of belief by stimulating the reader's awareness of his own interpretative faculties" (*A New History of French Literature*, 100).

Finally, since the *Rose* is a hybrid work, the question of its allegorical meaning ultimately raises the question of the unity or difference of the two parts. Again there are two major critical camps. Nearly all early scholars, and most contemporary ones, see an absolute divide between Guillaume's supposedly graceful, elegant idyll of courtly love and Jean's satiric, erudite, philosophical panorama of human behavior. Thus, Jean has usually been described as either insensitive to, uncomprehending of, or even as hostile to Guillaume's allegory (see Lanson, Lewis, Stone, Zumthor). Gunn and others, including Fleming (whose approach is very different from Gunn's), have argued on the contrary that Jean continued and completed Guillaume's beginning. Consequently, the question of sources, discussed in Section II, is further complicated by the fact that Guillaume is one of Jean's principal sources: Jean is rewriting Guillaume, however we understand that rewriting.

Poetic Technique

> ... couchier m'aloie
> une nuit, si con je souloie,
> et me dormoie mout forment,
> et vi un songe en mon dormant
> qui mout fu biaus et mout me plot

One of the great advances in *Rose* criticism, if we can speak of advances in criticism, is the recognition by contemporary scholars that the *Rose* is a poem and not a treatise or a collection of dissertations. Early scholars were generally content to label the parts of the *Rose* with a few adjectives ("elegant and naive," for the first; "rambling and pedantic," for the second) and neglected to look at how the *Rose* functioned as poetry. A large part of the problem was a long-standing antagonism toward the very heart of the *Rose*--its allegory. Early scholars had little sympathy for allegory and were often openly hostile to it as a literary form, even blaming the *Rose*'s popularity for "corrupting" late medieval literature. Fortunately, contemporary scholars have moved to a more sympathetic understanding of the *Rose*'s poetic and narrative qualities.

Since allegory is the quintessential medieval literary form, one of the primary tasks of modern scholars is to understand allegory as it appears in the *Rose*. A number of articles and monographs have attempted to place the *Rose* in the history of late classical and medieval allegorical works and to understand how medieval allegory functioned (see Barney, Jauss, Quilligan, Strubel, Van Dyke, Wetherbee). Others have studied the psychological and linguistic status of the personifications (C. S. Lewis, Batany, Frank, Kelly). What some scholars have criticized as inconsistent use of personification (for example, the fact that Guillaume's part includes characters of different levels or kinds of abstraction) has been praised by others as revealing his variety and flexibility.

More specifically, scholars are now studying the way the two parts rework medieval genres to produce a new synthesis. One of the breakthroughs in understanding what is new about Guillaume de Lorris's poem is the realization that he is reworking not only religious and romance approaches to personification but blending the romance quest with the lyric hero. Scholars such as Hult and Huot have explored how the romance hero in the first half of Guillaume's work modulates into the lyric voice after the episode of the Fountain of Narcissus. Others have examined generic questions such as the components of the dream-vision and the earthly paradise (Piehler, Lynch, Spearing). Studies of the second part have focused on how Jean de Meun plays with the "consolation" pattern represented by Boethius's *De consolatione Philosophiae* and Alain de Lille's *De planctu Naturae*, especially how he moves it toward satire and parody (see Bouché, Cherniss, Poirion).

Important studies have also appeared on the question of the complex relationship of the voices in the *Rose*. While Guillaume gives us the dreamer, the protagonist, and the narrator as aspects of one person, Jean adds both a distinct authorial voice and characters beyond the dreamer's ken. The question of voice is particularly thorny for the second part because of the number and importance of the speakers. The question of "decorum" (see above), which was first raised in the medieval debate on the *Rose*, has been raised again in the twentieth century. Scholars have asked to what extent Jean's personifications are characters, how they function as fictional creations distinct from their creator. This has led to a better understanding of how Jean de Meun composed, how he structured the discourses (Blangez, Patterson).

Finally, a number of scholars have looked at the conception of poetry implied by the *Rose*, especially in Jean's continuation, and have come to recognize a new consciousness of poetry's special power (Uitti). It is the *Rose*'s creation of a vernacular poetry capable of expressing cosmic themes that opened up the poetic enterprise for later poets.

Influence

> For in pleyn text withouten nede of glose,
> Thou hast translated the Romaunce of the Rose
> (Chaucer, *Legend of Good Women*)

The one fact of the *Rose*'s literary history that scholars agree on is its enormous influence: "the great foundation text of the European Middle Ages, the secular tree of Jesse upon which all illustrious poets sit" (Wallace, "Chaucer and the European Rose" 67), while C. S. Lewis called it "one of the most 'successful' books, in the vulgar sense, that have ever been written" (*The Allegory of Love* 156). Scholars have claimed that the *Rose* is "a unique and memorable work without which the course of Western culture would not have been the same" (Dunn, *The Romance of the Rose* xxvii), and "historically and perhaps esthetically the most important single work of literature produced during the medieval period " (Calin, *A Muse for Heroes* 125). Given the breadth and complexity of the *Rose*'s influence, I can only sketch its effect on later writers, a topic discussed by the studies in Chapter 4 of this bibliography.

Most love poetry in Europe after the thirteenth century shows the influence of the structure and personifications of the *Rose*. In particular we see this in the works of the fourteenth-century writers Guillaume Machaut and Jean Froissart, while echoes of the *Rose* are found even in the work of a mostly non-courtly poet like François Villon. In France, in the century after the composition of the *Rose*, writers not only referred to the *Rose* but rewrote it (Deguileville's *Pèlerinage de vie humaine* and the anonymous *Echecs d'amour* and *Echecs amoureux*). While the influence of the first part of the *Rose* on love poetry continues through the Renaissance, moralists and satirists appreciated Jean de Meun's anticlerical and misogynist satire. Badel's study of the *Rose*'s reception examines in detail the way the poem was read in the fourteenth century, while other monographs focus on the romance's influence on specific poets (Brownlee, Wimsatt).

About 1400, discussion of the *Rose* among clerics and members of the French court, including the prolific and varied writer, Christine de Pizan, led to what is usually called the first literary debate in medieval history. This exchange of letters and treatises arguing the qualities, defects, and dangers of the *Rose*, which I refer to in this bibliography as the Querelle de la Rose, raised a number of literary questions that still concern scholars, such as the author's ultimate responsibility for the characters he creates, the use of obscene language, and the concept of literary decorum.

The importance of the *Rose* for Chaucer is too well known to need to be pointed out here: as Cunningham phrased it, "if one were to look for the source of anything in Chaucer, the first place an experienced scholar would look is in the *Romance of the Rose* and its tradition" ("The Literary Form of the Prologue to the *Canterbury Tales*" 174). Early source studies often simply compared lines from the *Rose* with lines from Chaucer's works. More recently scholars have observed a more subtle dialogue between Chaucer and the authors of the *Rose* involving characterization, views of love, and poetic ambition.

The influence of the *Rose* has been studied in other literatures, particularly in the works of Italian poets (the *Fiore*, the *Detto d'amore*, the *Divina commedia*, among others) and in later periods. Jean de Meun, for example, has been compared to Rabelais and Voltaire.

No other medieval work, except perhaps the *Divina commedia*, has had such a long-lasting and varied effect on later writers as the *Roman de la rose*.

THE ORGANIZATION OF THE BIBLIOGRAPHY

Primary focus

Because virtually all aspects of European literature from the thirteenth to the sixteenth centuries were touched by the *Rose*, it is almost impossible for an annotated bibliography to include all that has been written about it. Consequently, this bibliography has as its primary focus modern scholarship on the romance from 1850 to works published in 1992. Nearly all critical and scholarly discussions of the *Rose* in this period are included.

The bibliography lists works alphabetically by author or translator in four chapters, except for the editions, which are listed chronologically by editor. Entries are numbered consecutively throughout. The first chapter, The Text of the *Roman de la rose*, includes virtually all editions of the *Rose* in the eighteenth, nineteenth, and twentieth centuries, as well as most translations and adaptations, descriptions of manuscripts and early editions, and concordances. For reasons of space, not all descriptions of *Rose* manuscripts have been included, but additional information can be found in the works listed. Studies that interpret manuscripts, rather than simply describing them, are included in Chapter 4, the Influence of the *Roman de la rose*. Specific incunabula are not listed; the reader is referred to Bourdillon's comprehensive study, *The Early Editions of the "Roman de la rose"*. The bibliography does not list editions of works influenced by the *Rose*, since it would be impossible to know where to draw the line (almost everything written in Europe after the *Rose* was "influenced" by it in one way or another). References to such editions can be found in the studies listed here.

The second chapter lists the editions and studies of Jean de Meun's extant translations and the *Testament* and *Codicile* attributed to him, including studies of the influence of these works on Chaucer. Although these works do not on the whole concern the *Rose* directly, they are of intrinsic interest both for the history of translation and its relation to vernacular literature and for the light Jean's other works may shed on his most celebrated one.

The third, and longest, chapter includes virtually all twentieth-century scholarship on the *Rose*, as well as many earlier studies. Unless the discussion presents some critical interest, brief references to the *Rose* in medieval and Renaissance works are largely omitted. These references are given by Badel for the fourteenth century and by many introductions to the *Rose* for later periods. Brief discussions in histories of literature are also generally omitted.

The influence of the *Rose* is the subject of the fourth chapter, which includes scholarship on the Querelle de la Rose and on the *Rose*'s influence on Villon, Chaucer, Dante, and others. Since in the past ten years scholarship on the Querelle has been appearing at a rate as fast as that on the *Rose* itself, I have not included every work

Introduction   xxix

relating to the Querelle, but scholars will find the essential ones. The Querelle could occupy by itself an annotated bibliography, as could the works on Chaucer and the *Rose*: almost every study of Chaucer mentions the *Rose* or its authors. Consequently I have attempted to give the essential entries on Chaucer; through these, scholars can find related works. Also I have included important recent bibliographies on Chaucer, all of which list works discussing the influence of the *Rose*.

A short final chapter lists miscellaneous works, mainly artistic.

The Entries

The organization and main ideas of each work are summarized as objectively and succinctly as possible and to a great extent in the words of the author. Generally the length of the entry reflects the importance of the work, but it may also be a reflection of the complexity of the ideas expressed. When a study discusses other literary works in addition to the *Rose*, they are mentioned only so far as they bear directly on the *Rose*. In order to distinguish my (rare) comments in the entry from the author's, mine are enclosed in square brackets. A few titles which I was not able to annotate for reasons of time or availability are included for completeness. All quotations from the *Rose* are from the Lecoy edition unless otherwise indicated. If another edition is used in the study cited, those line references are also given.

I was fortunate to have the help of other scholars who prepared some of the entries. Their initials are given after the entry. Kathryn M. Lorenz (English and French), Maria R. Brackett (Italian), Anita Suess-Kauschik and Judith S. Zollinger (German), and Keith Busby (Dutch) contributed entries. All others are mine.

Many dissertations on the *Rose* are listed, even if subsequently published, because they can be useful for specific topics, especially for their bibliographies. They are not annotated since in most cases the researcher can consult the abstract in *Dissertation Abstracts International*.

A small number of works could have been included in either of two sections, such as studies of both the *Rose* and Chaucer rather than simply of the *Rose*'s influence on Chaucer. Such works are cross-referenced in the bibliography. When there are a number of references to the same title, a short title is given after the first entry and the entry number of the complete title is given in parenthesis.

The reader will notice that the titles of works listed here give diverse spellings of the names of characters in the *Rose*, which may be in English, French, various forms of Old French, or Middle English, depending on the edition used. In order to avoid confusion and to achieve some consistency, the problem of spelling has been solved, arbitrarily perhaps, by adopting in the annotations either the modern French spelling of characters' names when possible or the most common Old French spelling. The following personifications are frequently mentioned in studies of the *Rose*: l'Amant, Oiseuse, Deduit, le Dieu d'Amour, Bel Accueil, Danger, Raison, l'Ami, Faux Semblant, la Vieille, Raison, Genius, and Venus. The author's spelling is respected, of course, in direct quotations and in titles of books and articles. Similarly, the spelling of classical and medieval authors' names and the titles of medieval works have been standardized to avoid confusion (scholars use three forms of Alain de Lille's name, for example).

Bibliographic information and citations follow the *MLA Handbook for Writers of Research Papers*, 3rd ed., with some minor variations.

The Index

The index lists by entry number all proper names and titles referred to in the entries; also indexed are important topics. The names of authors whose works are annotated in the bibliography are not indexed unless their work is discussed in another entry; they should be looked for alphabetically in the appropriate section of the bibliography. The entries themselves refer the reader to related studies only in exceptional cases, such as when authors comment on each other's work.

CHAPTER ONE

THE TEXT OF THE *ROMAN DE LA ROSE*

COMPLETE EDITIONS
listed chronologically

1   Marot, Clément, ed. *Le roman de la rose dans la version attribuée à Clément Marot.* See no. 36.

2   Lenglet Dufresnoy, Nicolas, ed. *Le roman de la rose, par Guillaume de Lorris et Jean de Meun dit Clopinel, revu sur plusieurs éditions et sur quelques anciens manuscrits, accompagné de plusieurs autres ouvrages, d'une préface historique, de notes et d'un glossaire.* 3 vols. Paris: Veuve Pissot; Amsterdam: Jean Fred. Bernard, 1735.

The first edition of the *Rose* after the Renaissance; the text reproduces the first quarto Vérard edition (1500). The Paris printing differs from the Amsterdam in the first twenty-eight pages, the text of which has been revised from manuscripts (see Langlois ed., no. 6, 45). Volume 1 includes a preface by Lenglet Dufresnoy, Marot's 1526 preface (see no. 36), and an essay on the life of Jean de Meun by André Thévet. Lenglet Dufresnoy's preface describes the importance and popularity of the *Rose* (called the masterpiece of Old French literature), extols Jean de Meun as "notre Homère" (i), and suggests that Jean was about twenty-two when he wrote the continuation. The preface also discusses various aspects of the *Rose*: conception of love, satire of society, style and versification. The first two volumes give the text of the *Rose*, the third reprints a number of works attributed to Jean de Meun, including the *Testament* and *Codicile*, "Les remontrances de Nature à l'alchimiste errant" and "La response de l'alchimiste à Nature," the "Petit traicté d'alchymie," and "La Fontaine des amoureux." All these works, including the preface and essay on the life of Jean de Meun, are reproduced in Méon's edition (see no. 4). Volume 3 also includes a glossary (shorter than Méon's).

3   Lantin de Damerey, J. B., ed. *Le roman de la rose, par Guillaume de Lorris et Jean de Meung, dit Clopinel: edition faite sur celle de Lenglet Dufresnoy, corrigée avec soin, et enrichie de la dissertation sur les auteurs de l'ouvrage, de l'analyse, des variantes et du glossaire publiés en 1737.* 5 vols. Paris: J. B. Fournier et fils and P. N. F. Didot, an septième [1798].

Virtually a reproduction of Lenglet Dufresnoy's 1735 edition, with the addition of Lantin de Damerey's "Dissertation sur le *Roman de la rose*," originally published in 1737 (the author was preparing an edition of the *Rose* when Lenglet Dufresnoy published his). The dissertation is reproduced in Méon's edition (no. 4), 1:65-109. Lantin de Damerey's dissertation talks more about what people have thought and said about the *Rose* than about the poem itself. Although he appears to admire the Middle Ages in some respects ("on pensoit plus sainement autrefois" [see Méon, no. 4, 71]), he reproaches the authors of the *Rose* for reproducing the bad taste of their time and for incorrect versification. Lantin de Damerey also supplied notes and a supplement to the glossary.

4   Méon, Dominique Martin, ed. *Le roman de la rose par Guillaume de Lorris et Jehan de Meung: nouvelle édition,*

revue et corrigée sur les meilleurs et plus anciens manuscrits. 4 vols. Paris: P. N. F. Didot l'aîné, 1814.

The first edition based on a study of the manuscripts. Méon, who claims to have worked for fifteen years on this edition, consulted forty mss., "les plus anciens que j'ai pu me procurer" (xxii); his base manuscript, unidentified, was dated 1330. The first volume includes a letter of dedication to the secretary of state, an Avertissement by Méon, the prefaces by Lenglet Dufresnoy and Clément Marot, Thévet's life of Jean de Meun, Lantin de Damerey's dissertation, an analysis of the romance, a "table de matières" of the four volumes (165-75; both an index and a summary), and the text and variants of the first part of the *Rose*. The second and third volumes give the text of Jean de Meun's part. The fourth includes the *Testament* and *Codicile* and a number of other texts attributed to Jean (reprinted from Lenglet Dufresnoy's edition [no. 2]) and a glossary.

5   Michel, Francisque, ed. *Le roman de la rose par Guillaume de Lorris et Jean de Meung: nouvelle édition revue et corrigée*. 2 vols. Paris: Firmin Didot, 1864.

A reprinting of Méon's edition (see no. 4), with a few changes in the text, some of which substitute errors for correct forms (see Langlois, no. 6, 47-48). In his preface Michel reprints Méon's Avertissement and the prefaces of Lenglet Dufresnoy and Clément Marot; the editor's original contribution to the preface consists of excerpts from other scholars on Chaucer and on the sources of the *Rose*, especially the troubadours and trouvères. However, Michel does give useful translations of difficult words in the margin.

6   Langlois, Ernest, ed. *Le roman de la rose par Guillaume de Lorris et Jean de Meun, publié d'après les manuscrits*. Société des Anciens Textes Français. 5 vols. Paris: Firmin

Didot (vols. 1-2) and Honoré Champion (vols. 3-5), 1914-1924. Rpt. New York: Johnson Reprints, 1965.

The first modern edition, still often used by scholars. The editor, who is also the first outstanding specialist of the romance (see nos. 66 and 358), used as his base manuscript, according to Lecoy (see no. 7, xxxix), Paris, B. N. fr. 1573, which he corrected and emended for clarity and uniformity. In the first volume, a good introduction to the literary history of the *Rose* discusses facts and conjectures about the authors, including a remarkable list of apocryphal works attributed to Jean de Meun, a short analysis (accurate, if unsympathetic to the second part), and an overview of the influence of the *Rose*. Volume 1 also includes a table of rhymes and a philological study. The other volumes contain the text, selected variants, and notes.

7   Lecoy, Félix, ed. *Le roman de la rose par Guillaume de Lorris and Jean de Meun*. 3 vols. Classiques Français du Moyen Age 92, 95, 98. Paris: Honoré Champion, 1965-1975.

The most frequently used edition of the *Rose* today, Lecoy's is a corrected transcription of Paris, B. N. fr. 1573, an early composite manuscript (to a copy of the first part was added, evidently not long after its composition, a copy of the second part by a different hand). Lecoy corrected the base ms. from four other mss.; both changes and principal variants are indicated. In addition, each volume includes a detailed summary and notes indicating allusions, citations, and texts that inspired Jean de Meun especially. A glossary and Table de Noms is given at the end of Volume 3. In the introduction, Lecoy discusses what we know of the authors; suggests dates based on historical allusions in the second part; and gives an overview and literary appreciation of each part (praising Guillaume for his "souci d'une vérité psychologique...ferme et solide" [xvi] but criticizing Jean for his lack of coherence [xvii]). Lecoy stresses Jean's naturalism as the key to understanding the second part. Furthermore, the introduction summarizes the Querelle de la Rose and describes the success of the *Rose* as measured by references to it in other works and by the number of manuscripts and incunabula (Lecoy lists mss. discovered since Langlois's study [no. 66]). Finally, Lecoy describes the manuscript tradition of the two parts ("mauvaise" for the first, "excellente" for the second [xxxvi]), and gives the plan of his edition.

8   Poirion, Daniel, ed. *Le Roman de la Rose*. Paris: Garnier-Flammarion, 1974. Pp. 576.

An edition based on a different manuscript than that of Lecoy and Langlois (see nos. 6 and 7)--Paris, B. N. fr. 25523 instead of B. N. fr. 1573--thereby offering another but equally interesting version of the romance. The editor has corrected the text only in the case of evident copyist's mistakes and has completed the numerous lacunae from other manuscripts. Page numbering follows Langlois. The edition includes a chronology, a twenty-one page analytical preface which discusses allegory, irony, and mythology in the *Rose*, a short bibliography, and a discussion of the language of the base manuscript.

9   König, Eberhard. *Der Rosenroman des Berthaud d'Achy: Codex Urbinatus latinus 376*. Codices e Vaticanis Selecti 71. 2 vols. Zurich: Belser, 1987.

Facsimile edition of a manuscript from the end of the thirteenth century in the Vatican Library, identified as the work of Berthaud d'Achy. Volume 2 includes the commentary by König (in German).

10   Tsuji, Sahoko, Nobutoshi Fukube and Takao Tsukada, eds. *Le roman de la rose*. Tokyo: Iwanami-Shoten; Vatican: Biblioteca Apostolica Vaticana, 1989.

An edition listed in *Encomia: Bibliographical Bulletin of the International Courtly Literature Society* 13 (1991):51 and described as the publication of ms. Urbinatus latinus 376. [I have not been able to see a copy.]

PARTIAL EDITIONS
listed chronologically

11   Püschel, Robert, ed. "Li Romanz de la rose, première partie par Guillaume de Lorris." In *Friedrichs-Gymnasium Jahresbericht für das Schuljahr von Ostern 1871 bis Ostern 1872*. Berlin: Gustav Lange (Otto Lange), 1872. Pp. 26.

   An edition of the first part of the *Rose* based on ms. 80 of the Bibliothèque Royale of Berlin, with variants from Francisque Michel's edition (no. 5) and Tyrwhitt's *Romaunt of the Rose*. A short introduction reviews earlier editions, the *Romaunt*, and the date of the *Rose*, which the author places, for the second part, between 1268 and 1277.

12   Doinel, Jules, ed. *Guy Fabi et Guillaume Rebrachien*. Orleans: H. Herluison, 1887. Pp. 28. [Extract from the *Annales de la Société historique et archéologique du Gâtinais* (3rd trimester 1887):153-80.]

   Reproduces the first thousand lines of Paris, B. N. fr. 1573. See no. 213.

13   Linker, Robert White, ed. *Guillaume de Lorris, Li romanz de la rose*. Chapel Hill, N. C.: [n. p.], 1937. Pp. 77.

   A typescript of the first part of the *Rose*, reproducing Langlois's text (no. 6) and including the anonymous 78-line conclusion. No editorial or critical material.

14   Bihler, Heinrich, ed. *Der Rosenroman von Guillaume de Lorris und Jean de Meun*. Sammlung romanischer Übungstexte

49. Tubingen: Max Niemeyer, 1966. Pp. xxiii + 110 + ill.

A selection of passages from the two parts, reproducing Langlois's edition (no. 6) with proportionately more excerpts from the first part. The introduction gives the history of the authors and an overview of the two parts. Includes a glossary and list of proper names.

15 Nichols, Stephen G., Jr., ed. *Le roman de la rose [par] Guillaume de Lorris.* New York: Appleton-Century-Crofts, 1967. Pp. 197.

An edition for American students which reproduces Langlois's text (no. 6), with difficult words translated into modern French at the bottom of the page. An introduction in French defines the goal of the romance--"montrer l'essence de l'amour entre deux personnes" (2), describes some of the personifications and how they function, discusses briefly the symbolism of the rose, and outlines the different forms and meanings assumed by the protean Fountaine Périlleuse [the Fountain of Narcissus], which "nous offre une vue du 'moi' jusqu'à présent inconnue" (10), the narrator's lack of love, and the young woman's eyes. The edition includes Fragment A of *The Romaunt of the Rose*, which Nichols attributes definitely to Chaucer; an introduction in English to the *Romaunt* which argues that Chaucer "captured the spirit and much of the freshness of the original" (151); a bibliographical note; and a list of proper names.

TRANSLATIONS
listed alphabetically by editor or translator
includes translations accompanied by the Old French text

The Romaunt of the Rose
(For other editions see no. 731. Studies of the *Romaunt* can be found in Section 3, The Influence of the *Rose*.)

16 Brunskill, Ann, illustrator. *The Romaunt of the Rose.* London: World's End Press, 1974. Pp. 77.

An art edition of the first 1670 lines of the *Romaunt*, accompanied by seven original etchings. The English and French texts are taken from Sutherland's edition (no. 20). Printed in a limited edition of seventy-five copies, the first twenty-five copies include the etchings and are printed on white mould-made paper; the others include one original etching and are printed on hand-made paper.

17 Furnivall, Frederick J., ed. *The Romaunt of the Rose: A Reprint of the First Printed Edition by William Thynne, A. D. 1532.* Intro. by W. W. Skeat. The Chaucer Society, First Series 82. London: Kegan Paul, Trench, Trübner, 1911. Pp. xi + 101.

A reprint of one of the two early texts of the *Romaunt*, published posthumously with a short introduction by W. W. Skeat. The introduction describes editorial practice ("The present print reproduces all Thynne's peculiarities" [v]), lists the lines in Thynne that are missing from the Glasgow ms., and describes the three fragments of the poem.

18 Henderson, Keith and Norman Wilkinson, illustrators. *The Romaunt of the Rose Rendered out of the French into Anglise by Geoffrey Chaucer.* 1908; rpt. New York: Henry Holt, 1911. Pp. 108 + 20 ill.

The text is that of Mark H. Liddell in the Globe Edition (1898). The first edition consisted of 512 copies in quarto. Includes colored frontispiece and colored plates, with plates mounted. The twenty illustrations show the influence of Belgian-French symbolism, seasoned with carefully observed details reminiscent of Pre-Raphaelitism.

19 Kaluza, Max, ed. *The Romaunt of the Rose from the unique*

Glasgow ms., parallel with its original, "Le roman de la rose". Part I The Texts. The Chaucer Society, First Series 83. London: Kegan Paul, Trench, Trübner, 1891. Rpt. New York: Johnson Reprints, 1967. Pp. 439.

A parallel-text edition; the Old French text is based on Francisque Michel's 1864 edition, with variants from a half-dozen manuscripts; the English text "closely follows the unique ms. V. 3. 7, Hunterian Museum, Glasgow" (3), with the text of the missing leaves supplied from Thynne's edition of 1532. Corrections from earlier editions are given in the notes, with Kaluza's emendations. (See also no. 668)

20   Sutherland, Ronald, ed. *"The Romaunt of the Rose" and "Le roman de la rose": A Parallel-Text Edition.* Berkeley and Los Angeles: U of California P, 1968. Pp. xxxix + 202.

An edition, based on the author's 1960 dissertation, of the Middle English translation which prints Thynne's edition across from "the most probable source lines in selected manuscripts of the *Roman de la Rose*" (v). The previous parallel-text edition was Kaluza's in 1891 (see no. 19), before Langlois's edition and manuscript study of the *Rose* (see nos. 6 and 66), and therefore a new edition of the *Romaunt* was needed. The introduction reviews the history of critical opinion on the question of Chaucer's authorship, describes in detail which manuscripts are closest to the various fragments, and proposes a theory of how the Thynne edition came to be constructed. Sutherland's findings support the hypothesis that Chaucer is the translator of Fragment A. Textual notes give variant readings and emendations. Includes bibliography.

Other Translations and Edition-Translations

21   Alvar, Carlos, ed. and tr. *Guillaume de Lorris, El libro de la*

rosa. Biblioteca filológica 5. Barcelona: Festin de Esopo, Quaderns Crema, 1985. Pp. 269 + ill.

The Old French text of the first part of the *Rose*, with parallel Spanish translation. Includes a prologue and notes.

22 Battaglia, Salvatore, tr. *Guillaume de Lorris, Le roman de la rose*. Speculum: Raccolta di Testi Medievali e Moderni 1. Naples: A. Morano, 1947. Pp. xxvi + 203.

Langlois's edition of the first part, accompanied by a prose translation in Italian and a glossary. In the introduction to his elegant translation, Battaglia dwells upon the question of the *Rose*'s fortune in the late Middle Ages and early Renaissance. He defines it as a work at the same time old and new, in some regards belated and in others anticipatory of new tendencies, a work which had immediate success by pleasing the literary taste of its contemporaries. For Battaglia, Guillaume starts from a scientific, didactic approach, as in a contemporary psychological study, and attains a reintegration of the poetic substance. The "intelligenza del fenomeno amoroso" (xiii) is the best quality of the *Rose*, since Guillaume is the only author of a treatise who "approda a rive liriche" (xv) though engaged in an exegetic itinerary. Guillaume's use of allegory fulfills a need to rescue mental images from the "provvisorietà della figurazione empirica e personale" (xxiv). The use of allegory, from Guillaume's *Rose* to Dante's *Comedia*, expresses the side of the medieval mind which aspires to "riconoscere e contemplare il reale in una prospettiva universale, extratemporale" (xxiv). Guillaume's intent was in fact that of objectifying amorous endeavors, thus detaching them from the frailty of personal experience. [MRB]

23 Cipriani, Lisi, tr. *Selections from the "Romance of the Rose": Introduction and Translations*. Urbana: [Carbon copy of typescript, about 1906].

An introduction to the *Rose* and translation of the first part. A note by Charles A. Williams dated 1943 and inserted at the beginning of the typescript states that these carbon copies were found about 1916 in a desk. They consist of three parts: a blank verse translation of large sections of the *Rose*, an introduction to the work, and a long study of the *Rose*'s influence on Chaucer, a shorter version of which appeared a year later in *PMLA* (see no. 601). The introduction describes briefly the influence of the *Rose* and its place in Old French literature, summarizes the romance, and reviews Langlois's study of its sources. Cipriani stresses Jean de Meun's originality and his uncompromising moralism, which, however, she has difficulty reconciling with obscene parts of the *Rose*. The translation, which stays close to the original, is "meant for students of English literature, and not for the general reading public" (78).

24   Dahlberg, Charles, tr. *The Romance of the Rose by Guillaume de Lorris and Jean de Meun*. 1971; rpt. Hanover and London: University Presses of New England, 1986. Pp. xviii + 450 + ill.

A generally accurate and readable prose translation which incorporates Fleming's approach to the *Rose* (see no. 246). Includes a good introduction. [Note that the exclusive reliance on patristic principles to interpret the Lover's experience is not accepted by many scholars of the *Rose*.] Illustrations from a number of manuscripts show some of the ways that the Middle Ages envisioned the *Rose*.

25   D'Angelo Matassa, Gina, tr. and preface. *Guillaume de Lorris, Il romanzo della rosa*. Postface by Enzo Giudici. Narciso di Novecento 12. Palermo: Novecento, 1984. Pp. 179.

A verse translation in Italian of Langlois's edition of the first part (see no. 6). In his generous *postfazione*, Enzo Giudici praises D'Angelo Matassa's translation as a personal reading of a "poema di cui si avverte tutta la fresca vitalità" (176), but the translator's attempt to render the medieval masterpiece into Italian with rhyming couplets of double pentasyllabic verses is desperate. The lack of perspective on the different historical use of metrics in the two Romance languages ultimately causes Guillaume's elegant verses to become unrecognizable in this whimsical, sing-song Italian recasting (not to mention the liberties, additions, and modernisms, such as *melodramma*, that it features). [MRB]

26 Ellis, F[rederick] S[tartridge], tr. *The Romance of the Rose by W. Lorris and J. Clopinel*. The Temple Classics. 3 vols. 1900; rpt. New York: AMS, 1975.

The first English translation after the *Romaunt*, a free rendering in octosyllabic rhyme based on the 1878 Marteau edition (see no. 37). Ellis, a book dealer and friend of William Morris (see no. 377, 24), translates most of the *Rose*, but he declines to give the ending, which he finds too offensive, and reprints the last 1100 lines of the French text in an appendix, in the belief "that those who read them will allow that he is justified in leaving them in the obscurity of the original" (212) [evidently they are not obscure enough]. Ellis supplies an ending of his own, based loosely on the original, in which Venus shoots her arrow into the rose's heart and transforms her into a beautiful damosel. A prologue reviews negative critical opinions of the *Rose*, expresses the translator's admiration, and suggests that Genius's doctrine of procreation was a response to the *Golden Legend*'s exaltation of celibacy. There is no critical apparatus, but Ellis gives summaries of the sections and an index of proper names and topics.

27 Fährmann, Heinrich, tr. *Das Gedicht von der Rose, aus dem Altfranzösischen des Guillaume de Lorris*. Foreword by Fr. Heinrich von der Hagen. Berlin: Vereins-Buchhandlung, 1839. Pp. xiv + 197.

The first German translation of the *Rose* (see also no. 28).

28   ----- and Joseph Gregor, tr. *Guillaume de Lorris, Der Roman von der Rose.* Essay by Emil Winkler. Vienna: Museion, Ed. Strache, 1921. Pp. lix + XVII + 8 leaves of plates.

Fährmann's early German translation of the first part, followed by an introductory essay by Emil Winkler. A note at the end identifies the translator as Heinrich Fährmann, with Joseph Gregor. A beautifully printed volume (issued in 200 copies), in large format with gothic letters and full-color reproductions of eight pages from the ms. Vienna, National Library Codex 2592.

29   Goublet, Juliette, tr. *Le roman de la rose d'après Guillaume de Lorris.* Paris: J. Carvo, 1963. Pp. 90.

An octosyllabic, mostly rhyming translation into Modern French of the first 3491 lines of the *Rose*, ending with the kiss, rather than with l'Amant's lament: "Et qu'importe si j'ai souffert/ Des ennuis de jour et de nuit / Puisque j'ai pu baiser la ROSE" (89). The translation, printed in script, stays close to the text, to the point of keeping Old French vocabulary such as *ouir*. The translator appends the following wish: "Puisse ce travail d'amateur plus hardi qu'un labeur savant, rendre odeur et couleur à la ROSE" (90).

30   Heeroma, K., ed. *De fragmenten van de tweede Rose.* Zwolle: N. V. Uitgevers-Maatschappij, 1958. Pp. 191.

An edition of the fragments of the "'seconde *Rose*'" (84), the anonymous Flemish version from about 1290. While the other medieval Dutch translation, that of Hein van Aken, follows the text of the *Rose* quite closely, the second translator makes many changes, to the point of eliminating the first-person narrator and creating a different frame story. The editor praises the translator, whom he sees as ameliorating the story. Heeroma considers the translator as "un des meilleurs poètes flamands du 13me [sic] siècle" (86). [Includes resumé in French.]

31 Huard, Etienne, tr. *Le roman de la rose: traduction libre et en vers.* Paris: Louis Rosier, 1835. Pp. 304.

The first rendering of the *Rose* into modern French. Huard's version, in alexandrine verse, is less a translation than an imitation: "nous n'avons puisé dans l'original que les pensées, que nous avons dépouillées de la haire et de la heuse pour les vêtir de l'habit français" (3). The translator took it upon himself to restore to the text all the suppressions and omissions made by the "rivaux des deux auteurs" (6). The second volume was supposed to include a life of Jean de Meun and portraits of the authors "dessinés d'après nature" (7). (The Bibliothèque Nationale has only the first volume, and I have not been able to locate any subsequent volumes.)

32 Hubert, André, illustrator. *Le roman de la rose, par Guillaume de Lorris.* Paris: Editions de l'Ibis, 1965. N. p.

An edition based on the incunabulum of Jean du Pré, with Marteau's translation (see no. 37), and illustrated by André Hubert.

33 Ineichen, Gustav, tr. and intro. *Guillaume de Lorris, Der Rosenroman.* Foreword by Wolfgang Stammler. Philologische Studien und Quellen. Berlin: Erich Schmidt, 1956. Pp. 86.

A German prose translation of the first part of the *Rose*, with lines numbered to correspond with Langlois's edition (see note 6). The introduction describes briefly the literary history of the romance and summarizes the first part. Ineichen points to a two-part structure: in the first part the dreamer is an impartial observer of the garden, in the second he becomes the lover. The Rose is seen as "Geschlechtssymbol" (15). The introduction stresses Guillaume's originality, which involves his shaping of the psychological processes of the love experience through the allegorical methods of medieval mental analysis and the actualization of this vision in an original world, "in einem Metakosmos" (18). Includes list of allegorical characters.

34 Jeanroy, B.-A., tr. *Le roman de la rose: principaux épisodes traduits par Mme B.-A. Jeanroy.* Intro. A[lfred] Jeanroy. *Poèmes et Récits de la Vieille France* 12. Paris: E. de Boccard, 1928. Pp. xxi + 133.

A selection of short passages from the *Rose* in a fairly literal prose translation (intervening material is summarized briefly). The first part receives as much attention as the second. The introduction relates briefly what is known of the two authors and indicates the artistic qualities and faults of the two parts: Guillaume is subtle but lacking in verbal power; Jean is interested in knowledge of all kinds and preaches an unchristian naturalism. Jeanroy praises especially Jean's "faculté d'observation et son sens dramatique" (xvi), which contributed to the survival of the *Rose* in the shipwreck of medieval literature.

35 Lanly, André, tr. *Guillaume de Lorris et Jean de Meun, Le roman de la rose.* Classiques Français du Moyen Age, Traductions 12. 2 tomes in 5 vols. Paris: Honoré Champion, 1971-76. 2nd ed. Paris: Honoré Champion, 1982-83. Rpt. Paris: Club du Livre, 1976.

A blank-verse translation in modern French of the Lecoy edition (see no. 7), which the translation generally follows line for line. Each volume includes notes on the text (largely lexical), a list of words discussed in the notes, and a summary. In Tome 1 a short "Notice de Présentation" gives basic information about the *Rose* and concludes that Guillaume's part suggests an antagonism between stern and conventional courtly views of love imposed on the unhappy lover and the "joie de vivre dans des plaisirs sans mélange -- et d'aimer" (xvi) which the superhuman personifications in the garden enjoy. The last volume includes a note (207-14) on the meaning of the personifications; Lanly reviews Louis's tempting proposal that everything in the garden of Deduit reflects the inner world of the young woman but cites lines from Jean de Meun's continuation that suggest that some characters, Jalousie in particular, represent forces outside her (see no. 376). The 1976 reprint includes an introduction by Georges Duby (see no. 219), twelve etchings by Leonor Fini, and woodcuts from the 1485 edition.

36 Marot, Clément, tr. *Le roman de la rose dans la version attribuée à Clément Marot.* Ed. Silvio F. Baridon. Intro. Antonio Viscardi. 2 vols. Testi e Documenti di Letteratura Moderna 1. Milan: Istituto Editoriale Cisalpino, 1954-1957.

The text, with variants and a preface by Baridon, of the modernization of the *Rose* first published in 1526 and attributed to the poet Clément Marot by Etienne Pasquier at the end of the century. In his long preface, Baridon summarizes the reception of the *Rose* in the sixteenth century, attributing a large part of its continued popularity to its misogynistic themes. He then discusses its influence on specific writers such as Villon, Rabelais, and particularly Marot, whose work shows many points of influence by the *Rose*. Finally, Baridon reviews the principal arguments for and against the attribution of this version to Marot and concludes that there is no good reason to deny him the authorship. Includes a bibliography of the early editions of the *Rose* (based on Bourdillon; see no. 49).

37 Marteau, Pierre [Jules Croissandeau], ed. and tr. *Le roman de la rose par Guillaume de Lorris et Jean de Meung: édition accompagnée d'une traduction en vers, précédée d'une introduction, notices historiques et critiques, suivie de notes et d'un glossaire.* Bibliothèque elzévirienne 39. 5 vols. Orleans: H. Herluison; Paris: P. Daffis [vols. 2-5], 1878-1880. Rpt. Nendeln: Kraus Reprints, 1970.

A reprinting of Méon's text (no. 4) with facing verse translation that attempts to be literal. A brief introduction explains the translator's desire to make this formerly popular but currently difficult text available to both scholars and the general public. After another scholar, M. Cougny, had abandoned the task of reediting the text, Marteau decided to reprint Méon's edition as "la meilleure que nous connaissions" (xv). In the biographical notice Marteau cites Méon to some extent but also brings the information on the poets' lives up to date. A long summary of the romance, interspersed with glosses, ends in a remarkably sentimental resume of the last 18 chapters. Marteau reproduces the "Vie de Jean de Meung" by André Thévet and discusses the critical work of other scholars, in particular J.-J. Ampère, Paul Huot, and Paulin Paris (see nos. 144, 307, and 423). The notes are in part original, in part taken from earlier editions.

38 Mary, André, tr. *Le Roman de la rose de Guillaume de Lorris and Jean de Meun*. Paris: Payot, 1928. New ed. 1949; rpt. Paris: Gallimard, 1969 and 1984 (Collection Folio 1518, with Postface and Bibliography by Jean Dufournet). Rpt. Paris: Club des Libraires de France [1960].

The first prose translation in modern French, according to the author (new ed., 365), and the only modern French translation of the entire romance in one volume before Strubel's (see no. 43). The translation, meant to make the *Rose* enjoyable to "le public d'aujourd'hui" (17), is generally accurate. The Preface reviews briefly responses to the work up to the nineteenth century and describes in laudatory terms the literary qualities of the two parts: One cannot conceive of anything more divine than Guillaume's "paradis d'amour" (10), while Jean de Meun, "le premier grand homme de lettres qu'ait produit la France" (10), is seen as embodying "l'esprit français" (11). Brief notes clarify certain references and difficult words. The 1960 edition includes eight color reproductions of miniatures from a fifteenth-century manuscript in Vienna.

39 Ott, Karl August, tr. *Guillaume de Lorris und Jean de Meun, Der Rosenroman*. Klassische Texte des romanischen Mittelalters in zweisprachiger Ausgabe 15, 1-3. 3 vols. Munich: Wilhelm Fink, 1976-1979.

A translation into unrhymed German verse based on Langlois's edition, corrected with Lecoy's (see nos. 6 and 7). The first volume includes an introduction which reviews *Rose* criticism, the arguments for the Christian interpretation, and the evidence for and against the presumed courtly perspective of the first part. Volume 3 includes a long bibliography and an index of proper names.

40 Redoli Morales, Ricardo, tr. *Guillaume de Lorris, Le roman de la rose*. Malaga: Universidad de Malaga, 1984. Pp. 79.

A Spanish prose translation of the first part, with notes and an introduction which reprints, with a few changes, the author's article in *Analecta Malacitana* (see no. 462).

41 Robbins, Harry W., tr. *The Romance of the Rose by Guillaume de Lorris and Jean de Meun*. Intro. by Charles W. Dunn. New York: E. P. Dutton, 1962. Pp. xxxiii + 472.

This English verse translation of the *Rose* was discovered and printed after Robbins's death. The language of the translation is slightly archaic, and the translator renders the Old French more freely than does Dahlberg (and with a few errors), but there are also some felicities of expression (see for example: Cerberus "with longing burns / And well-nigh dies of hunger-nourished rage / Unless the harlot hastens to his aid" [421]). Robbins's lines do not always correspond to the original, making it difficult to go from one to the other. The volume includes a short introduction for non-specialists (which tries to make the ending more acceptable), a selective bibliography, a descriptive table of contents with line numbers from the Langlois edition (see no. 6), fifteen black and white illustrations from three *Rose* manuscripts in the Pierpont Morgan library, and a selective list of proper and place names.

42 Sasaki, Shigemi, tr. *Le roman de la rose*. Tokyo: Daigaku-Shorin, 1988. Pp. 149.

A partial translation in Japanese, with commentary and notes.

Listed in *Encomia: Bibliographical Bulletin of the International Courtly Literature Society* 12 (1990):25. [I have not been able to see a copy.]

43 Strubel, Armand, ed. and tr. *Guillaume de Lorris et Jean de Meun, Le roman de la rose*. "Lettres gothiques." Paris: Le Livre de Poche, 1992. Pp. 1272.

An edition and translation in modern French of the complete *Rose* in one volume [a small, thick one; it would have been easier to handle in two volumes]. The editor chose for his base manuscripts two that had never before been edited (Paris, B. N. fr. 12786 for the first part, 378 for the second), but which he sees as representative of part of the manuscript tradition. The text is accompanied by a close prose translation in modern French, notes, variants, and rejected readings. An introduction presents briefly the literary history of the *Rose* but concentrates on analyzing the authors' poetics. Strubel stresses the differences between the two parts: Guillaume's "raffinement aristocratique" is followed by Jean's "ensemble apparemment chaotique de discours et de dissertations" (7). Strubel presents a good analysis of the themes and images which convey this "dialectique du désir" (18). [Note that the second manuscript lacks the ending, which Strubel translates from the Lecoy addition without, however, providing the text of the ending.] This edition-translation makes it easier to use the *Rose* in the classroom.

44 Vertut, Georges, tr. *Le roman de la rose par Guillaume de Lorris et Jean de Meung*. Collection Jacques Hamont. Paris: Editions d'Histoire et d'Art, Librairie Plon, 1956. Pp. 181.

A prose translation and condensation in modern French, with a few archaic words for atmosphere. Vertut evidently wanted to modernize the *Roman de la rose* in order to show how it is "la manifestation et la preuve du génie de l'âme française par excellence" (12). The second part of the *Rose* is considerably condensed--in Vertut's translation it is one-third shorter than the first part--and its bawdiness cleaned up. Nature's long discourse, for example, is summarized in one page, and the erotic elements of Genius's speech and of l'Amant's appearance as a pilgrim are eliminated. Two dozen woodcut illustrations from the fifteenth-century edition of Jean du Pré are reproduced.

45 Verwijs, Eelco, ed. *Die Rose van Heinric van Aken, met de Fragmenten der tweede Vertaling*. 1868; rpt. Utrecht: HES Publishers, 1976. Pp. xxxiv + 260.

An edition of the medieval Dutch translation of the *Rose* by the Brabançon cleric, Heinric van Aken; with variants and notes. A short introduction first looks at the popularity of the *Rose* in France in the Middle Ages and its rediscovery and reception in the nineteenth century. In the first section proper, Verwijs discusses the dating of the two parts with particular respect to contemporary allusions and concerns. The second section considers and evaluates the relationship of the Middle Dutch text with the original. Heinric van Aken translates Guillaume's text almost word-for-word, while he reduces Jean's to just over half. The reduction is achieved by both abbreviation and wholesale omission of passages. Includes the fragments of the other medieval Dutch translation (see no. 30). [KB]

STUDIES OF MANUSCRIPTS AND EDITIONS; CONCORDANCES

46 Bertrand, Roger. *Guillaume de Lorris, Le roman de la rose: concordancier complet des formes graphiques occurrentes*. 2 vols. Aix-en-Provence: CUER-MA, 1983-1984.

A key word in context concordance: each word of the first part is printed with the verse in which it is found. The text is divided into two parts, volume 1, treating vv. 1-2076; volume 2, vv. 2076-4028 (based on the Lecoy edition; see no. 7). Thus each word is listed twice. Special signs are used for the diacritical marks and certain grammatical forms are differentiated (the preposition *a*, for example, from the verbal form *a*). [The system of differentiation is not clearly explained.]

47 Bezzola, Reto R. "Fragment einer unbekannten Handschrift des *Roman de la rose*." *Vox romanica* 5 (1940):284-89.

48 -----. "Ein neues Zürcherfragment des *Roman de la rose*." *Vox romanica* 6 (1941/1942):371-73.

49 Bourdillon, F[rancis] W[illiam]. *The Early Editions of "The Roman de la rose"*. The Bibliographical Society Illustrated Monographs 14. 1906; rpt. Geneva: Slatkine Reprints, 1974. Pp. x + 212 + 34 illus. Appended: *A Vérard Fragment of the "Roman de la rose": Supplementary Note to Illustrated Monograph XIV "The Early Editions of the Roman de la rose"*. London: Printed for the Bibliographical Society at the Chiswick Press, 1913. N. p.

A meticulous study of the twenty-one editions of the *Rose* printed from about 1480 to 1538. Bourdillon describes in detail the editions, which include Marot's modernized version and Molinet's prose version, and traces the relationship both of the editions and the illustrations (woodcuts). The study includes much information on the history of printing and woodcuts in this period, providing intriguing insights into the *Rose* as a book. For example, all the editions are derived from the first edition (1481), which became the standard version of the text (supplanting the many manuscripts); one of the outstanding manuscripts in the British Museum, Harley 4425, was copied from a printed edition; and Lenglet Dufresnoy's 1735 edition (see no. 2), despite the editor's claims to have consulted the manuscripts, is "an almost verbatim reprint of Vérard's Quarto" (150). *The Early Editions* is beautifully printed to resemble an incunabulum and includes many reproductions of woodcuts from the early editions. Appended is a note on and facsimile of a fragment related to Vérard's folio edition. Bourdillon concludes that the fragment is not part of a lost edition but "a 'trial sheet' printed off to test the type, which proved, when tested, to be too much worn to use" [6].

50   Danos, Joseph R. "A Concordance of the *Roman de la rose* of Guillaume de Lorris, with a Dependent Semantic Study of Four Key Concepts of Courtly Love: 'Cortoisie,' 'Franchise,' 'Vilanie' and 'Felonie'." Diss. U of North Carolina, 1974.

51   -----. *A Concordance to the "Roman de la rose" of Guillaume de Lorris*. North Carolina Studies in the Romance Languages and Literatures: Texts, Textual Studies, and Translations 3. Chapel Hill, N. C.: University of North Carolina, Department of Romance Languages, 1975. Pp. 307.

A list of each word in the first part of the *Rose* in alphabetical order, followed by all the lines in which it occurs (both number and entire line are given). Homographs are distinguished by part of speech. The author has used the Langlois edition instead of the more recent edition by Lecoy (erroneously described in the preface as a diplomatic edition), but a table reconciling the verse numbers of the two editions is provided in Appendix IV (see nos. 6 and 7). The appendices also give an alphabetized word frequency list (the adjective *bel*, for instance, is found 31 times); a word frequency list arranged in descending order of frequency; and a reverse-alphabetized word list (i.e., by ending). One useful aspect of the concordance is that characters' names are listed separately, with multiple-word names, such as Bel Accueil, given as one word.

52   Dean, Ruth J. "Un manuscrit du *Roman de la rose* à Jersey." *Romania* 65 (1939):233-37.

A note about a manuscript that Langlois did not include in his study (see no. 66), one that was discovered in an old barn and given to the Jersey Public Library. Probably dating from the second quarter of the fourteenth century, the manuscript is missing several leaves and others are out of order (Dean indicates the correct order). She suggests Langlois's group II for the manuscript family and gives the first and last ten lines.

53   Dorgan, Cornelia W. "*Le roman de la rose*, 1526." *Boston Public Library Quarterly* 6 (1954):58-61.

A description of the library's recently acquired copy of the first edition (1526) of Clément Marot's revision of the *Rose* (see no. 36). In addition, Dorgan gives a brief overview of the importance of the *Rose* and its influence. The illustrations of the 1524 edition are also described.

54   Ewert, A. "Two Fragments of the *Roman de la rose*." *Modern Language Review* 26 (1931):182-87.

A description of two fourteenth-century manuscript fragments from the Merton College, Oxford, library, containing Langlois ll. 2398-2716 and 3031-3341 in the first, 16003-16162 and 16483-16642 in the second. Ewert also suggests the family of manuscripts to which they may belong (following Langlois's classification; see no. 66) and lists readings "calculated to clear up doubtful points" (187) or to support some of Langlois's readings.

55   Fawtier, R. "Deux manuscrits du *Roman de la rose*." *Romania* 58 (1932):265-73.

A description of two manuscripts in English libraries, neither of which were seen by Langlois (see no. 66). The first, that of the Count of Crawford, is described in some detail since it was in private hands. Completed on April 30, 1323 (not 1523, as Langlois states in his edition; see no. 6, 1: 49 n. l), it contains ninety-five miniatures which are a good example of the work of French miniaturists of the time, and is placed by Fawtier in the B family of manuscripts (Langlois's classification). The second manuscript, in the John Rylands Library in Manchester, is described briefly (see also no. 68). It dates from the end of the fourteenth century, has only four mediocre miniatures, and is incomplete.

56 Fourez, Lucien. "*Le roman de la rose* de la Bibliothèque de la Ville de Tournai." *Scriptorium* 1 (1946/1947):213-39.

A description of manuscript CI, dated 1330, one of the twenty-four manuscripts that escaped the destruction by German bombing of the library of Tournai in 1940 and one of those edited by Gui de Mori (see nos. 682 and 769). Fourez describes not only the ms. but also speculates on the patron for whom it was completed, one of the Pourrés family. He also includes a plot summary before completing a physical description of the ms. The major portion of the article is a description of the illustrations, including the drolleries, with the conclusion that these illustrations are entirely different from the "décoration classique" (234) of the *Rose* as described by Kuhn (no. 65). The article ends with a description of the manuscript's situation within the corpus of Tournai mss. [KML]

57 Ham, Edward Billings. "The Cheltenham Manuscripts of the *Roman de la rose*." *Modern Language Review* 26 (1931):427-35.

A concise description of five *Rose* manuscripts in the collection of Sir Thomas Phillipps in Thirlestaine House, Cheltenham. The author notes that these manuscripts have only casually been recorded by Haenel, Migne, and Durrieu. Of the five manuscripts, Ham calls 4363 the most important; he believes it to be the one used by Méon and dated 1375 (see no. 66, 120). After describing each manuscript, Ham attributes it to the appropriate grouping done by Langlois in *Les manuscrits du "Roman de la rose"* (no. 66). [KML]

58 Hawkins, Richmond Laurin. "The Manuscripts of the *Roman*

de la rose in the Libraries of Harvard and Yale Universities." *Romanic Review* 19 (1928):1-24.

A description of three manuscripts at Harvard and Yale, which Langlois failed to treat fully. The early, well-written Harvard Fr. 14.5 is by far the most important and receives a detailed description and evaluation, including biographical information on some of the previous owners, reproduction of the anonymous ending interpolated between the two parts, and a study of the scribal dialect. Hawkins classifies the manuscript in Langlois's family C and believes that it is close to the original text. The other two manuscripts are described briefly: Yale Z 111.015 reduces the first part to 1312 lines, to serve as an introduction to Jean's part; Harvard Fr. 14F, a late fifteenth-century manuscript, contains "nearly every blemish that it is possible for a scribe to introduce into a manuscript" (23). Includes five reproductions of pages of the manuscripts.

59 Hegman, W. E. "In margine het Cheltenhamse *Rose*-handschrift." *Spiegel der Letteren* 30 (1988):67-71.

A detailed description and brief history of ms. Brussels KB II-1171, containing texts of Middle Dutch versions of the *Sept Sages de Rome*, Vincent de Beauvais's *Speculum Historiale* (i.e., Maerlant's *Spiegel Historiale*), and the *Roman de la rose*. [KB]

60 Högberg, Paul. *L'édition du "Roman de la rose" par Nicolas Desprez*. Besançon: Impr. Jacques et Demontrond, 1925. Pp. 14. [Extract from the *Bibliographe moderne* 22 (1924/1925):97-111.]

A sequel to the author's discussion of the rare early printed edition of the *Rose* by Nicolas Desprez (see no. 61). Högberg surveys the known copies of Desprez's edition and describes the copy made for Clément Longis, now in the library of Harvard University. This copy cannot help resolve the question of the exact date of the printing, which must be after January 1503 and before May 15, 1510. More precisely, though, Höberg suggests dating it between October 10, 1504 and May 26, 1506 (see no. 49).

61 -----. "Une édition rarissime du *Roman de la rose* dans la Bibliothèque de l'Université Royale d'Uppsala." In *Uppsala Universitetsbiblioteks Minnesskrift, 1621-1921* [Uppsala, 1921]: 268-91.

A description of and attempt to date a very rare early edition of the *Rose*, printed by Nicolas Desprez for Guillaume Eustace. The only known copy at that time was in the Uppsala University library (see also no. 60). Two appendices list the publications of Guillaume Eustace and Nicolas Desprez.

62 Huot, Sylvia. "Notice sur les fragments poétiques dans un manuscrit du *Roman de la rose*." *Romania* 109 (1988):119-21.

A study of the fragments of text discovered on the last page of Paris, B. N. fr. 24390 by Joseph Morawski in 1922. Huot, a specialist in *Rose* manuscripts, identifies the fragments as related to the revised edition of the *Rose* made by Gui de Mori in the thirteenth century. Certain details of the fragments lead Huot to speculate on the way the copyist approached his work and to suggest that he was following a copy close to that of the Tournai manuscript. The fragments are further evidence of the "lecture comparée" (121) to which the *Rose* was subjected in the Middle Ages.

63 Jung, Marc-René. "Ein Fragment des *Rosenromans* in der Stiftsbibliothek Engelberg." *Vox romanica* 24 (1965):234-37.

A description of a two-folio fragment of Jean de Meun's part of the *Rose* (Langlois ll. 9351-494 and 10365-508) found in the Engelberg (Switzerland) library. Comparing the fragment to one in Zurich, Jung argues that both fragments are from the same late thirteenth- or early fourteenth-century manuscript but that the Engelberg fragment is too short to be placed in one of Langlois's families of manuscripts. A list of selected variants and corrections in the Engelberg fragment is given. The notes contain a useful list of fourteen articles that describe other manuscripts and fragments discovered since Langlois's *Manuscrits du "Roman de la rose"* (no. 66).

64   Kelly, Thomas E. and Thomas H. Ohlgren. "Paths to Memory: Iconographic Indices to *Roman de la rose* and *Prose Lancelot* Manuscripts in the Bodleian Library." *Visual Resources* 3 (1983):1-15.

A report on a collaborative project with the Bodleian Library to film and index eleven manuscripts of prose romances, predominantly the *Lancelot* in prose, and twelve manuscripts of the *Roman de la rose*. This project was undertaken to encourage studies of the "visual contents so central to the original conception" (1) of medieval illuminated manuscripts. The report outlines the constituent parts: microfiche reproduction of the manuscripts in color, commentaries and descriptions on black and white fiches, and a printed guide. In addition, the authors are preparing a machine-readable record for each manuscript in order to produce an iconographic index which will describe the distinctive features of each image, that is, both text-specific pictorial detail and extratextual elements. A set of descriptors will allow cross-references based on generic entries such as *costume* or *archery*.

65   Kuhn, Alfred. "Die Illustration des *Rosenromans*." *Jahrbuch der Kunsthistorischen Sammlungen des allerhöchsten Kaiserhausen* 31 (1912):1-66 + 15 plates and 45 figures.

A study of miniatures in *Rose* mss. Kuhn first describes in detail the physical appearance (size of pages, style of handwriting, number and size of miniatures, etc.) of the fourteenth-century ms. Codex 2592 of the Court Library in Vienna. The author gives color specifications for each miniature, elaborates on the various backgrounds, and traces the precise history of background patterns from antiquity to the period of the manuscript. Kuhn further concentrates on the various costumes represented in the mss., giving information about the clothes of men and women, their shoes, hairstyles, and in general, their physical aspect and facial expressions. Women have for instance a small mouth, a long, fleshy neck, and tender, white skin. The author then questions whether the entire ms. was written by one scribe. However, it is a fact that it was illustrated by more than one artist, and the technical details allow Kuhn to date it to Paris in the 1370s. In order to explain this information, Kuhn traces the history of the many illustrated mss. of the *Rose* and their characteristics. The oldest date from the last years of the thirteenth century and come from the north of France. There is still complete lack of realism in the colors: pink and blue trees are the rule. The depiction is entirely symbolic with frequent borrowings of schemes from sacred art. From the north the illustration cycle reached Paris in the first half of the fourteenth century and influenced the major development, the abandoning of the monastic tradition for a gradual conquest of realistic representation. In big ateliers the numbers of mss. increased drastically, while their quality declined. [ASK]

66 Langlois, Ernest. *Les manuscrits du "Roman de la rose": description et classement.* Travaux et Mémoires de l'Université de Lille n.s. I, Droit, Lettres 7. Lille: Tallandier; Paris: Honoré Champion, 1910. Pp. 548.

The only comprehensive description yet undertaken of the many *Rose* manuscripts. The catalogue describes 215 manuscripts found in thirteen countries, including some fragments, and classifies 116 of them. Langlois's descriptions, most of which are brief and include both manuscripts that he saw and some that he did not, give the size and date of the manuscript, the page format, and the first line of the second leaf. The presence of miniatures is noted, with sometimes a brief appreciation of their quality. Given in full are scribal additions (such as lines inserted between the two parts). There are also descriptions of manuscripts whose whereabouts are unknown and a number of lists: other works found in the same manuscript, copyists, owners of manuscripts, and incipits of second leaves. The second and third parts of Langlois's work attempt to group pre-fifteenth century manuscripts according to variants, omissions, etc. Each part includes an index of variants cited. Although Langlois's classification has been questioned (Lecoy, no. 6, xxxvii), it has served as a first description and grouping of the manuscripts.

67 Monnier, Philippe M. "Trois manuscrits à peintures ayant appartenu au duc de Berry." *Librarium* 11 (1968):125-37 + ill.

A description of a beautiful *Rose* manuscript dating from 1353 in the Bibliothèque Publique et Universitaire of Geneva, fr. 178, which also includes the *Testament*. The author praises the warm colors and lifelike composition and costumes of the miniatures and attributes the manuscript to "un excellent atelier parisien" (125). Two pages are reproduced.

68 Pickford, Cedric E. "The *Roman de la rose* and a Treatise Attributed to Richard de Fournival: Two Manuscripts in the John Rylands Library." *Bulletin of the John Rylands Library, Manchester* 34 (1951/1952):333-65.

A very detailed description of two *Rose* mss., neither of which were described by Langlois (see no. 66). The first, Rylands French 66, was described briefly by Fawtier (no. 55). It contains all but the last 773 lines of the romance and includes four miniatures. The first folios contain a short prose treatise on the nature of love, which is reprinted here. The manuscript also contains a 72-line version of the anonymous ending found in six other mss. and a large number of marginal notes; the language is Picard, from the first half of the fourteenth century; Pickford places it in Langlois's Group I. The other manuscript contains the complete *Rose* followed by *La Châtelaine de Vergy*. It is a conflated text (Groups I and II), dating probably from the latter half of the fourteenth century, and contains two miniatures.

69 Ponzio, Carla. "Un frammento del *Roman de la rose* a Montréal." *Pluteus* 2 (1984):79-83.

A transcription of a short fragment of the *Rose* (Langlois ll. 19062-19294) erroneously described by De Ricci and Wilson, *Census of Medieval and Renaissance Manuscripts in the United States and Canada*, as a dialogue or mystery play. The mistake was probably prompted by the presence of four rubrics about Nature inserted in the text. The fragment appears to be related to Langlois's group II, families M and N (see no. 66). [MRB]

70 Roques, Mario. "Fragments de manuscrits du *Roman de la rose*." *Romania* 55 (1929):263-65.

A brief description of five fragments of *Rose* manuscripts which the author dates from the end of the fourteenth through the fifteenth centuries and which are now in the Archives Nationales in Paris.

71 Ruggieri, Jole. "Uno sconosciuto frammento del *Roman de la rose*." *Archivum romanicum* 14 (1930):417-36.

A description of a fragment which was donated by Giulio Bertoni to the Biblioteca Estense of Modena and which consists of two parchments with the text in two columns by a French hand of the first half of the sixteenth century. The text corresponds to Langlois ll. 9454-607, 10502-651, 10800-949, and 11535-686. The fragment appears to be close to the large family of manuscripts designated by Langlois as L. An examination of linguistic features reveals that the amanuensis was originally from central-eastern France. The fragment contains a few rubrics (unknown to the critical edition) and also some marginal notes by an owner (probably a notary) in the sixteenth century. [MRB]

72   Samaran, Charles. "Fragments de manuscrits." *Romania* 76 (1955):240-43.

A note about a fourteenth-century *Rose* manuscript, unknown to Langlois (see no. 66), among a group of four fragments discovered by the archivist of the Marne. The fragment consists of four "feuillets doubles, en médiocre ou mauvais état" (241), containing six passages from the second part. Samaran mentions that they offer many variants but declines to reproduce them.

73   Spiele, I. and M. Drijkoningen-Leyh. "Quelques fragments inconnus du *Roman de la rose* conservés à Leyde (UB-BPL 2552,3)." *Neophilologus* 66 (1982):16-42.

A description and transcription of eight fragments from an apparently unfinished manuscript dating from the second quarter of the fifteenth century, probably Brabantine. In addition to the transcription, the article indicates the distribution of verses and the manuscript groups and families to which the copy is related (based on Langlois's classification, which the authors briefly summarize; see no. 66).

74   Van der Poel, Dieuwke [E]. "Over gebruikersnotities in het *Rose*-handscrift K. A. XXIV." *De Nieuwe Taalgids* 79 (1986):505-16.

A description of the manuscript The Hague K. B., K. A. XXIV containing Heinric van Aken's adaptation of the *Roman de la rose*, the *Roman van Cassamus*, and *De frenesie*. The manuscript contains three kinds of marginal annotations: two types of *nota* signs (pointing fingers, etc.), and sets of plus and minus signs. Van der Poel concludes that the latter may be by an adaptor who intended to abbreviate the passages thus designated so as to form a faster-moving narrative. [KB]

75 Vitale-Brovarone, Alessandro. "Un nuovo frammento del *Roman de la rose*." *Studi francesi* 60 [20] (1976):497-98.

A notice and brief description of a short fragment of the *Roman de la rose* found in the Archivio Comunale of the city of Asti. A list of the most important variants is given. [MRB]

76 Walters, Lori. "Author Portraits and Textual Demarcation in Manuscripts of the *Romance of the Rose*." In *Rethinking* (no. 182). 359-73.

An appendix to the volume of articles giving a detailed list of miniatures representing the *Rose*'s authors in 59 manuscripts (out of 91 mss. studied). The list also indicates whether the portrait occurs at the end of Guillaume's *Rose*, at the midpoint of the conjoined work, or in both places, and what rubrics are given. Walters believes that the author portraits became an acknowledged feature in *Rose* mss., more so than in the manuscript tradition of other works.

77 -----. "A Parisian Manuscript of the *Romance of the Rose*." *Princeton University Library Chronicle* 51 (1989):31-55.

A study of ms. Garrett 126 in the Princeton University Library. Walters notes that it is a typical example of mid-fourteenth-century Parisian editions of the *Rose*. Walters's study would be an excellent reading for students in a *Rose* seminar, since it opens with an outline of the poem and continues with a discussion of *Rose* manuscripts. Eight reproductions illustrate miniatures from the Garrett ms. and also from Paris B. N. fr. 1565 and 24388 and Pierpont Morgan 324. Tables describe individual miniatures in the four mss., comparing placement of those miniatures. In fact, the major portion of the article discusses the typicality of Garrett 126 as a fourteenth-century *Rose* ms., both in its "schedule of illumination and the placement of its author portrait" (55). [KML]

CHAPTER TWO

OTHER WORKS BY OR ATTRIBUTED TO JEAN DE MEUN

EDITIONS

Abelard and Heloise, *Les épîtres*

78 Beggiato, Fabrizio, ed. *Le lettere di Abelardo ed Eloisa nella traduzione di Jean de Meun.* Istituto di Filologia Romanza dell'Università di Roma; Studi, Testi e Manuali 5. 2 vols. Modena: STEM Mucchi, 1977.

An edition of the letters which gives the text in the first volume and an introduction, critical apparatus, notes, and glossary in the second. [The edition is flawed by many errors of transcription and by an inconsistent editorial procedure, such as in the resolution of u/v and i/j].

79 -----, ed. "La prima lettera di Eloisa ad Abelardo nella traduzione di Jean de Meun." *Cultura neolatina* 32 (1972):211-30.

A critical edition of Jean's translation of the first letter of Heloise to Abelard, with complete *apparatus criticus*, notes, and

34 The *Roman de la rose*: An Annotated Bibliography

a paleographical and linguistic description (from Paris, B. N. fr. 920). Beggiato argues that the criteria Jean followed in the translation of the *Consolatio* (see no. 103) are already applied in this earlier work: "aderenza al significato del latino e chiarezza funzionale del volgare" (215), and that Jean seems to reach a higher expressive intensity in Heloise's letters. Beggiato announces the forthcoming edition of the entire manuscript, which contains Jean's version of the *Historia Calamitatum*, seven of the eight letters, and three other texts related to the Abelard and Heloise story (see no. 78). [MRB]

80   Brook, Leslie C. "Jean de Meun's Translation of the Letters of Abelard and Heloise: A Critical Edition, with Introduction, Notes and Glossary." Diss. U of Bristol, 1968.

81   Charrier, Charlotte, ed. *Jean de Meun, traduction de la première épître de Pierre Abélard (Historia Calamitatum)*. Paris: Honoré Champion, 1934. Pp. 198.

An edition of Jean de Meun's translation of Abelard's first letter, with facing Latin text from earliest extant manuscript (originally the author's dissertation, University of Paris, 1934). Charrier's introduction describes the only extant manuscript of the translation, summarizes some facts of Jean's life and work, and speculates on the reason for his translation of the letters, which aroused little interest in the Middle Ages since they ran counter to medieval views of courtly love. She also gives an overview of the language of the copy and the strengths and weaknesses of the translation, which she sees as faithful and clear. The edition includes notes, information on works cited in the *Historia*, and an index of proper names. [Charrier is also the author of *Héloïse dans l'histoire et dans la légende*.]

82   Génin, François, ed. "Première lettre d'Abailard, traduction inédite de Jean de Meung." *Bulletin du Comité historique*

des monuments ecrits de l'histoire de France; histoire, sciences, lettres 2 (1850):175-91, 265-92.

The first edition of Abelard's *Historia calamitatum* in Jean de Meun's translation.

83 Hicks, Eric, ed. *La vie et les epistres Pierres Abaelart et Heloys sa fame: traduction du XIIIe siècle attribuée à Jean de Meun*. Nouvelle Bibliothèque du Moyen Age 16. 2 vols. Geneva: Slatkine; Paris: Champion, 1991. Vol. 1 (to date), pp. Lix + 161 double pages.

A complete edition of the only extant manuscript of the translation of the letters attributed to Jean de Meun, including the three added pieces which were probably not translated by him. The Latin text is given facing the translation; changes and corrections are given at the bottom of the page. In his introduction Hicks reviews modern critical opinion on the authenticity of the letters and of the attribution to Jean de Meun, which he is inclined to accept. After discussing briefly the translation and the problems it poses for editors, Hicks discusses at greater length all extant and lost Latin mss. of the letters. The second volume is to include a computer-generated lexicon of the letters.

84 Schultz, Elizabeth. "*La vie et les epistres Pierres Abaelart et Heloys sa fame*, a Translation by Jean de Meun, and an Old French Translation of Three Related Texts: A Critical Edition of MS 920 (Bibliothèque Nationale)." Diss. U of Washington, 1969.

85 Zink, Michel, ed. "Traduction française attribuée à Jean de Meun de la lettre de Pierre le Vénérable à Héloïse." In *Pierre Abélard-Pierre le Vénérable: les courants philosophiques, littéraires et artistiques en occident au milieu du XIIe siècle (Abbaye de Cluny, 2 au 9 juillet 1992)*. Ed. René Louis and Jean Jolivet. Colloques internationaux du

Centre National de la Recherche Scientifique 546. Paris: CNRS, 1975. 29-37.

The text of the translation attributed to Jean de Meun of a letter in Latin from Peter the Venerable to Heloise after Abelard's death. The translation is preceded by the Latin text printed as a "Texte liminaire" (23-27) and by an introduction which discusses the question of attribution and describes the numerous glosses in the translation which the editor believes show that this translation "vise moins au plaisir littéraire qu'à l'instruction et à l'édification du lecteur" (30).

Boethius, *La consolation de Philosophie*

86   Dedeck-Héry, V[enceslas]-L[ouis], ed. "Boethius' *De Consolatione* by Jean de Meun." *Mediaeval Studies* 14 (1952):165-275.

An edition of Jean de Meun's translation published after the editor's death by Alex J. Denomy, who wrote an introduction that includes a short biography of Dedeck-Héry, a list of the seventeen manuscripts, and a description of editorial practices. The edition also gives all ms. variants, "however minute, to provide the machinery for one day determining the definite Latin manuscript and French commentary that Chaucer used in his translation" (166).

87   -----. "Un fragment inédit de la traduction de la *Consolation* de Boèce par Jean de Meun." *Romanic Review* 27 (1936):110-24.

A transcription of a fragment of a Parisian manuscript of Jean de Meun's translation. Dedeck-Héry indicates the corresponding passages in the Latin original and in another manuscript of the translation and suggests that this manuscript served either a religious orator or a teacher of composition. The article also gives variants from the other manuscripts in the group to which this one belongs. The author believes that it was made from one of the earliest copies, perhaps during Jean de Meun's life [thus suggesting its immediate popularity].

Vegetius, *L'art de chevalerie*

88   Löfstedt, Leena, ed. *Li abregemenz noble honme Vegesce Flave René des establissemenz apartenanz a chevalerie: traduction par Jean de Meun de Flavii Vegeti Renati viri illustris Epitoma institutorum rei militaris.* Helsinki: Suomalainen Tiedeakatemia, 1977. Pp. 250.

A critical edition of Jean de Meun's translation, based on the best manuscript (Carpentras, Bibl. Inguimbertine ms. 332), with important variants at the bottom of the page. An introduction describes briefly Jean's translation, the dedicatee, and the manuscripts (with stemma); the language of the base manuscript is discussed at length. The edition marks interpolated passages (perhaps added by Jean de Meun's patron, Jean I, Count of Eu) and includes a commentary (mainly linguistic notes); indexes of proper names, Latin words, and subjects discussed in the commentary; and a short bibliography.

89   Robert, Ulysse. *L'art de chevalerie: traduction du "De re militari" de Végèce par Jean de Meun.* Société des Anciens Textes Français. Paris: Firmin Didot, 1897. Pp. LVi + 205.

An edition of the ms. Paris, B. N. fr. 2063, with modern punctuation. The introduction explains that Jean de Meun's translation is printed only to serve as a comparison to the verse translation of Jean Priorat, which is based closely on Jean de Meun's and followed it by a few years (Jean de Meun's version dates from 1284). Also discussed are some of the difficulties in translation that Jean de Meun met and numerous interpolations by him or copyists. The editor points out that Priorat's translation can be used to determine which parts of Jean de

Meun's were added by later hands.

Works Attributed to Jean de Meun

(The Méon edition of the *Roman de la rose* reprints alchemical works, the *Testament*, and the *Codicile*; see no. 4.)

90 Bourneuf, Aimee Celeste. "The *Testament* of Jean de Meung: Vatican MS 367." Diss. Fordham U, 1956.

91 Buzzetti Gallarati, Silvia, ed. *Le testament maistre Jehan de Meun: un caso letterario*. Scrittura e Scrittori, Serie Monografica 4. Alessandria: Edizioni dell'Orso, 1989. Pp. 261.

An annotated edition of the *Testament*, a work attributed to Jean de Meun in some manuscripts. The editor's introduction reviews the literary debate on the attribution of the work, its structure, themes, and rhetorical procedures. After exploring its 2,120 verses from different perspectives in order to define the cultural environment in which it was conceived, the author concludes that the attribution to Jean de Meun represents the most economical solution to the open question of attribution. A variety of factors, thoroughly analyzed by the author, point to Jean Clopinel: the familiarity with the language of scholasticism, the surfacing philosophical culture, the adherence to Thomist positions, all prove that the author is a cleric linked to the University of Paris, possibly a *maistre*, but at the same time his elaborations on the moralistic and didactic literature which constitutes the *Testament's* background and his virtuoso use of rhetoric reveal the *uomo di lettere*. Moreover, the *Testament* and the *Rose* present lexical and stylistic similarities, isomorphism of expository structure, and extensive formal correspondence. The *Testament* is to the *Rose* an "interlocutore da cui intende prendere una qualche distanza sul piano ideologico attraverso il sottile ed allusivo esercizio dei 'distinguo,' pur nell'atto di ribardirne varie idee, temi, immagini..." (112). In other words, if the *Rose* was inspired by radical Aristotelianism, at odds with Catholic orthodoxy, the *Testament* moves, if with some uncertainty, towards less Averroistic positions, closer to Thomas Aquinas and farther from hedonistic theories by condemning lust repeatedly and severely. The copyist of the base manuscript (dated 1353), was Girart de Biaulieu, a cleric of St. Sauveur. The notes are mostly aimed at elucidating the chosen text but also provide an historically sound commentary. Includes a glossary and bibliography. [MRB]

CRITICAL, LINGUISTIC, AND MANUSCRIPT STUDIES

General studies

92   Lucas, Robert H. "Mediaeval French Translations of the Latin Classics to 1500." *Speculum* 45 (1970):225-53.

A list of manuscripts containing medieval French translations of the Latin classics. The author believes the list to be "the first attempt at as complete an inventory...as the state of manuscript cataloguing will allow" (227). Included are the manuscripts of Jean's translations of the letters of Abelard and Heloise, Boethius's *De consolatione Philosophiae*, and Vegetius's *Epitoma rei militaris*. Lucas also lists some earlier studies of the manuscripts. Because of the uncertainty about which of the two translations of Boethius attributed to Jean de Meun was the authentic one, Lucas points out that even in recent catalogues "mss are often indiscriminately listed as those of Jean de Meun" (230 n. 26); only the incipit of the text can establish whether it is Jean de Meun's.

93   Paris, Paulin. "Jean de Meun, traducteur et poète." In vol. 28 of

Histoire littéraire de la France. 1881; rpt. Paris: H. Welter, 1900. 391-439.

A bio-bibliographical study of Jean de Meun which describes his translations and the works attributed to him and summarizes what was known of his life at the time. Paulin sees Jean as one of the earliest translators from Latin to French and praises his translations for their precision and elegance, despite the difficult texts with which he was working. The author has doubts about "la sincérité rigoureuse" (399) of the attribution of the famous letters to Abelard and Heloise (see also no. 100); he believes that the mixed prose-verse translation of Boethius, rather than the all-prose translation, is Jean's [scholars today generally believe the opposite; see no. 118]. Excerpts from all three translations are given, as well as from the *Testament*, which is seen as a document for "l'étude des moeurs anciennes" (426). Paulin gives evidence for rejecting the other works attributed to Jean and reviews the documents relating to Jean's house and his death (see also no. 455).

Abelard and Heloise, *Les épîtres*

94 Bozzolo, Carla. "L'humaniste Gontier Col et la traduction française des *Lettres* d'Abélard et Héloïse." *Romania* 95 (1974):199-215.

A two-part study which describes codicologically the sole manuscript of the French translation of the letters (attributed to Jean de Meun) and examines the manuscript's relation to the early fifteenth-century humanist, Gontier Col, and his milieu. Although the author declines to evaluate the authenticity of the translation, she does conclude that the last three pieces in the collection were originally an independent text, translated at a later date than the first eight letters, probably in the second half of the fourteenth century. Furthermore, she argues that it was Gontier Col who joined the two parts when he made the copy. Finally Bozzolo points to evidence of interest among French and Italian humanists of the period and suggests reasons for Col's decision to copy the letters.

95 Brook, Leslie C. "Comment évaluer une traduction du treizième siècle? Quelques considérations sur la traduction des lettres d'Abélard et d'Héloïse faite par Jean de Meun." In *The Spirit of the Court*. Selected Proceedings of the Fourth Congress of the International Courtly Literature Society (Toronto 1983). Ed. Glyn S. Burgess and Robert A. Taylor. Dover, New Hampshire: D. S. Brewer, 1985. 62-68.

A discussion both of the literary history of Jean de Meun's translation of the letters and of the criteria for judging a medieval translation. The single manuscript includes many errors of different kinds, which Brook briefly describes. Nonetheless, he believes that we can see that Jean followed in the letters his philosophy of translation as outlined in the prologue to his translation of Boethius, but more study is needed in order to appreciate Jean's qualities as a translator.

96 -----. "Reiterated quotations and statements in Jean de Meun's translation of the Abelard-Heloise Correspondence." *Zeitschrift für romanische Philologie* 105 (1989):81-91.

A study that aims to "uncover some of Jean de Meun's working methods" (81). Brook compares reiterated quotations in the letters, that is, passages cited from earlier letters or repeated citations of the same biblical, patristic, or secular passages. The study shows considerable variation in the reiterated quotations, beyond what can be attributed to scribal changes. Brook suggests several explanations, including the translator's medieval (i. e., non-modern) standards of consistency and the problem caused by copying procedures in which completed sections of the translation "might have been dispatched immediately to professional copyists" (91) and so have been unavailable to the translator in his later work.

97 -----. "Synonymic and Near-Synonymic Pairs in Jean de Meun's Translation of the Letters of Abelard and Heloise." *Neuphilologische Mitteilungen* 87 (1986):16-33.

A description of the form and function of synonymic and near-synonymic pairs of words as the commonest form of the broader phenomenon of the "expansion of the Latin wording" (16) in the letters. An appendix gives all examples of such pairs, which Brook analyzes for evidence of the author's stylistic purpose. The pairs have a variety of functions, such as clarifying the Latin word, often by indicating two possible meanings; adding rhetorical or emotional emphasis; and softening a Latinism. This analysis also suggests which French words Jean thought of as neologisms. Brook compares briefly his list with that given by Löfstedt for Jean de Meun's translation of Vegetius (see no. 124). He concludes favorably for Jean's skill as a translator: "the device of synonymic or near-synonymic pairs makes a positive contribution both to the clarity and the elegance" (28) of the translation. [Such an analysis may be helpful in studying Jean's use of synonymic pairs in the *Rose*.]

98 -----. "The Translator and his Reader: Jean de Meun and the Abelard-Heloise Correspondence." In *The Medieval Translator II*. Ed. Roger Ellis. Westfield Publications in Medieval Studies 5. London: Queen Mary and Westfield College, 1991. 99-122.

A continuation of the study [begun in no. 95] of Jean's approach to and skill in translation. The author focuses on ways in which Jean attempted to clarify for his readers the meaning of the Latin text. These ways include using two French terms to translate one Latin term and explaining classical names and difficult terms. Despite having made a few mistakes and mistranslations, Jean is judged by Brook to be "a meticulous but flexible translator" (103), whose prose is energetic and expressive.

99 Hicks, Eric and Jean R. Scheidegger. "Le corpus abélardien de

Jean de Meun: recherches et méthodes." *Bulletin de la Section de linguistique de la faculté des lettres de Lausanne* [University of Lausanne] 6 (1984):117-45.

A report on a project to produce a computer-generated concordance of Jean de Meun's translation of the letters of Abelard and Heloise. The printout lists not only the specific words in the French text but a dictionary entry for them, the corresponding words in the Latin text with dictionary entries, and the line numbers. After pointing out the importance of translations not only for Jean de Meun's literary activity but for medieval French literature generally, the authors devote most of the article to a discussion of the difficulties of determining what is a word in Old French. A sample of several pages of the concordance is appended.

100 Silvestre, Hubert. "L'idylle d'Abélard et Héloïse: la part du roman." *Bulletin de l'Académie royale de Belgique; classe des lettres et sciences morales et politiques* 5th series 71 (1985): 157-200.

An excellent review of scholarship on the authenticity of the Abelard and Heloise dossier, the *Historia calamitatum*, and the letters of the famous couple of which Jean de Meun is believed to be the first translator (the *Rose* makes also the first literary mention of their story). Because the evidence for a forgery is strong, Silvestre proposes to clarify the possible motivation for such an act in order to help determine its source. After linking Heloise's famous statement that she would rather be Abelard's concubine than his wife to contemporary ecclesiastical concerns with clerical celibacy and continence in Jean de Meun's time, Silvestre suggests that Jean (or an associate) was, rather than simply the translator, the actual author of the documents.

Boethius, *La consolation de Philosophie*

101 Atkinson, J. K. "Les compléments prédicatifs dans *Li livres de*

confort de philosophie de Jean de Meun." *Studia neophilologica* 46 (1974):391-408.

An analysis of a type of phrase, labeled by the author "complément prédicatif" (392), and used by Jean de Meun in his translation of Boethius to translate Latin absolutes, participles, and adjectives. The author describes the phrase as a kind of non-propositional, semi-independent, secondary predicate (as in "Lors, *la nuit chaciee*, me laisserent tenebres" [404]). The article also studies their function and place in the sentence, and speculates on whether this type of construction became an accepted part of French syntax largely through Jean de Meun's translation.

102 Cline, James M. "Chaucer and Jean de Meun: *De consolatione Philosophiae.*" *ELH 3* (1936):170-81.

A review of arguments for and against the attribution to Jean de Meun of the prose translation of Boethius's work (see in particular no. 118) and an analysis of the stylistic goals that the prologue to the translation proposes. In response to the argument that the prose translation does not meet the prologue's supposed literal/free criteria, or that it does not do so as well as the other translation attributed to Jean de Meun (the prose and verse translation), Cline interprets Jean's terms *mot à mot* and *plainement la sentence* (173) by comparing them to similar terms in the prologue to the Second Recension of the Wycliffite Bible. He concludes that the medieval "theory of open translation" (178) does in effect describe both the prose translation in French and Chaucer's version of the *De consolatione Philosophiae*, and that such a translation is what we mean by a literal rather than a free one. Therefore arguments against the prose translation based on its literalness are mistaken.

103 Crespo, Roberto. "Jean de Meun traduttore della *Consolatio Philosophiae* di Boezio." *Atti dell'Accademia delle scienze*

di Torino 103 (1969):71-170.

An analysis of the work of Jean de Meun as a translator, based on Crespo's intuition that a more accurate profile of the development of his literary personality can be traced by studying how the pedagogic penchant already shown in the *Rose* shapes his later activity as a vulgarizer. Crespo demonstrates how Jean targeted Boethius's translation for the needs of the lay people and especially the clerics of mediocre culture who wanted to "entendre le latin par le françois" (91). Jean systematically intervenes in the elegance of Boethius's style with the intent of making the *De consolatione Philosophiae* accessible to his medieval readers while respecting the true mind of "l'ultimo dei classici" (71). [MRB]

104 -----. "Il prologo alla traduzione della *Consolatio Philosophiae* di Jean de Meun e il commento de Guglielmo d'Aragona." In *Romanitas et Christianitas: Studia Iano Henrico Waszink A.D. VI Kal. Nov. a. MCMLXXIII, XIII lustra complenti oblata*. Ed. W. den Boer et al. Amsterdam: North-Holland, 1973. 55-70.

A critical edition of the Latin prologue to Boethius's *De consolatione Philosophiae* and of Jean de Meun's translation of it. Prior to Crespo's study the prologue was hardly known, although examined by Courcelle with other unpublished commentaries to the *De consolatione*. Crespo also brings to our attention two manuscripts of the Bibliothèque de l'Arsenal in Paris (737 and 738) which carry recto/verso the Latin original and Jean's translation of Boethius's masterpiece. [MRB]

105 Cropp, Glynnis M. "A Checklist of Manuscripts of the Medieval French Anonymous Verse-Prose Translation of the *Consolatio* of Boethius." *Notes and Queries* n.s. 26 [224] (1979):294-96.

A list of the known manuscripts of this translation, of which the author was preparing an edition [evidently never completed], and some corrections of earlier lists. The list of fifty-eight manuscripts is arranged in two parts, according to whether the manuscript contains a gloss or not.

106 -----. "*Le livre de Boece de consolacion*: From Translation to Glossed Text." In *The Medieval Boethius: Studies in the Vernacular Translations of "De consolatione Philosophiae"*. Ed. A. J. Minnis. Cambridge, England: D. S. Brewer, 1987. 63-88.

A study of an anonymous fourteenth-century verse-prose translation of *De consolatione Philosophiae* which situates it in its period, discusses style and use of glosses, and compares it to Jean de Meun's translation. A review of Jean's goals for his translation as expressed in his prologue (which was appropriated by the later translator) shows that his ideas were shared by other translators, including the one studied here. One scribe of the anonymous translation even substituted Jean's prose translation after Book V, Meter 2. In general, though, the verse-prose translation fills out the text with "examples, explanations, summaries of meaning, and rubrics" (84), making it less austere and more accessible for a lay audience (as distinguished from a learned audience, such as Jean's). An appendix lists the known manuscripts of the anonymous translation.

107 -----. "Manuscripts of the Old French Translation of Boethius." *Notes and Queries* n.s. 23 [221] (1976):393-94.

A note identifying three manuscripts of the French verse-prose translation of Boethius, earlier referred to by R. A. Dwyer as unidentified (no. 115), in the Libraries of the former East Berlin Deutsche Staatsbibliothek; Turin, Biblioteca Nazionale Universitaria; and Jena Universitätsbibliothek. Cropp also eliminates one of Dwyer's manuscripts, which does not contain the French translation and states that a Leningrad ms. can no longer be traced.

108   -----. "Le Prologue de Jean de Meun et *Le livre de Boece de Consolacion.*" *Romania* 103 (1982):278-98.

A study of the relation of Jean de Meun's prologue to both the anonymous French one and several Latin ones. Jean de Meun's prologue to his translation of Boethius also appears as the prologue to a later anonymous translation (*Le livre de Boece de Consolacion*). Cropp points out that a large portion of Jean's prologue corresponds to one by William of Aragon, thereby suggesting that a very limited part of the former was written by Jean. The text of several relevant Latin prologues is given. Includes many bibliographical references.

109   Dedeck-Héry, V[enceslas] L[ouis]. "Le Boèce de Chaucer et les manuscrits français de la *Consolatio* de J. de Meun." *PMLA* 59 (1944):18-25.

An attempt to discover which manuscript Chaucer may have used for his translation of Boethius. After summarizing the findings from his early study of mss. of Jean de Meun's translation (see no. 111), the author compares Chaucer's translation to the secondary groups of mss. and concludes that his manuscript was related to B (Besançon 434). This manuscript was prepared for Charles V of France in 1372; since Chaucer's translation dates from c. 1377-1378, he may have used an analogous manuscript.

110   -----. "Jean de Meun et Chaucer, traducteurs de la *Consolation* de Boèce." *PMLA* 52 (1937):967-91.

A review of previous scholarship on the question of whether Chaucer used Jean de Meun's translation of Boethius's *Consolation* when making his own and a study of several kinds of linguistic and stylistic evidence that support the hypothesis that he did. The evidence includes identical additions and doubling of translated terms, stylistic similarities, and Chaucer's errors which reflect a misreading of Jean de Meun. The author's conclusion is categorical: "Ces preuves d'imitation sont indiscutables" (991), and therefore Chaucer's debt to Jean de Meun is considerable.

111 -----. "The Manuscripts of the Translation of Boethius' *Consolatio* by Jean de Meung." *Speculum* 15 (1940):432-43.

A brief description of seventeen manuscripts containing all or part of Jean de Meun's translation (as established by Langlois; see no. 66). The description gives the date and length of the ms. and whether it contains both Latin text and translation or only the translation. The author also classifies the mss. and suggests that Paris, B. N. fr. 1097 can give us "a good text as close to the original as possible" (443). [This ms. serves as the base for the author's edition of the translation; see no. 86.]

112 Delisle, Léopold Victor. "Anciennes traductions françaises de la *Consolation* de Boëce conservées à la Bibliothèque Nationale." *Bibliothèque de l'Ecole des Chartes* 34 (1873):5-32. Rpt. in Delisle, *Inventaire général et méthodique des manuscrits français de la Bibliothèque Nationale*, 2 vols., 1878; rpt. Hildesheim and New York: Georg Olms, 1975; 2:317-46.

A list of manuscripts of Boethius's work, including those of the versions attributed to Jean de Meun. Delisle gives brief excerpts from several parts of the translation so that the specific translation can be determined. Manuscripts of the *Consolation*, the *Testament*, and other works attributed to Jean de Meun are also listed on other pages of the *Inventaire* (see 1:103-105, 2:167-170).

113 Denomy, Alex J. "The Vocabulary of Jean de Meun's Translation of Boethius' *De consolatione Philosophiae*." *Mediaeval Studies* 16 (1954):19-34.

A list of 106 words from Jean de Meun's translation that are given in their earliest known occurrence or in a form different from the standard Old French form. Denomy also indicates which of nine dictionaries give these words and the dates they assign and refers the reader to other studies of them. The author suggests a date of about 1300 for the translation.

114 Donaghey, B. S. "Another English Manuscript of an Old French Translation of Boethius." *Medium aevum* 42 (1973):38-42.

A description of a manuscript of an anonymous medieval translation, offered as a "small contribution" to a "complete checklist of known manuscripts" (38) of the *De consolatione Philosophiae*. The manuscript studied is preserved in York Minster Library XVI.D.14 and "almost certainly belongs to the first decade of the fifteenth century" (41). Donaghey describes and ascribes it, offering also in the notes to the article a comprehensive list of related manuscript studies. [KML]

115 Dwyer, R. A. "Manuscripts of the Medieval French Boethius." *Notes and Queries* n.s. 18 [216] (1971):124-25.

A list of manuscripts of Boethius's work that Dwyer suggests adding to Robert H. Lucas's inventory. To the list of manuscripts of the version "identified as 'Jean de Meun's translation'" (124), Dwyer would add ms. Paris, Arsenal 738; he also eliminates ms. Bergues, France, 27. [See also no. 107.]

116 Kaylor, Harold. "John Walton's 1410 Verse Translation of the *De consolatione Philosophiae* in the Context of its Medieval Tradition." *Fifteenth-Century Studies* 6 (1983):121-48.

A study of the only fifteenth-century English translation of Boethius's work in its literary context and the earlier translations that may have influenced it, including Jean de Meun's. Kaylor defines three attributes of the *De consolatione* that "are adequate as a gauge to measure the amount and type of deviation the translations make from the Latin text" (123): the formal aspect (the combination of prose and poetry), the argument (the universe is ruled by reason), and the "very human biographical/historical dimension" (124). Kaylor studies Jean's "utilitarian" (133) translation both from these three aspects and in its influence on later translations and concludes that it was the model, through Chaucer, of Walton's translation. Furthermore, Jean de Meun's version is judged "the best of the medieval translations of the *Consolatio*" (143). Includes a good bibliography of the subject.

117 Langlois, Charles-Victor. "La *Consolation* de Boèce d'après Jean de Meun et plusieurs autres." In *La vie spirituelle: enseignements, méditations et controverses d'après des écrits en français à l'usage des laïcs*. Vol. 4 of *La vie en France au moyen âge du XIIe au milieu du XIVe siècle*. Paris: Hachette, 1928. 269-326.

A review of the importance of Boethius's *Consolation* in the Middle Ages. Langlois describes briefly the medieval translations known at the time, including Jean de Meun's (274-77), and paraphrases passages in the *Rose* that are based on Boethius (303-18).

118 Langlois, Ernest. "La traduction de Boèce par Jean de Meun." *Romania* 42 (1913):331-69.

An important reexamination of the problem of determining which of two translations of the *De consolatione Philosophiae* was made by Jean de Meun (though very different, they both have Jean's dedication). After reviewing scholarship on the question, Langlois examines the arguments in favor of the manuscript that combines prose and verse, many of which are based on stylistic appreciations or on what scholars believed Jean de Meun would have done. The examination involves a comparison of the Boethius translations with both Jean's translation of Vegetius and his part of the *Rose*. Langlois finds certain special expressions, such as *perdurableté* for *aeternitas*, in the *Rose* and the prose translation of Boethius but not in the prose and verse translation. Consequently he argues in favor of the authenticity of the prose translation. [Unfortunately many of Langlois's arguments based on versification or linguistic forms are made questionable by the lack of information on the text of the *Rose* that he used (it was evidently not the text of his own edition), since there is much variation among manuscripts. Nonetheless Langlois's conclusions in favor of attributing the prose translation to Jean de Meun seem sound.]

119   Lowes, John Livingston. "Chaucer's *Boethius* and Jean de Meun." *Romanic Review* 8 (1917):383-400.

A comparison of passages of Chaucer's translation of Boethius's *De consolatione Philosophiae* with the prose translation attributed to Jean de Meun and the Latin original, in order to demonstrate that Chaucer used the French version in his translation. After reviewing critical opinion for and against the hypothesis, Lowes prints a long excerpt from the French version in parallel lines with the English and Latin versions, indicating significant words and phrases with bold-faced type and asterisks. Lowes concludes that while Chaucer had both the French and Latin texts before him, "it is obvious that it is Jean de Meun whom he is supplementing by the Latin, not the reverse" (396) and suggests further study of this and other translations from the French by Chaucer.

120   Minnis, Alastair. "Aspects of the Medieval French and English Traditions of the *De consolatione Philosophiae*." In *Boethius: His Life, Thought and Influence*. Ed. Margaret Gibson. Oxford: Basil Blackwell, 1981. 312-61.

121   Thomas, Antoine and Mario Roques. "Traductions françaises de la *Consolatio Philosophiae* de Boèce." Vol. 37 of

Histoire littéraire de la France. Paris: Imprimerie nationale, 1938. 419-88.

A series of brief comments on the French translations of Boethius's *De consolatione Philosophiae* from the early thirteenth to the mid-fourteenth century. An introduction also reviews earlier translations. The discussion of Jean de Meun's version (436-41) touches on the manuscripts, the literalness of the translation, the date, proposed editions, and Chaucer's use of the translation. The beginning of Book 2, Meter 5 is printed as a sample.

Vegetius, *L'art de chevalerie*

122 Buridant, Claude. "Jean de Meun et Jean de Vignay, traducteurs de l'*Epitoma rei militaris* de Végèce: contribution à l'histoire de la traduction au Moyen Age." In *Etudes*...*Lanly* (no. 230). 51-69.

A review of medieval translations of Vegetius's treatise and a comparison of the versions of Jean de Meun (1284) and Jean de Vignay (c. 1320?), whose translation reworks Jean de Meun's by collating it with the Latin text. This comparison serves the purpose of situating the two works "dans l'histoire des traductions médiévales et dans leur conditionnement linguistique" (52). While Jean de Meun reacted against word-for-word translation, Jean de Vignay was concerned to give a more literal rendering. The author shows how Jean de Vignay stayed closer, lexically and syntactically, to the Latin text, thus producing a "relatinisation" (61) of the more colloquial version of his predecessor.

123 Knowles, Christine. "A 14th Century Imitator of Jean de Meung: Jean de Vignay's Translation of the *De re militari* of Vegetius." *Studies in Philology* 53 (1956):452-58.

A comparison of the two translations in order to see how Jean de Vignay used the earlier version. Jean de Vignay, a prolific translator at the court of Philippe VI, evidently undertook his translation of Vegetius as a youthful exercise, for he uses Jean de Meun's translation "extremely unintelligently" (454), although sometimes Knowles deems his version better than the earlier one. The author believes that Jean de Meun's version, including the mistakes, passed through Jean de Vignay to Christine de Pizan and finally into Caxton's translation.

124 Löfstedt, Leena. "La réduplication synonymique de Jean de Meun dans sa traduction de Végèce." *Neuphilologische Mitteilungen* 77 (1976):449-70.

A semantic and stylistic study of synonymic verbal pairs in Jean's translation of Vegetius, *L'art de chevalerie*. After reviewing similar studies on other medieval French and Latin works, Löfstedt defines synonymic pairs and examines in detail the two main types, "explicatifs" (454) and rhetorical (motivated by stylistic concerns). The author refers to similar expressions in the *Rose*, in particular those involving the verb *chuer*, "le verbe favori" (461) de Jean de Meun. Includes a list of the examples found in *L'art de chevalerie*. (See also no. 97.)

125 -----. "*Res* et *causa*: étude lexicographique sur la base de trois traductions." *Archiv für das Studium der neueren Sprachen und Literaturen* 209 (1972):310-26.

Essentially a list of passages involving *res* or *causa* in three medieval translations of Vegetius's *Epitoma rei militaris*, including Jean de Meun's from 1284. The study includes a few passages from Jean Priorat's versification of Jean de Meun's translation. Brief comments on the differences in the translations include little linguistic analysis. The author concludes that Jean de Meun's translation is the best of the three and the most comprehensible to his contemporaries.

126 -----. "La traduction des mots abstraits dans le Végèce de Jean de Meun." In *Actes du 6e Congrès des Romanistes Scandinaves, Upsal, 11-15 août 1975.* Ed. Lennart Carlsson. Studia Romanica Upsaliensia 18. Uppsala: University of Uppsala, 1977. 191-96.

A study of translation problems posed for Jean de Meun by certain abstract words (names of qualities or actions) in Vegetius's military treatise. Jean handles the problems in several ways: he may translate such words freely; give the equivalent French word (*raison* for *ratio*, for example, regardless of the meaning of the Latin word); or substitute a simpler, more concrete French word (*isnel* for *velocitas*). Löfstedt observes "une tendance prononcée à concrétiser, actualiser ses expressions" (196) on Jean's part, which she sees as the principal stylistic difference between the Latin and the French texts.

127 -----. "Le Végèce de Jean de Meun: essai de classement des manuscrits." *Studia neophilologica* 43 (1971):500-20.

A description and classification of the manuscripts of Jean de Meun's translation of Vegetius in preparation for a new edition (see no. 88). The author gives examples of the kinds of variants on which her classification is based, discusses the principles that distinguish an edition of a translation from that of an original work, and proposes a stemma for the manuscripts.

128 Meyer, Paul. "Les anciens traducteurs français de Végèce et en particulier Jean de Vignai [sic]." *Romania* 25 (1896):401-23.

A description of manuscripts containing medieval translations of Vegetius's *Epitoma rei militari*. A brief notice about Jean de Meun's translation, the most popular one, precedes the sections describing manuscripts of the anonymous translation from 1380 and of Jean de Vignay's translations of Vegetius. Jean de Vignay's translation was evidently consulted by Christine de

Pizan in her version entitled *Le livre des fais d'armes et de chevalerie.*

129 Mongeau, Rene Guy B. "*Li Chevaliers*: Jean de Meun's Translation of *Epitoma rei militaris*." *Proceedings of the PMR Conference: Annual Publication of the International Patristic, Mediaeval and Renaissance Conference* 6 (1981):89-99.

A semantic study of Jean's translation of "terms related to Roman military personnel, specifically *miles, tiro* and *eques*" (89). Mongeau shows specifically how Jean's use of the term *chevalier* to translate various Latin words for soldier caused him difficulties due to the ideological value placed on the knight in the Middle Ages. To maintain the positive connotations of *chevalier* as well as to preserve medieval custom, Jean was forced to find substitutes for *chevalier* in passages where he deemed the behavior described by Vegetius as inappropriate for a knight. In his conclusion Mongeau suggests that Jean "advocated profound changes in the composition of medieval armies, specifically the selection of the knights" (97).

130 -----. "Jean de Meun's Translation of Military Terminology in Vegetius' *Epitoma rei militaris*." Diss. Fordham U, 1981.

131 -----. "Thirteenth-Century Siege Weapons and Machines in *L'art de chevalerie*." *Allegorica* 7 (1987):123-43.

A description of the difficulties Jean de Meun encountered in translating certain Latin expressions for siege weapons and machines that lacked exact French equivalents, due to the fact that despite the remarkable continuity between Roman and medieval siege equipment, some new machines had been developed. For example, Jean often translated Latin *onager*, a catapult, by the anachronistic *trebuchet* since it would be clearer to his public. Thus, while in a few cases Jean created neologisms when referring to specific Roman machines, he often substituted anachronisms "in his effort to update the Latin treatise" (134).

132 Segre, C. "Jean de Meun e Bono Giamboni, traduttori di Vegezio." *Atti dell'Accademia delle scienze di Torino; classe di scienze morali* 87 (1952/1953):119-53.

A comparative study of Jean de Meun's and Bono Giamboni's translations of Vegetius. Segre suggests that the first signs of the "razionalismo analitico" (300) typical of French prose, are to be seen in Jean's translations: with his "programma divulgativo" (275), he occupies a "posto d'onore" (275). Vegetius' translation reveals that he searches in the Latin language for a model or inspiration leading to syntactical and logical coherence. The rich and well established tradition of the French language allows him to work without an inferiority complex towards Latin, and to transform its syntax (synthetical and subordinating) into the analytical and coordinating modes of French. The result is a dry, descriptive clarity which has a didactical, technical quality. [MRB]

133 Wisman, Josette. "L'*Epitoma rei militaris* de Végèce et sa fortune au Moyen Age." *Le moyen âge* 85 (1979):13-31.

A review of Vegetius's life and work, a survey of extant Latin manuscripts of the *Epitoma* and of medieval translations of it, and a summary of its influence as reflected in the works of some medieval authors. Vegetius's treatise is the only complete work about Roman military institutions that has been passed down. The author summarizes current information about Jean de Meun's translation and the manuscripts. Includes a discussion of Christine de Pizan's version, *Le livre des fais d'armes et de chevalerie.*

Le Testament

134 Buzzetti Gallarati, Silvia. "'Mots sous les mots': una firma per il *Testament*." *Medioevo romanzo* 15 (1990):259-76.

A continued discussion, from her edition of the *Testament* (see no. 91), of the possible author of the work. Buzzetti Gallarati had earlier identified the author with a figure so close to that of Jean de Meun as to remove nearly any doubt about the paternity. In this article she looks for a hidden signature and having chosen three key passages, she undertakes an anagrammatic journey into the text. This approach allows her to discover a number of alleged sequences of graphemes and phonemes which reveal Jean's name and title (*mai/s/tre*). Unfortunately their presence seems to be accidental, as she, with reference to Starobinski (270), comes close to admitting herself. [If it is true that the literary artifice of hiding one's name in the text was often used as a demonstration of skill by medieval French authors (see the examples of Jean Renart, Guillaume de Machaut, and Christine de Pizan), it is also true that in this particular case the evidence is not completely convincing.] [MRB]

135 -----. "Nota bibliografica sulla tradizione manoscritta del *Testament* di Jean de Meun." *Revue romane* 13 (1978):2-35.

A description of the manuscript tradition of Jean's *Testament*. The author located 116 codices which contain this and other works by Jean de Meun, a fact that bears witness to the wide circulation of the *Testament* in the Middle Ages. Information was collected in three ways: by examining the catalogues of manuscripts in French and foreign libraries and in the archives of the Institut de Recherche et d'Histoire des Textes in Paris; by conducting inquiries in person in the Parisian libraries; and by analyzing the answers to a questionnaire that the author sent to libraries commonly or allegedly known to preserve manuscripts containing works by Jean de Meun. For each codex, Buzzetti

Gallarati gives a brief description that includes information on content and paleography. [MRB]

136   Rice, Winthrop Huntington. *The European Ancestry of Villon's Satirical Testaments*. Syracuse University Monographs 1. New York: The Corporate Press, 1941. Pp. 244. (See no. 732.)

Alchemical works

137   Badel, Pierre-Yves. "Alchemical Readings of the *Romance of the Rose*." In *Rethinking* (no. 182). 262-85.

A study of the *Rose* that includes a comprehensive list of alchemical works attributed to Jean de Meun over the centuries. (See no. 570.)

138   Frati, Lodovico. "Poesie alchimistiche attribuite a Jean de Meun." *Archivum romanicum* 3 (1919):321-26.

A description of short alchemical works in a collection of manuscripts in the Biblioteca Universitaria di Bologna. The collection, once belonging to the Caprara family, was put together in France in the first half of the sixteenth century. Among these mss., all on alchemical subjects, there are several attributed to Jean de Meun. The codices n. 179, n. 457, n. 458, and n. 1445 contain a variety of works, including lines from the *Rose* on alchemical subjects, verses from the *Testament*, the *Complainte de Nature* and *La table d'esmeraude* also attributed to Jean de Meun, and some ballads attributed to him. [MRB]

139   Vernet, André. "Jean Perréal, poète et alchimiste." *Bibliothèque d'humanisme et renaissance* 3 (1943):214-52.

An examination of Jean de Meun's supposed alchemical works.

Vernet argues that the author of the *Complainte de Nature* (also called the *Remontrances de Nature*) is in reality Jean Perréal, a painter, sculptor, and architect.

CHAPTER THREE

CRITICAL STUDIES OF THE *ROMAN DE LA ROSE*

140 Accarie, Maurice. "La vie n'est pas un songe: théorie et pratique chez Guillaume de Lorris." In *Contemporary Readings of Medieval Literature*. Ed. Guy Mermier. Michigan Romance Studies 8. Ann Arbor: Department of Romance Languages, University of Michigan, 1989. 115-44.

A reconsideration of the long-debated question of whether Guillaume's part of the *Rose* is complete. Accarie approaches the problem on two levels--through the structure of the *récit* and the evolution of its allegorical system. After discussing briefly Gunn's and Lejeune's readings of the structure (see nos. 274 and 369), Accarie proposes divisions of the poem that point to the following conclusions: the first part is incomplete, lacking about 750 verses, and the text juxtaposes successively the two large ensembles of initiation (theory of love) and adventure (practice of love) (the two ensembles are marked by an abrupt change at l. 2749). A second structural analysis, of narrative versus discursive (didactic or descriptive) "modes d'écriture" (122), further establishes the distinction between the two sections. Finally, this distinction is explored through a useful, detailed analysis of Guillaume's allegorical system, which, static and serene in the first section, becomes dynamic and confused in the second through the increased humanization of the characters: the psychological universe replaces the allegorical one.

141 Allen, Peter L. "*Ars amandi, Ars legendi*: Love Poetry and Literary Theory in Ovid, Andreas Capellanus, and Jean de Meun." *Exemplaria* 1 (1989):181-205.

An analysis of the three authors' treatises on love, which are, according to Allen, not about love but about reading poetic works about love; further, they are "documents of literary theory" (182). The author finds evidence for this interpretation in the relationship of these works to other works about love; their use or rejection of literary love conventions; the reader's direct relation to the narrator; the art of seduction which the works teach, based on deception and manipulation; and especially the "rifts" (191) between opposing sections, opposing preceptors, opposing views of love. The possible reading strategies suggested by the transition from the praise of love to the rejection of it are described as a stimulus to the questioning of the treatise's truthfulness. Finally, this questioning becomes "an exercise in the power of fiction" (194) which makes of the treatises works of literary theory, that is, both fiction and commentary.

142 ------. *The Art of Love: Amatory Fiction from Ovid to the "Romance of the Rose"*. Middle Ages Series. Philadelphia: U of Pennsylvania P, 1992. Pp. xi + 178.

143 Alvar, Carlos. "Oiseuse, Vénus, Luxure: trois dames et un miroir." *Romania* 106 (1985):108-17.

A discussion of the meaning of Oiseuse, the character who opens the garden gate to the dreamer in the *Rose*, and especially of the significance of her mirror. Because the Robertsonian view of the mirror as a representation of lust has not been accepted by scholars (see no. 473), Alvar reviews evidence from art, theology, and literature to suggest other possible meanings of the mirror, such as the contemplative life, and other attributes of Luxure (Lust). Oiseuse's mirror, he concludes, is used by Guillaume as a symbol of beauty, "sans aucune arrière-pensée moralisante" (113). Furthermore, Oiseuse is modeled on the figure of Venus in Ovid's *Remedia amoris*, but because Guillaume has given the mirror, Venus's attribute, to Oiseuse, he gives the goddess "un attribut tout à fait nouveau dans l'iconographie de Vénus" (114), a torch. Thus Oiseuse and Venus are two very different characters in the first part of the *Rose*.

144   Ampère, J.-J. "Poésie du Moyen Age: *Le roman de la rose.*" *Revue des deux mondes* n. s. 3 (1843):253-83.

An early overview of the *Rose* in a venerable review. Ampère summarizes what he considers the best parts of the poem (leaving out the offensive ending) for his educated but not scholarly audience. In addition, he comments both on specific passages and on the general style and approach of the two authors. Guillaume's delicate and ingenious allegory of "amour chevaleresque" (280) is followed by Jean's "incroyable mélange de brutalité, de pédanterie et de verve" (254). Recognizing in Jean a pioneer in the use of the French language for serious ideas, Ampère describes those ideas as materialistic and epicurian. Consequently, the *Rose* is "l'évangile de la matière et des sens" (283).

145   Arden, Heather. *The Romance of the Rose*. Twayne's World Authors Series 791. Boston: Twayne Publishers, 1987. Pp. 135.

A scholarly introduction to the *Rose* which includes an outline and a summary, a discussion of literary and philosophical traditions that influenced the authors, an analysis of the major personifications, an overview of the *Rose's* influence on French, English, and Italian literature, and a history of *Rose* criticism. The final chapter compares the allegorical approach of the two authors and proposes a new interpretation of the character Genius, whom Jean poses as a means of foregrounding epistemological questions. [See also no. 299.]

146 Armitage, Isabelle. "La philosophie de la plénitude dans le *Roman de la rose*." *Chimères* (Winter 1970):22-33.

An introduction to the *Rose* [incorporating a number of errors of fact] and a brief discussion of what the author sees as Jean de Meun's philosophy of plenitude or "remplissage" (28): the universe must include all possible forms of life, which are emanations from God; through procreating their kind, creatures not only help to realize this plenitude but "participent à la bonté et à la vertu du créateur" (28); as a corollary, the organs of procreation are precious. The author's remarks are based on Gunn's work (see no. 274). [Unfortunately the bibliographical references are not complete.]

147 Auvray, Lucien. "Origines et sources du *Roman de la rose*." *Bulletin de la société archéologique et historique de l'Orléanais* 10 (1891):26-27.

A brief discussion of Langlois's doctoral dissertation, which became *Origines et sources du Roman de la rose* (see no. 358). Auvray feels that Langlois's work on the many sources used by the authors of the *Rose* diminishes their originality but flatters their erudition, especially Jean de Meun's: "il a tout connu" (26). The success of the romance was due, therefore, less to its originality than to its relative formal perfection.

148 Badel, Pierre-Yves. "Au Moyen Age dire et vouloir-dire." *Corps écrit* 18 (1986):53-59.

An introduction to medieval meanings of the term *allégorie* (as opposed to examples of modern usage that the author cites), and in particular a description of the ways that medieval authors distinguished "entre un dire et un vouloir-dire du texte" (59). Badel gives examples from two allegorical works, the *Songe du vieil pèlerin* and the *Rose*, of the ways in which the letter of the text could be made to point to its latent significance. These ways include emblematic description whose meaning may or may not be articulated, life-like portraits, and metaphors such as armor or chess. Badel concludes that allegory runs the risk of either reducing the letter to its latent truth, or freeing the letter from the intended meaning.

149 -----. "Raison 'fille de Dieu' et le rationalisme de Jean de Meun." In *Mélanges de langue et de littérature du Moyen Age et de la Renaissance offerts à Jean Frappier par ses collègues, ses élèves et ses amis.* Publications Romances et Françaises 153. 2 vols. Geneva: Droz, 1970. 1:41-52.

An introductory discussion of the significance of Raison's divine origin for understanding Jean de Meun's place in medieval literary and intellectual history. After a brief critical description of personified abstractions as a literary mode, Badel suggests that Raison in Guillaume de Lorris's part represents society, experience, age, and common sense. In the second part, Raison and Nature, as the "interprètes autorisées" (44) of the author, condemn the hedonism of courtly love. The phrase, "fille de Dieu" (l. 5786), suggests the divine grandeur which Jean de Meun imparts to Raison, but her relation to humanity is ambiguous: a force superior to man, she is also an interior voice speaking to him, though a voice that is ineffectual unless supported by man's belief (will). Above all, Badel stresses the religious orthodoxy of Jean's Raison: "Aimer Raison, c'est aimer Dieu" (50).

150 Baig, Bonnie Pavlis. "Vision and Visualization: Optics and Light Metaphysics in the Imagery and Poetic Form of Twelfth and Thirteenth Century Secular Allegory, with Special Attention to the *Roman de la rose*." Diss. U of California, Berkeley, 1982.

151 Baker, David Jeffrey. "Allegory and Exegesis in Jean de Meun's *Roman de la rose*." Diss. Yale U, 1978.

152 Bambeck, Manfred. "*Cire vierge* (*Rosenroman*, V. 19490): Jean de Meun und die mittelalterliche Deutungstradition eines christlichen Symbols." *Romanistisches Jahrbuch* 33 (1982):97-110.

An analysis of the meaning of Jean's phrase, "cire vierge" (Lecoy, l. 19460), taking into consideration a large number of mostly religious Latin writings which deal with the symbolism of burning candles in church, with special emphasis on the Candlemas celebration. Bee-mysticism was used to illustrate the ideal of virginity; thus wax is referred to as being virgin because it is a product of the bee, an insect believed to be created exclusive of any sexual act. Wax signifies therefore Mary's virgin womb which bore Christ in human form. The light of the candle relates to the divine nature of Christ, linked however to the human through the wick. If we are aware of this tradition, Jean de Meun's parodic use of the image in reference to Genius, Venus's priest, becomes evident. [ASK]

153 Bargreen, Melinda Lueth. "The Author in His Work: The Priest/Pupil Narrative Topos." Diss. U of California, Irvine, 1972.

154 Barnett, John D. J. "Rationalism and Naturalism in Jean de Meung's *Roman de la rose*." *University of Cape Town Studies in English* 4 (1973):45-55.

An interpretation based on the premise that the "most productive method of approaching this incredible poem...is the historical one" (45). Barnett reviews the intellectual milieu of Jean's *Rose* through a summary of contemporary Parisian teaching methods and scholastic vocabulary and the influence of major questions of thirteenth-century Aristotelianism on Jean's thought. His conclusion is that Jean de Meun was a rationalist ("a devotee of Reason" [49]), in part because of his profession, and a naturalist in his heterodox sexual beliefs, but that he was orthodox in his other philosophical beliefs (such as free will). Jean's naturalism, which Barnett does not define, appears to consist mainly of an emphasis on the continuation of the species and on the value of procreation, expressed through Jean's condemnation of unnatural sex [not a heterodox belief, however]. [The author also refutes F. W. Müller's arguments (see no. 401).]

155   Barney, Stephen A. *Allegories of History, Allegories of Love*. Hamden, Conn.: Archon Books, 1979. Pp. 323.

A study of "the best works of allegory" (14), in which Barney examines how allegory functions in the *Rose*, in particular in relation to rhetorical elements and to the theme of plenitude. The "rhetoric of plenitude" (186) in the first part, manifested, for example, in Guillaume's descriptive catalogue, is a stylistic expression of a natural, harmonious love which l'Amant is unable to understand. The various kinds of allegory in the *Rose* (personification, topographical and architectural allegory, typology, classical myth, and "continued metaphor" [190]) are described in relation to the themes of plenitude and love. (Many of the terms and ideas in this analysis are presented in the book's useful introduction.) A long section discusses Jean's response to Guillaume, which in Genius's sermon becomes "the conflict of worlds" (196). Barney then studies the three myths of Narcissus, Adonis, and Pygmalion as organizing elements of the romance, leading to the conclusion that Guillaume's part harks back to the Fall, while Jean's recollects the Creation. Barney often relates the allegory of the *Rose* to other European works.

156   Batany, Jean. *Approches du "Roman de la rose"*. Bordas Etudes 363. Paris: Bordas, 1973. Pp. 124.

Essays on the *Rose*, destined primarily for French students, that place the work in its literary, social, and intellectual contexts. The first three chapters focus on medieval literary views of love; on medieval allegorical works, especially those of Bernard Silvestre; and on the framework of the work, defined as the key concepts of romance, dream, rose, mirror, and *summa*. While these chapters consider primarily the first part of the *Rose*, the next four--on marriage, power, wealth and poverty, and hypocrisy--explore some of the principal themes of the second part. Many of the essays treat the topic broadly, in effect giving the reader also an introduction to medieval French literature (a discussion of Saint Alexis introduces the chapter on Faux Semblant, for example). Batany believes that the entire work is dominated by "une conception joyeuse et simple, dirigée vers la vie plus que vers la mort, n'opposant pas la chair et l'esprit" (24).

157 -----. "Miniature, allégorie, idéologie: 'Oiseuse' et la mystique monacale récupérée par la 'classe de loisir'." In *Etudes...Lorris* (no. 231). 7-36.

A rapid perusal of subjects more or less related to the personification, Oiseuse. The author analyses Guillaume's technique of portraiture and description, the polyvalent function of the personification, and the ideological implications of Guillaume's courtly ideal of *oisiveté*, particularly the possible relation between Oiseuse, the monastic concept of *otium*, and the leisure class. Rejecting Ott's hypothesis of Guillaume's bourgeois origins, Batany seems to argue that Oiseuse represents both the aristocracy's erotic ideal and its self-justification of a life of leisure. [The author's arguments are often presented quickly and elliptically.]

158 -----. "Paradigmes lexicaux et structures littéraires au Moyen Age." *Revue d'histoire littéraire de la France* 70 (1970):819-35.

A detailed analysis of lexical series in the *Rose* and later medieval works. The study relates "paradigmes lexicaux," such as the portraits on the wall of the garden and Deduit and his followers inside, to Greimassien *actants*, in particular to the *adjuvant*, *opposant*, and *destinateur*. The metonymic or metaphoric lexical units both define Guillaume's understanding of certain concepts and help to structure the work. Thus, the first part of the *Rose* shows a subtle interaction of linguistic and literary structures. Furthermore Guillaume's flexible use of the two procedures of allegorical designation by moral notion (Chasteté) or by proper name (Ami) is seen not as a weakness but as a sign of creative flexibility lacking both in his predecessors and in later writers. In contrast, the use of lexical paradigms (the series of vices, for example, or the estates) in later works offers a revealing but somewhat rigid approach to lexical series as literary structuring devices.

159 Baumgartner, Emmanuèle. "L'absente de tous bouquets...." In *Etudes...Lorris* (no. 231). 37-52.

An approach that places the first part of the *Rose* in the context of other courtly works, in particular Chrétien's *Chevalier de la charrete*, the *Lancelot en prose*, and trouvère lyrics. Guillaume's ambition was to write a text that was at the same time a romance, a treatise on love, and above all "la trace d'un itinéraire poétique" (39). The stages of Guillaume's quest for love are analyzed, from the seductive but facile lyricism of the beginning, through the fecundity of Deduit's garden, to the three *destors* (isolated places) of Deduit, the Fountain of Narcissus, and the rosebushes. Baumgartner sees Guillaume as transforming, at the Fountain, the quest for the rose into a poetic quest for the way to write love's mystery, to communicate what was only a dream (to make present, in Mallarmé's words, "l'absente de tous bouquets").

160 -----. "De Lucrèce à Héloïse, remarques sur deux exemples du *Roman de la rose* de Jean de Meun." *Romania* 95 (1974):433-42.

A comparison of Jean de Meun's version of the story of Lucretia to his source, Titus Livius (Livy). Baumgartner finds divergences in the motives for the heroine's suicide that suggest that Jean saw her as choosing to die in order to free all women from the loss of liberty resulting from masculine aggression. This retelling of the story, however, creates a dissonance between the story's new significance and the mentality of the teller, the jealous husband (who desires only to limit his wife's freedom). Furthermore, a similar development can be seen in the jealous husband's version of the motives for Heloise's resistance to marriage and for Abelard's castration, both of which are reworked in the direction of defending women's liberty. The author concludes that we need to nuance Jean's misogyny, for he appears to argue that both partners in a relationship must respect the other's *franchise*.

161 -----. "The Play of Temporalities; or, The Reported Dream of Guillaume de Lorris." Tr. Benjamin Semple. In *Rethinking* (no. 182). 21-38 [given as 22-38 in table of contents].

A study of the representation of time in Guillaume's dream fiction and of the special status that this dream confers on the narrator. The triple beginning of the dream includes the lyric springtime motif, which suggests a predisposition of the dreamer for the erotic narrative which follows. The complexities of the narrator's relation to this narrative--he "speaks in the present, rewrites his past, and projects himself into the future" (23)-- makes it difficult to situate him in time. In the Garden itself Guillaume first creates the effect of time suspended through techniques of accumulation and description, then suggests that time flows again after the episode of the fountain, which is "the locus at once of unmediated vision and of an experience of possession" (33). In his quest for the object of his desire, the lover strives to recapture the original eternity of time. Thus, only in the moment outside of time--the dream--can the writer master time and its mystery.

162 Bellessort, André. *Heures de parole: sujets anciens--questions modernes*. Paris: Perrin, 1929. Pp. 312.

A collection of essays on literature, based on lectures by the author, that includes an introduction to the *Rose*. Bellessort stresses the differences between the two parts: the *Rose* is "l'oeuvre d'un poète anémique, continuée par un orateur gras et sanguin" (148). After a brief discussion of the authors' biographies and of the significance of the poem, Bellessort summarizes and comments on the *Rose* itself. Though very appreciative of Guillaume's aristocratic refinement, he expresses bewilderment at Bel Accueil's masculine gender. He believes that Guillaume was the first, however, to describe the sentimental battle waged in the heart of a young woman. Jean's most original creation is la Vieille, for whom Bellessort expresses a disgusted admiration. While Jean is not a poet, according to Bellessort, he does have the talent of a satirist. Finally, Bellessort suggests that the success of the *Rose* was its undoing, that everything it contains was said again later and better.

163   Beltrán, Luis. "La Vieille's Past." *Romanische Forschungen* 84 (1972):77-96.

A reconsideration of the character of the old woman that first reviews similar characters in medieval romance, fabliau, and elegiac comedy (and considers the relation between the last two), then describes how Jean de Meun gives la Vieille, in addition to a synthesis of the traditional traits of the duenna and the go-between, a past that makes her more human and more real. Both the joy and the sorrow that she has experienced in love "appear masterfully reflected in her narrative" (91). Perhaps Jean's greatest accomplishment is that in la Vieille he has closed the gap between the character and the reader. Thus Beltrán argues that the portrait of the old woman is not misogynistic; instead Jean de Meun is bringing men and women together in a way that denies the validity of the old hierarchy, of the old antagonisms.

164   Benedetto, Luigi Foscolo. "Per la cronologia del *Roman de la rose*." *Atti della Reale Accademia delle scienze di Torino* 44 (1908/1909):471-87.

An exploration of the somewhat neglected issue of the chronology of the *Rose* through a study of the relationship between Jean de Meun and Brunetto Latini, whose *Tesoretto*, heavily influenced by Jean's masterpiece, was composed between 1260 (the Guelph defeat of Montaperti) and 1266 (the *Tresor*). After dismissing the two objections against 1262 as the *terminus ad quem* (the first being the mention of the end of the Swabian family, which he considers a later addition by both Jean de Meun and Brunetto dictated by political considerations; the second the question of Robert d'Artois (who, for the authors, must be identified with the first and not the second of his family), Benedetto demonstrates how Jean started to work on the *Rose* at the relatively young age of twenty and completed its first version within four to five years [this last point is not very convincing]. As for the *terminus a quo*, Benedetto, who accepts the authority of the *Testament* in corroboration of his theory, stresses the fact that the only date mentioned in the *Rose*, 1255, is related to the *Evangile pardurable* and the troubles that followed. Jean de Meun describes those events with "il sacro spavento" (486) of a witness, just as his loyalty to Guillaume de Saint-Amour shows in him "oltre che il contemporaneo, lo scolaro" (487). Thus the *Roman de la rose* would have been continued and finished by Jean between 1255 and 1262. [MRB]

165 Bermejo, Esperanza. "Notas sobre las modalidades retóricas de inserción de anécdotas en el *Roman de la rose de Jean de Meun.*" In *La lengua y la literatura en tiempos de Alfonso X*. Actas del Congreso Internacional, Murcia, 5-10 marzo 1984. Ed. Fernando Carmona and Francisco J. Flores. Murcia, Spain: Departamento de Literaturas Románicas, Facultad de Letras, Universidad de Murcia, 1985. 91-108.

A study of the exempla--defined as "historias que cuentan un incidente sucedido a un(os) personaje(s)" (92-93)--their rhetorical presentation and function, and their relation to the ideologies of the *Rose*'s authors. Bermejo first distinguishes between the only two fables told by the narrator (Narcissus and Pygmalion) and the many *exempla* embedded in characters' speeches. Her analysis of the rhetorical function and the rhetorical presentation of the fable highlights Guillaume's reduction of the fable of Narcissus by replacing direct discourse with narratization, contrasted with Jean de Meun's amplification, by expansion of direct discourse, in his version of Pygmalion. These antithetical presentations suggest an ideological parallel with the movement in the *Rose* from a conception of love related to death to one connected to life. This movement is also illustrated by the contrast in the two fountains. Furthermore, the use of exempla by Jean's personifications shows symmetry and "ciertas conexiones temáticas" (103) that contradict the scholarly charge of capriciousness or lack of cohesion. The author believes that Jean's use of exempla shows that "La armonía preside la composición del *Roman de la Rose*, desde la organización del marco--conquista de la Rosa--, hasta la de las historias en él englobadas" (101).

166   Blangez, Gérard. "Comment composait Jean de Meun (à partir d'une étude du *Discours d'Ami*)." In *Etudes...Lanly* (no. 230). 31-36.

An essay that asks whether it is possible to determine Jean's methods of composition, in particular, how the "digressions" (32)--whether secondary clauses in sentences or larger sections--were incorporated. Blangez outlines three possible compositional procedures: that the digressions were included in the conception of the work, that they were added in the course of its composition, or that they were added later. He then studies the speech of l'Ami in terms of its two major sections and describes how they incorporate material from Ovid, Valerius, and Juvenal. Based on this evidence and on the way the various subdivisions are stitched into the speech, the author concludes that Jean de Meun often added elements after the writing of a section, and that the passages on the Golden Age and the tirade of the jealous husband may have been previously composed pieces that were incorporated later into the *Rose*.

167   Bodenham, C. H. L. "The Nature of the Dream in Late

Mediaeval French Literature." *Medium aevum* 54 (1985):74-86.

An exploration of the conception of dreaming that underlies the *Roman de la rose* and other late medieval works from the point of view of "the new learning derived from Aristotle and more particularly from the medical teaching of an Avicenna schooled in the Aristotelian view of things" (75), rather than from the question of Macrobius's influence. In a somewhat disjointed discussion of thirteenth-century theories of the soul, the author appears to suggest that the dedicatee of the *Rose* is the rational soul (and both Guillaume's and Jean's "mocking references to *cele*" [83] reveal reason's implicit powerlessness) and that it is the irrational sleeping mind that creates the dream, in which all events "must be the substance of the mind that dreamt them" (76).

168 Bossuat, Robert. *Le moyen âge*. Ed. J. Calvet. Histoire de la Littérature Française. Paris: del Duca, 1962. Pp. 368.

An introduction to the *Rose* which stresses the differences between the two parts despite their coherence. Information on the authors places the first in a courtly milieu, the second in a bourgeois context. The author mentions Guillaume's possible courtly and clerical sources but sees in his poem the expression of the poet's "âme juvénile et charmante, encore fleurie d'illusions" (197). For Jean de Meun, it was the digressions that were important, for they permitted him to convey his knowledge and his philosophy, which is contained in Nature's confession. Jean was above all interested in the moral education of his readers. Bossuat summarizes briefly the Querelle de la Rose and explains the work's continuing popularity as a result of its being the epitome of medieval thought. Includes brief indications of the *Rose*'s influence on later French writers.

169 Bouché[-Picart], Thérèse. "Amour et écriture dans le *Roman de la rose* de Jean de Meun." Diss. U of Paris, Sorbonne, 1985.

170 -----. "Burlesque et renouvellement des formes: l'attaque du château dans le *Roman de la rose* de Jean de Meun." In *Hommage à Jean-Charles Payen: farai chansoneta novele: essais sur la liberté créatrice au Moyen Age*. Caen: Centre de Publication de l'Université de Caen, 1989. 87-98.

A close look at the artistic structure and function of the allegorical battle between the forces of le Dieu d'Amour and of Jalousie (ll. 15273-599), an episode which scholars have often considered a concession to the reader in need of action after so much talk. The author reviews medieval examples of allegorical battles, then describes Jean's tourney as a burlesque set-to, meant to "détruire au moins partiellement les modèles imités" (89). Jean treats the basic epic pattern of individual combat with stylistic dissonance and parody of situation, characterization, or speech which involves the "intrusion du trivial dans le conventionnel noble" (91). Furthermore, Jean's skillful transformation of the battle's epico-allegorical structure is seen as infusing new meaning in a cliched convention. Through a detailed analysis of description, discourse, and action in the combat, Bouché finds evidence that Jean was illustrating Raison's view of the chaotic instability of love, in other words, "les contradictions et la complexité du sentiment amoureux" (98).

171 -----. "L'obscène et le sacré ou l'utilisation paradoxale du rire dans le *Roman de la rose* de Jean de Meun." In *Le rire au moyen âge dans la littérature et dans les arts*. Ed. Thérèse Bouché et Hélène Charpentier. Bordeaux: Presses Universitaires de Bordeaux, 1990. 83-95.

An examination of Jean de Meun's use of comedy, especially of the kind that Mikhail Bakhtine called "le 'réalisme grotesque'" (83; see *L'oeuvre de François Rabelais et la culture populaire au Moyen Age et sous la Renaissance*). Examples of Jean's humor can be found in the tirade of the jealous husband, in la Vieille's fabliau-like instructions to young women, in the farcical episode of the killing of Male Bouche, and in the charlatan's harangue of Genius's sermon. But Bouché argues that it is in the disconcerting union of the sacred and the obscene at the end of the romance that Jean reaches a vision of life where the comic and the tragic are intertwined. In an analysis of three major episodes of the final section--Genius's sermon, the story of Pygmalion, and the conquest of the rose, Bouché shows that through the paradox of laughter Jean has made "de l'obscène l'instrument de la saisie du sacré, du sacré le mode d'expression de l'obscène" (87); through laughter Jean exalts the contraries of the body and the spirit, which are harmoniously fused.

172 -----. "Ovide et Jean de Meun." *Le moyen âge* 83 (1977):71-87.

A discussion of the importance of Ovid to the first part of the *Rose*, following previous scholars, including E. K. Rand. Bouché shows in particular the Latin author's metamorphosis in the discourses of Jean de Meun's characters, l'Ami and la Vieille. A thoughtful confrontation of corresponding passages from the *Ars amatoria* and the *Rose* show how Jean adapted, amplified, actualized (brought up-to-date), and personalized Ovid's advice on love. Jean's great talent lay in his power to dramatize, as shown in la Vieille's description of a little scene involving a woman who has to deal with two lovers at the same time, which Bouché retells in dramatic form. Rather than simply translating Ovid, Jean transformed the older material in a way that expressed his own originality.

173 Bouhours, Dominique. *Entretiens d'Ariste et d'Eugène.* 1671; new ed. Paris: Bossard, 1920. Pp. 254.

A brief appreciation of Jean de Meun, found in the dialogue entitled "La langue française." A respected expert on French grammar and style in his day, Bouhours points to Jean as "le père et l'inventeur de l'éloquence française" (113), whose continuation of the *Rose* was admired not only "pour l'élégance du style, mais aussi pour le fonds de la doctrine" (113). Bouhours recognizes, however, that some of the allegories scholars have found in the *Rose* were not thought of by the author.

174 Braet, Herman. "Der Roman der Rose, Raum im Blick." In *Träume im Mittelalter: Ikonologische Studien*. Ed. Agostino Paravicini Bagliani and Giorgio Stabile. Stuttgart and Zurich: Belser, 1989. 183-92; color plates 20-23.

An analysis of several aspects of illustrations in *Rose* manuscripts, such as the scenes chosen for the title page, the different representations in a triptych or a quadriptych, and the various facets of the countryside and the animals. The author concludes that the miniature on the title page is not only an introduction to distinct narrative elements but also a synthesis which contains what the artist--the privileged reader--considers the most important aspects or moments of the romance. The illustrator proceeds hermeneutically, leading us to a certain comprehension of the text and hence contributing to its reception. [AKS]

175 Braun, George M. "Old French 'Dangier': A New Interpretation of its Semantic Origin." *French Review* 7 (1934):481-85.

A study of *dangier* (or *dongier*), which from its first occurrences in the mid-twelfth century carried the two meanings of power and refusal. The author points out both its "frequent use in connection with erotic effusions" (481-82) and the greater frequency of its second meaning, that of a woman's refusal or resistance. Braun accepts Langlois's explanation of the personification Dangier in the *Rose* as meaning "la Pudeur de la femme" (484; see no. 6, 5:335). He concludes that *dangier* "seems to be a neologism of gynocracy" (485) and that it "owes its genesis to a scholarly coinage of the commencing lyrical art poetry" (485).

176 Brook, Leslie C. "The Continuator's Monologue: Godefroy de Lagny and Jean de Meun." *French Studies* 45 (1991): 1-16.

A comparison of examples of monologues written by authors "who knowingly assumed another's mantle and completed an unfinished tale" (1), that is, Godefroy de Lagny's monologue in his continuation of Chrétien de Troyes's *Chevalier de la charrete* and Jean de Meun's continuation of l'Amant's soliloquy after l. 4028. After reviewing the monologues found in the first part of the *Rose*, Brook describes, line by line, how Jean both binds the two parts of l'Amant's lament together and subtly changes the tone. Brook stresses Jean's skillful widening of the monologue "on the levels of style, tone, lexis, and content" (14), a development which is a microcosm of the continuation as a whole.

177 -----. "Love's External Foes: From the Lyric to the *Roman de la rose*." In *L'imaginaire courtois et son double*. Ed. Giovanna Angeli and Luciano Formisano. Pubblicazioni dell'Università degli Studi di Salerno, Sezione Atti, Convegni, Miscellanee 35. Naples: Edizioni Scientifiche Italiane, 1992. 255-69.

A study of the meaning and behavior of the lover's opponents, often called *losengiers*, *medisants*, or *jaloux*, in medieval lyric and romance, in particular in the first part of the *Rose*. After surveying references to these enemies of love in lyric poetry, Brook analyzes in detail references to *losengiers* (flatterers, gossips, and other evil-speakers) in the *Rose* and to their personification in Male Bouche and Jalousie, two allies whose "role and portrayal owe something to the *losengiers* and *gelus* of the lyric" (259). As Male Bouche seems to suggest both general gossip and specific tale-telling, Jalousie also suggests the different concepts of an external guardian or of the rose herself, "jealously guarding her person against any intrusion from an outsider" (265). Finally Brook points out that in the continuation Male Bouche must be eliminated early on in order to prevent Jalousie from being alerted.

178 Brownlee, Kevin. "Jean de Meun and the Limits of Romance: Genius as Rewriter of Guillaume de Lorris." In *Romance: Generic Transformation from Chrétien de Troyes to Cervantes*. Ed. and intro. Kevin Brownlee and Marina

Scordilis Brownlee. Hanover and London: University Presses of New England for Dartmouth College, 1985. 114-34.

A discussion of the "poetics of continuation" (114) in the *Rose* through a detailed analysis of Genius's critique of Guillaume's garden of Deduit and of his courtly discourse. Through a three-part rhetorical strategy Genius rewrites Guillaume as *écriture*, reworking and deforming the earlier text. In the second part of the *Rose* we see a radical change in the narrator-protagonist relationship and, with the introduction of Nature, we pass beyond the limits of Guillaume's romance. Genius thus provides "the final and most explicit instance of Jean de Meun's expansion of the generic limits of romance" (130), an expansion which makes the production of meaning in romance synonymous with the reading process.

179 -----. "Orpheus' Song Re-Sung: Jean de Meun's Reworking of *Metamorphoses*, X." *Romance Philology* 36 (1982):201-09.

A consideration of how the only two Ovidian stories told by Jean's narrator serve to define Jean's relation to Guillaume de Lorris and to the Orphic role of vernacular poet. Jean's reworking of the story of Adonis complements Guillaume's Narcisse and exploits Ovid's Orpheus as subtext. Jean's retelling of the Pygmalion story departs from Ovid in three important ways: by stressing the artist figure as a commentary on the earlier discussion of Art and Nature; by commenting again on Guillaume's story of Narcissus; and by transposing the order of the two Ovidian stories to call attention to Jean himself as a new Orpheus.

180 -----. "The Problem of Faux Semblant: Language, History, and Truth in the *Roman de la rose*." In *The New Medievalism*. Ed. Marina S. Brownlee, Kevin Brownlee, and Stephen G. Nichols. Baltimore: The Johns Hopkins UP, 1991. 253-71.

A close study of the character Faux Semblant that raises

questions about his "narrative or diegetic status; his historical subtext; and his linguistic-poetic significance" (254). These three questions are intimately related and reflect Faux Semblant's complex relationship with le Dieu d'Amour, who poses seven sets of questions concerning both Faux Semblant's nature and certain theological concerns, such as mendicancy. Faux Semblant's answers reveal "a series of conflicting voices which are repeatedly played off against each other" (264). Furthermore Brownlee points to Faux Semblant's discussion of two books, "one by a Guillaume; the other associated with a Jean" (264), that is, Guillaume de Saint-Amour's *De periculis* and Joachim de Fiore's *Evanglium eternum* [important texts in the conflict between the Mendicant Orders and the University of Paris]. Brownlee argues that Faux Semblant's presentation of these texts "involves a commentary on and a reworking of the God of Love's presentation of the *Roman de la Rose*", thus raising "questions of textual and discursive authority" (265). [Note that the earlier source of this article, *Romantic Review* 79, as stated on the copyright page, is incorrect.]

181 -----. "Reflections in the *Miroër aus Amoreus*: The Inscribed Reader in Jean de Meun's *Roman de la rose*." In *Mimesis: From Mirror to Method, Augustine to Descartes*. Ed. John D. Lyons and Stephen G. Nichols, Jr. Hanover: University Presses of New England for Dartmouth College, 1982. 60-70; notes 257-58.

A discussion of the inscribed audience in Jean de Meun's *Rose* which raises three questions: the mimetic function of the text for the presumed audience of lovers, the authorial stance that Jean assumes before that audience, and the expansion of the public to include society as a whole. The mimetic function--how readers relate to the text--suggests three kinds of status for the text: didactic (how to), representational (how it is), and imitative (how it should be). From an analysis of Jean's apologia and its prologue (ll. 15105-272), which is his "most elaborate direct address to his readers" (61), Brownlee argues that Jean claims for "his vernacular poetic enterprise all the authority associated with the canonical Latin poetic texts" (68).

Through his address not only to "seigneur amoreus" (ll. 15129), but to women and clerics, Jean expanded Guillaume's courtly public "into a potentially universal audience" (70).

182 Brownlee, Kevin and Sylvia Huot, ed. *Rethinking the "Romance of the Rose": Text, Image, Reception*. Middle Ages Series. Philadelphia: U of Pennsylvania P, 1992. Pp. x + 386.

A collection of articles (two of which had appeared previously) on the *Roman de la rose*, based on papers given at the 1987 Newberry Library (Chicago) Renaissance Conference on the *Rose*. The articles are grouped into three topics: literary approaches, the iconographic tradition, and the reception of the *Rose* in France, Italy, the Low Countries, and England. The editors' introduction summarizes the articles and argues that they present a double orientation, a "collective reevaluation of past work during a particularly rich period" and the suggestion of "new connections and new syntheses" (3). See entries on Pierre-Yves Badel, no. 570; Emmanuèle Baumgartner, no. 161; Kevin Brownlee, no. 590; John V. Fleming, no. 239; Robert Pogue Harrison, no. 645; David F. Hult, no. 304; Sylvia Huot, no. 655; Stephen G. Nichols, no. 404; Lee Patterson, no. 718; Daniel Poirion, no. 445; Karl D. Uitti, no. 528; Dieuwke E. van der Poel, no. 761; and Lori Walters, nos. 76 and 769.

183 Burchardt, A. "Beiträge zur Kenntnis der französischen Gesellschaft in der zweiten Hälfte des XIII. Jahrhunderts auf Grund der Werke Rutebeufs, des *Roman de la rose*, des *Renart le nouvel* und des *Couronnement Renart*." Diss. U of Leipzig, 1910.

184 Butturff, Diane and Douglas. "*Le roman de la rose* and the Sophistry of Love." *French Review* 45 (1971):52-58.

An interpretation based on the hypothesis that Fleming did not take far enough his analysis of sophistry in the *Rose* (see no. 243). The authors quickly review what they see as the sophistic arguments of l'Ami, la Vieille, Faux Semblant, and Bel Accueil, who all misuse rhetoric and dialectic in order to please their listeners. Even Franchise and Pitié are prone to sophistry. In the other camp the authors place Raison and Nature, whose appeals to reason and character, respectively, fail to move the lover. (Nature is absolved of Genius's call to procreation: see the discussion of "Genius's misinterpretation of Nature's confession" [58]). Thus l'Amant, having lost the ability to distinguish sophistry from true wisdom, "falls into deadly sin" (58).

185 Cahoon, Leslie. "Raping the Rose: Jean de Meun's Reading of Ovid's *Amores*." *Classical and Modern Literature* 6 (1986):261-85.

As much an interpretation and condemnation of the "worldly and irreverent Amator" (283) of Ovid's *Amores* as a study of Jean's version and use of the Pygmalion myth and the militaristic, architectural, and religious context in which it is set. Cahoon proposes that it is the lover of the *Amores*, rather than the Pygmalion of the *Metamorphoses*, who lies behind Jean's retelling of the myth. In the end, both Ovid and Jean de Meun sought to "revivify traditional values and traditional religion in an increasingly loveless world" (284), and it was through irony that they called on their readers to see the serious purpose behind their irreverent, urbane, and insensitive depictions of love.

186 Caie, Graham D. "An Iconographic Detail in the *Roman de la rose* and the Middle English *Romaunt*." *The Chaucer Review* 8 (1974):320-23.

An interpretation of the dreamer's "interesting and curious gesture" (320) of sewing on his sleeves before setting out--a detail portrayed in many miniatures--as suggestive of his readiness for *fol'amour*. Close-fitting sleeves, according to the author, were "a mark of the servants of the God of Love" (321). Furthermore, Guillaume's source may have been Jerome's

"Epistle to Eustochium," which associates such sleeves with lechery. [Although the author labels it "curious," sewing in the sleeves of a garment after it was put on was common practice in the Middle Ages.]

187   Calin, William. "La comédie humaine chez Jean de Meun." In *Mélanges offerts à Charles Rostaing par ses collègues, ses élèves et ses amis*. Ed. Jacques De Caluwé et al. 2 vols. Liege: Association des Romanistes de l'Université de Liège, 1974. 1:101-14.

A humanistic and naturalistic overview of the second part of the *Rose* which stresses the variety, deceptiveness, and humor of its characters. In "ce monde brutal où règnent l'or et la luxure" (105), everyone must learn to deceive or be deceived. Yet Jean de Meun is striving to strip off the masks, to reveal the falseness of received ideas. Thus the Narrator learns, to Jean de Meun's approval, that *fin'amors* is a lie and that he has a sensual nature whose expression is life-affirming. Jean's Balzacien portrait of the world is offered with much humor, however, and Calin concludes by describing, in accord with Bergson's principles, the comic side of the principal personifications, including (especially) Raison, and of the character types, such as l'Ami and la Vieille.

188   -----. "Contre la *fin'amor*? Contre la femme? Une relecture de textes du Moyen Age." In *Courtly Literature: Culture and Context*. Selected Papers of the 5th Triennial Congress of the International Courtly Literature Society, Dalfsen, The Netherlands, 9-16 August, 1986. Ed. Keith Busby and Erik Kooper. Amsterdam: John Benjamins, 1990. 61-82.

A discussion of medieval French works which offer views of women that appear both misogynistic and antagonistic to the principles of *fin'amor* (the medieval term which corresponds roughly to "courtly love," although Calin rejects this neologism). Between a rereading of the romance *Ipomedon*, the pastourelle, and several *dits* of Guillaume de Machaut, the author considers briefly the question of Jean de Meun's misogyny, for which he cannot accept Friedman's mitigating arguments (see no. 253). Although Jean's "polymodalité" (73) prevents us from identifying a single interior vision in his continuation, the repetition of certain key ideas about women and love suggests that "antiféminisme constitue une des bases de la structure intellectuelle du *Roman de la rose*" (74). Ultimately Jean's debasing of women is intended to unmask the illusory exaltation of women and to propose "la liberté dans l'égalité" (75).

189 -----. *A Muse for Heroes: Nine Centuries of the Epic in France.* Toronto: U of Toronto P, 1983. Pp. 513.

An interpretation of the personifications, imagery, and world view of the two parts of the *Rose* as part of a long study of the epic poem in France. A section on medieval allegory introduces the discussion of Guillaume's "blatantly aristocratic" (117) view of love and his exploration of the psychology of young people, especially of "the ideal potential courtly lover" (116). Jungian and phenomenological approaches suggest that the garden--a feminine landscape--reflects nostalgia for the Mother. Jean de Meun's vision of the world is totally different from Guillaume's: his comic treatment of the social effects of money, deception, and manipulation is the other side of the author's urging the Narrator and his public "to go beyond appearances and seek the truth" (129). Furthermore, Calin sees in Jean an important proponent of the philosophy of plenitude (fecundity)--all the characters "favor some kind of sexual intercourse" (134). Finally, Jean is seen as an early humanist and precursor of Rabelais and Voltaire.

190 Callay, Brigitte L. "The Road to Salvation in the *Roman de la rose*." In *Pascua Mediaevalia: Studies voor Prof. Dr. J. M. De Smet.* Ed. R. Lievens, E. Van Mingroot and Werner Verbeke. Mediaevalia Lovaniensia, Series I, Studia X. Louvain: Presses Universitaires de Leuvain, 1983. 499-509.

An analysis of conflicting critical views on whether the character

Genius speaks for his author or is treated ironically. Callay argues that Jean de Meun, contrary to Alain de Lille, intended "to discredit Genius' moral authority" (502). Genius, as a priest in Nature's church rather than the Christian God's, cannot fit his teaching into "the framework of orthodox Christian faith" (503). This unorthodoxy, according to Callay, demonstrates Genius's inadequacy as a moral authority: his reasoning, of obtaining Heaven through natural means, can no longer be true since the Fall. The narrative setting of Genius's sermon, which condemns love *par amors* (as represented by le Dieu d'Amour), while enabling l'Amant to achieve his immoral goal, further shows Genius to be a victim of delusion.

191 Camille, Michael. *The Gothic Idol: Ideology and Image-making in Medieval Art*. Cambridge New Art History and Criticism. Cambridge: Cambridge UP, 1989. Pp. xxxii + 407 + 181 ill.

A detailed study that "charts the complex interdependence of scriptural and visual traditions" (xxvii) with regard to images, especially those considered idols, from the mid-twelfth to the end of the fourteenth century. During the High Middle Ages "the function and production of images underwent profound and permanent change" (xxvii), a change that is discernible in important passages toward the end of the *Rose*. In his analysis of the ambiguous Dieu d'Amour, of Venus shooting her arrow at the "figurative castle of the female body" (320), and especially of the episode of Pygmalion-the-artist, Camille argues "for the celebration rather than the denial of love-idolatry in Jean de Meung's *Roman de la Rose*" (xxix). Jean's Pygmalion is not an idolater; his passion is "anti-idolatry, because as idols women are far too dangerous" (333). Thus, while Jean seems to play on the positive language of natural love, his celebration of sculptural and sexual artifice is nonetheless "ideologically constructed" (333).

192 Cénac-Moncaut, Justin Edouard Mathieu. "Les jardins du *Roman de la rose* comparés avec ceux des Romains et ceux

du Moyen Age." *L'investigateur* 8 (1868):225-42. Rpt. Paris: Auguste Aubry, 1869. Pp. 21.

A comparison of the garden of Deduit in the *Rose* to the fourteenth-century gardens of the kings of Navarre in the little town of Tafalla, Spain (the author also dates the *Rose* from the fourteenth century). After reviewing the garden topography in the *Rose* (with some inaccuracies), the author describes in detail the walled gardens of Tafalla, which are concerned with security, the dominant preoccupation of the Middle Ages. If this Spanish garden were replanted with trees and flowers, we would have "une reproduction fidèle des jardins du *Roman de la Rose*" (18). A plan of the Tafalla gardens is appended. There is only a very brief reference to Roman gardens, of which Cénac-Moncaut believed that Middle Ages knew little.

193 Cherniss, Michael D. "Irony and Authority: The Ending of the *Roman de la rose*." *Modern Language Quarterly* 36 (1976):227-38.

An interpretation which focuses on the many kinds of inadequate, i.e., secular, love in the garden of Deduit. This view of love underlies the ironic status of the authorities on love (in particular Raison, Nature, and Genius), none of whom is wholly adequate (they are looking for love in the wrong places). One of them, however--Genius--suggests to the reader the possibility of a divine order through his contrast of the Park of the Lamb with the garden of Deduit. Although Genius is incapable of leading anyone to the Christian paradise, he does suggest, according to Cherniss, that the natural procreative force "is the link between the natural order in which he [Genius] exerts his influence and the divine order toward which he aspires" (232). The rhetorical techniques of contraries and contrast structure Genius's and the other authorities' views of love, thus making of Jean de Meun's remarks on the importance of knowing "contreres choses" (l. 21543), "a key passage for the entire poem" (238). Although irony is seen as the major literary mode of the *Rose*, the author does not apparently see Genius's use of the description of the Park of the Lamb as ironic. [Is Genius simply unaware of his inadequacy as a guide, or is he using Christian imagery to manipulate his audience?]

194 -----. "Jean de Meun's Reson and Boethius." *Romance Notes* 16 (1975):678-85.

A study of Jean de Meun's reworking of Boethius's *De consolatione Philosophiae* in Raison's second dialogue with l'Amant, in order to understand "the process by which Meun might have been drawn into continuing the poem in the first place" (685 n. 17). L'Amant's lamentation at the end of the first part, which reminded Jean of the opening complaint of the *De consolatione*, became the point of departure for a Boethian dialogue on rational and irrational loves. Thus Guillaume's narrative became "a sort of prologue to Amant's complaint" (681), corresponding to Boethius's account of his imprisonment. However, because Jean could not end his work with a rationalistic resolution to l'Amant's problem if he wanted to explore the experience of sensual love in a "realistic" way, and because Raison's wisdom is not Christian, he must make her fail to convince l'Amant: "Amant is no Boethius, and Reson is wasting her time" (685).

195 Cohen, Gustave. *Le roman de la rose.* "Les cours de Sorbonne." 1928; rpt. Paris: Centre de Documentation Universitaire, 1973. Pp. 227.

An introductory study prepared for French university students. Although the work is largely a summary of the *Rose*, with long, modernized excerpts, Cohen surveys critical opinion on the romance and earlier erotic and allegorical vernacular literature. For each part of the *Rose* Cohen reviews what was known about the author and delineates the work's principal ideas [without regard for the character expressing the idea]. The first part, "la principale, la plus agréable" (64), is a treatise on civility and refined pleasure as well as a perceptive depiction of the emotional conflict in the heart of a young woman. Jean de Meun, on the other hand, is an "anti-Guillaume de Lorris"

(199); his didacticism, undigested erudition, and naturalistic ideas oppose the courtly love of the first part. Cohen judges the second part as unequal but robust and realistic.

196 -----. "Le Roman de la rose (XIIIe siècle)." In *Tableau de la littérature française.* 2 vols. Paris: Gallimard, 1962. 1:89-101.

An introductory essay for the general French public which stresses the differences between the two parts: the first is poetic and courtly, the second erudite and "naturiste" (98). The author's sympathies clearly lie with the first part, on which he spends much more time than on the second. He accuses Jean de Meun of ruining the first part by crushing the rose's petals "sous les grosses pattes de sa massive érudition" (98). However, he does recognize in Jean "notre premier humaniste" (101). [Cohen attempts to bring to life Guillaume de Lorris, his romance, and its courtly background but in so doing he sometimes offers hypotheses as facts.]

197 Cohn, Norman. *The World-View of a Thirteenth-Century Parisian Intellectual: Jean de Meun and the "Roman de la rose".* Inaugural Lecture of the Professor of French delivered in the Chemistry Lecture Theatre on 11 October 1960. Durham: University of Durham, 1961. Pp. 22.

An introduction to the *Rose* and an appreciation of three major themes in the second part by an intellectual historian of the Middle Ages, author of *The Pursuit of the Millenium*. The author stresses Jean de Meun's importance as both a popularizer and a pioneer in three areas of inquiry: scientific knowledge of the cosmos, propaganda in favor of sexual procreation, and democratic social theory. Unfortunately this elaboration of Jean's world view rarely recognizes the distinction between a character's ideas and the author's. While Cohn recognizes Jean's debt to previous thinkers, he emphasizes Jean's originality in using French for the first time "as a vehicle for the most lofty philosophical thought" (11).

Finally, Cohn argues for Jean's importance as a predecessor of modern political and social thought.

198 Cortes Vazquez, Luis. *El episodio de Pigmalión del "Roman de la rose": Etica y estética de Jean de Meun.* Acta Salmanticensia, Filosofia y Letras 122. Salamanca: Ediciones Universidad de Salamanca, 1980. Pp. 167 + ill.

A detailed study of Jean's retelling of the Pygmalion story from Ovid's *Metamorphoses* (ll. 20787-21156), which includes the text of the Lecoy edition, a Spanish translation, the Latin text, and a sampling of later versions, including a poem by Voltaire. When comparing the episode in the *Rose* to Ovid's, Cortes Vazquez argues that Jean's version, "muy elegante y delicado," was "un brillante ejercicio escolar" (155) later inserted into the *Rose*, "una obra juvenil" (9) which displays all the young cleric's rhetorical knowledge and skills. While the author points to important differences between the Pygmalion episode and the rest of the continuation, such as absence of misogyny and acceptance of marriage of a sort, he also argues that the episode reveals important facets of Jean's ethical (materialistic) and esthetic ideas (in particular the rhetorical concept of *amplificatio*). The analysis includes a discussion of what the text tells us about medieval life, especially about details of clothes and music.

199 Curtius, Ernst Robert. *European Literature and the Latin Middle Ages.* Tr. Willard R. Trask. New York: Harper and Row, 1963 [originally published Bern; A. Francke, 1948]. Pp. xv + 658.

A brief discussion of Jean de Meun's attitude toward nature and procreation, which reflects borrowings from Alain de Lille, Boethius, and Virgil. Curtius appears to rebuke Jean, who "warns against love" (125), for sinking "to the level of a sexual liberalism which concocts a spicy stew out of erudite tinsel and philistine pruriency" (126). Further, Curtius suggests that Bishop Tempier's condemnation of 1277 was aimed at the *Rose*'s heresy; he points out that Jean's philosophy is found in the Wife of Bath's prologue and in Shakespeare's eleventh sonnet. Other brief references to the *Rose* include a discussion of the "quinque lineae" of love (512-14).

200 Dahlberg, Charles. "First Person and Personification in the *Roman de la rose*: Amant and Dangier." *Mediaevalia* 3 (1977):37-58.

A study of the narrator in the *Rose* that highlights supposed ambiguities in l'Amant's point of view. The author hopes to show the "traditional scriptural implications" (49) of certain characters in the *Rose*, in particular of the first-person narrator and Danger. If l'Amant is wrong-headed, his negative perceptions of his enemies, such as Danger, are also wrong: Danger is in effect the lover's ally. Dahlberg argues for the "fair interior" (44) of Danger through an analysis of such iconographic details as his hairiness and his thorny club. The article suggests the concept of "unlike images" (37) as an explanatory tool, a concept which will be developed in a later work (see no. 201).

201 -----. *The Literature of Unlikeness*. Hanover and London: University Presses of New England, 1988. Pp. xiv + 207.

An examination of the theme of unlikeness, of exile from God, from Augustine's *Confessions* through a number of medieval works, including the *Rose*, where the garden is seen as a "land of unlikeness" (100). After a discussion of first-person voices in other medieval works, in particular the Latin poem, *The Apocalypse of Golias* (c. 1200?), the various first-person voices in the *Rose*-- poet(s), narrator, lover, characters, inner characters--are shown to be ambiguous and contradictory. Analyzed in detail are the voices of le Dieu d'Amour, Faux Semblant, and Genius. In order to develop parallels with Augustine's voice in the *Confessions*, Dahlberg offers such arguments as refusing Jean his stated sources (Cicero) in favor of more Augustinian ones (Aelred of Rievaulx's work, *On Spiritual Friendship*). The article's final argument makes of the

Rose a "confession without repentance" (123) in which the "absurd self-deceptions of the Lover in his garden of unlikeness" (121) are reflected in all the other characters except in Jean's Augustinian Raison, who reflects God. [Ultimately Dahlberg's use of the idea of the garden of unlikeness, "where all is turned upside down" (124), appears to suggest that nothing in the garden, not even Raison, can be taken to mean what it seems to mean.]

202 -----. "Love and the *Roman de la rose.*" *Speculum* 44 (1969):568-84.

An analysis of various kinds of love portrayed in the *Rose*, in particular l'Amant's "classic form of cupidity" (575). The author turns "to the theologians for illumination" (577); Alain de Lille, Augustine, and Pierre de Blois are among those whose thought clarifies, according to Dahlberg, the kinds of love found in the *Rose*. Since natural affection is the starting point for both charity and cupidity, both authors of the *Rose* suggest that l'Amant, by choosing cupidity, reenacts the pattern of the Fall. Some analysis of structural and symbolic elements in the poem, such as the five arrows of le Dieu d'Amour, are offered as further evidence of l'Amant's cupidinous love. [The author relies heavily on Robertson's *Preface to Chaucer* (no. 473).]

203 -----. "Macrobius and the Unity of the *Roman de la rose.*" *Studies in Philology* 58 (1961):573-82.

An interpretation of the *Rose*'s opening reference to Macrobius's theory of dreams which leads Dahlberg to suggest that the lover's belongs to the category of enigmatic dreams. Furthermore, the lover's dream is a kind of fabulous narrative whose purpose "is to reveal an art of love, but a philosophical rather than a pornographic art of love" (576). Following D. W. Robertson (see no. 473), Dahlberg argues that the *Rose* is really about the Fall, in particular about the three-stage process through which man comes to sin: "the suggestion to sense, the delight of the heart, and the consent of the reason" (578).

Guillaume developed the first two stages, Jean the third (the overthrow of reason). Thus the reference to Macrobius suggests that "the two authors were in fundamental agreement" (582) over the ultimate meaning of the lover's experience.

204 -----. "The Secular Tradition in Chaucer and Jean de Meun." Diss. Princeton U, 1953.

205 Dauphine, James. "Pygmalion dans *Le roman de la rose*." *Razo, Cahiers du Centre d'Etudes Médiévales de Nice* 3 (1982):89-92.

An interpretation of the significance of the Pygmalion story in the second part of the *Rose*, an approach based on a striking difference between Jean's version and Ovid's: whereas the Latin author stresses the transformation of stone to living woman, Jean concentrates on detailing Pygmalion's artistic expression. Thus Jean's retelling is a reflection on art that suggests not only the power of love but that of writing. The author proposes that Pygmalion be seen as the "emblème" (91) that Jean has chosen for himself and every artist.

206 Defourny, Michel. "Observations sur la première partie du *Roman de la rose*." *Mélanges offerts à Rita Lejeune*. 2 vols. Gembloux: Duculot, 1969. 2:1163-69.

A review of the critical debate over the nature (abstract or individual) of the personifications in the first *Rose*, with particular attention to Hans Robert Jauss's contribution in "La transformation de la forme allégorique" (no. 319). Defourny raises several questions about what he calls the "incohérences" (1166) in Guillaume's use of personification: characters are found inside the garden that would seem to be proscribed by the paintings on the outside; some characters, such as the masons who build the tower, the Norman soldiers of fortune who guard it ("D'où viennent tous ces gens?" [1166]), and la Vieille who watches over Bel Accueil, are not allegorical personifications;

many personifications act or speak at times in a manner inconsistent with their names. These "petites imperfections" (1169) are ultimately attributed to the limitations of the allegorical system; not Guillaume de Lorris but the supposed "lois du genre allégorique" (1169) are to blame.

207 -----. "Le *Roman de la rose* à travers l'histoire et la philosophie." *Marche romane* 17 (1967):53-60.

A bibliographical study offering an introduction to important editions of the *Rose* and works of scholarship up to Gunn's *Mirror of Love* (no. 274). Defourny summarizes the *Rose*'s popularity up to the sixteenth century (when Etienne Pasquier believed it superior to Dante), surveys the history of the major editions from Marot (1526) to Langlois (1914-1924), and briefly appraises the contributions of half a dozen seminal critical studies, including those of Gaston Paris, Ernest Langlois, M.-M. Gorce, G. Paré, and Alan Gunn [see nos. 422, 358, 265, 419, and 274].

208 Demarolle, Pierre. "Remarques sur le texte de Jean de Meun et de Villon." In *Etudes...Lanly* (no. 230). 85-93.

A discussion of two difficult verses in the *Rose* (ll. 6624 and 19637) and of one in Villon's *Testament* (l. 952). The first verse, "d'un tret de paonet errant," concerns the description of Manfred's death, the second, Genius's metaphoric description of male sexual organs as "l'aumosniere et les estalles." Demarolle uses the *Grandes Chroniques de France* to clarify Jean's references to Manfred, but the term "estalles," despite similar terms in other works, remains obscure.

209 Demats, Paule. "D'*Amoenitas* à *Deduit*: André le Chapelain et Guillaume de Lorris." In *Mélanges de langue et de littérature du Moyen Age et de la Renaissance offerts à Jean*

Frappier par ses collègues, ses élèves et ses amis. 2 vols. Geneva: Droz, 1970. 1:217-33.

A study which focuses on how the gardens in the *De amore* (c. 1185) and the *Roman de la rose* materialize their authors' ambiguous views of love. Most of the article deals with the narrative section in Book 1 of the *De amore* in which appears the marvelous garden of Amoenitas. The author brings out perceptively André le Chapelain's conflicting views of love--as a rational choice and an inborn passion, as a source of virtue (for the lover) or enslavement (for the beloved). The last four pages discuss the transposition of elements in the earlier work to the garden of Deduit in the *Rose*, including the moral of Amoenitas, which reappears as the moral of the Fountain of Narcissus. The differences in the two conceptions are also described: one is an eschatological vision aimed at softening hard-hearted ladies, the other an initiation and an adventure both personal and exemplary. The final discussion of the meaning of the crystals in Narcissus's fountain (which Demats argues represent the lover's eyes) is a careful reading of the way the fountain serves as intermediary between "la forme pure de l'idéal courtois" (233) and the realization of this ideal in the hero's experience.

210 -----. "Poésie et doctrine courtoise au XIIIe siècle: Le *Roman de la rose*." In *Histoire de la littérature française*. Ed. Jacques Roger and Jean-Charles Payen. Collection U. 2 vols. Paris: Armand Colin, 1969. 1:70-81.

A good short introduction to Guillaume's part of the *Rose*. In a few pages (see especially 70-77), Demats describes how the poem works as doctrine, model, and mystery. The first part of the *Rose* is "une éthique toute profane et mondaine, une morale du paraître" (75) which suggests the antagonism between *fin'amor* and Christian morality. The author also situates the first part in the evolution of courtly lyrics and treatises and sketches its influence. The second part is treated in one paragraph (Jean's "dessein anticourtois ne fait aucun doute" [79]), as is Christine de Pizan's role in stimulating the Querelle de la Rose.

211 Denkinger, T. "Die Bettelorden in der französischen didaktischen Literatur des 13. Jahrhunderts, besonders bei Rutebeuf und im *Roman de la rose*." *Franziskanische Studien* 2 (1915):286-313.

212 Di Stefano, Giuseppe. "Situation de la *Rose*." In *Littératures: mélanges littéraires publiés à l'occasion du 150e anniversaire de l'Université McGill de Montréal*. Montreal: Hurtubise, 1971. 61-71.

A discussion of two editions and twenty-seven critical works on the *Rose* which groups them according to the questions that concerned scholars at the time. The principal topics are the Querelle de la Rose, the *Roman*'s sources, and the differences in the two parts, all of which Di Stefano suggests need further study. While stressing Jean de Meun's "démesure" (67) and lack of system, Di Stefano points out that it was the second part to which most subsequent writers responded. He also argues that it is simplistic to attribute the differences in the two parts to class or generational influences. [A few serious errors mar the bibliographical information: the information given for Jean Frappier's article, "Aspects de l'hermétisme dans la poésie médiévale," is that for his article on the theme of the mirror (no. 247).]

213 Doinel, Jules. *Guy Fabi et Guillaume Rebrachien*. Orleans: H. Herluison, 1887. Pp. 28. [Extract from the *Annales de la Société historique et archéologique du Gâtinais* (1887):153-80.]

Geneological information, gathered by the archivist of the Loiret region, on the de Lorris family and others who may have been related to or in contact with the authors of the *Rose*. Fabi was the uncle of Guillaume Rebrachien, the son of Guillaume de Lorris, "dit Le Doyen, ancien sergent du roi Philippe-Auguste" (5); this Guillaume may have been the author of the first part. The wife of Evrard de Chateauneuf, who was named Rose, "est peut-être la *Rose* du célèbre roman" (9). Includes the first thousand verses of the ms. Paris, B. N. fr. 1573.

214 Dornbush, Jean M. *Pygmalion's Figure: Reading Old French Romance.* The Edward C. Armstrong Monographs on Medieval Literature 5. Lexington, Ky.: French Forum, Publishers, 1990. Pp. 151.

A wide-ranging essay in which Dornbush approaches the *Rose* as "above all an exercise in mirror imagery" (52); the lover's quest reflects on the imaginative and interpretative principles of the romance as a whole, just as one part of it, Pygmalion's story, is both "a miniature analogue of the entire *Rose*" (53) and a mirror of the activities of poetic creation and re-creation. Dornbush explores this principle of mirroring through similarities and differences in a number of relationships: between the myths of Narcissus and Pygmalion (and by extension between the two parts of the *Rose*); between Ovid's version of Pygmalion and Jean de Meun's; between Pygmalion's imaginative art and the "analogous interpretive activities of the narrator, poet, and reader" (57); and finally between texts within a tradition. It is the *Rose*'s "conflation of amatory and rhetorical arts" (62) that makes possible such complex analogies. Finally, the author stresses the "invertible reverence and audacity" (85) at play in poetic creation and in the reader's response.

215 Dragonetti, Roger. "Une métaphore du sens propre dans le *Roman de la rose*." *Digraphe* 21 (1979):67-85. Rpt. in *La musique et les lettres: études de littérature médiévale.* Publications Romanes et Françaises 171. Geneva: Droz, 1986. 381-97.

An abstruse analysis of the passage in which Raison uses a bawdy word ("coilles," l. 5507), introduced by means of a summary of the medieval theory of rhetorical ornamentation based on *ornatus difficilis* and *ornatus facilis*. Various views of language are expressed in Raison's argument that although she names things according to her good pleasure, those names designate the literal meaning of the word. Thus two languages confront each other in Raison's view of language: the metaphorical level (the gloss) and common usage which acts as if "la chose même se donnait dans le nom et inversement" (391). The author concludes that the proper meaning "recouvre de sa fable édenique la réalité scripturale de la lettre musicalement liée" (394).

216 -----. *Le mirage des sources: l'art du faux dans le roman médiéval*. Paris: Editions du Seuil, 1987. Pp. 267.

An exploration of the ambiguous status of the literary text in the Middle Ages. The study focuses on romances attributed to Jean Renart, including the *Roman de la rose ou de Guillaume de Dole,* sometimes confused in bibliographies with the *Rose* of Guillaume de Lorris and Jean de Meun, to which the author also devotes a chapter. The first section describes the ways in which medieval texts seem to be false to modern positivist scholars, a falseness that the author summarizes as "le mirage des sources" (10). For example, in "cette fraude textuelle généralisée" (18) of the Middle Ages, texts pretend to divulge their sources but rarely do, or they are falsely attributed, or they pretend to be what they are not. A chapter on the *Roman de la rose* scrutinizes what we know about the text from the remarks of le Dieu d'Amour at the midpoint of the romance. Dragonetti argues that Jean is practicing "une véritable stratégie de brouillage" (203) to create confusion about the author(s) of the *Rose*. The text becomes "une écriture virtuelle" (205) of "contraires choses" (l. 21543), a text and its gloss, a double game which is in reality the creation of a single poet (Jean de Meun).

217 -----. "Pygmalion où les pièges de la fiction dans le *Roman de la rose*." In *Orbis medievalis: mélanges de langue et de littérature médiévales offerts à Réto Radulf Bezzola*. Ed. Georges Güntert et al. Bern: Francke, 1978. 89-111. Rpt. in *La musique* (no. 215). 345-67.

A discussion of the Pygmalion passage at the end of the second part of the *Rose*, which is part of an essay on (among other subjects) the specular dimension of the text (Jean de Meun calls his continuation "le *Miroër aus Amoreus*" [l. 10621]); "la bipartition et l'unité, conjointes" (346) of the work, signs of which include the two fountains and Nature's discussion of optics; le Dieu d'Amour's prophecy concerning the second author and his relation to the first (there are not two authors but one); and metaphors of clothing. The retelling of the myth of Pygmalion reflects these themes, seen as means of distancing the desired object. The author stresses, for the romance as a whole, its all-pervasive ambiguity, "incohérences" (351), and antitheses: "C'est donc à l'intérieur d'un langage toujours mensonger que se joue en effet le jeu de la vérité" (353).

218 -----. "Le 'Singe de nature' dans le *Roman de la rose*." *Travaux de linguistique et de littérature* [Strasbourg: Centre de Philologie et de littératures romanes de l'Université de Strasbourg] 16 (1978):149-60. Rpt. in *La musique* (no. 215). 369-80.

An analysis of the passage in the second part in which Art is seen as an ape attempting to imitate Nature (ll. 15992-16000), an image which has significance for Jean's attitude toward the relation of artistic creation to divine and natural creation. Instead of agreeing with Jean's apparent assertation that art is sterile, Dragonetti suggests that the passage is "une espèce de provocation" (369). He points out the relevance of the detailed passage on alchemy as an "art véritable" (l. 16054), which is inserted in the discussion of the letter of art as a lifeless reflection of the living letters created by Nature and God. Far from simply copying nature, "le 'Singe' met au jour le statut fictionnel de la nature vivante" (378) by making of the copy the model which creates its double. Art's power is further realized through the textual play with pre-existing texts: "la quête du *Roman de la Rose* est essentiellement une traversée des écritures par l'écriture" (379). The final feat of skill that Jean brings off is to produce the very dream which the poem pretends is anterior to it.

219 Duby, Georges. "Le roman de la rose." In *Mâle Moyen Age: de l'amour et autres essais*. Paris: Flammarion, 1988. 83-117.

A remarkable and challenging synthesis by the great French historian of the economic and social underpinnings of both parts of the *Roman de la rose*. On the assumption that the means of production support high culture and its ideology, Duby describes the first part of the *Rose* as the crowning reflection of the landed aristocracy (and its peasant base), especially that of the royal court. The complex interaction of the landed lords and the subculture of the *jeunes* is conveyed in this brilliant synthesis of Duby's long study of the topic. He argues that Guillaume's *Rose* shows both the troubled class ideology of "la chevalerie" and how it became "desarmée" (101). Between the two parts of the *Rose* profound economic and social changes affected the outlooks of the upper class and the intellectuals, thereby suggesting reasons for Jean de Meun's very different continuation of the *Rose*. While Guillaume proposes a model of behavior, Jean, "Admirable vulgarisateur" (110), proposes a new joy in knowing the world. Consequently Jean argues for the rehabilitation of Nature: Nature's laws are "la voie du salut" (114). Denying Jean's antifeminism, the study ends in a panegyric of Jean de Meun, so generous, so "fraternel" (117).

220 Dufeil, M.-M. *Guillaume de Saint-Amour et la polémique universitaire parisienne, 1250-1259*. Paris: A. et J. Picard, 1972. Pp. xxxii + 468.

An exhaustive study (originally a dissertation) of Guillaume de Saint-Amour's role in the conflict between the University of Paris and the mendicant orders, a series of events that are reflected in the *Rose*, in particular in Jean de Meun's character, Faux Semblant. Among the author's brief comments on Jean's relation to the events are some speculations on the date of the *Rose* based on how it reflects the conflict: the author believes that the *Rose* "n'a pu être écrit dans son ensemble et même publié qu'entre 1263 et 1269" (352). The author further sees Jean not only as a disciple of Guillaume de Saint-Amour but of the Averroistic philosophers at the University of Paris [without, however, giving any textual evidence]. The study also discusses in detail the works of Rutebeuf, who created the character Faux Semblant.

221 Dufournet, Jean. "Le dessein et la philosophie du *Roman de la rose*." *Acta litteraria academiae scientiarum hungaricae* 23 (1981):177-214.

An introduction to the *Rose*, including large sections of plot summary, which also delineates the two major components and the philosophy of the second part. After an overview of the *Rose*'s influence and some of the critical clichés that have become attached to it, the author describes the first major component, the allegorical quest for the rose, as a lover's sentimental education. The second component, "exposition directe par personnages" (182), is the subject of most of the article (relying heavily on Gunn's *Mirror of Love*, no. 274): Dufournet summarizes the positions of the various authorities and argues for Jean's sympathy for all of them, including le Dieu d'Amour. Jean's overall design, in addition to portraying different psychological states, is to "faire éclater les contradictions" (201). Dufournet outlines Jean's philosophy of plenitude and regeneration and concludes with a summary of John Fleming's very different approach to the *Rose* (see no. 243). [Dufournet does not try to reconcile his approach to Fleming's].

222 Durrieu, Paul. "Jean de Meun et l'Italie." *Académie des inscriptions et belles lettres; comptes rendus* (October 1916):436-45.

A report on a document that may relate to Jean de Meun's biography. Durrieu reinterprets the name given in a notarized act made in Bologna in 1269 and relating to a shipment of law books to Paris as in fact that of Jean de Meun ("Magister Johannes de Mauduno, Aurelianensis dyocesis" [438]). If Durrieu's reading is correct, it places Jean in Italy at the time of the historical events referred to in the *Rose*, those concerning

Charles d'Anjou and Manfred and Conradin Hohenstaufen and their allies. It also suggests that Jean had some affluence and that it was in Italy that he may have become familiar with many classical authors, such as Virgil, Cicero, and Suetonius.

223   Eberle, Patricia J. "The Lovers' Glass: Nature's Discourse on Optics and the Optical Design of the *Romance of the Rose*." *University of Toronto Quarterly* 46 (1976/1977):241-62.

An interpretation of Nature's discourse on optics which is not another digression, according to Eberle, but "the very centre of [Nature's] self-revealing monologue" (253); further, it is the key to the design of the poem as a whole. The author reviews the science of optics in the thirteenth century, in particular the theory of Robert Grosseteste, in which light is "the ultimate 'corporeal form' of all being" (249). Jean combines this theory with Seneca's moral applications of optics in order "to increase our distrust of our senses" (257). Rhetoric and art parallel, by analogy, the powers of mirrors by revealing our illusions. Thus, Jean's alternate title, *Le mirouer aus amoureus* (a glass for/of lovers), suggests that the poem is a multifaceted optical device which multiplies and transforms the many perspectives on love that it offers. Far from being a collection of digressions, Jean's poem reflects the artistic ideal of "coherent multiplicity" (256) rather than simple unity.

224   Economou, George D. "The Character Genius in Alain de Lille, Jean de Meun, and John Gower." *The Chaucer Review* 4 (1970):203-10.

An examination of the evolution of three medieval manifestations of the character Genius to show how each author adopted and modified his predecessor's conception. Alain de Lille's Genius in the *De planctu Naturae* is both Natura's priest and "an aspect of Natura herself" (205), a Nature who has authority over man's reason and who places sexuality firmly in the marriage bed. Jean de Meun removes these two important aspects of Nature, authority over man's reason and moral concerns, to make of her priest and confessor a spokesman for unrestrained procreation. In the process, Genius unwittingly becomes the priest of Venus and her son, le Dieu d'Amour. Gower's Genius is also Venus's priest, because "that is where he found him in Jean's *Roman*" (209), but Gower makes of Venus the goddess of love rather than of lust. Thus, in Gower, Genius becomes "the moral agent that bridges the worlds of true religion and the religion of love" (209).

225 -----. *The Goddess Natura in Medieval Literature*. Cambridge, Mass.: Harvard UP, 1972. Pp. ix + 213.

A broad analysis of the complex of ideas associated with the goddess Natura in classical and medieval literature--in Aristotle, Plato, Plotinus, Macrobius, and Chalcidius; in Boethius and the Chartrian allegorists; and finally in Jean de Meun and Chaucer (*The Parliament of Fowls*). Jean de Meun's figure of Nature is compared with Alain de Lille's, since the latter "did more than any other writer to establish Natura as the most heroic figure in medieval personification allegory" (72). Jean combines his predecessor's conception with contemporary ideas of nature to create an individual character who, while lacking Alain's connection of Natura with marriage and reason, is more human (i.e., female). Like Alan, Jean uses Genius to complete "the expression of Natura's position in the poem" (111). Economou also examines Nature's relation in the *Rose* to Raison, who more closely embodies Alain de Lille's conception of Natura, and to Venus and Cupid, in an attempt to determine whether Nature and Genius speak for their author. His conclusion suggests that it is Raison who has the more complete view of human sexuality, Nature's and Genius's views being limited to procreative desire.

226 Egbert, Virginia Wylie. "Pygmalion as Sculptor." *Princeton University Library Chronicle* 28 (1966/1967):20-23.

A study of portraits of Pygmalion in *Rose* manuscripts. After briefly describing the two basic types of miniatures that portray

Pygmalion at work on a life-size statue or carving a relief sculpture, as in the miniature found in a Princeton University Library manuscript, the author speculates on the meaning of a miniature in a British Library manuscript which appears to represent the maiden as dead. She suggests, referring to Fleming's approach (see no. 243), that this image may be a gloss on the Pygmalion story, indicating "the ephemeral aspect of physical pleasure or the association of death" (22) with the sin of lust. Includes black and white reproductions of six miniatures.

227 Emmerson, Richard Kenneth and Ronald B. Herzman. "The Apocalyptic Age of Hypocrisy: Faus Semblant and Amant in the *Roman de la rose*." *Speculum* 62 (1987):612-34.

A consideration of Faux Semblant in a broader context than that of the historical dispute over the mendicant orders at the University of Paris in Jean de Meun's time. The authors argue that textual evidence links Faux Semblant and his girlfriend with apocalyptic imagery, in particular with the Fourth Horseman, a symbol of hypocrisy: "the extraordinarily rich tradition of apocalypticism energized [the] continuation of the *Roman de la Rose*" (614). They further integrate the seemingly anomalous Faux Semblant into Jean's poetic conception by pointing out parallels between this character and l'Amant, whose hypocrisy and lust can be seen as signs of the "last days" (619). Thus, by showing how Faux Semblant is the key to a "moralized reading" (630) of the *Rose*, the authors argue against splitting Jean's work into the private world of love and the public world of eschatology.

228 ----- and Ronald B. Herzman. *The Apocalyptic Imagination in Medieval Literature*. Philadelphia: U of Pennsylvania P, 1992. Pp. 282 + ill.

A unifying approach to the *Rose* based on apocalyptic concerns in the text. While the study incorporates material from the authors' earlier *Speculum* article (no. 227), additional analyses include the twelfth-century *Apocalypse of Golias* and the connection between history and eschatology: "Jean cannot turn to history without also turning to eschatology" (101).

229 Ettmayer, Karl R. v. *Der Rosenroman (Erster Teil): Stilistische, grammatische und literarhistorische Erläuterungen zum Studium und zur Privatlektüre des Textes*. Repetitorien zum Studium altfranzösischer Literaturdenkmäler 1. Heidelberg: Carl Winter, 1919. Pp. 42.

An introductory study of the text, including a plot summary as well as stylistic, syntactical, morphological, and phonological comments. The author, while recognizing the great literary success of the *Rose*, points to what he sees as the many weaknesses in the first part's composition and attributes the popularity of the romance to Jean de Meun's continuation. [The stylistic and morphological remarks seem questionable, even more since the author himself admits the lack of a critical edition of the text at the time of his writing.] [JSZ]

230 *Etudes de langue et de littérature française offertes à André Lanly*. Ed. Bernard Guidoux. Nancy: Université de Nancy II, 1980. Pp. xvi + 593. [Referred to here as *Etudes...Lanly*.]

Includes articles on the *Rose* by Gérard Blangez, no. 166; Claude Buridant, no. 122; Pierre Demarolle, no. 208, Pierre Miguet, no. 395; Jean-Charles Payen, no. 430; Colette Rimlinger-Leconte, no. 471.

231 *Etudes sur le "Roman de la rose" de Guillaume de Lorris*. "Textes recueillis" (collected) by Jean Dufournet. Collection Unichamp 4. Paris: Honoré Champion, 1984. Pp. 179. [Referred to here as *Etudes...Lorris*.]

A collection of articles on the first part of the *Rose*: see entries on Jean Batany, no. 157; Emmanuèle Baumgartner, no. 159; Eric Hicks, no. 288; Georgette Kamenetz, no. 328; Jean-Charles Payen, no. 426; and Armand Strubel, no. 513.

232 Faral, Edmond. "Le *Roman de la rose* et la pensée française au XIIIe siècle." *Revue des deux mondes* 7th ser. 35 (September 1926):430-57.

An early and influential attempt to evaluate the literary characteristics and importance of the *Roman de la rose* for a general audience. For both authors Faral considers the question of originality (in the post-Romantic sense in which it was understood in his time) and decides that though Guillaume de Lorris and Jean de Meun lacked originality, each had his own special genius. Guillaume de Lorris succeeded in expressing, through cumbersome personified abstractions but with exquisite psychological finesse, the courtly doctrine of his time. Jean de Meun not only wrote an "anti-Guillaume" (439), but imbued his "oeuvre difforme" (441) with a naturalistic doctrine that would influence thinkers for centuries. Although Faral emphasizes that no element in Jean de Meun's thought is original, he argues that Jean's personal choice of ideas and themes from classical and medieval authors and his vigorous, earthy expression of them created a unique, even revolutionary, work. The second part of the *Rose* is thus "la première grande oeuvre en langue française à porter vraiment des idées" (457).

233 Faughnan, Mary Ellen. "Morality in the *Romance of the Rose*: The Misunderstood Figure of Nature." *Proceedings of the PMR Conference: Annual Publication of the Patristic, Mediaeval and Renaissance Conference* 4 (1979):137-41.

An interpretation of Nature's role in the *Rose* in which Faughnan, after arguing that the character has been misinterpreted, proposes that "a defeated, not triumphant, Nature emerges at the romance's end" (137). Jean altered the figure of Nature found in three important predecessors (Plato, Bernard Silvestre, and Alain de Lille), to create a character to meet his own purposes, which are to show the horrors of self-love: Nature is tricked into unknowingly helping l'Amant in his sinful quest. [Faughnan does not see the plucking of the rose as a procreative act; but see Hill, no. 295]. Because Nature's understanding is limited, she must be aided by her partner

Raison "in his [sic] attempt to bring rationality to Fallen Man" (139).

234 Ferrante, Joan M. *Woman as Image in Medieval Literature from the Twelfth Century to Dante*. 1975; rpt. Durham, N.C.: Labyrinth Press, 1985. Pp. 166.

An approach to the *Rose* from the perspective of the portrayal of women and love, based on the significance of gender for understanding the poem. The gender of the characters, for example, is not simply a function of their grammatical gender but has meaning for understanding their behavior. Furthermore, the dreamer's love is judged negatively as hypocritical, self-indulgent, and self-delusive--lust "disguised in courtly behavior" (109). In the second part, l'Amant tries "to justify his lust by fitting it into a larger context" (113). The women characters are universally portrayed in derogatory terms, except Raison, whom l'Amant rejects in favor of the Rose, who wants him but is restrained by fear. Finally, the poem, according to Ferrante, shows that "man is seduced by his own desire" (117), that man is susceptible to women only if he wants to be.

235 Fialova, Maria. "Les expressions de la laideur dans le *Roman de la rose*." *Etudes romanes de Brno* 5 (1971):63-68.

An excerpt from the author's manuscript study of the esthetic vocabulary of the *Rose*, focusing on expressions of ugliness. The author points out both differences in meaning and use of such expressions in the two parts of the poem. The various meanings of the words in the "champ conceptuel de la laideur" (64) (Old French *lait* and its derivatives) and in the peripheral expressions (Old French *vil*, *ort*, etc.) include not only physical but moral ugliness and simple repugnance. A chart shows frequency of occurrence of the expressions and their relative distribution in the two parts.

236 Fleming, John V. "Carthaginian Love: Text and Supertext in the *Roman de la rose*." *Assays* 1 (1981):51-72.

A study of Jean de Meun's possible sources for the discussion of friendship by Raison and l'Amant. Based on the concept of the "supertext," that is, "a secondary literary presence of a specially, and often uniquely, privileged authority" (53), a concept developed in *Reason and the Lover* (no. 241), Fleming argues that Jean's source is not Cicero, who is named in the text, but Aelred of Rievaulx and Augustine, who are not. L'Amant's brief reference to Carthage is, Fleming suggests, an indication that Jean de Meun wants us to think of Augustine's *Confessions*, where Carthage is also mentioned: an Augustinian source is "the poem's inexorable implication" (62). The article includes a discussion of medieval Christian authors' attitudes toward and uses of pagan writers.

237 -----. "Further Reflections on Oiseuse's Mirror." *Zeitschrift für romanische Philologie* 100 (1984):26-40.

In part a rebuttal to Earl Jeffrey Richards's argument that Old French *oiseuse* in Chrétien de Troyes and the *Rose* meant "verbal folly or frivolity" (see no. 469), in part also a reiteration of Fleming's views of the ultimate Christian significance of the *Rose*. Using both philological and textual evidence from authors preceding and following Guillaume de Lorris, Fleming argues that Guillaume's Oiseuse personifies idleness in the Christian sense of sloth and that this is the way medieval readers would have understood her.

238 -----. "The Garden of the *Roman de la rose*: Vision of Landscape or Landscape of Vision?" In *Medieval Gardens*. Ed. Elisabeth B. MacDougall. Dumbarton Oaks Colloquium on the History of Landscape Architecture 9. Washington, D. C.: Dumbarton Oaks Research Library and Center, 1986. 201-34.

A discussion of images, mirrors, and vision in the *Rose* rather than of the garden itself (seen as an echo of the Garden of Eden). The central image, the "most prominent clue to the meaning of the garden" (203), is the Fountain of Narcissus, whose crystals are interpreted as metaphors for the anatomy and physiology of human sight. In addition, the Fountain exemplifies the vulnerability of the eye to deception, especially through lustful sight. The subsequent discussion of vision concerns Jean de Meun's assertion that his *Rose* is a "Miroër aus Amoreus" (l. 10621), which Fleming interprets in the sense of a moral warning. In the course of the article Fleming criticizes what he considers the wrong-headed theories of those who disagree with him, including David Hult, Alan Gunn, C. S. Lewis, and Frederick Goldin (see nos. 301, 274, 375, and 264).

239 -----. "Jean de Meun and the Ancient Poets." In *Rethinking* (no. 182). 81-100.

An analysis of how Jean de Meun incorporated the Latin classics into his poem; the author's goal is to show that Jean was a subtle and moral reader of pagan texts. After disputing Langlois's three assertions in *Origines et sources du "Roman de la rose"* (no. 358) that Jean was a vernacular, encyclopedic, and unpoetic poet, Fleming argues that Jean was "a careful reader of antique Latin texts" (84) and that he took "as a principal poetic theme the moral and poetic relationship between the pagan past and the Christian present" (85). For textual evidence Fleming examines Jean's use of certain passages from Ovid (from whom Jean learned much of his "impishness" [99]), Boethius, and Virgil. Fleming points out that Jean, in his use of Boethius to critique Ovid, set up the conflict between love and reason "that was to be the main event in a good deal of European erotic poetry until the time of Shakespeare's sonnets and beyond" (89). Finally, Fleming reiterates his contention that Jean's theme was "the pursuit of sexual gratification as an idolatrous religion" (99).

240 -----. "A Poetic Gambit in the *Roman de la rose*." *Romance Philology* 33 (1979/1980):518-22.

A note that points to one of Jean de Meun's "previously unnoticed literary relationships" (518), a twelfth-century Latin poem by Henry of Septimello, the so-called *Elegia*, in which Fortune compares Henry VI's invasion of Italy in 1191 to a game of chess. According to Fleming, there can be "little doubt that Jean de Meun had this conceit in mind when he was writing the long dialogue between Reason and the Lover" (519). In both works allusions to historical events in Italian campaigns are illustrations of Fortune's power, against which "no gambit is successful" (522).

241 -----. *Reason and the Lover*. Princeton: Princeton UP, 1984. Pp. xii + 196.

A study of selected passages in the dialogue between Raison (mostly Jean de Meun's character) and l'Amant in the light of their ideas, both implied and stated, on love, friendship, and language. As a "test" (ix) of ideas proposed in his earlier studies of the *Rose* and to demonstrate that Raison is the single voice to be believed--"we must believe her" (64)--Fleming finds unimpeachable credentials for her, that of Augustine and several medieval Augustinian writers. This process involves the concept of the "supertext," "the secondary literary presence of a specially, and often uniquely, powerful authority" (69; see also no. 236). This authority in the case of Jean de Meun most often goes unacknowledged, but Fleming argues that when Jean cites Cicero, he is in reality quoting Augustine and Aelred de Rievaulx; when his source appears to be Boethius, it is in reality Augustine, and when Virgil, Lactantius. Secondary discussions include an attack on critics who question the sapiential status of Raison, the relation of reason to sexuality (irrationality in sex is limited to orgasm), and a final chapter on what Petrarch's *Secretum* owes to Jean de Meun.

242 -----. "The *Roman de la rose* and Its Manuscript Illustrations." 2 vols. Diss. Princeton U, 1963.

243 -----. *The "Roman de la rose": A Study in Allegory and Iconography.* Princeton: Princeton UP, 1969. Pp. xv + 257 + 42 figures.

An important, often quoted, if "minority view" (vi) of the *Rose* which interprets its moral meaning on the basis of theological texts and iconographic evidence from the manuscripts. Starting from the principle that "a convincing interpretation of the most popular poetic work of late medieval Christendom" (x) must condemn passionate love and sex outside of Christian marriage, Fleming offers a medieval reading of the *Rose* by demonstrating that both parts portray l'Amant's lechery and idolatry. Raison, associated with Divine Sapience, must be the authors' authority; the other characters simply reveal various aspects of love's sinfulness. In Fleming's view all other approaches to the *Rose* are "fundamentally wrong-headed" (vi), and he rejects any reading, even a medieval one, that does not see the *Rose* as a conventionally moral work. Thus, Fleming asserts that Gerson, one of the *Rose*'s critics, was "thoroughly trounced" (47) in the Querelle de la Rose, and that Christine de Pizan's arguments and "her manner show the acumen (in the words of Jean de Montreuil) of 'the Greek whore who dared to write against Theophrastus'" (47). Includes black-and-white reproductions from illuminated manuscripts.

244 Frank, Robert Worth, Jr. "The Art of Reading Medieval Personification-Allegory." *ELH* 20 (1953):237-50.

An exploration of principles for reading personification-allegory that first distinguishes between symbol-allegory and personification-allegory. The author also distinguishes between the more literal allegory of the personification that speaks or acts according to type (Nature or Gluttony) and the more clearly allegorical status of the metaphoric actions of moral types and abstractions: "Only the action is allegoric... Characters are never allegoric" (243). Furthermore, the reader should recognize that not all characters in an allegorical work need be personifications, contrary to C. S. Lewis's complaint about Guillaume de Lorris's *Rose* (see no. 375). Finally, Frank warns readers of allegories about several possible interpretative errors, such as treating the personification as though it were a symbol, or over-estimating the relevance of the four-fold exegetical method (which has been suggested for the *Rose*). [Although oversimplifying perhaps the polyvalence of medieval personifications, Frank's remarks can help introduce a reader to some of the interpretative questions the form raises.]

245 Frappier, Jean. "Aspects de l'hermétisme dans la poésie médiévale." *Cahiers de l'Association internationale des études françaises* 15 (1963):9-24.

A brief overview, in a paper to a congress on hermeticism and poetry, of possible forms of hermeticism in medieval literature, including the *fatrasie*, the *trobar clus* of the troubadours, and the *Roman de la rose*. Deviating from the principle that hermeticism suggests a key to its hidden meaning, both poets of the *Rose* promise the key but do not give it, an omission for which Frappier suggests possible reasons. Although allegory is unhermetic in being at the same time *letre* and *sen* (letter and meaning), fable and truth, there nonetheless remains a "halo d'incertitude" (18) around the *Rose*'s personifications. In any case, Frappier argues that symbols in Genius's disconcerting Park of the Lamb are easily explained by Christian beliefs, and that the general meaning of the *Rose* is clear: courtly in the first part, "naturalisme évangélique" (20) in the second.

246 -----. "Le thème de la lumière, de la *Chanson de Roland* au *Roman de la rose*." *Cahiers de l'Association internationale des études françaises* 20 (1968):101-24.

A study that traces the use of light imagery in major works of medieval French literature, including the romances of Chrétien de Troyes, the *Queste del saint graal*, and the *Roman de la rose*. Frappier divides light images into the hierarchical categories of precious metals and jewels, the ideal landscape, physical beauty, love and related sentiments, and religious feelings. Light in the first part of the *Rose* is discussed in relation to the eternal spring morning in the garden of Deduit which takes on a spiritual clarity, the radiance or lack of it in the description of certain personifications, and, briefly, the crystals in the Fountain. The article concludes with a short discussion of light in Jean de Meun's part, which Frappier describes as both intellectual enlightenment and as a poetic vision of natural light, as in the description of clouds after a storm (Langlois ll. 17987-18000; Lecoy ll. 17957-70).

247 -----. "Variations sur le thème du miroir, de Bernard de Ventadour à Maurice Scève." *Cahiers de l'Association internationale des études françaises* 11 (1959):134-58.

A discussion of the *Rose*, in particular the first part, in the context of poetic images of the mirror in medieval and Renaissance French literature. Much of the discussion focuses on retellings of the Narcissus myth and the meaning of his watery self-reflection. Guillaume de Lorris enriches the Ovidian story with "une élaboration propice au symbolisme" (149)--Narcissus's pool becomes the Fountain of Love in which all who gaze are caught. When l'Amant looks into the Fountain, he feels intuitively the idea of love before he has chosen a beloved. The crystals that reflect the garden suggest for Frappier the lover's view of the lady's eyes. The author concludes that the variations of the theme from the twelfth to the sixteenth century indicate a growing introspection in the poetic meaning of mirrors.

248 Freeman, Michelle A. "Problems in Romance Composition: Ovid, Chrétien de Troyes, and the *Romance of the Rose*." *Romance Philology* 30 (1976):158-68.

An application of the theory of poetic composition described in the *Metalogicon* of John of Salisbury--*iuncturae dictionum* (joining words together), *translatio* (the elaboration of metaphor), critical reading, and creative imitation--to two medieval works, Chrétien de Troyes's *Conte du graal* (*Perceval*) and Guillaume de Lorris's *Roman de la rose*, in particular to their re-reading of Ovid's story of Narcissus. After describing many parallels between Ovid's myth and Chrétien's blood drops scene, Freeman describes how the *Rose*, through the Fountain of Narcissus, "builds upon a creative reading of these two texts" (160). She analyzes at length the various poetic resonances of the two crystals, which reflect "the dialectic between the two courtly genres" (166) of romance and lyric, by transforming the twenty-year-old lyric persona into the romance persona of the lover. The Fountain thus becomes an *essample* (l. 1552) not only of the lover's experience but of the process of poetic invention of the "clerkly romance poet-narrator" (164).

249 Friedman, Albert B. "Jean de Meun an Englishman?" *Modern Language Notes* 65 (1950):319-25.

A study that traces the history of the idea, repeated by English writers from 1557 to at least the end of the eighteenth century, that the author of the second part of the *Rose* was in effect an Englishman named John Moon (also spelled Mone or de Moon), who supposedly was a student in Paris in the thirteenth century. Friedman attributes the earliest example of the claim, found in John Bale's *Scriptorum illustrium majoris Britanniae catalogus* (1557-1559), to a misreading of Hoccleve's *Letter of Cupid*, in which Hoccleve refers to "mayster Johan de Moone" (323).

250 Friedman, John B. "L'iconographie de Vénus et de son miroir à la fin du moyen âge." In *L'érotisme au moyen âge.* Etudes présentées au troisième colloque de l'Institut d'Etudes Médiévales. Ed. Bruno Roy. Montreal: Editions de l'Aurore, 1977. 51-82.

A study, with nineteen illustrations of medieval iconography, of the evolution of Venus from a goddess to the symbol of fleshly desire as shown in her attributes, in particular the mirror. Mirrors in the *Rose* are mentioned briefly; Oiseuse as a reflection of Venus-Luxuria (lust) is discussed at more length. Adopting the Robertson-Fleming interpretation of the *Rose* (see nos. 473 and 243), Friedman equates Oiseuse to Venus-Luxuria because of the mirror and chaplet of roses. Despite some inaccuracies, such as the mention of a comb in Oiseuse's hair, the article provides background information on medieval associations concerning the mirror, Venus, and female sexuality.

251 Friedman, Lionel J. "Gradus Amoris." *Romance Philology* 19 (1965):167-77.

An examination of the topos of the stages of love (that is, seduction) and its historical transmission from Horace to the early Middle Ages and a discussion of these steps or stages, of which there are usually five (*visus, alloquium, contactus, osculum,* and *factum*), in medieval literature. The literary topos found in Latin elegiac comedy and the *Carmina burana* became associated with sin in the writings of moral theologians. Variant forms of the concept of stages of love are also described. When discussing the *Rose*, Friedman argues that the first four stages (sight, conversation, touch, and kiss) are found in the first part of the *Rose*, and that Jean de Meun took over at the stage of *factum*: "the dénouement of the romance could only be that which Jean finally supplied" (175). Consequently, Jean was continuing the plan of his predecessor.

252 -----. "Jean de Meun and Ethelred of Rievaulx." *L'esprit créateur* 2.3 (1962):135-41.

An analysis of Raison's remarks on friendship which argues that Jean de Meun was following the *De amicitia spirituali* of Ethelred of Rievaulx, a work which Jean translated (the translation has been lost). Although Jean indicates that Cicero is his source, Friedman attempts to depaganize him by showing that both Jean's words and ideas, in particular Raison's remarks on absolute discretion and on proofs in friendship, are closer to Ethelred's. [A good knowledge of Latin is necessary to evaluate Friedman's arguments.]

253 -----. "'Jean de Meung,' Antifeminism, and 'Bourgeois Realism'." *Modern Philology* 57 (1959/1960):13-23.

An important study of Jean de Meun's misogyny. The author asks if we can attribute antifeminist (i.e., misogynistic) attitudes to Jean de Meun based on the tirade of the jealous husband embedded in l'Ami's second speech. Friedman argues that literary principles such as fitting the doctrine to the character, generic constraints, and "strictly conventional characters" (16) suggest rather that "Jean de Meun" (a "bizarre modern personification of the genius of the *Rose*" [14] created by critics) was not expressing his own opinion through this character. Although Friedman's argument appears to remove the element of authorial choice, he believes that despite generic constraints and conventions, Jean de Meun's characters have "a human quality, individuality, and completeness" (19) that Guillaume's characters lack. [Surprisingly there is no reference to similar arguments in the Querelle de la Rose; see no. 575, 19-21.] Yet the source of the antifeminist remarks of the jealous husband, la Vieille, and others, is shown to be not bourgeois realism (the observation of real people), but books by churchmen. That is, their remarks are "a commonplace of the sermon or of moral, didactic literature" (23).

254 Fritz, Jean Marie. "Du dieu émasculateur au roi émasculé: métamorphoses de Saturne au Moyen Age." In *Pour une mythologie du moyen âge*. Ed. Laurence Harf-Lancner and Dominique Boutet. Collection de l'Ecole Normale Supérieure de Jeunes Filles 41. Paris: Ecole Normale Supérieure de Jeunes Filles, 1988. 43-60.

An examination of Jean de Meun's singular version of the mythic castration of Saturn in the context of other classical and medieval versions. Fritz describes in detail the "redoublement du geste mythique" (45) through two generations of gods, and the evolution of its main traditions (learned and popular), which offered physical, historical, and moral interpretations of the myth. By refusing the spatial or temporal traditions that had formed around Saturn and Jupiter, Jean de Meun gives back to the myth its Platonic "valeur génétique" (53), thereby explaining the advent of law, morality, and the word as the consequences of the first infringement of Nature's order.

255 Galpin, Stanley Leman. "Dangiers li vilains." *Romanic Review* 2 (1911):320-22.

A note proposing that the descriptive detail of Danger's "iex rouges comme feus" (l. 2907) indicates a fusion of "the usual characteristics of the ill-favored *paĩsant*" (320) with stock features of the devil, particularly as described in monastic literature. Guillaume may have been trying to make the peasant Danger more repellant than ever.

256 -----. "Fortune's Wheel in the *Roman de la rose*." *PMLA* 24 (1909):332-42.

A rapid sketch of the Latin background of the image of Fortune's Wheel, including Boethius's *De consolatione Philosophiae*, followed by a listing of all references to the Wheel in the *Rose*. Galpin distinguishes various components of the image, such as locomotion and realistic detail (which he attributes to "the loss of the aesthetic sense generally in the middle ages" [333]). The study compares passages in Jean de Meun's part to his sources in Boethius and Alain de Lille, concluding that Jean borrowed from both, though more from the former.

257 -----. "Geber and the *Roman de la rose*." *Modern Language Notes* 23 (1908):159.

A correction to Langlois's identification of "l'arabe Geber" (see 358), the author of one of Jean's sources on alchemy, as "'Djabar al Koufi,' an Arabian alchemist who flourished in the eighth or ninth century" (159). Pointing to the important but overlooked work of Berthelot on alchemy, Galpin argues that Geber's treatise was in reality the work of an anonymous Latin author of the thirteenth century.

258 -----. "Influence of the Mediaeval Christian Visions on Jean de Meun's Notions of Hell." *Romanic Review* 2 (1911):54-60.

A discussion of Jean de Meun's remarks concerning hell which places them in the context of medieval Christian visions of the afterlife. The references to partial immersion as a punishment, the marsh and the pit of hell, the stench and the variety of physical torments have parallels in *The Vision of Saint Paul*, *The Vision of Tundal*, and similar works. Since no one of these visions contains all the details of hell found in the *Rose*, Galpin concludes that Jean "was acquainted with a number of them" (60).

259 Garvey, Sister M. Calixta. *The Syntax of the Declinable Words in the "Roman de la rose"*. Catholic University of America Studies in Romance Languages and Literatures 13. 1936; rpt. New York: AMS Press, 1969. Pp. xi + 232.

A study (originally a dissertation for the Catholic University of America) which investigates the syntax of nouns (excluding proper names and personified abstractions), articles, adjectives, and pronouns in both parts of the *Rose*. Standard Old French usage is described (based largely on Foulet's *Petite syntaxe de l'ancien français*), followed by ten consecutive examples from each part. Frequent internal and final summaries indicate "the conformity or the non-conformity of the syntactical usage" (v) to Old French usage. The author notes that although the two parts are generally in accordance with such usage, small differences reveal the evolution of the language in the thirteenth century.

260 George, F. W. A. "Jean de Meung and the Myth of the Golden Age." In *The Classical Tradition in French Literature: Essays Presented to R. C. Knight by Colleagues, Pupils and Friends*. Ed. H. T. Barnwell, A. H. Diverres, G. F. Evans, F. W. A. George, and Vivienne Mylne. London: Grant and Cutler, 1977. 31-39.

A study of the Golden Age described by three characters in the second part of the *Rose* and alluded to by a fourth. The article reviews the earlier history of the myth, particularly in the works of Virgil and Ovid; summarizes briefly how Raison, l'Ami, la Vieille, and Genius use the myth; and attempts to establish the relevance of the myth "to the over-all conception of the love affair" (32). Raison sees the end of the Golden Age as justice replacing love; l'Ami, as venality and conflict between the sexes replacing free love; la Vieille, as male domination and marriage replacing women's freedom; and Genius, as unnaturalness in sex replacing naturalness. George concludes that Nature and Genius represent "a point of view Jean de Meung is seeking to exemplify" (37), an idealistic view in which both man and woman are "to be liberated and to devote their love to the safeguarding of the human race" (37).

261 Giamatti, A. Bartlett. *The Earthly Paradise and the Renaissance Epic*. 1966; rpt. New York: Norton, 1989. Pp. 374.

An examination of major literary traditions concerning the earthly paradise and the Golden Age. Giamatti describes briefly the two gardens in the *Rose* as reflecting the earthly paradise, which is both an aesthetic model for Guillaume's garden of Deduit and for Jean's Good Pasture [Park of the Lamb] and "a touchstone for their reliability and veracity" (66). [Although the author does not discuss the passages in the *Rose* describing the Golden Age, his review of classical and medieval traditions is useful in approaching that theme.]

262 Glier, Ingeborg. "Allegorische, didaktische und satirische Literatur." In *Europäisches Spätmittelalter*. Ed. Willi Erzgräber. Wiesbaden: Akademische Verlagsgesellschaft Athenaion, 1978. 427-54.

An analysis of the importance of allegorical, didactic, and satiric literature in the late Middle Ages. Even though there are few remaining works, they dominated the literary life of that era and obviously corresponded specifically to the expectations and interests of the audience. The *Rose* is quoted as a model: the development from the romances of chivalry to Guillaume's highly courtly part to Jean's rational-satirical view of the world illustrates beautifully the passage from the high to the late medieval period and is representative not only of changing literary interests but also of a noticeable modification of the entire spiritual climate. [ASK]

263 Glunz, Hans H. *Die Literarästhetik des europäischen Mittelalters: Wolfram--"Rosenroman"--Chaucer--Dante.* 1937; rpt. Frankfurt: Vittorio Klostermann, 1963. Pp. xvi + 608 + ill.

A discussion of allegorical poetry in the context of thirteenth-century neoplatonic esthetic theories. The author analyzes the different levels of literal and allegorical meaning in the text, which he links to the individual cognitive capacities of the readers. He further contrasts the allegorical poetry with courtly literature where symbolic meaning is represented through the action (inherent in the quest) and thus less accessible to the non-initiated public, a difference which is shown to have also a sociological dimension in that the allegorical poetry appears at the time of the dissolution of the aristocratic and cultural elite of knighthood. [JSZ]

264 Goldin, Frederick. *The Mirror of Narcissus in the Courtly Love Lyric.* Ithaca: Cornell UP, 1967. Pp. xiv + 272.

A study of Narcissus in the medieval lyric that includes brief discussions of both parts of the *Rose*. The introduction gives a good summary of the three major developments of the mirror theme in the Middle Ages (ideality, passivity, and matter and form together). After a detailed review of the twelfth-century lay of *Narcisus*, Goldin analyzes l'Amant's thoughts and behavior at the Fountain of Narcissus in the first part of the *Rose*. While looking in the water, l'Amant appears to alternate between admiring the vision of the garden and fearing the effects of the Fountain. He escapes Narcissus's fate, though, because he knows Narcissus's story and turns to a living reflection of himself in the Rose. Thus Goldin sees the Rose as the lover's "future identity" (59), an idealized image of what he is to become. Like the *Ovide moralisé*, Jean de Meun is described as seeing in the story of Narcissus a moral lesson which includes the "antithetical meanings" (65) of the lifeless, deceptive image and the life-giving Mirror of God, which is expressed in Nature's confession and in Genius's sermon on procreation.

265 Gorce, M.-M. *Le roman de la rose: texte essentiel de la scolastique courtoise*. Paris: Fernand Aubier, Editions Montaigne, 1933. Pp. 254.

A presentation of the *Rose* in short modernized excerpts preceded by an introduction which argues the necessity of placing Jean de Meun in the context of the intellectual turbulence occurring at the University of Paris around 1277. Somewhat scandalized by the goings-on, Gorce offers little textual evidence for Jean de Meun's heterodoxy. Instead he interprets Jean's part of the *Rose* as scholastic (that is, pedagogical), courtly (that is, erotic), and Christian (of a hedonistic kind). The *Rose* is thus the "Roman de la Joie" (29)--that of the Virgin Mary, of woman as erotic object, and of Paradise. The excerpts from the *Rose* are chosen to support Gorce's interpretation: he finds the erotic ending too realistic to be included but concludes nonetheless that the lover has become "un homme selon Dieu" (235). An appendix gives the text of *Le jardin amoureux de l'âme dévote* by Pierre d'Ailly.

266 Gorra, Egidio. *Fra drammi e poemi: saggi e ricerche*. Milan: Ulrico Hoepli, 1900. Pp. x + 527.

A treatment of medieval theories of love in which Gorra sees the *Roman de la rose* as the one work which epitomizes the characteristics of the new era, which "chiude il passato ed apre l'avvenire" (209) and represents the synthesis of a broad analysis. The reception of the classical heritage (especially Ovid), the ideas of courtly love, the new lay spirit and its satire of the traditional religious mind, all of these elements qualify the *Rose* as a work which occupies "una pagina importantissima nella storia del pensiero e dell'antica letteratura di Francia"

(207). It is worth noting that Gorra represents an exception to what Contini would have called the structural inability of romance philologists to "receive" the *Rose* in its entirety (see no. 605). [MRB]

267 Goujet, Claude-Pierre. *Bibliothèque françoise, ou histoire de la littérature françoise.* 18 vols. 1741-1756; rpt. Geneva: Slatkine Reprints, 1966. 9:26-71.

An introduction to the *Rose* for the general public which talks around the romance more than about it (discussed directly only on 39-45). The author gives information [much of it inaccurate] about the poets' lives and Jean de Meun's other works, calls Jean "un des plus savans hommes de son siècle" (34), and states that the continuation was written in 1300. Goujet also relates apocryphal anecdotes about Jean de Meun and discusses medieval reactions to the work, including the Querelle de la Rose [but does not mention Christine de Pizan]. He cites frequently the studies of Lantin de Damerey, Lenglet Dufresnoy, and Massieu whose edition appeared ten years earlier (see nos. 2, 3, and 384).

268 Gowan, Patricia. "L'énigme temporelle du *Roman de la rose*." *Chimères* 13.1 (Fall 1979):47-63.

A consideration of two aspects of time in the *Rose*: shifting temporal perspectives in the three levels of narration (dreamer, narrator, author; see also Pickens, no. 439); immortal vs. mortal time in the images of the two crystals in the Fountain of Narcissus (first part) and of the three-faceted carbuncle in the Park of the Lamb (second part). The most complex use of different temporal perspectives is found in the central speech by le Dieu d'Amour, whose ability to foresee the future reveals his immortality. The author associates le Dieu d'Amour with Genius's carbuncle and with Jean de Meun, who sees his poetic creation as immortal. [Note that although the author discusses tenses in the *Rose*, she quotes from an English translation.]

269 Gregory, Robert. "Reading as Narcissism: *Le roman de la rose*." *SubStance* 39 [12.2] (1983):37-48.

A wide-ranging essay that approaches the *Rose* through some of Freud's ideas concerning narcissism and dream interpretation, in particular the concepts of latent content and displacement. The question of figurative versus literal levels is raised with regard to both parts of the poem: Guillaume's idealization is an invitation to look beneath, for "base love" (42) lurks beneath the figure of noble love. Jean de Meun demystifies Guillaume's poem, which is somehow another mystification; he does not reach the latent content but merely displaces it. Both writing and reading are seen as a kind of narcissism, and the text and the lady (equally elusive) figure a desire for the self.

270 Gröber, Gustav. *Grundriss der romanischen Philologie*. Strasbourg: Karl J. Trübner, 1902. Pp. 1286.

A discussion of the *Rose* as a turning point in the history of French literature. After a short introduction to the historical and social context of the period 1240 to 1350, Gröber concludes that one can see in the ascendant role of the *menestrel* at the expense of the *jongleur* a passage from lyric poetry to more serious, moral literature with didactic purposes. This new and learned literature, through which the clerics transmsit their knowledge of classical sources to a lay public, appears mostly as *romans* or *dits*, where allegory is more and more used as a mode of representation for entire texts. Thus, in a chapter on profane allegorical-didactic literature, Gröber presents the *Rose* as the passage from early Old French literature to a new period: whereas Guillaume's allegorical description of love is still close to the spirit of earlier writers like Chrétien de Troyes, the theme of love is supplanted in Jean de Meun's continuation by a didactic discourse which has no relation to the first part of the romance. After a few biographical notes and a short comparison of the authors, Gröber proceeds to a separate content analysis of the two parts where he discusses the style and prevalent themes of the romance as well as its classical sources. [JSZ]

271 Gros, Gaston. *L'amour dans le "Roman de la rose"*. Bibliothèque du lettré. Paris: Editions Baudinière, 1925. Pp. 220.

A personal, informal essay on the *Rose* whose goal is to give people of intelligence and taste a better appreciation of the poem and of medieval literature generally. The author's agnostic, esthetic, and insurrectionist approach praises Jean de Meun's egalitarianism, anticlericalism, and practical wisdom, but scolds him for believing in the noble savage and for separating love from marriage. The rose symbol is seen as an avatar of the cult of Demeter, while women in love are described as "l'égoïsme dans la recherche du plaisir" (166). In Gros's soliloquy, short excerpts from the *Rose* [in modern French; edition or source of translation not indicated] are interspersed with personal comments on the validity of the two *Rose* poets' ideas and on contemporary manners.

272 Guillon, Félix. *Etude historique et biographique sur Guillaume de Lorris, auteur du "Roman de la rose", d'après documents inédits et révision critique des textes des auteurs*. Orleans: H. Herluison; Paris: Dumoulin, 1881. Pp. viii + 132.

A biographical-literary essay that contests the traditional attribution of Guillaume's origins to the town of Lorris-en-Gâtinais. The author proposes instead the Orleans town of Lory or Loury, based in part on his interpretation of the two towns' feudal status. Since Lorris was a *châtellenie royale*, Guillon believes that the particle *de* in Guillaume's name cannot indicate proprietorship of a fief in Lorris. This hypothesis has not been accepted by scholars (see Jarry, whom Guillon virtually accuses of plagiarism [nos. 313 and 314]; Lejeune [no. 370] does not mention Guillon's theory). Furthermore, Guillon reads Deduit's supposed coat of arms (see ll. 817-19) as "celle des *armes brisées*" (26) of the Counts of Loury. He also argues for a late date for the continuation (c. 1305) based on his interpretation of certain references to historic persons in the *Rose* [this theory also has not been accepted]. The second half of the book is an imaginative reconstruction of Guillaume de

Loury's life, based on historic information, lyric poetry, and the *Rose* itself, which Guillon argues is completely autobiographical. A review of various sixteenth- and seventeenth-century authors inspired by the *Rose* completes this section. The appendices include the geneology of the Lords of Loury-aux-Bois, various charters relating to the Lorris/Loury family, a translation of a poem by Pierre Vidal which Guillon believed inspired the *Rose*, and an excerpt from a critical work linking Guillaume to the Albigensian heresy.

273 -----. *Jean Clopinel dit de Meung: "Le roman de la rose" considéré comme document historique du règne de Philippe le Bel*. Paris: A. Picard et fils; Orleans: J. Loddé, 1903. Pp. xii + 219.

A sequel to no. 272, a biography of Jean de Meun and analysis of his part of the *Rose* in the context of the social and political ideas of Philip IV of France (1285-1314). Because the author saw parallels between some of the ideas expressed in the *Rose* and those of Philip IV, he concluded that Jean must have written the continuation toward the end of his life, specifically in 1296, rather than twenty years earlier, as scholars usually believe. Furthermore he asserts that Jean wrote his part on the command of the king. Guillon places Jean's birth in a bourgeois family, a milieu which may have encouraged his critical views of society, the nobility, and the church: "au moyen âge, [Jean] osa le premier s'élever hautement contre les abus dont la société était alors remplie" (ix). The study constructs a hypothetical biography and summarizes Jean's ideas on social questions, including that of women. The last chapter is a compilation of opinions concerning the *Rose* from the thirteenth century to Guillon's day.

274 Gunn, Alan M. F. *The Mirror of Love: A Reinterpretation of "The Romance of the Rose"*. Lubbock: Texas Tech Press, 1951. Pp. xvi + 592.

A monumental work in size, scope, and importance, one of the few all-encompassing interpretations of the *Rose* and the first to argue seriously for its unity, coherence, and poetic power. In Books I through IV, Gunn shows that "the line of narrative" (66)--the story of the love quest and its principal themes and imagery--expresses an organic conception of a lover's growth, maturing, and replenishment in happy, mutual, reproductive love. The author describes the rhetorical structure of the *Rose* by means of the medieval concepts of exposition and amplification in order to demonstrate that all parts are coherently connected. Everything in the *Rose*, both narrative and argument or discourse, is expository, a means for "representing and illustrating the different aspects of [the] theme" (72) of love. Gunn was one of the first to recognize that such apparently digressive material as the stories of Narcissus and Pygmalion do in fact express fundamental themes in the poem. Thus, rather than opposing Guillaume's poem, Jean's continuation amplifies and completes his art of love, primarily by enlarging its meaning to encompass the philosophical principles (whose historic development is described in A. O. Lovejoy's *Great Chain of Being*) of cosmic plenitude, continuity, replenishment, and phallicism. On these principles is based the underlying structure of the poem, the lover's *entelechy*, the maturing "not of the body only but of the whole man" (283). Consequently, the romance's rhetorical, narrative, thematic and poetic structures are analogous: on all levels the *Rose* expresses the organic unfolding symbolized by the Rose itself, which is "the fountain of God's bounty transformed into a flower" (303). Book V describes the line of argument, that is, the symposium or disputation carried on by the major speakers, all of whom attempt to convince their audience of the correctness of their views of love, while Book VI places this disputation in the context of medieval social tensions and literary traditions. While Jean's "many-mindedness" (466) leads him to express fully the views of each character, Gunn suggests that it is Nature and Genius who "expound more clearly than their predecessors the meaning of the Rose-quest" (405). Gunn's conclusion argues for a reversal of critical judgment of the *Rose*: not only did Jean achieve "a high degree of expressive and unified design" (489), but this life-affirming design may still have value for us. Includes an outline of the rhetorical scheme of the *Rose* and a long bibliography.

275 -----. "Le roman de la rose." In *Collier's Encyclopedia*. 24 vols. New York: Macmillan Educational Co.; London and New York: P. F. Collier, 1988. 20:147-48.

A brief overview of the *Rose* that incorporates the author's major ideas from *The Mirror of Love* (no. 274): the thematic unity of the two parts achieved by Jean de Meun despite the "amplifications and transformations in scope and mood" (147); the close alliance of love and Nature; and the "one grand debate" (148) created by the discourses of the major personifications.

276 -----. "Teacher and Student in the *Roman de la rose*: A Study in Archetypal Figures and Patterns." *L'esprit créateur* 2.3 (1962):126-34.

A further exploration of a pivotal idea in the author's *The Mirror of Love* (no. 274)--that of the *Rose* as a didactic work. Here Gunn examines the functions of the "archetypal elements" (126) of Teacher and Student in the *Rose*, in particular the use of explicit instruction (the fourth of the methods of poetic *enseignement* described). Discussed are the two authors of the *Rose*, seen as Teacher-Poets; le Dieu d'Amour, divine teacher, culture-centered god, and pedagogue; and the major personifications, especially Nature, the "supreme authority," "a wiser mother-teacher than virginal Raison," and a metamorphosis of the great Mother-Goddess (132). Finally the article considers the archetypal meaning of the Youth-Lover-Student. Gunn's valorisation of the archetype of the Teacher leads to positive views of all the incarnations of the archetype, despite the possible negative content of their teachings (la Vieille, for example, is seen as "wise" [131]) and despite the author's stereotypical views of women. Within this general valorization, Gunn suggests a hierarchy of authorities, with Nature and Genius at the top.

277 Ham, Edward B[illings]. "Régionalismes dans le *Roman de la rose*." In *Mélanges de linguistique française offerts à M.*

Charles Bruneau. Geneva: Droz, 1954. 235-39.

An evaluation of Langlois's edition of the *Rose* (see no. 6) which is convinced of its value, while at the same time pointing out some of its weaknesses. The author sees the need of a text that would preserve the regionalisms of the two authors as well as for a linguistic study of those regional traits. Since only a few of these regionalisms are noted in this article, it serves simply as a starting point for such a linguistic study. [KML]

278 Hanscom, Elizabeth Deering. "The Allegory of de Lorris' *Romance of the Rose*." *Modern Language Notes* 8 (1893):151-53.

A review of Guillaume's allegorical characters which stresses the gap that divides the two parts of the romance (the author argues that Jean de Meun "desecrated the soul" [151] of Guillaume's poem). In addition Hanscom proposes modern English translations or paraphrases the difficult names of some of Guillaume's characters. Bel Accueil is glossed as Comradery, or Chumminess "in current American" (152); Danger is Reserve; Jalousie becomes Suspicion; and Doux Regard is seen first as Friendliness when a dancer in the garden, then as Pleasant Vision when an arrow of le Dieu d'Amour.

279 Hanson-Smith, Elizabeth Ann. "Be Fruitful and Multiply: The Medieval Allegory of Nature." Diss. Stanford U, 1972.

280 Harley, Marta Powell. "Narcissus, Hermaphroditus, and Attis: Ovidian Lovers at the Fontaine d'Amors in Guillaume de Lorris's *Roman de la rose*." *PMLA* 101 (1986):324-37.

An analysis of the myth of Narcissus in which Harley argues that in addition to Narcissus two other Ovidian myths, those of Hermapproditis and Attis, were sources of inspiration for Guillaume de Lorris. Based on similarities of detail and general themes, the author argues that "Amant indeed enters a mythologically mined setting" (328), a setting which leads us to a negative reading of l'Amant's experience at the Fountain. Further, homosexual elements in the three Ovidian myths are called on to suggest, along with certain elements in the text itself, that Guillaume is "conscientiously flirting with sexual ambiguity and homosexuality" (333). However, the article concludes that Guillaume's poem does not portray a homoerotic fantasy but l'Amant's self-absorption, his egocentrism.

281 Harrison, Ann Tukey. "Echo and Her Medieval Sisters." *The Centennial Review* 26 (1982):324-40.

A study of the character Echo in her six major appearances in medieval French and English literature. Guillaume de Lorris's version of her story shows that he adopted the moral addressed to ladies found in the earlier lay of *Narcisus*, thus proposing Narcissus, not Echo, as the role model for medieval women. The popularity of the *Rose* "assured that this version of the story supplanted Ovid, and its moral became the authorized lesson, especially in short lyric verse" (329). After surveying the other medieval occurrences of Echo, including in Gower, the author suggests the principal ways that medieval authors reworked the story, redesigning Echo according to three criteria: the message or allegorical meaning to be conveyed, the setting, and the roles of other characters, especially Narcissus.

282 Hatzfeld, Helmut. "La mystique naturiste de Jean de Meung." *Wissenschaftliche Zeitschrift der Friedrich-Schiller-Universität Iena* 5 (1955/1956):259-69.

An interpretation of Jean de Meun's part of the *Rose* both as an aggressive parody of medieval mysticism, especially that of Saint Bonaventure, and a radical affirmation of a "mystique naturiste" (259), a celebration of nature and man's natural instincts. Hatzfeld builds his case by treating all characters as the author's spokespeople and by eliminating any distance between the author and his characters. Thus Hatzfeld extracts statements from any speech to set against the mystical writings of Saint

Bonaventure, in order to show Jean de Meun in competition with medieval mystical thought. The opposition of the two mysticisms includes ideas, such as the value of asceticism, and symbols, such as the Phoenix and the Fountain of Deduit. [Although disregard for the *Rose* as a literary work undercuts Hatzfeld's arguments, what stands out from his analysis is the lack of sympathy for mysticism felt by most of the characters.]

283 Heeroma, K. "*Reinaert* en *Rose.*" *Tijdschrift voor nederlandsche Taal- en Letterkunde* 74 (1957):251-55.

284 Heffernan, Carol F. "The Bird-snare Figure and the Love Quest of *The Romance of the Rose.*" In *The Spirit of the Court.* Selected Proceedings of the Fourth Congress of the International Courtly Literature Society (Toronto, 1983). Ed. Glyn S. Burgess and Robert A. Taylor. Cambridge, Eng.: D. S. Brewer, 1985. 179-84.

A discussion, following a Robertsonian approach (see no. 473), of the bird-snare image in the description of the Fountain of Narcissus (ll. 1586-95): the author sees the image as a sexual metaphor, specifically referring to the cupidinous love that will entrap l'Amant. Other images in the romance, such as the water of the fountain (dyed with menstrual blood?) and the rose itself/herself are interpreted as metaphors for female sexuality (see also Stablein, no. 503). Consequently l'Amant must look to "the celestial rose of the garden in Jean de Meun's continuation" (183) for a worthy love object. [It should be noted that Heffernan makes the common mistake of asserting that l'Amant sees the rosebud itself in the Fountain.]

285 Heinrich, Fritz. *Über den Stil von Guillaume de Lorris und Jean de Meung.* Ausgaben und Abhandlungen aus dem Gebiete der romanischen Philologie 29. Marburg: N. G. Elwert'sche, 1885. Pp. 54.

A listing of hundreds of metaphors, comparisons, and figures from both parts of the *Rose*, each section of which is followed by a brief commentary on the respective styles of the two authors. The author concludes that Jean's style is livelier and bolder than Guillaume's but that his tendency toward artificiality and ornateness sometimes passes the bounds of good taste. Includes a list of metaphors and comparisons cited.

286 Heisig, K. "Arabische Astrologie und christliche Apologetik im *Rosenroman*." *Romanische Forschungen* 71 (1959):414-19.

287 Helling, William Patrick. "The Transformation of the Rose Guardians from Guillaume de Lorris to Jean de Meun." Diss. U of Kansas, 1986.

288 Hicks, Eric. "La mise en roman des formes allégoriques: hypostase et récit chez Guillaume de Lorris." In *Etudes... Lorris* (no. 231). 53-81.

A discussion of the nature of allegory which emphasizes its hidden meaning. The author offers a diagram of the four ways to "parler autrement" (60) (based on the relation of the individual to the class): symbol, persona, exemplum, and maxim. Hicks then studies semantically and logically the allegory of the *Rose*, in particular the two series of *hypostases* (a form of personification in which an abstract quality is spoken of as something human) on the wall and in the garden. The discussion includes a consideration of static versus dynamic allegories, or description versus narrative. Hicks argues that the description of the allegories on the wall of the garden is "tributaire d'une narration sous-jacente" (67-68), that is, the language of the portraits suggests the beginnings of a story. Hicks then describes the linguistic difficulties created by personification, where the notion of semantic class becomes merged with that of essence. Consequently all attributions in the *Rose* are either pleonastic or contradictory. Hicks concludes that allegory is inherently unsuited for narrative. Nonetheless, he softens his apparently critical view of Guillaume's allegory by adding that we enjoy Guillaume's "modulation" (80) of abstract and rigid characters. [Note that the title given in the table of contents, "La mise en prose...," is incorrect.]

289 -----. "Proverbe et polémique dans le *Roman de la rose* de Jean de Meun." In *Le proverbe au Moyen Age*. Vol. 1 of *Richesse du proverbe*. Ed. Claude Buridant and François Suard. Lille: Université de Lille III, 1984. 113-20.

A discussion of the nature of proverbs followed by an analysis of how Jean de Meun uses the various forms of the proverb, the "locution gnomique" (117), or quotations from classical authors. Although Jean has a gift for pithy sentences, the occurrence of proverbial expressions in the *Rose* is less frequent than expected for a number of reasons, including a certain incompatibility of Meun's proverbial expression with allegory, and especially because the author is more concerned with the message, with convincing the reader, than with "la rhétorique de la dispute" (118). Furthermore, he hates "le vulgaire profane" (118).

290 -----. "Sous les pavés, le sens: le dire et le décorum allégoriques dans *Le roman de la rose* de Jean de Meun." *Etudes de lettres* 2-3 (1987):113-32.

An analysis of the difficult problem of the meaning of the second part of the *Rose*, the answer to which has caused much disagreement among scholars. Hicks reviews the conflicting judgments of the critics who see in Jean a precursor of the Enlightenment, and the "école robertsonienne" (119), for whom Jean is profoundly medieval. These difficulties of interpretation result in part from the nature of Jean's "allégorie à vocation satirique" (115), in part also from two different understandings of the idea of decorum (appropriate characterization or moral appropriateness). In the last part, Hicks suggests the usefulness of the speech act approach, in particular the concept of "présupposition" (125) or what is implicit in a statement (such as "Jean a-t-il cessé de battre sa femme?" [125]). Presupposition allows Hicks to bring out the importance of the theme of

Fortune for understanding the underlying meaning of the *Rose*.

291 -----. "Le visage de l'antiquité dans le *Roman de la rose*; Jean de Meung: savant et pédagogue." Diss. Yale U, 1965.

292 Hilary, Christine Ryan. "The 'Confession' Tradition from Augustine to Chaucer." Diss. U of California, Berkeley, 1979.

293 Hilder, Gisela. "Abu Ma'shars 'Introductorium in astronomiam' und der altfranzösische *Roman de la rose*: Ein Beitrag zur Tradition arabischer Astrologie und ihrer christlichen Deutung im 12. und 13. Jahrhundert." *Zeitschrift für romanische Philologie* 88 (1972):13-33.

294 -----. *Der scholastische Wortschatz bei Jean de Meun: Die Artes Liberales*. Beiheft of the *Zeitschrift für romanische Philologie* 129. Tubingen: Max Niemeyer, 1972. Pp. xvi + 213.

A study of Jean de Meun's role as mediator of scholastic vocabulary in Old French. His continuation shows a considerable change in mentality which has less to do with the generation gap between him and Guillaume de Lorris than with Jean's academic formation which, the author suggests, was based not only on classical and medieval literature as several scholars maintain, but above all on theological, philosophical, and scientific writings of the twelfth and even more of the thirteenth century. Hilder's linguistic examination provides more evidence about Jean's formation. In Jean's part of the *Rose* there are about 200 words, concepts, activities, objects, and characteristics from the domain of the liberal arts. In order to determine Jean's contribution to this terminology, terms which appear also in older Old French texts with the same meaning were eliminated. From this reduced material (110 terms), central words used by high scholasticism and generally by the universities were analyzed with closer attention. Hilder investigates how this vocabulary is distributed in the different disciplines, which words are new in Jean's continuation, and to what extent they appear before the continuation of the *Rose*. [ASK]

295 Hill, Thomas D. "Narcissus, Pygmalion, and the Castration of Saturn: Two Mythographical Themes in the *Roman de la rose*." *Studies in Philology* 71 (1974):404-26.

An examination of the paradoxical nature of Jean de Meun's view of sexuality through the juxtaposition of two significant mythographical themes in the second part of the *Rose*, the Narcissus-Pygmalion contrast and the castration of Saturn followed by the birth of Venus. Pygmalion is more fortunate than Narcissus in that he achieves his love and founds a family; Venus, representing natural sexuality, is the result of the fall, the loss of the Golden Age. These two myths about human sexuality are best understood in the light of l'Amant's apparent impregnation--with Venus's help--of the rose (l. 21690). For Hill, the "fact of generation at the conclusion of the *Roman* is a significant detail which must be accounted for in any serious interpretation of the poem" (416). That is, despite the folly and sinfulness of l'Amant's passion, a great good comes from it. Thus the major theme of the *Rose* is the paradoxical nature of human sexuality in the postlapsarian world. (For a reply by Fleming, whose views Hill questions, see no. 243, 17-24.)

296 -----. "La Vieille's Digression on Free Love: A Note on Rhetorical Structure in the *Romance of the Rose*." *Romance Notes* 8 (1966/1967):113-15.

An analysis on the underlying structure in the second part of the *Rose*, focusing on a passage in la Vieille's lecture in which she interrupts her telling of the story of how Venus and Mars were caught in Vulcan's net to discourse on the inherent freedom of sexuality. Rather than a digression, the old woman's plea for free love--which leaves the lovers hanging, as it were--makes of the mythological exemplum an ironic frame, for the episode of Vulcan's net was often interpreted in the Middle Ages to signify the bondage, not the freedom, of irrational desire. That la Vieille is unaware of love's bondage is also implicit in the pattern of her life, in which she exploited and was exploited. Thus her life story becomes an ironic frame for the Venus and Mars story, which is in turn an ironic frame for the discussion of free love.

297 Hillman, Larry H. "Another Look into the Mirror Perilous: The Role of the Crystals in the *Roman de la rose*." *Romania* 101 (1980):225-38.

A reexamination of the Fountain of Narcissus in the first part of the *Rose*. Seeking "an analysis in closer accordance with the text" (225), Hillman first gives a useful review of previous scholarship on the Fountain and in particular on the meaning of its two crystals. Most interpreters (C. S. Lewis, Jean Frappier, Erich Köhler, D. W. Robertson, among others; see nos. 375, 247, 348, and 473) have attempted to see the crystals as someone's eyes: the lady's, or l'Amant's vision of her eyes; l'Amant's eyes, or their reflection in the lady's, etc. Hillman argues that all these theories over- or mis-represent the text. He points out both textual details that jar with these approaches and a lack of textual evidence that the crystals represent anyone's eyes. Instead, he suggests that the Fountain and the crystals are the final test of l'Amant's "ability to choose an appropriate love object and in so doing, prove himself worthy of being Amour's vassal" (236). [See also no. 341.]

298 Hipolito, Terrence. "*Roman de la rose*: Nature's Grace." *Comitatus: A Journal of Medieval and Renaissance Studies* 1 (1970):47-79.

A wide-ranging and somewhat disconnected essay on a number of topics, in three sections: the unity of the *Rose*, Jean de Meun's philosophy, and his use of formal elements. Jean recognized in the first part "a partially submerged intellectual structure" (53) which he could develop. The ultimate statement of the relationship of the two parts is found in Genius's contrasting of the Park of the Lamb and the garden of Deduit, which are both comparable and incomparable; the contrast creates "the unity and the tension" (52) of the *Rose*. The author asserts, with little supporting evidence, that Jean owed much to, but diverged greatly from, Alain de Lille. He claims that Jean's philosophy saw love as paradoxical and immoral, but that "the raptures of love" (69) are Nature's grace. Finally, the author labels Jean's allegory "gothic" (72), which appears to involve the joining of microcosmic and macrocosmic visions, and concludes with a brief discussion of *persona* and satire in the *Rose*.

299 Hollier, Denis, ed. *A New History of French Literature*. Cambridge, Mass.: U of Harvard P, 1989. Pp. xxv + 1150 + ill.

An introduction to the *Rose* which discusses each part in a separate section. In an essay on thirteenth-century narratives that are generic hybrids, Kevin Brownlee describes Guillaume de Lorris's "brilliant structural innovation" which "conflates the first-person lover of courtly lyric with the first-person narrator of courtly romance" (89) to create a new kind of autobiographical work. This structural combination suggests that the work is "simultaneously unfinished as narrative and finished as lyric" (90). In a later section, Jean de Meun's continuation is set by David Hult in the context of the vibrant intellectual life of Paris. He argues that the "massive and centrifugal text...defies attempts to control its meaning" (99), and that the text's "irreducible intellectual heterodoxy" (100) raises broad epistemological questions. The "troubled relationship between intention and linguistic expression" (101) points to the power of the written word and the danger of the act of interpretation.

300 Huizinga, Johan. *The Waning of the Middle Ages: A Study of the Forms of Life, Thought and Art in France and the Nether-*

lands in the XIVth and XVth Centuries. 1949; rpt. Garden City, N. Y.: Doubleday Anchor Books, 1954. Pp. 362.

A brief overview of the place of the *Rose* in late medieval culture and the reasons for its continuing popularity, which "determined the aristocratic conception of love in the expiring Middle Ages" (108) and "satisfied the needs of erotic expression of a whole age" (112). Huizinga describes the romance both as the "treasure-house whence lay society drew the better part of its erudition" (108) and the expression of an ideal of civilization amalgamated with an ideal of love. The two parts juxtapose two conceptions of love--the first courtly, the second cynical and skeptical: "It is impossible to imagine a more deliberate defiance of the Christian ideal" (114). The author also summarizes the Querelle de la Rose [with some exaggeration and inaccuracy].

301 Hult, David F. "The Allegorical Fountain: Narcissus in the *Roman de la rose*." *Romanic Review* 72 (1981):125-48.

A good introduction to the "curious textual enigmas" (146) posed by Guillaume's retelling of the myth of Narcissus (in particular, ll. 1423-1612). Hult considers, among other problems, the conceptual difference between exemplum and personification, the peculiarities in the narrator's account of the Narcissus story, the surprising moral, the meaning of the crystals, and the episode's importance for understanding the romance as a whole. Guillaume's "subversive vision" (142), which underlies the ambiguities of the episode, points to the "recurrent theme of subjective judgment" (143); "the faculty of perception, and not the object perceived, is the central concern" (145). Thus Hult sees Narcissus's fountain as the image of fiction itself. Includes excellent bibliographical notes.

302 -----. "Closed Quotations: The Speaking Voice in the *Roman de la rose*." *Yale French Studies* 67 (1984):248-69.

A study of voice in the *Rose* that first discusses the stylistics of direct quotation in literature generally (referring to the work of

Gérard Genette, Antoine Compagnon, Harald Weinrich, and others) and in medieval literature. The difficulties, especially for modern audiences, of determining the voice in a medieval text is further complicated by the first-person quasi-autobiographical multi-referential *je* of the *Rose*. Hult analyzes in detail the mechanics of quotation in the passages that link the first part to both the anonymous continuation and to Jean de Meun's and compares these passages to similar transitions from introspection to narration (Lover to Narrator) in Guillaume's poem. Jean adds another referential level to the first-person pronoun, making it both personal (Jean) and impersonal (Guillaume). Guillaume's entire text becomes the direct quotation on which Jean builds his continuation, which is "a reabsorption of a *type* of discourse and not a simple critique of courtly ideology" (269), with the result that Guillaume's voice ultimately differs little from that of other personifications in Jean's romance.

303 -----. "In Quest of the Rose: Guillaume de Lorris and Jean de Meun." Diss. Cornell U, 1978.

304 -----. "Language and Dismemberment: Abelard, Origen, and the *Romance of the Rose*." In *Rethinking* (no. 182). 101-30.

An analysis of the discussion of obscene language in Raison's dialogue with l'Amant that proposes to see Jean de Meun's "unrelenting fascination with castration and, in broader terms, physical dismemberment" (115) as a model for his "poetics of dismemberment" (122), for the disjunction of words and things. After an eight-page "suggestive preamble" (109) that reviews disjunctive readings of the *Rose* during the fifteenth-century Querelle de la Rose [Hult clearly sides with Jean's defenders], the author summarizes the dialogue on language and its tale of Saturn's castration, a tale which lets in "a number of topics of central importance to the *Rose*" (112). These topics include obscene wordplay in the discussion of obscenity itself, the continued presence of the castrated member in language, and the sense of fullness or productivity that follows the stories of castration. The article argues that Jean's images of linguistic and physical dismemberment point to the dismemberment of language, to the production of sense "by the operations of language and not by the prior existence of things" (110).

305 -----. *Self-Fulfilling Prophecies: Readership and Authority in the First "Roman de la rose"*. Cambridge England: Cambridge UP, 1986. Pp. xiv + 321 + ill.

A reconsideration of the question, Is the first part of the *Rose* in fact unfinished? In considering from many angles the long-standing critical assumption that the first *Rose* is incomplete, Hult takes up several more or less related topics of *Rose* criticism and of medieval literary history, such as the status and role of the medieval author, intertextuality, Guillaume de Lorris's use of allegory, the *Rose*'s reworking of lyric and romance, and Guillaume's reinterpretation of the myth of Narcissus. Hult also attempts to make explicit the literary assumptions--the "self-fulfilling prophecies"--which underlie all criticism, including his own. The author's conclusion appears to be that the first *Rose* is unfinished, but that the author intended it that way.

306 -----. "Vers la société de l'écriture: *Le roman de la rose*." *Poétique* 50 (1982):155-72.

An examination of the prologue to the *Roman de la rose* as a way of approaching medieval works that were based on oral culture and written in the vernacular (as opposed to Latin) and of the repercussions of this evolution from spoken to written language on the composition of the works themselves. Hult points to four movements in the 44-line prologue: a general truth (the truth of dreams) or *sententia* supported by an authority (Macrobius); subjective opinion about the truth of dreams; a movement from general to specific discourse (personal experience); the writing of the dream which gives its value to the double event of dream and realization. By rhyming (writing) his own dream, Guillaume becomes an authority like

Macrobius, who "wrote" Scipio's dream, and thereby reduces a living personal quest to "une aventure purement livresque" (171). It is this written truth which is the "sens de la rose" (171). [Note that in Hult's analysis the beautiful people in the garden are mistakenly placed on the outside wall in place of the undesirables.]

307 Huot, Paul. *Etude sur "Le roman de la rose"*. Orleans: Alex. Jacob for the Société Archéologique de l'Orléanais, 1853. Pp. 67.

An early introductory study of the *Rose*, generally unreliable in its factual information and in the summary of the poem, which omits the pilgrim section, and in which are interspersed excerpts from Molinet's allegorization of the *Rose*. Huot suggests that Jean removed Guillaume's ending in order to add his own of 18,000 lines. Jean's "sorte d'encyclopédie" (14) proposes ideas so audacious that they would get him arrested today: he attacks religion, the family, private property, and women, the latter because he had "une vieille rancune contre les dames de son temps" (55). The author reproaches Guillaume for his long descriptions, for "les longueurs et les allégories" (9), and he regrets the period's taste for allegory and personification. Jean is criticized for Nature's disordered and capricious confession and for Genius's sermon, in which Huot sees "rien de saillant" (63). Molière, he suggests, must have studied the *Rose* when he developed his character Tartuffe, and Marot's theological interpretation outlined in the preface to his modernization of the *Rose* was an attempt to win the favor of church authorities.

308 Huot, Sylvia. *From Song to Book: The Poetics of Writing in Old French Lyric and Lyrical Narrative Poetry*. Ithaca: Cornell UP, 1987. Pp. x + 372 + 31 figures.

A detailed and perceptive study of "the relationship between poetics and manuscript format" (1) in Old French lyric and lyrical narrative works. The *Rose* played an important part in the "gradual establishment of the writer's primacy over the singer" (4). Huot uses both textual and manuscript evidence to describe how the two *Rose* poets conceive of the interplay of lyric and narrative, of poet-lover-singer and poet-narrator-writer. Guillaume's persona moves from narrator (observer) to lyric poet (lover); in the second half of his poem, narrative discourse "has given way to lyric discourse" (89), as epitomized in the myth of Narcissus, which Guillaume retells. On the other hand, Jean de Meun, who has become the omniscient author observing the protagonist-lover, conveys the idea that writing is more productive, more valuable than singing through his retelling of the myth of Pygmalion and through Genius's sermon on procreation as writing. Analysis of the rubrics and illuminations of a number of *Rose* manuscripts gives further evidence of the new kind of poetic authority that the poem was seen as embodying. The study also describes subsequent transformations of the *Rose*'s poetics by poets such as Baudouin and Jean de Condé, Guillaume de Machaut, and Jean Froissart.

309 Ineichen, Gustav. "Le discours linguistique de Jean de Meun." *Romanistische Zeitschrift für Literaturgeschichte* 2 (1978): 245-51; discussion 252-53.

A textual analysis of the linguistic and philosophical concepts underlying the discussion of proper and improper words by Raison and l'Amant (ll. 6898-7200). The author points to a number of problems in the passage concerning the Aristotelian or Augustinian basis of Raison's statements and the cognitive or metaphoric levels of language (science versus poetry). Jean de Meun's linguistic discourse is described as "très restreinte et conventionnelle" (250). Ineichen questions Poirion's interpretation of Jean's linguistic approach as "une volonté de rupture sur le plan du style et au niveau de la doctrine" (249). [The work by Poirion that Ineichen refers to is not included in the bibliography but is probably "Les mots et les choses;" see no. 448].

310 Irribarria-Huettig, Maria S. "Le système métaphorique du *Roman de la rose*." Diss. U of Kansas, 1975.

311 Jackson, W. T. H. "Allegory and Allegorization." *Research Studies* 32 (1964):161-75. Rpt. in *The Challenge of the Medieval Text: Studies in Genre and Interpretation.* Ed. Joan M. Ferrante and Robert W. Hanning. New York: Columbia UP, 1985. 157-71.

An approach to medieval allegory as a literary genre which argues that allegorical works should be placed in a literary frame. Such a frame "imparts authority" (162) to the work and enables the reader to make sense of it. For the *Rose* Jackson proposes the frame of the courtly romance, which involves the adventures and instruction of the young hero. He also discusses the differences between allegorization [allegoresis] as a kind of reading and allegory as a genre stemming principally from personification. Jackson concludes with a discussion of non-literary frames such as the hunt and proposes a definition of allegory based on the two elements of personification and framing.

312 Jager, Eric. "Reading the *Roman* Inside Out: The Dream of Croesus as a *caveat lector.*" *Medium aevum* 57 (1988):67-74.

An analysis of Raison's exemplum of Croesus's dream and the different interpretations offered by him and his daughter, Phania (one literal, the other figurative). Jager interprets this exemplum as a gloss on the *Rose* itself, thereby suggesting a resemblance between Croesus and l'Amant, both of whom through self-love suffer from "faulty spiritual eyesight" (70). Further applying Robertsonian exegetical principles (see nos. 472 and 473), Jager argues for a typological resemblance between the "tree" of Croesus's dream (a gallows) and the ones near the Fountain of Narcissus and in the Garden of Eden. Thus Raison's exemplum becomes also a *caveat* to the reader to understand the *Rose* spiritually.

313 Jarry, Louis. "Guillaume de Lorris et le testament d'Alphonse de Poitiers." *Mémoires de la Société d'agriculture, sciences,*

belles-lettres et arts d'Orléans 22 (19 November 1880):5-53.

A biographical investigation into the Lorris family, its relations with the French royal family, and the possible identification of one of its members with the author of the first part of the *Rose*. Jarry points to a Guillaume de Lorris (a bow-and-arrow maker, appropriately enough), mentioned in 1245 as being in service to Alphonse de Poitiers, the brother of Louis IX. The study also discusses briefly whether the author of the *Rose* was from the town of Lorris-en-Gâtinais or Loury-aux-Bois (see also no. 272); he argues strongly for the former. Includes two documents from 1384 relating to the heirs of Guillaume de Lorris.

314 -----. "Note supplémentaire pour le mémoire intitulé 'Guillaume de Lorris et le testament d'Alphonse de Poitiers'." *Mémoires de la Société d'agriculture, sciences, belles-lettres et Arts d'Orléans* 23 (3 March 1882):189-200.

The transcript of an oral communication in which Jarry defends himself against Guillon's accusations that the former stole the latter's discoveries concerning the biography of Guillaume de Lorris (see no. 272).

315 Jauss, Hans Robert. "Allégorie, 'remythisation' et nouveau mythe: réflexions sur la captivité chrétienne de la mythologie au moyen âge." In *Terror und Spiel: Probleme der Mythenrezeption*. Ed. M. Fuhrmann. Poetik und Hermeneutik 4. Munich: W. Fink, 1971. 188-209. Rpt. in *Mélanges d'histoire littéraire, de linguistique et de philologie romanes offerts à Charles Rostaing par ses collègues, ses élèves et ses amis*. Tr. Janine Delcourt-Angelique. Liege: Association des Romanistes de l'Université de Liège, 1974. 469-99.

An exploration of the reception of classical myths in the Middle Ages which includes remarks on Prudentius's *Psychomachia*, the *Tournoiement Antecrist*, Alain de Lille's *Anticlaudianus* and *De planctu Naturae*, the *Roman de la rose*, Latini's *Tesoretto*, and

Dante's *Vita nuova*. Jauss describes the various stages through which pagan gods and myths passed in medieval literature and suggests distinctions between myth and personification. Of particular importance are the myths of Cupid and Venus, which became "un noyau de cristallisation" (470) around which courtly love elaborated its new mythology. Also noteworthy was the development of a myth involving Nature, Venus, and Genius, which in the *De planctu Naturae* become "un nouveau mythe en milieu chrétien" (495). Jauss points to the influence of the classical epithalamium on allegories of love such as Guillaume's *Rose*, in particular on the garden of love. Jean de Meun is seen as denouncing the courtly mythology of his predecessor by means of the new myths of the twelfth-century school of Chartres: to Guillaume's Dieu d'Amour Jean opposes the higher reality of "la trinité mythique Vénus-Natura-Genius" (488-89).

316 -----. "Form und Auffassung der Allegorie in der Tradition der *Psychomachia* (von Prudentius zum ersten *Romanz de la rose*)." In *Medium Aevum Vivum*: *Festschrift für Walther Bulst*. Ed. Hans Robert Jauss and Dieter Schaller. Heidelberg: Carl Winter, 1960. 179-206.

An early study in the author's continuing analysis of medieval allegorical works (see Note Préliminaire to "La transformation de la forme allégorique" in no. 319). After an introductory review of critical discussions of symbol and allegory, Jauss analyzes the conception of the *bellum intestinum* in Prudentius's *Psychomachia*, then considers more briefly important examples of medieval allegory, such as Raoul de Houdenc's *Voie d'Enfer* and *Voie de Paradis* and Huon de Méry's *Tournoiement Antecrit*, concluding with a brief discussion of allegory in the first part of the *Rose*. Jauss's interest lies in the way Guillaume maintains both the general allegory of an art of love and the individualized allegory of the lover's sentimental adventures.

317 -----. *Genèse de la poésie allégorique française au moyen-âge (de 1180 à 1240).* Heidelberg: Carl Winter, 1962. Pp. 55.

A sample chapter from the *Grundriss der romanischen Literaturen des Mittelalters* (see no. 318), describing the major allegorical works that preceded and prepared the first part of the *Rose*. Jauss argues that between 1180 and 1240 a new allegorical poetry in French developed, using religious texts and themes. This poetry began with allegorical interpretations of religious texts, continued with original religious poetry in allegorical form, and culminated in the profane allegory of the *Roman de la rose*. The major texts discussed include the *Songe d'enfer* of Raoul de Houdenc, the *Château d'amour* of Robert Grosseteste, Renclus de Moiliens's *Roman de Miserere*, which Jauss sees as offering many elements surprisingly similar to the *Rose*, and Huon de Mery's *Tournoiement Antecrist*, a *psychomachia* of the virtues and vices that includes Venus and Arthur's Knights of the Round Table. The ways is which the *Rose* uses this tradition are outlined (21-23). Detailed documentation on the works discussed is given at the end of the chapter.

318 -----. *La littérature didactique, allégorique et satirique.* Vol. 6, Tomes 1 and 2, of *Grundriss der romanischen Literaturen des Mittelalters*. Heidelberg: Carl Winter, 1968.

A two-part introduction to the *Rose* by a specialist in the history of medieval allegory, as part of a massive history of medieval Romance literatures. The historical introduction describes Guillaume's poem (Tome 1, 232-34) in terms of its merger of diverse traditions: the courtly art of love (it is "eine vollständige und abschliessende Summa aller Konventionen der höfischen Liebe" [233], the biographical vision, and the system of personifications first seen in the *Psychomachia*. Jauss also discusses how Guillaume frees his allegory from the constraints of the *bellum intestinum* to create for the first time "eine reine Fiktion" (233), as illustrated by the various means used to portray the Lady--she is represented by the arrows of le Dieu d'Amour, by the personification of conflicting tendencies, and by the unveiled mystery of her being. The overview of Jean de Meun's part (236-38), after summarizing adverse critical judgments, describes how Jean modifies the first part. Jauss argues that Jean attempts to reach a mystical parallel between human and divine love in Genius's description of the Park of the Lamb. The documentation (see Tome 2, 271-76) gives succinctly much information about the *Rose*, including editions, major studies, biographical information, date of composition, history of the text, and generic and stylistic characteristics.

319 -----. "La transformation de la forme allégorique entre 1180 et 1240: d'Alain de Lille à Guillaume de Lorris." In *L'humanisme médiéval dans les littératures romanes du XIIe au XIVe siècle*. Colloque organisé par le Centre de Philologie et de Littératures romanes de l'Université de Strasbourg du 29 janvier au 2 fevrier 1962. Ed. Anthime Fourrier. Paris: Klincksieck, 1964. 107-44; discussion 145-46.

A synthesis of Jauss's work on allegory before Guillaume de Lorris, earlier versions of which appeared in nos. 315, 316, 317. A brief review of theories of allegory (symbolism/allegory, form/meaning, typological/abstract allegory) and of critical hostility to allegory precedes the survey of works from Prudentius's *Psychomachia*, through the allegorical epics of the twelfth-century school of Chartres and personifications in vernacular lyric and romance, to the crucial development of allegory in religious poetry, which gave rise to the new allegorical style. The relation between the *abstractum agens* and the human soul is different in each text: only Guillaume de Lorris will realize a balance between "allégorie générale et allégorie particulière," between "le destin supraindividuel de l'amour et la route propre aux amants" (137).

320 Jeanroy, Alfred. *Histoire des lettres*. Vol. 12 of *Histoire de la nation française*. Ed. Gabriel Hanotaux. Paris: Société de

l'Histoire Nationale and Plon-Nourrit, 1921. Pp. 590.

A history of French literature which includes a short introduction to the *Rose* for the general public; it gives information about the authors (some of it erroneous), plot summaries, and an evaluation of the authors' literary strengths. Guillaume is credited with "un esprit d'observation et une finesse d'analyse" (410) which those who mapped the seventeenth century Carte de Tendre would have admired; Jean was "le premier des humanistes" (414). His simple philosophy of "suivre la nature" (417) put him outside of Christianity without his realizing it. His writing, despite the digressions, could be picturesque and nuanced and could reach "la sobre et rude éloquence du drame" (418).

321 Jernigan, Charles. "*Arma, Arme, Arm*: The Literary Use of a Bawdy Pun in the Middle Ages and the Renaissance." *Fifteenth-Century Studies* 5 (1982):99-116.

A word study that traces the use of various forms of *arm(s)* as a bawdy phallic pun, including at least two occurrences in the *Rose*, one during the assault on the castle, the other in l'Amant's speech as a pilgrim. Other sources of the pun include Arnaut Daniel's famous sestina and several of Shakespeare's plays.

322 Joret, Charles. *La rose dans l'antiquité et au moyen âge: histoire, légendes et symbolisme*. 1892; rpt. Slatkine Reprints, 1970 and 1989. Pp. x + 480.

A detailed history of the rose in ancient, oriental, and medieval history, literature, and folklore that helps to understand its moral and poetic connotations in the *Roman de la rose*, although there is little direct discussion of the *Rose*. Among the connotations indicated are the rose's association with spring, love and joy; with the beloved; with paradises both terrestrial and heavenly; with beauty, excellence, and virginity. Joret cites many medieval Latin and vernacular works that express these associations with the rose.

323 Jung, Marc-René. *Etudes sur le poème allégorique en France au moyen âge.* Romanica Helvetica 82. Bern: Francke, 1971. Pp. 334.

A collection of essays studying "sans préjugés" (9) the major late classical and medieval allegories, including works by Prudentius, Martianus Capella, Bernard Silvestre, Alain de Lille, Huon de Mery, and many anonymous Occitan and French allegories. The studies are intended to describe the allegorical tradition which prepared Guillaume de Lorris's part of the *Rose* (discussed in the last section). Jung's approach divides allegory into static (descriptive) and dynamic (narrative) types. The "centre et le moteur du poème allégorique" (21), however, are according to Jung, the personifications. In his analysis of the first part, Jung suggests referents for events and personifications without adhering to a rigid system: "Il n'existe pas de clé pour lire l'allégorie du *Roman de la Rose*" (310). Thus the rose suggests three possible meanings, the lady herself, her love, or "une valeur érotique très précise" (308), depending on the circumstances. Guillaume's allegory is not "froidement calculée" (297) and remains closer to the romance than to the didactic model.

324 -----. "Jean de Meun et l'allégorie." *Cahiers de l'Association internationale des études françaises* 28 (1976):21-36.

A study that argues that the "grand artiste qu'est Jean de Meun" (23) calls on us in a number of ways to see beyond the *sensus litteralis* of his poem, something which some of his characters, l'Amant, for example, have trouble doing. Pygmalion's story and Raison's remarks on language suggest that we go beyond l'Amant's extended metaphor of relics for sexual organs in the final scene. In Jean's text the gloss (of Guillaume's text, of Boethius's, of Cicero's, etc.) is found in the exempla: "L'exemple narratif remplace la glose discursive" (25). Furthermore, the incorrect syllogisms ("sophismes") of many characters, the idea of definition by contraries, the complex play between Jean's source and his use of it, all indicate that he is putting us on guard against arguments that rest on authority.

The "subtilités métaphoriques, allégoriques, typologiques et exemplaires" (27) of Jean's *Rose* make of it "une allégorie de la lecture" (28).

325 -----. "Jean de Meun et son lecteur." *Romanistische Zeitschrift für Literaturgeschichte* 2 (1978):241-44; discussion 244-45.

An approach to the *Rose* as a series of readings (glosses, interpretations, teachings) by the major characters. Their teachings are not conveyed directly, however, but through the narrative itself and its metaphors and exempla. Jung first discusses briefly l'Ami's precepts on love as an example of how a character reads a source, then the theme of the Golden Age as an example of how Jean de Meun creates a "structure réflexive" (243), characterized by the return of the same motifs in the lectures of different characters in different contexts, leading to different solutions.

326 -----. "Der Rosenroman in der Kritik seit dem 18. Jahrhundert." *Romanische Forschungen* 78 (1966):203-52.

A study that traces the evolution of *Rose* criticism since the edition of 1735. After an account of eighteenth- and nineteenth-century editions and of early discussions of the poem (which seem to have been mainly interested in the legends about Jean de Meun), Jung reviews the first serious studies, in particular those of J.-J. Ampère and Gaston Paris, whose judgment "wird für fast fünfzig Jahre wegweisend sein" (221). The author stresses the importance of Langlois's three-part work on the *Rose* (source study, manuscript study, edition). The final section, on modern criticism, begins with Jean de Meun and summarizes major studies concerning his possible naturalism (including the theories of Lanson, Faral, Françon, and Hatzfeld), his scholastic perspective (Gorce and Paré), his heterodox opinions (Müller), his philosophy of plenitude (Gunn), and finally, his Christian allegory (Fleming). Jung reviews more briefly works on Guillaume de Lorris's use of allegory (C. S. Lewis, Benedetto, Jauss, and Frappier) and concludes with the hope that the new edition by Lecoy will stimulate discussion of the romance. A short and eclectic annotated bibliography is appended.

327 Kamenetz, Georgette. "L'ésotérisme de Guillaume de Lorris." Diss. U of Paris, 1980.

328 -----. "La promenade d'Amant comme expérience mystique." In *Etudes...Lorris* (no. 231). 83-104.

A study, based on the author's dissertation, which proposes to read the first part of the *Rose* as an allegory of a mystical itinerary that passes through five phases: awakening to another reality, purification, illumination, identification, and union. The portraits on the wall, the struggle between the personifications (Danger, Male Bouche, Courtoisie, etc.), the Fountain of Narcissus, the fortification in which Bel Accueil is imprisoned--all represent some aspect of l'Amant's soul, while le Dieu d'Amour and the rose suggest divine love. The force of the parallels rests on the fact that passionate love does in some respects resemble the mystical experience. [To make her case, the author suggests general analogies (the springtime motif, for example, is seen as representing the awakening of the soul to a higher reality), but she considers neither other possible interpretations nor details that appear to contradict the idea of a mystical experience.]

329 Kaminska, Alexandra B. "Literary Confessions from 1215 through 1550: Development in Theme and Form of French, German and English Confessions from the Fourth Lateran Council Through the Reformation." Diss. U of Maryland, 1972.

330 Kanduth, Erika. "Der Rosenroman--ein Bildungsbuch?" *Zeitschrift für romanische Philologie* 86 (1970):509-24.

A detailed discussion of the problematic nature of the

educational aspects of the *Roman de la rose*. The didactic basis is common to both authors, but they confront us with different concerns and forms. Hence, the question whether this allegory is in fact a *Bildungsbuch* does not depend on its content but rather on its form and structure. For both parts the author carefully analyzes and compares such elements as antithesis, irony, and satire. On the assumption that literature is part of education, Guillaume de Lorris created a poetic masterpiece whose didactic content was already passé, whereas Jean de Meun addressed with his contribution a profoundly bourgeois world opening up to useful erudition more easily than to poetry with its exclusive demands. [ASK]

331 Kauke, Rainer. "Jupiter et Saturne chez Jean de Meun." *Romanistische Zeitschrift für Literaturgeschichte, Cahiers d'histoire des littératures romanes* 2 (1978):258-63.

A brief but revealing confrontation of the diverse references to Jupiter in the second part of the *Rose* and to the difficulties of interpretation that they pose. Jean's myth(s) of Jupiter's castration of Saturn are compared to the different mythographic versions that he knew. For Jean "le vrai sens du vieux mythe" (259) is the castration itself and not the birth of Venus. The derogatory accounts of Jupiter by Raison and Genius make of the god "le mauvais représentant d'une humanité dégénérée" (261), but in Jean's laudatory association of himself with Jupiter in the midpoint speech of le Dieu d'Amour, he is following a different tradition, an astrological rather than a mythological one. Thus he has reshaped the mythographic material to create his own myths.

332 Keck, Sylvia. "Faux Semblant--Guerrier du Dieu d'Amour." *Romanistische Zeitschrift für Literaturgeschichte, Cahiers d'histoire des littératures romanes* 2 (1978): 263-65.

A brief summary of the narrative importance and historical background of Faux Semblant. The author asks whether Faux Semblant really commits himself to a cause that is morally good, but the answer is pragmatic: only a Faux Semblant would be effective in killing Male Bouche, "la plus grande ennemie du Dieu d'Amour" (265). It is necessary to realize that Faux Semblant is parodic, as are other passages of the romance, in order to arrive at an adequate interpretation of the *Rose*.

333 Kelly, Douglas. *The Art of Medieval French Romance*. Madison: U of Wisconsin P, 1992. Pp. xvi + 471.

An erudite and wide-ranging study of how medieval French authors thought about questions of literary technique. The author points to the *Rose* a number of times when discussing such subjects as use of sources, amplification and truth, order in dreams, metaphor, topical order, and the late-medieval transition from romance to *dit*. The two-part *Rose* can tell us much about how a medieval author viewed a predecessor's creation. In addition, both parts of the *Rose* prepare for the *dit*, Guillaume "by making romance into a topical art of love, thus opening the way for the *traitié*" (308), Jean by rationalizing the mystery of the rose at the heart of Guillaume's poem.

334 -----. "'Li chastiaus...Qu'Amors prist puis par ses esforz': The Conclusion of Guillaume de Lorris' *Rose*." In *A Medieval French Miscellany*. Papers of the 1970 Kansas Conference on Medieval French Literature. Ed. Norris J. Lacy. Lawrence: University of Kansas Publications, 1972. 61-78.

An imaginative exploration of the possible ending of the first part of the *Rose*. Kelly finds the key to understanding how Guillaume may have intended the *Rose* to end in the concept of courtly love, an ideal which le Dieu d'Amour teaches and toward which l'Amant must move if he wishes to win the rose. It is significant that in Guillaume's projected ending, it is love, not Venus or himself, who will take the castle of Jalousie. The stages through which the lover must pass are compared to the categories of love defined by André le Chapelain's *De amore*: from *rage* (simple desire to love) to *folie* (physical desire) to *fin'amors*. L'Amant must rise above *folie* "not by eschewing love, but by a better love" (68). The profound difference between the intentions of the two authors of the *Rose* is found in the role of Venus, who has only temporary effectiveness in Guillaume's poem but whom Jean makes the key to taking the rose. These two views of love--courtly and sexual--show that the two poems are "fundamentally different in perspective" (76).

335 -----. *Medieval Imagination: Rhetoric and the Poetry of Courtly Love.* Madison: U of Wisconsin P, 1978. Pp. xvi + 330.

A study of medieval theories and the practice of imagination, "the invention, retention, and expression of Images in the mind" (xii), especially in relation to the literature of courtly love. The author examines the three major groups of images in the first part of the *Rose*: the figures painted on the wall of the garden, the courtly personifications in Deduit's company and the personifications that appear in the allegorical narrative itself. Detailed rhetorical analysis of the first two groups shows that Guillaume was attempting topical description, that is, the description of the "most obvious, appropriate, and characteristic features" (70) in order to contrast those images outside of the garden, all of which connote hate, with those inside, which connote joy and love. Among the personifications that contribute to the narrative, Kelly singles out Oiseuse, Jalousie, Danger, and the rose as illustrative of the ambiguity and suggestiveness of certain images, their "possible discursive meaning in different settings" (93). Ultimately it is authorial intention that controls the organizing Image both of the repetitive figures in the descriptions and the ambiguous, shifting ones in the narrative. In the subsequent discussions of major courtly poets, such as Machaut, Froissart, and René d'Anjou, Kelly frequently makes brief comparisons of their works to the two parts of the *Rose*. Jean de Meun's criticism of courtly love is credited with "the general breakup of courtly values" (199) in the late Middle Ages.

336 Kessler, Joan. "La quête amoureuse et poétique: la fontaine de Narcisse dans le *Roman de la rose.*" *Romanic Review* 73

(1982):133-46.

An analysis of the Fountain of Narcissus episode in terms of its larger meaning for the structure of Guillaume's *Rose*. Using as her point of departure Freeman's article, "Problems in Romance Composition..." (no. 248), the author describes how Guillaume moves from the lyric view of love to the narrative. This move involves the techniques of "dépassement" (135) of the lyric model and "répétition" (137) or reliving the subjective experience, techniques which structure l'Amant's relation to Narcissus, the narrator's relation to his protagonist, and the relation of "tout bon lecteur" (141) to the romance. [Despite the oversimplification of the voice of the lyric poet (is there really no distinction "entre poète et amant" [146]?), and despite the disturbing number of serious typographical errors (missing footnotes, unintelligible words, incorrect genders, etc.), Kessler's close reading of the Narcissus episode is often perceptive.]

337 Ketcham, Herbert Eugene. *Nature in Old and Middle French Poetry and in the First Poet of the Renaissance.* Foreword by Urban T. Holmes, Jr. Williamsport, Pennsylvania, 1950 [multigraphed]. Pp. 112.

A survey of descriptions of "nature elements" (1) in works in various genres, in both Latin and French, from the fourth to the sixteenth century, concluding with Jean Lemaire de Belges. The author cites the descriptions of the garden in the first part of the *Rose* but stops his analysis when the allegorical portion begins (he distinguishes "true descriptions" [80] from allegories). Guillaume goes beyond a compilation of elements found in earlier works to create new images, such as the earth's robe and the colors of the spectrum in the refracting crystals of the fountain, about which Ketcham claims that "no such image has occurred in all the poetry examined" (83).

338 Kievits, Bridget. "'To have and have not': Rijkdom und armoede in de *Roman van de roos*." In *In onse scole:*

Opstellen over Middeleeuwse leterkunde voor Prof. Dr. Margaretha H. Schenkeveld. Ed. Fred De Bree and Roel Zemel. Amsterdam: Stichting Neerlandistiek VU, 1989. 175-96.

339 King, Peter. "*Flos Veneris.*" In *Essays presented to G. I. Lieftinck. Litterae textuales: A Series on Manuscripts and Their Texts.* Ed. J. P. Gumbert and M. J. M. de Haan. 2 vols. Amsterdam: A. L. van Gendt, 1972. 2:61-72.

A review of medieval and later works in which the rose figures as an erotic symbol. Following Knuvelder (see no. 346), King acquits Jean de Meun of a vulgar association of the rose with female genitals because the poet was "too clearly aware of a paradoxical mystery" (61) surrounding beauty, youth, virginity, and transitoriness. The author then proposes a new reading for the medieval Latin poem, *Pervigilium Veneris* (he provides reproductions of several manuscripts), and traces the erotic/virginal imagery of the rose in later authors, especially Dutch, including Gorter and Hooft. King concludes that "wherever love generates a tension between an instinctive urge and contemplative wonder, the rose has expressed this hybrid quality" (71).

340 Knoespel, Kenneth J. "Fable and the Epistemology of Expanding Narrative: An Example from the *Roman de la rose.*" *University of Hartford Studies in Literature* 17.2 (1985):28-48.

An examination of Nature's retelling of the fable of Mars and Venus caught in Vulcan's net (ll. 18031-099) in the context of a broad discussion of the narrative function of fables. The author argues that since Guillaume de Lorris and Jean de Meun see in Ovid's fables an invitation "to discover meaning" (30), the Ovidian fable of Mars and Venus is "not a simple rhetorical embellishment" (31) but a means of knowledge. It is specifically Nature's remarks on the use to which the lovers might have put a magnifying glass--an example of human technological innovation--that makes us reformulate the meaning of the fable. The fable is thus a lens both for "viewing our subsequent experience of the narrative" (41) and for integrating scientific knowledge.

341 -----. *Narcissus and the Invention of Personal History*. New York: Garland Publishing, 1985. Pp. xii + 160.

A study of Echo and Narcissus and their reception in the Middle Ages, in particular in the *Roman de la rose*. More specifically, the author looks at the way Ovid's fable "encourages the invention of narrative strategies that would explain and finally transcend Narcissus's experience" (ix). The first chapter analyzes the fable in the *Metamorphoses* by dividing it into nine sections and linking it to Theban history, psychological disturbance, and speech as a disruptive agent in history. Chapter 2 reviews some approaches to the fable by medieval mythographers, principally Arnulf of Orleans, John of Garland, and the *Ovide moralisé*. While showing ways to study fables, these commentaries "provided a ready body of exempla that could be drawn on, they created ground fertile for further meaning" (58). The third chapter describes both Guillaume's exploration of the physical phenomena of sight and the process of falling in love, and Jean's "ongoing strategy to criticize and finally replace Narcissus as the central fable in the *Roman*" (98), in part by the fable of Pygmalion. Thus the *Rose* as a whole uses fable to depict "adolescent change within amorous settings" (108). An appendix discusses the Narcissus fable in Renaissance epics by Boiardo, Spenser, and Milton.

342 Knowlton, Edgar C. "The Allegorical Figure Genius." *Classical Philology* 15 (1920):380-84.

An outline of "the presumable early history of Genius" (380) in the works of Bernard Silvestre, Alain de Lille, and Jean de Meun, with brief discussions of Claudian's *Second Panegyric on the Consulship of Stilicho* and Gower's *Confessio Amantis*. The author sees Jean's Genius as "peculiar" and "highly humorous"

(384). He is a "stump orator" (384) who re-parodies the courtly parody of church forms. [The article continues with no. 677, "Genius as an Allegorical Figure."]

343 -----. "The Goddess Nature in Early Periods." *Journal of English and German Philology* 19 (1920):224-53.

An introduction to the general study of the allegorical figure Nature. Knowlton shows the origin of the figure among the Greeks and Romans and traces its history in writings through the Middle Ages up to the Renaissance. In particular, Knowlton discusses the pre-Socratic idea of Physis and the Platonic notion of Natura. He also studies the Roman use of the figure Natura, including the texts of Seneca, Cicero, and the Elder Pliny. Noting that Natura had become a common personification used to adorn literature by the time of Seneca and Pliny, he presumes that it thus stimulated medieval writers. Works such as those of Bernard Silvestre, Alain de Lille, and Jean de Hauville are treated at length. Only brief mention of the *Roman de la rose* is made, noting that with the thirteenth century came a decline in the allegorical use of Natura in Latin and thus "the exuberance of the Latin literary enthusiasm over the device had passed and only the regular philosophical definitions or the brief conventional formulae were used" (251). [KML]

344 -----. "Nature as an Allegorical Figure." Diss. Harvard U, 1918.

345 -----. "Nature in Old French." *Modern Philology* 20 (1922/1923):309-29.

A review of the use of Nature as an allegorical figure in French literature of the thirteenth century. Citing his earlier article (see no. 343), Knowlton assumes that the medieval figure was based on Latin literature and tradition. He then discusses the use of the personification of Nature as hyperbole, as in Gautier d'Arras and Chrétien de Troyes. Knowlton also treats the use

of the figure by Simond de Freine, Alain de Lille, Alain
Chartier, and Jean Robertet. The *Roman de la rose* is studied in
a section noting that both the *Rose* and another work, *L'image
du monde*, combine encyclopedic interest with allegorical use of
Nature. The *Rose* is cited as the "Old French work which
employs Nature most extensively" (318). Knowlton discusses
both the principal meanings of the figure as used by Guillaume
de Lorris and Jean de Meun and also the scope of its use, the
philosophic background, and the "extension of the principle to
many aspects of life" (319). In concluding his discussion,
Knowlton also discusses alchemy and a few other uses of
Nature. In each case, he makes comparisons between those
examples and the use of the figure in the Rose. [KML]

346 Knuvelder, Gerard. "Het slot van de *Roman van de roos*."
Spiegel der letteren 9 (1965/1966):241-51.

An analysis of connotations of the rose symbol in the second
part of the romance. Knuvelder argues that Jean de Meun
probably intended the Rose to be viewed as the female
pudendum. The adaptors of the two Middle Dutch versions of
the *Roman van de roos* de-allegorize the narrative and stress the
physicality of the action. It is made clear that the Rose does *not*
stand for the beloved or her love, but for the female genitalia,
and that the plucking of the Rose represents the act of sexual
intercourse. [KB]

347 -----. "Roman van de Roos." *Handelingen van de
Zuidnederlandse Maatschappij voor Taal- en Letterkunde
en Geschiedenis* 22 (1968):263-303.

An introduction to the *Rose* for the Dutch-speaking reader that
takes as its point of departure a passage from Huizinga's
Herfsttij der Middeleeuwen (*The Waning of the Middle Ages*) with
which Knuvelder disagrees. In order to correct the false
impression of the representation of love in the *Rose* left by
Huizinga, Knuvelder gives narrative summaries of both parts of
the romance, followed by some critical analysis stressing their

conventional and innovative elements. With regard to Guillaume, Knuvelder stresses literary technique, and with respect to Jean, he considers that the idea of a coherent theocentric universe underlies all of the latter's work. Johannes Scotus Eriugena and Alain de Lille are seen as fundamental influences on Jean's world-view. For Knuvelder, Guillaume and Jean have basically antithetical conceptions of love--the former belonging to the twelfth century, the latter to the thirteenth--this in contrast to Huizinga's view. The final section of the study deals with the relationship of the two Middle Dutch versions, *Die Rose* of Heinric van Aken and the *Tweede Rose*, to the French original. [KB]

348 Köhler, Erich. "Narcisse, la fontaine d'amour et Guillaume de Lorris." In *L'humanisme médiéval dans les littératures romanes du XIIe au XIVe siècle*. Colloque organisé par le Centre de Philologie et de Littératures Romanes de l'Université de Strasbourg du 29 janvier au 2 février 1962. Ed. Anthime Fourrier. Actes et Colloques 3. Paris: Klincksieck, 1964. 147-66.

A reexamination of the meaning of the Fountain of Narcissus and its crystals. After summarizing articles by Jean Frappier and Hans Robert Jauss, the author points out that the only motif which Guillaume takes from Ovid's myth is the call for vengeance on those who scorn their lovers: reciprocal love has become law. Referring to medieval interpretations of the symbolic meanings of water, Köhler argues that the Fountain of Narcissus, which is also called the Fontaine d'Amors, is in effect a source of life in the *Rose*, not of death. Furthermore, the author argues that the two crystals magically reflect the dreamer's eyes, or rather his lady's eyes reflecting both his own and her soul, by means of which the dreamer gains self-knowledge. Thus Guillaume portrays "un amour courtois purifié" (162), sublimated by its detachment from concrete life and from history.

349 Kolb, Herbert. "Oiseuse, die Dame mit dem Spiegel." *Germanisch-Romanische Monatsschrift* n.s. 15 [46] (1965):139-49.

A study of the allegorical figure Oiseuse that focuses on her name and function. Her appearance, and especially her mirror, remind us of Luxuria, the vice that is the counterpart of Chastity or of other personifications like Vanitas and Prudentia. The author also does a comparative study of characters in medieval German literature. He goes on to interesting considerations of *vita activa*, *vita contemplativa* and its association with *speculum* and *speculatio*, and the derivation of Oiseuse's name from *otium*. Her function is related to knighthood's debate about the importance of leisure in a life full of action. Oiseuse symbolizes the transition from the *vita activa* of a secular society to a *vita contemplativa* separated from it. Her only role therefore consists in assuring the passage across this border. [ASK]

350 König, Eberhard. "'Atant fu jourz, et je m'esveille': Zur Darstellung des Traums im *Rosenroman*." In *Träume im Mittelalter: Ikonologische Studien*. Ed. Agostino Paravicini Bagliani and Giorgio Stabile. Stuttgart and Zurich: Belser, 1989. 171-82.

A study of the iconography of dreaming in *Rose* manuscripts. In the history of the romance's illustration, König argues that one can trace an important development of the iconography of dreams as well as a gradual change in what one thought to be a picture. In the beginning, the representations were a series of concepts juxtaposed in a rather syntactical manner. They could be read like sentences which, without any unity of space and time, were able to describe any type of reality. Most frontispieces, for example, show the awakening of the hero in a very realistic world. A few exceptions, however, contribute to the iconography of dreams, and in only one ms., from around 1405, the illustrator refers to the parallel with Macrobius mentioned by the poet and complements the lover's dream with the classical one, hence elevating the dream to a concept. [ASK]

351 Kubota, Katsuichi. "Sur la 'continuation' du *Roman de la rose*: monument d'un idéalisme." *Etudes de langue et littérature françaises* [Tokyo] 40 (1982):1-22.

An appreciation and synthesis of the ideas and language of Jean de Meun's continuation. The satiric spirit, exemplified by Faux Semblant and l'Ami, is an expression of "la pure volonté de connaître" (3). Faux Semblant, who reveals contradictions, expresses both a denunciation and an idealism concerning lay piety. Jean's "philosophie naturelle" (9) sees natural liberty as good if guided by reason and culture. The need for reconciling nature and reason leads Jean to condemn, through Genius, absolute asceticism. The author also points to Jean's respect both for experience and for books: in Jean's philosophy "l'esprit critique est fortifié par le respect de la littérature, de l'expérience et de la raison" (13). (When discussing Jean's sources the author suggests sources in Ovid and Virgil for two difficult lines, 15366 and 16256.) The final section is a study of certain linguistic aspects of Jean's "unité féconde" (19), such as negation and *tutoiement* or *vouvoiement*.

352 Kuhn, Alfred. "Die Illustration des *Rosenromans*." See no. 65.

353 Kunitzsch, Paul. "Das Abū Ma'šar-Zitat im *Rosenroman*." *Romanische Forschungen* 82 (1970):102-11.

354 Kupka, Paul. *Zur Chronologie und Genesis des "Roman de la rose"*. Beilage zum Jahres-Bericht der Städtischen Realschule zu Gardelegen. Gardelegen, 1901. Pp. 28.

A review of hypotheses concerning the date and method of composition of Jean de Meun's continuation and a summary of what can be stated with some certainty. In particular Kupka discusses assertions by the early editors of the *Rose*, by Paulin and Gaston Paris, and by Ernest Langlois, who disagree on such basic questions as Jean's age and the dates when he was working on the second part. Kupka evaluates several kinds of evidence, including statements in the prologues to Jean's translations, references to historical people and events in the *Rose*, and passages in which a character or the author discusses himself. Kupka concludes that unfortunately we can say little with confidence, except that "Jehan Clopinel ungefähr von 1256 bis 1285 an seinem Werke gearbeitet hat" (27). He believes that Jean must have worked on the romance for a long period of time and that this explains the apparent digressions and interpolations.

355 Lagarde, Georges de. *Secteur social de la scolastique.* Vol. 3 of *La naissance de l'esprit laïque au déclin du moyen âge.* 4 vols. Saint-Paul-Trois-Châteaux: Eds. Béatrice; Paris: E. Droz, 1934-1942. Pp. 422.

An inquiry into social theory in the thirteenth century that begins with an overview of the main tenets of Averroistic philosophy at the University of Paris. Lagarde cites brief passages from Jean de Meun's *Rose* on the influence of the stars, poverty, and the origin of royal power as examples of the "averroïsme estudiantin" (47) of the author. Jean is seen as invoking Aristotelian naturalism in order to scoff at Christian supernaturalism, and as calling on Christian traditions "pour rappeler à la modestie les autorités 'naturelles'" (58).

356 Lange, M. "Aus dem Roman von der Rose." *Schachzeitung* [Berlin] 15 (1860):30-39, 137-42.

357 Langlois, Ernest. "Anc. franç. *vizele.*" *Romania* 33 (1904):405-07.

A discussion of Old French *vizele* in which Langlois argues that earlier editors were mistaken in giving *videle* at l. 98 in the *Rose* instead of *vizele* or *visele,* which is found in more manuscripts and makes better sense. "A vizele" he believes can be translated by "a lacet" [basting or lacing?] and may refer either to laced sleeves or to a type of stitching. The Middle English *Romaunt of the Rose* gives a faithful translation: "With a threde basting my slevis (Skeat ed., 1.98)."

358 -----. *Origines et sources du "Roman de la rose"* [followed by *De artibus rhetoricae rhythmicae*]. 1890; rpt. Geneva: Slatkine Reprints, 1973. Pp. viii + 203.

One of three important works by this pioneer of *Rose* studies (see also nos. 6 and 66), and the first modern critical work that attempts to describe in detail the *Rose*'s sources. *Origines* is both an account of the classical and medieval works that the authors of the *Rose* may have used, and an attempt to understand how they used them (i.e., through translation, imitation, echoing, or transformation). In discussing Guillaume's part, Langlois believes that little or nothing is original; that the frame and everything it encloses--the precepts on love, the symbolism of the rose, the personifications, etc.--are imitated or inspired by earlier works, thereby limiting Guillaume's claim that "La matire est et bone et nueve" (l. 39) to a combination of earlier elements. Lack of knowledge about dates of composition, however, leads Langlois to posit as sources works that may in fact have been imitations (see his discussion of the "fableau du Dieu d'Amours," 32-34). In contrast to Guillaume's delicacy and elegance, Jean de Mcun's erudition and didactism are stressed. The second part is, according to Langlois, "un recueil de dissertations" (93) for which Jean borrowed from thirty-eight named authors, the most important of whom were Ovid, Boethius, and Alain de Lille, and from various mythographers and poets. Langlois often simply lists line-by-line borrowings, but he does at times attempt to find the specific medieval texts from which Jean drew his knowledge of Greek and Latin authors. By focusing on simple indications of borrowings, Langlois unfortunately misses the significance of these passages for the romance as a whole, as shown in his remark that in the Pygmalion episode (now believed to be a key to the second part) Jean "semble avoir perdu de vue le Roman de la Rose" (181). Includes a table of lines discussed from the *Rose* and a lexicon.

359 -----. "Le roman de la rose." In *Histoire de la langue et de la littérature française*. Ed. L. Petit de Julleville. 8 vols. Paris: Armand Colin, 1878-1900. 2:105-61.

An introduction to the *Rose*, including excerpts with notes translating difficult words, bibliographical information on the authors, and literary judgments. In agreement with most scholars before Gunn's *Mirror of Love* (no. 274), Langlois stresses the differences between the two parts: Guillaume combines a biographical plot with an art of love (that is, example and precept) in a gracious but transparent allegory; Jean is learned, immoral, prolix, and derivative, but a master of language ("un poète, le plus grand peut-être du XIIIe siècle" [147]). Langlois speculates that Jean's midpoint discourse on the two authors was added after the fact, that Jean suppressed the original ending, and that the continuation is so long because, lacking a plan, Jean did not know how much he was going to write. In a discussion of the success and influence of the *Rose*, Langlois tries to discredit the idea of the supposed pernicious influence of the allegory on later works by questioning the extent of that influence and by arguing that poets of genius could escape from it.

360 Lanly, André. "La hardiesse de pensée de Jean de Meun." *"Linguistique et philologie" (applications aux textes médiévaux)*. Actes du Colloque des 29 et 30 avril 1977, Université de Picardie, Centre d'Etudes Médiévales. Ed. Danielle Buschinger. Paris: Honoré Champion, 1977. 345-58.

An examination of the audaciousness of Jean de Meun's thought, which the author believes follows Plato and Aristotle while opposing certain aspects of Christian dogma. Through a discussion of some of the speeches of the second part of the *Rose*, especially that of Faux Semblant, Lanly stresses that Jean affirms natural (i.e., procreative) love but refers rarely or not at all to major Christian beliefs, such as resurrection. Jean is seen as a predecessor of the Reformation and of the Enlightenment, especially of Montesquieu, Diderot, and Rousseau.

361 Lanson, Gustave. *Histoire de la littérature française*. 3rd ed. Paris: Hachette, 1895. Pp. 1164.

An introduction to the *Rose* seen as the culmination of the didactic literature of the period. Guillaume's aristocratic code of courtly love reflects the cleric's mania for abstraction and allegory. Though all individualism has been removed from the story, the poet is still capable of individualizing characters and of expressing an almost pagan joy in the physical world. Between the two parts there is an absolute incompatibility, for Jean de Meun is characterized as a bourgeois pedant who pours "toute la science cléricale du XIIIe siècle" (127) into his poem. And his bourgeois thinking is reflected in his misogyny, anticlericalism, and criticism of the nobility. He is also an original and daring thinker who sees Nature as the source of all virtue. Although Jean's poem is "une suite de morceaux, qui s'accrochent comme ils peuvent" (133), it does not lack vigor and psychological drama. Finally, Lanson sees Jean as the first link in the chain that passes through Rabelais, Montaigne, and Molière to Voltaire.

362 -----. "Un naturaliste du XIIIe siècle: Jean de Meung." *La revue bleue* 4th ser. 2 (1894):35-41.

The first modern study which attempts to distinguish the distinctive characteristics of Jean de Meun's *Rose* and his place in literary history. Although the article presents conclusions to a reading of the text rather than the supporting arguments, it was influential for many years, in particular in two of its claims--that the two parts of the *Rose* are incompatible, and that Jean de Meun's part shows a vigorous natural philosophy while lacking a coherent structure. Like many scholars before and after him, Lanson attributes many of Jean's ideas--in particular his misogyny--to his supposed bourgeois origins. Jean de Meun was also a cleric, and his knowledge was encyclopedic: the second part is "une *somme*...des connaissances et des idées de l'auteur sur l'univers, la vie, la religion et la morale" (35). But this knowledge is given to the reader in a chaotic way; the work is "une suite de morceaux" (39). However, this lack of composition, of proportion, does not prevent Jean de Meun's "sérieux et solide naturalisme" (35) from coming through, nor does it destroy the poetry of his creation of memorable characters and scenes.

363   Larmat, Jean. "Le jardin de Déduit dans le *Roman de la rose* de Guillaume de Lorris." In *Mélanges de langue et de littérature médiévales offerts à Alice Planche*. Annales de la Faculté des Lettres et Sciences Humaines de Nice, Centre d'Etudes Médiévales, 48. 2 vols. Paris: Les Belles Lettres, 1984. 1:263-72.

A Christian reading of the first 1678 lines of the *Rose* which takes up, in order, the portraits on the wall of the garden (Tristesse, Vieillesse, and Pauvreté can be fitted into a Christian interpretation if they are given allegorical--spiritual--meanings); Oiseuse (the contemplative life); the carole (the dancers, Beauté, Richesse, and Largesse, are interpreted as attributes of God); the garden (paradise); and the rose (the Virgin Mary). Larmat's reading rests on two exegetical procedures: the text is sometimes read metaphorically (i.e., allegorically), as when the "joyeuse union de corps" (267) becomes an allegory for spiritual union; at other moments the metaphors of the text are taken literally, when, for example, Guillaume's comparison of birds to angels turns them into real angels. The author also uses other medieval works, in particular the *Tournoiement Antecrist* and Gautier de Coinci's *Miracles de Notre-Dame* to interpret the *Rose*.

364   Larsen, Judith Clark. "Proverbial Material in the *Roman de la rose*." Diss. U of Georgia, 1978.

365   Lecoy, Félix. "Sur la date du *Roman de la rose*." *Romania* 89 (1968):554-55.

The author had proposed, in the introduction to his edition of the *Rose* (see no. 7), the period of 1269-1278 for the composition of the second part. Based on the reference to the mendicant order called "les Sacs" in l. 12107, Lecoy proposes 1274, the date at which the order was abolished, as the *terminus ante quem* of the second part. Thus the *Rose* should have been well advanced, if not finished, about 1275.

366 -----. "Sur un passage délicat du *Roman de la rose* (v. 5532 de l'édition Langlois)." *Romania* 85 (1964):372-76.

"Por ce Amor a meilleur renon" (Langlois ll. 5532, Lecoy ll. 5502) presents a number of variants occasioned in part by the difficulty of the rhyme word, which Lecoy proposes to be the old form of the verb *renomer*, meaning "to name, declare to be, describe" rather than the noun meaning "fame," as Langlois gives in the glossary. After discussing the readings found in the major manuscript families, Lecoy considers some of the morphological and syntactic reasons for the difficulties that scribes had with the line.

367 Le Gentil, Pierre. *La littérature française du moyen âge*. Paris: Armand Colin, 1963. Pp. 207.

An introduction to the *Rose* seen as embodying the evolution of medieval literature and society in the thirteenth century. Guillaume's achievement was the creation of an art of love that was at the same time "le récit circonstancié d'un cas exemplaire" (132). His principal poetic qualities are youth, freshness, and charm: "Tout l'idéalisme médiéval est là, avec ses naïvetés et ses profondeurs" (133-34). Le Gentil, stressing the differences between the two parts, points to the numerous lengthy digressions which he believes interrupt the story in the continuation. Underlying the digressions is Jean's philosophy, whose best interpreter is Genius, a philosophy based on confidence in reason and nature and on physical love as necessary and good. Thus Guillaume satisfied a conservative courtly public while Jean interpreted the confusion and malaise of his time.

368 Leicester, H. Marshall, Jr. "Ovid Enclosed: The God of Love as *Magister amoris* in the *Roman de la rose* of Guillaume de Lorris." *Res publica litterarum* 7 (1984):107-29.

A perceptive study of le Dieu d'Amour as a character in the first part of the romance, as a teacher whose instructions reflect both the medieval view of Ovid as a compendium of amorous lore and Guillaume's questioning of the god's behavioral approach to love. After describing how Guillaume's relation to his courtly audience shapes the "performance" (114) of the poem, Leicester analyzes in detail the performance of le Dieu d'Amour, stressing his emphasis on external signs and institutions and his consequent insecurity in the face of possible betrayal. Guillaume suggests that the "*magister amoris* is out of date: he has lived so long that he now presides, not over a psycology [sic], but over a set of conventions" (123). [The article is marred by a number of misprints.]

369 Lejeune, Rita. "A propos de la structure du *Roman de la rose* de Guillaume de Lorris." In *Etudes de langue et littérature du moyen âge offertes à Félix Lecoy par ses collègues, ses élèves, et ses amis*. Paris: Honoré Champion, 1973. 315-48.

A detailed commentary on the first part of the *Rose* which proposes that a balanced structure underlies the work (see diagram, 346). Guillaume's courtly poem falls into seven parts: discovery of the garden, discovery of the earthly paradise, discovery of the fountain, discovery of the rose, the art of love, the kiss, and Jalousie's revenge, plus a prologue and epilogue. In her commentary, Lejeune emphasizes the poetic and oneiric effects of Guillaume's art of composition. Frequent references are made to similar medieval works and to the interpretations of other scholars. Finally, the author offers as evidence that the work is complete as it stands both the well-proportioned structure she has described and the lyric epilogue which brings the poem into the narrator's present time and which parallels the unsatisfiable desire expressed at the end of medieval *chansons courtoises*. (For a response, see no. 393).

370 -----. "Propos sur l'identification de Guillaume de Lorris, auteur du *Roman de la rose*." *Marche romane* 26 (1976):5-17.

An investigation into the identity of the historic Guillaume de Lorris. Scholars have almost invariably based their remarks concerning Guillaume on Jean de Meun's assertions in the second part of the *Rose*. Lejeune attempts to add to the historical background of this "personnage mystérieux, isolé" (5) in two ways: by describing the important relations that his native town, Lorris, entertained with the royal family, especially during the supposed period of composition of the *Rose* (ll. 1220-1236), and by bringing attention to Abbot Bernois's theory, proposed in 1914, that identified the author of the *Rose* with one of two men named Guillaume de Lorris, members of a noble family in the thirteenth century. Although Lejeune does not choose either Guillaume I le Sergent or II le Balistier, she argues that the investigation should be reopened.

371 Le Merrer, Madeleine. "Le sens éducatif du *Roman de la rose* de Guillaume de Lorris." In *L'enfance et les ouvrages d'éducation*. Ed. Paule-M. Penigault-Duhet. 3 vols. Nantes: Université de Nantes, 1983. 1:29-50.

For the author, the educational goal of the first part of the *Rose* proves to be the description of the lover's religious, even mystic, development. After a brief discussion of elements that point to Guillaume de Lorris's educational orientation (the narrator's promise to reveal what the allegory means, the hero's youth, the use of verbs such as *savoir* and *connaître*), the author compares the *Rose* to religious works, in particular to the second-century apocalyptic vision, the *Pasteur* of Hermas. Although she does not argue for direct influence, Le Merrer believes that both works participate in "un mode d'écriture symbolique, caractéristique d'une écriture apocalyptique" (42). Thus the *Roman* is "sans doute le lieu du passage du disciple à l'autonomie de l'être" (46), before the disciple becomes the Master and diffuses the divine word.

372 Lenient, C[harles Félix]. *La satire en France au moyen âge.* 3rd ed. Paris: Hachette, 1883. Pp. xviii + 437.

A survey of satire in French medieval literature that includes brief analyses of satire in the two parts of the *Rose*. The author can see no reason for the *Rose*'s popularity except the fact that it appeals to the two most popular passions in France, "la médisance et l'amour" (120). Lenient stresses the differences between the parts: the first expresses "toute la métaphysique amoureuse" (115) of chivalric society, the second is an audacious satire foreshadowing the Philosophes of the eighteenth century. Lenient approaches Jean's continuation in economic and political terms, interpreting Raison's remarks on avarice and Nature's on celibacy in terms of the politics of Philippe le Bel. After reviewing anticlerical and misogynistic satire in the second part, Lenient concludes with a discussion of Faux Semblant, the ancestor of Moliere's Tartuffe and "la création la plus vivante, la plus originale et la plus populaire du *Roman de la Rose*" (159).

373 Lepage, Yvan G. "Le *Roman de la rose* et la tradition romanesque au moyen âge." *Etudes littéraires* 4 (1971):91-106.

An analysis of how each part of the *Rose* expresses the aspirations and beliefs of a certain social milieu at a certain time in its history. Guillaume de Lorris's composition is "le dernier joyau de la tradition courtoise" (93), but it is not so much courtly love as "volupté" (93) which motivates l'Amant. The author explores the consequences for the romance's structure of the fact that the beloved is not the lofty lady of the lyric but a young girl. The second part of the *Rose* is a realistic and demystifying work, the expression of the spirit of an antifeminist, antifeudal, and anticourtly bourgeoisie. An Aristotelian naturalist, Jean de Meun was sympathetic to such diverse causes as the bourgeois communal movement, Guillaume de Saint Amour, and the autonomy of the University of Paris. His work is "le premier et unique *roman de moeurs urbaines* du Moyen Age français" (106; author's emphasis).

374 Levy, Raphael. "Le rôle de la charaierresse dans le *Roman de la rose.*" *Neophilologus* 36 (1952):75-79.

A philological discussion of the word "charaierresse" (l. 9300), a term of abuse which the jealous husband applies to his wife. In opposition to the generally accepted translation of "sorcière," Levy proposes something more like "prostituée" (78). His evidence comes both from French and Judeo-French occurrences of the word and is, he argues, more appropriate to the context in which it appears in the *Rose*.

375 Lewis, C. S. *The Allegory of Love: A Study in Medieval Tradition.* 1936; Oxford: Oxford UP, 1958, 1977, and 1978. Pp. 378.

A landmark study of the *Rose* in the context of allegorical love poetry by the well-known English medievalist and writer. Lewis attempts to reconstruct "that long-lost state of mind for which the allegorical love poem was a natural mode of expression" (1). He reads both as a literary historian, concerned to understand the literary work in its context and traditions, and as a critic, willing to pronounce on matters of quality and taste. Chapters on courtly love and the development of allegory from the late classical period through the school of Chartres prepare the modern reader to approach the *Roman de la rose* (Chapter 3) with "sympathetic understanding" (112) (at least for the first part; Lewis has little sympathy for the second). Because Lewis sees allegory as painting our inner world of conflicting sentiments, he responds warmly to Guillaume de Lorris's depiction of the emotional qualities of the lover and especially of the beloved, the "most important actors in the drama" (122). He has less interest in the "neutral qualities" (120) (le Dieu d'Amour, Deduit, Courtoisie, and the like), none at all in the "doctrinal part of [Guillaume's] work" (130). This same principle underlies Lewis's treatment of Jean de Meun's "huge, disheveled, violent poem" (137), whose major failing is lack of unity: the major characters in the second part are seen as "digressions" (141). Disinterested in allegory, Jean was a writer of instruction ("the best of popularizers" [143]), satire, and nature poetry, among other subjects. His misfortune was "to have read and remembered everything" (151) and to have incorporated it into his poem. Thus while describing in often memorable phrases the distinctive characteristics of the two parts of the *Rose*, Lewis stresses their profound stylistic and thematic differences. *The Allegory of Love* also contains chapters on Chaucer, Gower, and *The Faerie Queene*.

376 Louis, René. *Le roman de la rose: essai d'interprétation de l'allégorisme érotique*. Nouvelle Bibliothèque du Moyen Age 1. Paris: Honoré Champion, 1974. Pp. 150 + 3 figures.

An essay on the erotic significance of the *Rose*. Although Louis examines both parts, he clearly favors the first, for which he proposes an original interpretation: virtually all the allegorical elements--the garden, all the personifications, the rose bush, the castle--represent the young woman, her interior world, her feelings and characteristics. Oiseuse is her portrait, and the rosebud itself represents simply "le charme le plus désirable" (28), that is, her sexual favors, with which the narrator falls madly in love. Thus social milieu, family, and friends "ne jouent strictement aucun rôle dans l'action" (13). Citing Virgil and Tibullus, Louis argues that the ambiance of the first part is "profondément païenne" (45), in contradiction with the Christian spirituality of the period. Jean de Meun is seen as a traitor for destroying this hedonistic creation through his "conception dépoétisée et dépersonnalisée" (93, chapter title) of the romance, in particular through his crude language, misogynistic view of women, and parody of pious practices. The study includes many passages rendered in modern French and references to many other writers and artists, including Charles d'Orléans, Botticelli, and Apollinaire.

377 Luria, Maxwell. *A Reader's Guide to the "Roman de la rose"*. Hamden, Conn.: The Shoestring Press, Archon Books, 1982. Pp. xiv + 282.

A good introduction that includes a great deal of information.

172 The *Roman de la rose*: An Annotated Bibliography

Luria discusses nearly all the basic topics, such as manuscripts, editions, and translations; allegory and satire in the *Rose*; the poem's reception; Chaucer and the *Romaunt*. Aids to reading include outlines and a summary of the work, glossaries of personifications and allusions, excerpts (in English) from relevant Latin, French, and English works, and an excellent basic bibliography.

378 Lynch, Kathryn L. *The High Medieval Dream Vision: Poetry, Philosophy, and Literary Form*. Stanford: Stanford UP, 1988. Pp. xiv + 263.

An approach to Jean's part of the *Rose* in terms of the subgenre of the philosophical vision and the way the *Rose* reshapes earlier examples of the vision. Lynch argues for the need to reexamine Jean's thinking in the context of the profound philosophical challenge to the medieval world view occurring in the latter part of the thirteenth century (as exemplified by the Condemnation of 1277). Jean responded to Guillaume's generic conflict between le Dieu d'Amour and Raison by affirming Raison as the true guide. The dreamer's rejection of her is indicative of his incapacity for moral development, which is "a controlling theme in the poem" (129). He cannot see, for example, that all other authorities in the poem are defective. Thus Jean sought to modify Bishop Tempier's condemnation of reason by conservatively arguing for the synthesis of reason and faith. Yet despite Jean's belief in reason, the poem sees the visionary quest as a failure, and this failure reflects pessimistically on poetry's ability to yield truth.

379 Lyons, Faith. "Some Notes on the *Roman de la rose*--the Golden Chain and Other Topics in Jean de Meun." In *Studies in Medieval Literature and Languages in Memory of Frederick Whitehead*. Ed. W. Rothwell et al. Manchester: Manchester UP; New York: Barnes and Noble, 1973. 201-08.

Brief discussions of three philosophical topics touched on by the character Nature: the Golden Chain that binds creation, man's free will, and the phoenix. After pointing out that the idea of the Golden Chain has been misunderstood by earlier scholars, in particular by Paré (see no. 419), Lyons traces the idea in medieval writers from Macrobius to Bernard Silvestre. Unlike his immediate source, Alain de Lille, Jean "uses the golden chain in a context that is entirely physical, and devoid of any spiritual feeling" (202). As with this topic, those of free will and of the phoenix (an example of the eternity of species) are given original expression in the *Rose*. Lyons concludes that the poet "handles general truths in unique fashion, however time-worn his material" (208).

380 Maler, B. "La prophétie d'Albumasar dans le *Roman de la rose*." *Studia neophilologica* 11 (1945/1946):47-48.

381 Mancini, Mario. "Servo e padrone in Jean de Meun." In *XIV⁰ Congresso internazionale di linguistica e filologia romanza, Napoli, 15-20 aprile 1974; Atti V*. Ed. Alberto Várvaro. Naples: Macchiarolli; Amsterdam: John Benjamins, 1981. 469-79.

A new interpretation of Jean de Meun's references to the Golden Age. Mancini rejects Milan's conclusion (see no. 396) that the opposition between nature and the social or political covenant, already present in Seneca and Augustine, is typical of medieval thought. To strengthen his argument, Mancini quotes Thomas Aquinas, for whom man is essentially a political animal: the question, then, becomes that of dominance, a central issue in the philosophical debate of the second half of the thirteenth century. In evaluating Jean's views, it is necessary to take into account this ongoing *questio*: if Raison preaches "sofisance" (479), resignation to Fortune's will, Nature is the voice of "franchise" (472), which once, under Saturn's rule (see Genius's monologue), was the original condition of both men and women. [MRB]

382 Marcinkowska, Zuzanna. "La prison amoureuse de Guillaume de Lorris." *Médiévales* 14 (1988):103-12.

An approach to the first part of the *Rose* through the idea of "l'espace artistique" (104). Several important places--the prairie, the garden, the fountain, the castle--are shown to be "noeuds dramatiques" (111) which reflect psychological movements in l'Amant. Furthermore, Guillaume's spatial language translates the rules of courtly love. The progressive narrowing of the l'Amant's space suggests, for Marcinkowska, changes in the emotional climate and l'Amant's loss of liberty.

383 Mason, Patricia E. "The Pronouns of Familiarity and Respect in the *Roman de la rose* and its Middle English Translation." In *Literary and Historical Perspectives of the Middle Ages*. Proceedings of the 1981 SEMA Meeting. Ed. Patricia W. Cummins, Patrick W. Conner, and Charles W. Connell. Morgantown: West Virginia UP, 1982. 66-77.

A comparative study of the use of *tu* and *vous* (based on manuscript readings given in Langlois's edition; see no. 6) in the *Rose* with *thou* and *ye* in the late fourteenth-century English translation. Both regularities of usage and "a number of cases of switching between *thou* and *ye*" (69) are described. Although Mason argues that it is an oversimplification to say that "the Old French use of *tu* and *vous* reflects semantic distinctions made solely on the basis of the speaker's feelings of respect or familiarity towards his interlocutors" (72), she does indicate that pronoun usage in most cases reflects relationships of hierarchy or equality. The main difference between the two versions is the English use of *thou* as the pronoun of address among "friends and power equals" (72), while the French version uses *vous* in that context. Charts of French and English usage are given in appendices.

384 Massieu, Guillaume. *Histoire de la poësie françoise*. Paris: Prault fils, 1739. Pp. viii + 349.

An introduction to the *Rose*, focusing on the authors' strengths and weaknesses and on the poem's influence. In Massieu's time the *Rose* was considered "le meilleur de tous les Ouvrages de Poësie qui ont été faits avant François I" (165). Guillaume's poetic talent lay in description and portraits, and his language was more pure and flowing "qu'on ne devroit l'attendre de la grossiereté de son siècle" (169). Jean de Meun was, according to common opinion, a Doctor in Theology and, Massieu assures us, limped [it seems we know less about Jean de Meun today than we did in Massieu's time]. Both authors are criticized for the goal of their work, to teach the art of the most dangerous of passions, whose pains and dangers they described to the point of discouraging would-be lovers. Massieu points to the digressive form of the poem ("Jean de Meun s'égare à l'infini" [191]) and its disdain for women, and he criticizes Jean further for using improper language, for joining frivolous and religious topics, and for speaking ill of women and clerics. Although anathematized "dans toutes les Chaires" (192) in the Middle Ages, the poem's reputation continued to grow. Finally, Massieu proves that Abelard could not have been the author of the romance, as some Moderns claim.

385 Mazzoni Peruzzi, Simonetta. *Il codice laurenziano Acquisti e Doni 153 del "Roman de la rose"*. Società Dantesca Italiana: Centro di Studi e Documentazione Dantesca e Medievale 3. Florence: Le Lettere, 1986. Pp. 76 + ill.

A study of the corpus of eighty-nine illustrations which decorate the Laurenziano manuscript of the *Rose*, second only, by number of miniatures, to the Parisian codex B. N. fr. 24892, which has 115. Langlois and Kuhn recognized the importance of this manuscript, but the analysis of the relationship between text and illustration, especially close in the Laurenziano codex (see use of sideheads), represents the novelty of Mazzoni Peruzzi's work. As for authorship Mazzoni Peruzzi advances the hypothesis of a "maestro della *Rose* laurenziana" (72) with a personality different from Jean Pucelle's but probably also working in one of the "ateliers" of rue Eremburg-de-Brie where this manuscript might have been conceived as a shop sampler:

this function would explain its format, atypical for such a precious codex. [MRB]

386 McCaffrey, Phillip. "*Le roman de la rose* and the Sons of Narcissus." *Mediaevalia* 11 (1985 [1989]):101-20.

An approach to the perennial question of l'Amant's relation to Narcissus through a reexamination of the Ovidian myth and its "sons," that is, other classical and medieval versions. These versions allow McCaffrey to distinguish three significant features of l'Amant's experience which differ from those of Ovid's Narcissus: the nature of the love object, the possibility of winning that object, and l'Amant's lack of awareness that "the rosebud may be a displaced narcissistic reflection" (101). With the additional aid of developmental psychology, the author defines and clarifies the narcissistic Idol and l'Amant's relation to it in the *Rose*. His conclusion points to the lady of courtly literature as also a form narcissistic Idol: "romance [sic] love is, by definition, narcissistic" (112).

387 McKean, Sister M. Faith, R.S.M. "The Role of Faux Semblant and Astenance Contrainte in the *Roman de la rose*." In *Romance Studies in Memory of Edward Billings Ham*. California State College Publications 2. Hayward: California State College, 1967. 103-07.

A discussion of Faux Semblant's reflection in the "Miroër aus Amoreus" (Jean's alternate title for his part; l. 10621). The author argues that this mirror is limited in that it reflects human love "to the deliberate exclusion of the supernatural" (104); therefore, it is consistent that the romance's only representatives of chastity are in effect the enemies of chastity. It is not consistent, however, that Faux Semblant's gravest sin is avarice instead of lust, an inconsistency that must be understood in the light of Jean's opposition to the mendicant friars. Thus Faux Semblant and *amie* are "the snarl in the allegory" (106). In the end, the author suggests, in opposition to Gunn's views (no. 274), that while the *Rose* is only about human love, Faux

Semblant is not about love at all.

388 Means, Michael H. *The Consolatio Genre in Medieval English Literature*. University of Florida Humanities Monograph 36. Gainesville: U of Florida P, 1972. Pp. v + 105.

A brief discussion of the *Roman de la rose* (32-43) as background to a number of medieval English poems that incorporate elements of the "consolatio genre" (1), as established by Boethius's *De consolatione Philosophiae*. The impact of the genre was reinforced by the *Rose*, which offered English poets "a new model" (32) because it incorporates most of the consolation elements into a poem differing in subject and intent from Boethius's. Means's study, based on his doctoral dissertation, focuses on Guillaume de Lorris's part, arguing that le Dieu d'Amour's instructions are the first and most important consolation in the poem and that everything in the dream that precedes it is preparation for it. Jean de Meun saw the dialectical materials as the most important part of his predecessor's poem and developed them at the expense of allegorical action. The book also treats the *Divina commedia*, *Pearl*, *Confessio Amantis*, and other works.

389 Méla, Charles. "Le miroir périlleux ou l'alchimie de la rose." *Europe* 654 (October 1983):72-83.

A dense meditation on the alchemical secret that is mystically expressed in Guillaume's dream primarily through "la Rose mystique" (77) and the liquid mirror and crystals of the Fountain of Narcissus. The author's interpretation relies on various kinds of word play and reading between the lines which allow him to make connections between images in the *Rose* and alchemical concepts and images. Thus l'Amant's quest for the Rose is seen as a quest for the joy/jewel (*joyau*) of the philosopher's stone: a joy that "brille au coeur de sa joie de tous les feux d'un joyau pur, pierre philosophale ou pierre de paradis" (83).

390 Ménard, Philippe. "Jardins et vergers dans la littérature médiévale." In *Jardins et vergers en Europe occidentale (VIIIe - XVIIIe siècles)*. Flaran, Journées internationales d'histoire 9. Auch: Comité Départemental du Tourisme du Gers, 1989. 41-69.

A brief discussion of the garden in the first part of the *Rose* (62-64)--the pleasure garden as men long imagined and wished it to be--in the context of an historical and philological review of garden information and terminology in France in the twelfth and thirteenth centuries, based both on scientific and literary works. Guillaume includes traditional elements--the walls, grass, trees, birds, flowers, and pool--while developing them into "un assemblage rêvé" (62) which mixes native and exotic species. This abundant, generous nature, where lovers are shaded from harsh elements, expresses the festive, voluptuous setting desired by refined people of the time. [Includes eleven reproductions of garden scenes in medieval mss.]

391 -----. "Les représentations des vices sur les murs du verger du *Roman de la rose*: le texte et les enluminures." In *Texte et Image*. Actes du Colloque international de Chantilly (13 au 15 octobre 1982). Paris: Les Belles Lettres, 1984. 177-90.

A study of the relation of text to iconography based on forty *Rose* manuscripts (selected from the estimated 100 illuminated manuscripts of the *Rose*), and focusing on the series of miniatures which depict the vices on the wall of the garden. Ménard reviews the meanings of the terms used to designate the vices, technical difficulties in representing the figures, and the interplay of traditional and original elements. The last section discusses possible sources for Guillaume's ensemble: the author rejects Kuhn's theory of the *Psychomachia*'s influence (see no. 65) and stresses the originality of Guillaume's invention: "Une bonne moitié des personnifications... paraît inconnue de l'art chrétien et semble tout à fait neuve" (189). Includes four color reproductions of *Rose* miniatures at the end of the volume.

392 -----. *Le rire et le sourire dans le roman courtois en France au Moyen Age.* Geneva: Droz, 1969. Pp. 802.

A wide-ranging study of various manifestations of "le comique, le burlesque, la satire, la parodie, le badinage, l'ironie, l'humour" (11) in courtly romances, including the first part of the *Rose*. The subjects of humor in the *Rose* include old age and the other infirmities on the wall of the garden, which represent "défauts abhorrés du monde courtois" (161) and which appear only in Guillaume's *Rose*. Ménard also discusses briefly such topics as courtly gaiety and good humor, picturesque metaphors, and the hyperbole of the lovers' paradise (in which he sees no "irréligion" [646]).

393 Meyer, Gertrud. "A propos de la structure du *Roman de la rose* de Guillaume de Lorris." *Romanistische Zeitschrift für Literaturgeschichte* 2 (1978):265-68.

A critique of the structural analysis of the first part of the *Rose* proposed by Rita Lejeune (see no. 369), particularly of the use of Provençal lyric as an interpretive tool for northern French romance and the use of the narrator's remarks ("insertions du narrateur" [266]) to mark divisions in the romance. In turn, Meyer proposes a structure based on the principle of a series of obstacles followed by a) "éléments statiques" (267), all of which are messages of one kind or another, b) overcoming the obstacles, usually with the help of a "gatekeeper," and c) a new experience. Thus, according to Meyer's proposed structure, "l'oeuvre n'est pas achevée" (268).

394 Miguet, Thierry. "L'escarboucle médiévale, pierre de lumière." *Marche romane* 29.3-4 (1979):37-60.

A sometimes mystical meditation on the meaning of the legendary carbuncle in medieval literature. Miguet twice touches on the *Rose*: first, to suggest that the use of "chambrière" (l. 16748) to describe Nature's relation to God is an alchemical reference to the carbuncle, often seen as the

Philosopher's Stone; second, to refer the reader to the long passage in which Genius describes the marvelous carbuncle that illuminates the Park of the Lamb (ll. 20495-566). [While Miguet does not discuss this passage in detail, his comments on the carbuncle's meanings in medieval literature help to explain the characteristics of Genius's gem.]

395 -----. "L'ésotérisme de Villon." In *Etudes. . . Lanly* (no. 230). 239-62.

Includes a discussion of possible alchemical allusions in Jean de Meun's part of the *Rose* (see no. 701).

396 Milan, Paul B. "The Golden Age and the Political Theory of Jean de Meun: A Myth in *Rose* Scholarship." *Symposium* 23 (1969):137-49.

An examination of what validity there may be in scholarly theories that references to the Golden Age reveal Jean de Meun's supposed bourgeois or Averroistic ideas on government and society. (Four characters--Raison, l'Ami, la Vieille, and Genius--refer more or less openly to the myth of the Golden Age.) The study comprises a review of scholarly opinion from Lanson to Müller, a summary of the characters' discourses in the *Rose*, and a brief history of classical and medieval ideas on the Golden Age and on equality, including those of the church fathers and medieval lawyers. Milan concludes that the theme of the Golden Age is neither bourgeois nor Averroist, and that the characters' use of the myth for purposes of argumentation do not constitute "a program of radical social reform" (148). Certainly we cannot say that their ideas are "the personal views of Jean de Meun" (148).

397 Miller, James Lester. "Vision of the Cosmic Dance in Western Literature from Plato to Jean de Meun." Diss. U of Toronto, 1979.

398 Mölk, Ulrich. "Deux livres récents sur le *Roman de la rose*." *Romanistische Zeitschrift für Literaturgeschichte* 2 (1978):269-74.

A review article discussing Karl August Ott's introduction to his translation of the *Rose* (see no. 39) and Jean-Charles Payen's *La rose et l'utopie* (no. 433), both of which speak to nonspecialists and focus on Jean de Meun's part. After a summary of Payen's analysis of Jean's continuation, in which Mölk finds "le vrai centre de son idéologie" (270) in the fact that Jean was a cleric living in an urban, university milieu, Mölk summarizes Ott's arguments for Jean's conservative, orthodox, clerical thought. Finally, Mölk evaluates Ott's arguments for the bourgeois origins of Guillaume de Lorris and concludes that Guillaume's romance reflects Latin, especially goliardic, poetry, which expresses a "rêve d'un bonheur érotique tout privé" (274).

399 Morel-Fatio, A. "Châteaux en Espagne." In *Mélanges offerts à M. Emile Picot par ses amis et ses éléves*. 2 vols. Paris: Librairie Damascène Morgand, 1913. 1:335-43.

A discussion of whether Guillaume de Lorris invented the phrase "châteaux en Espagne" (Langlois l. 2432), as part of a discussion of Robert Gaguin's contacts with Spain (c. 1465-1468). The author points to the often ironic use of the expression or similar ones in French epics beginning in the thirteenth century, to refer both to Charlemagne's legendary generosity and to noble lords' empty promises. Morel-Fatio believes that the spirit in which the phrase is used "consiste à tourner en ridicule la machinerie déjà usée de notre vieille épopée" (342). Therefore he argues that the meaning of the phrase in the *Rose* is clearly "se repaître de chimères" (340) (contradicting Thuasne's interpretation of the phrase as equivalent to doing something useless; see no. 522) and that it was current in Guillaume's time.

400 Muela Ezquerra, Julián. "Técnicas retóricas y producción del sentido en el episodio de Pigmalión del *Roman de la rose*."

In *La lengua y la literatura en tiempos de Alfonso X*. Actas del Congreso Internacional, Murcia, 5-10 marzo 1984. Ed. Fernando Carmona and Francisco J. Flores. Murcia, Spain: Departamento de Literaturas Románicas, Facultad de Letras, Universidad de Murcia, 1985. 373-92.

An analysis of rhetorical techniques in the Pygmalion episode and their relation to the larger poetic meaning of the romance. The first part focuses on important changes and amplifications that Jean made in Ovid's briefer version of the myth, in particular on the significant shift from presenting Pygmalion as a woman-hater to an overreaching sculptor. The author argues that the themes of open/hidden and of natural/ornamented which recur in Jean's retelling are linked to his conception of the limits of art. The second part of the analysis describes the techniques and structure of Pygmalion's love monologue, again showing that what appear to be imbricated rhetorical passages of questioning, comparison, and digression reflect the character's relation to other mythical-literary lovers.

401 Müller, Franz W. *Der "Rosenroman" und der lateinische Averroïsmus des 13. Jahrhunderts*. Frankfurt am Main: Vittorio Klostermann, 1947. Pp. 47.

An interpretation which advocates that Jean de Meun's continuation is not simply a reflection of the cultural atmosphere of his time, or a harmless vulgarization of scholastic commonplaces, but is directly affected by the radical Aristotelianism of the arts faculty of which he was a member. In that period there were three philosophical currents at the Sorbonne: the first was the traditional, scholastic philosophy of Neoplatonic-Augustinian influence, the other two were linked to the reception of Aristotelianism. However, while the Dominicans under the direction of Albertus Magnus and his disciple Thomas Aquinas pursued the reconciliation of religious belief with the system of the Stagirites, a large number of the arts faculty represented the radical Aristotelism called Latin Averroism. This heresy contravened the Christian teachings in four main points: the denial of divine providence in the realm of contingency; the denial of the Creation through the concept of the eternity of the world; the denial of free will because of the influence of the stars on human actions; the numeric unity of the soul, thus the denial of individual mortality. Müller argues that most of these points are present in a disguised form in the *Rose*. To mention one example, Jean's knowledge of the eternity of species results in a triumph of life in Eros and leads to a radical vitalism, where God as the highest good is replaced by lust. [ASK]

402 Müntz, Eugène. "Iconographie du *Roman de la rose*." *Académie des inscriptions et belles-lettres, comptes rendus* 4th series 27 (13 January 1899):15-16.

A brief summary of a paper on the importance of the *Rose* in medieval art. In addition to illuminated manuscripts, Muntz mentions tapestries and ivories which portray characters and scenes from the romance, including the siege of the Castle of Jalousie. The author also suggests the influence of the *Rose* on Petrarch's *Trionfi*.

403 Muscatine, Charles. "The Emergence of Psychological Allegory in Old French Romance." *PMLA* 68 (1953):1160-82.

An analysis of allegory that, following C. S. Lewis's leading remark that romance before Guillaume de Lorris adapted or borrowed allegory, traces in detail the development of psychological (as distinguished from moral or cosmological) allegory in dozens of romances preceding the *Rose* in order to show how extensive allegory was in romance and how it developed certain specific literary techniques. After describing realistic situations in medieval romances that parallel those of the *Rose* and mentioning the literary and cultural conditions relevant to the development of psychological allegory, including the introspection of mysticism, Muscatine shows how the inner monologue developed in Old French romance to include techniques of dialogue that became debates or conflicts between more or less personified voices. In many romances, the inner voices became full-fledged dramatic personifications, but Muscatine argues that, unlike moral allegory, these personifications remain expressions of individual psyches, not prescriptive abstractions. Thus it is not the Prudentius tradition that explains the allegory of the *Rose* but "the romance matrix" (1179); the "procedures of romance psychology" (1181) prepared Guillaume's audience for his poem, "our first full-scale psychological novel" (1182).

404 Nichols, Stephen G., [Jr.] "Ekphrasis, Iconoclasm, and Desire." In *Rethinking* (no. 182). 133-66.

A study of the function of ekphrasis ("the description of a visual art work" [133]) as a conflict between word and image in Virgil's *Aeneid* and in the first part of the *Rose*. Nichols predicates a tension between the sensual and immediate (the image) on the one hand, and the rational and conceptual (the word) on the other. The comparison of the *Aeneid* and the *Rose* is based on the perception that both Aeneas and l'Amant "encounter a set of ekphrastic portraits painted on walls of spaces in which each will undergo a formative lesson in love" (136). While Aeneas learns through Virgil's ekphrasis to privilege logic over emotion, l'Amant's ekphrastic rhetoric is the beginning of the *Rose*'s exploration of "the venereal gaze" (150). Nichols turns to an analysis of six illuminations of the uncourtly vices on the garden wall, and in particular illuminations of Envy, from three manuscripts in the Pierpont Morgan and the University of Pennsylvania Libraries, in order to show how "the illuminations reveal the psychodrama inherent in the poetic allegory" (152). The miniatures reveal, he concludes, how ekphrasis is "ever on the verge of being parodied by the allegory of its own mimetic desire to be image" (157).

405 -----. "The Rhetoric of Sincerity in the *Roman de la rose*." In *Romance Studies in Memory of Edward Billings Ham*. Ed.

Urban T. Holmes. California State College Publications 2. Hayward: California State College, 1967. 115-29.

An analysis of the authority of the narrator and the characters in the *Rose*. Whereas Guillaume de Lorris invests authority equally in the "three-way hookup between author, lover, and Amour" (118), Jean de Meun both distances himself from the lover and compromises his characters' authority by revealing their subjectivity: in Jean's world, "no single code is privileged" (125). Nichols illustrates this argument with an analysis of Raison's lecture. Thus Jean, the "master rhetorician" (120), forces us to discover the meaning of the work for ourselves, something l'Amant never seems to do.

406 Nisard, Désiré. *Histoire de la littérature française*. Vol. 1 of 4 vols. 10th ed. Paris: Firmin Didot, 1883. Pp. 502.

An introduction to the *Rose* [with some errors], in the context of the development of French literature from its infancy to maturity. Guillaume's part is seen as the transposition of a *roman de chevalerie* into the framework of a dream; simply a kind of art of love, it is inoffensive. Nisard praises the delicacy and "la naïveté d'une langue naissante" (175) of the poet. Jean, on the other hand, is praised for his encyclopedic knowledge, satiric verve, and independence of thought. His characters, who differ greatly from Guillaume's, appear to be the same people grown older. A long section analyzes the vigorous portrait of Faux Semblant, compared several times to Molière's Tartuffe. A short section reviews the influence of the *Rose* and includes a summary of Jean Gerson's treatise. After defending Jean de Meun against charges of being boring or decadent, the final section explains his success as a result both of his expression of general ideas (the only basis of progress in the arts: "la poésie antérieure n'était qu'un sommeil" [193]) and of "l'esprit français" (195), comprised of clear-sightedness, humor, and "l'amour du mot propre" (197).

407 Nitzsche, Jane Chance. *The Genius Figure in Antiquity and the*

Middle Ages. New York: Columbia UP, 1975. Pp. xi + 201.

A study of the "bewilderingly diverse array" (ix) of forms and associations linked to the allegorical figure, Genius, in classical and medieval literature and thought. Nitzsche focuses on "representative types and forms" (x) in the works of Bernard Silvestre, Alain de Lille, Jean de Meun, and Gower. These figures are analyzed in terms of the "four descents" (44) of man with which Genius is associated: the descent into the sublunary realm at birth, the descents of man's soul into fleshly desires or into knowledge, and the artificial descent into the demonic. In answer to the critical difficulty of relating Genius's two roles of generation god and priest in the *Rose*, Nitzsche proposes that Jean "links both roles by using the natural and virtuous descents as analogues" (117), thereby sidestepping the apparent contradiction between the roles. Thus Genius's dual role is seen as a brilliant synthesis of the ideas of Bernard Silvestre and Alain de Lille.

408 Notz, Marie-Françoise. "*Hortus conclusus*: réflexions sur le rôle symbolique de la clôture dans la description romanesque du jardin." In *Mélanges de littérature du Moyen Age au XXe siècle offerts à Mademoiselle Jeanne Lods par ses collègues, ses élèves et ses amis.* Collection de l'Ecole Normale Supérieure de Jeunes Filles 10. 2 vols. Paris: L'Ecole Normale Supérieure de Jeunes Filles, 1978. 1:459-72.

An essay on the symbolism of certain elements in the traditional motif of the enclosed garden as a place of happiness in medieval French literature. In her discussion of "une phénoménologie de l'espace" (460), the author focuses on the meaning of enclosure and of the tree-fountain pattern at its center. Evidence from authors both medieval (Chrétien de Troyes, the *Rose* poets) and modern (Louis-Ferdinand Céline) suggests that the circumference of the garden is not imposed from without but results from a movement of appropriation from the center, and that enclosures exist in medieval literature to be entered. Notz further analyzes the symbolic meanings of the contrast between the overall shape of the gardens and their central trees in the two parts of the *Rose*--a square enclosure around a pine in Guillaume's part, a circular one around an olive tree in Jean's.

409 Nouvet, Claire. "Dangerous Resemblances: The *Romance of the Rose*." *Yale French Studies*, Special Issue "Contexts: Style and Values in Medieval Art and Literature" (1991):196-209.

An analysis of the "peculiar play of resemblance between speech and song" (197) in the first part of the *Rose*, in particular through examination of the passages describing birds and birdsong. The cliché of the birds recalls the courtly song, in which birds figure the lyric voice. In the *Rose*, the song of the birds "transports" (198) the dreamer both emotionally, as a sign of joy, and physically, by leading him up to and into the garden. Nouvet interprets the detail of the birds being placed in the four corners of the garden as indicating not only the "inaudible spacing" (201) of music but also the relation of difference and of spacing set up between sounds in speech. The concept of spacing or difference is further suggested by the nonresemblance of the birds to birds (they are said to resemble angels) and of Deduit to himself (he is said to resemble a portrait). The author argues finally that the speaking voice in the *Rose* "seems to be discreetly and quite elegantly cut off" (207) at the point where it asserts itself, thereby suggesting "an infinite movement toward speech, toward the possibility of addressing speech" (209).

410 -----. "Les inter-dictions courtoises: le jeu des deux bouches." *Romanic Review* 76 (1985):233-50.

A complex analysis of the linguistic gaps, suppressions, and breaks between the signifier and the signified in both courtly and non-courtly language in the *Rose*. Certain characters illustrate this "coupure" (235)--the Rose, le Dieu d'Amour, Courtoisie and her dress, and the courtly lover himself, who must mutilate his speech into silence or autocensorship. The

Rose thus realizes "l'impossibilité structurale de représenter la jouissance" (240), an impasse which makes possible the proliferation of courtly writing. Nouvet argues finally that the *Rose* represents "l'évacuation de *tout* signifié" (241), that desire itself is shown to be a missing signified.

411 Nykrog, Per. *L'amour et la rose: le grand dessein de Jean de Meun*. Harvard Studies in Romance Languages and Literatures 41. Cambridge: Department of Romance Languages and Literatures of Harvard University, 1986. Pp. 98.

An analysis of Jean de Meun's *dessein* (meaning both design and intention), in the course of which the author considers a number of related questions. An introductory chapter argues, from the fact that Jean de Meun waited for 6,500 lines to identify himself (in ll. 10565-66), that the continuation has a "structure compositionnelle" (9). After a chapter on Guillaume's *Rose*, Nykrog gives a "lecture analytique" of the continuation in eight short chapters that discuss such topics as the differences between Jean's rosebud and Guillaume's; the false counselors, including Raison, l'Ami, and la Vieille; the allegorical meaning of the hand-to-hand combats; Nature's view of man's "aberrations" (53); Genius as spokesman for the author; the misogyny of the pilgrim passage; and finally, in a few pages, the historical and theological context in which Jean was writing. Nykrog argues that Jean's "structure textuelle intégrée" (79) combines *l'amour, la morale*, and *la cosmologie*, and that Jean's most deeply-held belief is that we should all return to making love joyfully and freely, without any sense of sin (see especially 70 and 81), an hypothesis which rests on Nykrog's acceptance of Genius as Jean's spokesman.

412 O'Leary, Susan Jane. "A Semiotics of Allegory (an Allegory of Semiotics): A Study of Guillaume de Lorris' *Roman de la rose*." Diss. U of Wisconsin, 1980.

413 Ott, Karl A. *"'Armut' und 'Reichtum' bei Guillaume de Lorris."* In *Beiträge zum romanischen Mittelalter.* Ed. K. Baldinger. Tubingen: Max Niemeyer, 1977. 282-305.

A study of the crucial roles of poverty and wealth in Guillaume's part of the *Rose*, an aspect neglected by nearly all critics except Batany and Poirion (see nos. 157 and 451), with whose analyses though Ott does not agree. He argues that most critics take for granted that the *Rose* is a courtly work and are therefore startled by Jean's uncourtly continuation. Ott points out that the garden of Deduit includes the qualities of pleasure generally rather than specifically courtly virtues, and this garden of pleasure is equal to a garden of wealth. The narrator is surprised at his entry into that paradise because he is not used to such luxury and wealth. The lover is taught how he can obtain esteem (for example, le Dieu d'Amour tells him to put on better clothes but not to ruin himself for this reason); he has to appear distinguished and noble. Therefore, these are not inherent qualities of our protagonist. Furthermore, the beloved lady is never characterized in her individuality but only by belonging to a rich and noble family. Thus this dream about the acceptance into a beautiful world would logically not be dreamed by a youth born into the higher ranks of society. Hence the *Roman de la rose* is about the conception that a bourgeois has of courtly life; this is the reason for its unrealistic, idealized picture of courtly life, its juxtaposition of reality and dream. [ASK]

414 ------. "Jean de Meun und Boethius: Über Aufbau und Quellen des *Rosenromans.*" In *Philologische Studien: Gedenkschrift für Richard Kienast.* Heidelberg: Carl Winter, 1978. 193-227.

An article that deals mainly with the structure and sources of the *Roman de la rose*. Ott objects strongly that scholars, in order to determine the social status, historical situation, or interpretation of the romance, have hardly ever used the fact that Jean de Meun gave preference to specific sources in his continuation. Instead, critics speak merely of the heterogeneous, encyclopedic accumulation of ancient knowledge. However, the unusually high number of sources is in glaring contradiction to the evident predilection for only four authors: Ovid, Boethius, Alain de Lille, and Guillaume de Saint Amour. Ott says further that the question of why there are three theological works besides Ovid should represent a basic problem in any analysis of sources. He also agrees, to a certain extent, with Gunn (see no. 274) that Jean de Meun has respected the thematic and formal unity of the first part of the romance, composing the continuation according to the rhetorical principle of *amplificatio*. [ASK]

415 -----. "Neuere Untersuchungen über den *Rosenroman*: Zum gegenwärtigen Stand der Forschung." *Zeitschrift für romanische Philologie* 104 (1988):80-95.

A review article that examines six recent books on the *Rose*: Badel's *Le roman de la rose au XIVe siècle* (no. 572), Strubel's *Le roman de la rose* (no. 515), Dufournet's collection of articles (no. 231), Fleming's *Reason and the Lover* (no. 241), Hult's *Self-fulfilling Prophecies* (no. 305), and Nykrog's *L'amour et la rose* (no. 411). While summarizing some of the main points of each study, Ott also subjects it to an often stern evaluation. For example, he points out that Badel took so long to complete his study that he was unable to take recent studies into account; Struble is accused of saying the same old thing in new jargon; Hult's language is attributed to the demands of the American university system; the articles in Dufournet's collection contradict each other; and Fleming's discussion of l'Amant's reference to Carthage misses the point of the passage on friendship. Ott also refers at points to his own work on the *Rose*.

416 ------. "Pauvreté et richesse chez Guillaume de Lorris." *Romanistische Zeitschrift für Literaturgeschichte, Cahiers*

d'histoire des littératures romanes 2 (1978):224-39; discussion 239-40.

The French version of no. 413. The author raises the question of Guillaume's almost universally accepted courtly origin and concludes that if "c'est le monde courtois que Guillaume idéalise, ce monde serait vu par quelqu'un qui n'y appartenait pas" (240). In support of his argument that Guillaume was bourgeois, the author discusses the importance accorded to Richesse and the incompatibility of this figure with the courtly world and courtly love; the narrator's wonder before the marvels of the garden of Deduit and its life of pleasure; possible allusions to a city (Paris?); Guillaume's recommendations for reasonable spending on gifts; the meaning of the dream framework and of Guillaume's claims for the dream's veracity. Going beyond questions of literary history, Ott explores the literary consequences of his hypothesis for the *Rose*. [Although he overstates the evidence at times, generally avoids talking about the courtly aspects of love in the *Rose*, and makes improbable assumptions about medieval classes (that the nobility did not value wealth, for example), Ott does raise fundamental questions about the complex meanings of courtliness for *Rose* criticism.]

417 -----. *Der Rosenroman von Guillaume de Lorris und Jean de Meun*. Erträge der Forschung 145. Darmstadt: Wissenschaftliche Buchgesellschaft, 1979. Pp. vi + 222.

A synopsis and critique of modern criticism of the *Rose*, with all its contradictions and uncritical premises. Ott believes that scholars have not understood the reasons for the *Rose*'s amazing popularity: it characterized a style which was its own antithesis, that is, it was historically an exceptional case. The author argues that one source of scholarly error has been assumptions about the courtliness of the first part and the bourgeois views of the second. Ott argues that this hypothesis leads to a too-easy explanation of the immense difference between the two parts. He also points out the need to consider a work of the thirteenth century in its context, contrary to traditional critics, who tried to find their own ideas in the *Rose*. Consequently Ott emphasizes the importance of Jean's sources for any interpretation. A chapter is devoted to the Robertsonian interpretation (see no. 473), its advantages and errors. The Robertsonians recognize the importance of manuscript illustrations, of the different voices of the author, the narrator, and the lover, and finally of the romance's ironical structure. But Ott rejects certain Robertsonian interpretations, such as the association of the garden of Deduit with Eden. The author, who feels that we are still far from the crucial interpretation of the romance as a whole, argues that Jean wrote an ironical continuation, and this can only be proved by comparing identical elements in the two poems. Ott concludes that Jean postulated against a total idealization of love in which the conquest of the rose is equivalent to the entrance to an earthly paradise. [ASK]

418 Paré, Gérard. *Les idées et les lettres au XIIIe siècle: "Le roman de la rose"*. Bibliothèque de Philosophie 1. Montreal: Université de Montréal, Centre de Psychologie et de Pédagogie, 1947. Pp. 363.

An examination and synthesis of Jean de Meun's ideas on God, the physical universe, human nature, and love as expressed by the major personifications, especially Raison and Nature (the study consists in large part of summaries of ideas expressed by the personifications). Paré begins with a semantic and philosophical study of key words and themes in the *Rose*, then places them in their scholastic context, that is, in the turbulent currents of thirteenth-century Aristotelianism at the University of Paris. The components of Jean's cosmology and morality are compared to the ideas of his twelfth-century Chartrian predecessors (i.e., Alain de Lille) and to contemporary thinkers such as Albertus Magnus and Thomas Aquinas. Paré finds that in all respects but one Jean's thinking is both orthodox and not particularly original--the one exception is the primordial importance of procreation in his system of values. Thus Paré argues that we must modify earlier appreciations of Jean's "rationalisme ou...naturalisme intégral" (304): his views on nature and reason are compatible with the Christianized

Aristotelianism of his time. Furthermore Jean's emphasis on procreation is seen as the basis for his "négation radicale de l'amour courtois" (341), while his interest in cosmology and moral philosophy lies behind his desire to popularize current scientific theories for the lay public.

419 -----. *Le "Roman de la rose" et la scolastique courtoise.* Publications de l'Institut d'Etudes Médiévales d'Ottawa 10. Paris: J. Vrin; Ottawa: Institut d'Etudes Médiévales, 1941. Pp. 210.

An earlier version of *Les idées et les lettres* (no. 419), which discusses the scholastic context of Jean de Meun's ideas on man, nature, God, and the cosmos. (For the phrase "scolastique courtoise," see Gorce, no. 265).

420 Paris, Gaston. *Esquisse historique de la littérature française au moyen âge (depuis les origines jusqu'à la fin du XVe siècle).* Paris: Armand Colin, 1907. Pp. 319.

A short introduction to the *Rose* which stresses both the differences between the two parts and what Paris sees as their failings. Guillaume de Lorris, "un jeune clerc de l'Orléanais" (194), invented the personification of the "dispositions momentanées" (196) of an individual in order to express refined love, but unfortunately his invention gave the impetus to a completely false allegorical literature in the following centuries: his new style of mythology was "funeste à la poésie française" (196). Jean de Meun, on the other hand, was a bourgeois thinker whose poem, "hardi, cynique, nullement religieux" (198), is characterized by prolixity, platitudes, and digressions. Paris sees, surprisingly, la Vieille's discourse as the center of the poem. While strongly attacked, according to Paris, in the fourteenth century, Jean's romance inaugurates modern literature, characterized by "la pensée philosophique et la connaissance de l'antiquité" (201).

421 -----. *La littérature française au moyen âge (XIe-XIVe siècle)*. 5th ed. Paris: Hachette, 1914. Pp. 352.

A short section on the *Rose* introduces and summarizes the poem and evaluates the differences between the two authors and their merits. Paris stresses the predecessors and influences on the first part but sees originality in Guillaume's creation of personifications which are "des manières d'être passagères" (162) rather than general qualities. While praising Guillaume's ingenious and subtle art, Paris's hostility to allegory leads him to blame the poem as preventing realistic observation and true sentiment. Jean de Meun, called "le Voltaire du moyen âge" (166), receives a harsher judgement for his lack of form and taste. [Note that Paris mistakenly gives the source of Nature's speech as Alain de Lille's *Anticlaudianus* rather than his *De planctu Naturae*.]

422 Paris, Paulin. "Le roman de la rose." In *Histoire littéraire de la France*. Vol. 23. Paris: H. Welter, 1895. 1-61.

An overview of what was known about the *Rose* and its authors at the time and a summary of the love story which emphasizes the "physiologie" (3) of love, omits the episode of the Fountain of Narcissus, and reduces the importance of the Art of Love. While Guillaume is described as clear and precise, Jean de Meun is erudite and libertine and talks about everything except real love. L'Ami's speech is praised for its boldness and originality, and Nature's confession is "un grand poëme didactique" (40). As for the ending, since according to Paris everyone knows it, he cites only the last two lines. He suggests that many of the apparently gratuitous episodes may have been composed by Jean earlier and inserted in his continuation. Paris also reviews the Querelle de la Rose and discusses the manuscripts and incunabula of the *Rose*. A final section discusses the Marot and Molinet versions.

423 Patch, Howard R. *The Goddess Fortuna in Mediaeval Literature*. Cambridge: Harvard UP, 1927. Pp. xii + 215 + ill.

A detailed study, based on the author's dissertation, of "the composite portrait of Fortuna in the Middle Ages" (35), which Patch traces "not chronologically but *en masse*" (35). The *Rose* is frequently cited among the many French, English, Latin, and Italian works surveyed, thereby suggesting that Fortune, as she appears in Raison's long description, shares many characteristics not only with her direct predecessor in Alain de Lille's *Anticlaudianus* but also with many other medieval works that discuss the goddess. These characteristics include her blindfold; her daughter, Nobility; the unceasing turning of her wheel; her connection with love; and her assistant, Poverty. Patch points out that Raison's description of her dwelling begins the French tradition which "appears again in Lydgate's *Disguising at London*, where, with an acknowledgement of indebtedness to the *Roman*, the author speaks of Fortune's dwelling" (128).

424 Paulmy, Antoine René, Marquis de. *De la lecture des livres françois, considérée comme amusement*. First part. Vol. 4 of *Mélanges tirés d'une grande bibliothèque*. Paris: Moutard, 1780. Pp. 379.

A brief discussion of the *Rose* in a history of the progress "de notre stile & de notre langage" (6), for the amusement of ladies. The author suggests that Guillaume de Lorris's real name was Guillaume de Machaut [proving that there is progress in literary scholarship] and that he died in 1260; Jean de Meun is believed to have written at the beginning of the fourteenth century. Paulmy describes the *Rose* as eclectic, containing morality both good and bad, portraits, and critical reflections, among other things. A few excerpts are given to show Guillaume's style; while admiring the meditation on time and the portraits on the garden wall, the author finds the most remarkable passage to be la Vieille's proclamation of free love [which he apparently attributes to Guillaume de Lorris]. A later section on Jean de Meun recounts the apocryphal story of how he outwitted a group of ladies outraged by his misogynistic remarks. Paulmy attributes to Jean works on alchemy, in addition to his translations, and refers several times to Jean's lameness which earned him the surname Clopinel [the spelling given in some manuscripts].

425 Payen, Jean-Charles. "Amour, mariage et transgression dans le *Roman de la rose*." In *Amour, mariage et transgressions au moyen âge*. Actes du Colloque des 24, 25, 26 et 27 mars 1983, Université de Picardie, Centre d'Etudes Médiévales. Ed. Danielle Buschinger and André Crépin. Goppingen: Kümmerle, 1984. 335-47.

An interpretation of the second part of the *Rose* which sees it as proclaiming the universal law of procreation, as Nature, Genius, and Venus tell us. The author views Jean de Meun as a "provocateur" (335) engaged in transforming "la loi en transgression et *vice versa*" (335). Man's original transgression, the "vrai péché originel" (337) which lost him the Golden Age, was the breaking of Nature's laws. Because sexuality that leads to fecundity is the ideal, Jean de Meun condemns homosexuality and abstinence, thereby implicitly rejecting the Christian conception of virginity as saintliness. Payen suggests a carnivalesque inspiration, also manifested in the fabliaux and goliardic poetry, in Jean's inversion of official values in favor of "un environnement social plus libre" (341).

426 -----. "L'art d'aimer chez Guillaume de Lorris." In *Etudes...Lorris* (no. 231). 105-44.

A long, close reading of Guillaume's teachings on love, seen as a lesson for and model of the "'honnête homme' du XIIIe siècle" (144). The "stratégie aristocratique" (108) revealed in the *Rose* euphemistically hides l'Amant's physical desires. Sources of this carnal-courtly view of love are discussed, in particular the goliardic poem, "Carmen de Rosa," André le Chapelain's *De amore*, and Bernard de Ventadour's Chanson 31. Despite the assertion of love's physicality, however, Payen also argues that the personifications in the *Rose* spring from a diffuse Platonism. Further comments on love include: the arrows of le Dieu d'Amour follow the medieval five stages of love; the god's commandments teach a worldly sociability; *fin'amors* (courtly love) is an heroic adventure in which only the most worthy triumph; and the Rose is an adolescent girl awakening to desire (and enjoying being forced...). This study of the *Rose* as both a *Bildungsroman* and a manual for the well-bred suitor presents an image of the Lover as an adventurous, hot-blooded, and egocentric young womanizer who will not take "no" for an answer.

427 -----. "Attention au *Roman de la rose!*" *Les nouvelles littéraires* 2561 (2 December 1976):8.

A pre-publication announcement and summary of the author's book, *La rose et l'utopie* (no. 433). Payen stresses Jean de Meun's theory of utopic communism and sexual liberation and sees in him a precursor of the Philosophes of the eighteenth century, the socialists of the nineteenth, and the ecologists of the twentieth.

428 -----. "Le comique de l'énormité: goliardisme et provocation dans le *Roman de la rose*." *L'esprit créateur* 16 (1976):46-60.

A study of the presence, in the *Roman de la rose* and other French works in the period 1250-1280, of *goliardisme,* defined both as Biblical parody and a naturalistic philosophy opposed to Christian *contemptu mundi*. Payen, arguing that the influence of goliardic texts "a été déterminante" (47) on Jean de Meun, gives as principal examples Genius's monologue and the recurring image of the two paths to salvation. Jean de Meun is not simply amusing his audience--rather, he is intentionally if indirectly attacking the church's rejection of the pleasures of this world. In comparison to the more superficial parody found in other works of the period, such as *Aucassin et Nicolette*, which Payen discusses briefly, Jean de Meun's provocation is "un projet corrosif qui se fonde sur une revendication plus ou moins humaniste" (57). Finally, Jean's goliardism masks itself behind the enormity of its provocation.

429 -----. "Eléments idéologiques et revendications dans *Le roman de la rose*." In *Littérature et société au moyen âge*. Actes du Colloque des 5 et 6 mai d'Amiens 1978. Ed. Danielle Buschinger. Amiens: Université de Picardie, 1979. 285-304.

A summary of the author's ideas on the ideological claims of the *Rose*, in which Payen describes the poem as "une série de revendications" (285). While Guillaume de Lorris expresses the aspirations of a young urban cleric who hopes to gain admission to the courtly garden, Jean de Meun, also an urban cleric, has much loftier demands, including material and political advantages for clerics, the end of sexual repression, and especially the utopian ideal "de bonheur et de plaisir" (290). By selecting from a number of characters' speeches, especially from Nature's, whom Payen considers beyond doubt "le porte parole du poète" (288), the author argues for Jean de Meun's "épicurisme très charnel" (290) and his hedonism "qu'il justifie par la procréation" (291). And although Jean does not make any demands on behalf of women, Payen argues that he believes in conjugal love and equality as part of his hope for a better humanity.

430 -----. "L'espace et le temps dans *Le roman de la rose*." *Romanistische Zeitschrift für Literaturgeschichte* 2 (1978):253-58. Rpt. in *Etudes...Lanly* (no. 230). 287-99.

An analysis of the "spatiotemporalité respective" (287) of the two parts of the *Rose*, with emphasis on Jean de Meun's. Payen focuses on the three spatiotemporalities of "le récit," "le discours," and "le locutif" (287), that is, of the speakers in the text. Beginning with the prologue, Guillaume superimposes several levels of time. The spatiotemporality of the second part, however, is much more complex, for Jean de Meun questions and enlarges his predecessor's dream world by introducing distances foreign to the garden of Deduit and new temporal levels of myth and contemporary history: "L'intemporalité du roman allégorique est alors corrigée par son insertion dans un contexte à la fois intellectuel et politique" (292). Finally, the Pygmalion myth holds the key to the meaning of the second part, for it suggests a utopic spatiotemporality constituted by "un faisceau chaleureux de tendresse entre l'homme, la femme et l'enfant" (296), that is, a better mankind.

431 -----. "Genèse et finalités de la pensée allégorique au Moyen Age." *Revue de métaphysique et de morale* 19 (1973):466-79.

A series of philosophical observations on medieval allegory, and on the *Roman de la rose* in particular, as "toute une représentation du réel" (466) which is profoundly ideological. Allegory, that is, personification, is seen as a projection of thought "dans l'univers des essences" (467), a pedagogical mode of discourse, a revelation of higher truths, and a view of the world and the mind as the site of conflict between forces more powerful than the individual. Allegory's goal of rendering in concrete images the abstract essence of things leads to a utopian view of "un univers rêvé, rectifié, corrigé" (477) where absolute evil cannot exist. However, this Platonic goal of the representation of essences through images leads Payen to criticize medieval allegory as a form of alienation through fantasy.

432 -----. "Le *Roman de la rose* et la notion de carrefour idéologique." In *Romanistische Zeitschrift für Literaturgeschichte* 1 (1977):193-203.

An analysis of the ways in which Jean de Meun's part of the *Rose* is a crossroad of medieval ideologies, in particular the bourgeois, the clerical, and the courtly. Selected passages illustrate ideas or values associated with each of these ideologies, thereby suggesting that the poet attempted "une synthèse de ces héritages dispersés, sans tout à fait parvenir à les organiser de façon cohérente" (193). The ideas which Payen finds in the *Rose* on work and exchange, on spending or hoarding, suggest that Jean had fairly conservative bourgeois attitudes. Yet he is also described as "une sorte de goliard en langue vernaculaire" (200), inclined to criticize power and to celebrate sexuality. Finally, according to the author, Jean combatted a courtly ideology which denatured man, while accepting implicitly its principles of transgression and "dépassement" (202).

433 -----. *La rose et l'utopie: révolution sexuelle et communisme nostalgique chez Jean de Meung*. Classiques du Peuple "Critique". Paris: Editions Sociales, 1976. Pp. 271.

An introduction to the *Rose* that is at once summary, source study, and interpretation of Jean de Meun's philosophy. Through the analysis of ten characters, Payen traces a progressively provocative conception of society and morals. The resistance of Danger and friends to l'Amant is simply a way of glorifying his conquest of the rose; Raison's speech "s'attaque à la fois la *fin'amors* et à la morale chrétienne traditionnelle" (28), thus preparing "une sexualité triomphante" (36); l'Ami describes by means of the myth of the Golden Age a new sexuality and a utopic anarchism; Faux Semblant is a protestation "contre les manoeuvres et les combines des intrigants et des imposteurs" (104); la Vieille, Nature, Genius, and Venus express the omnipotence of natural law, especially concerning sexuality. Furthermore Genius makes pleasure innocent by associating it with God in a return to the Golden Age. Thus, Guillaume is seen as cultivating an egocentric passion while Jean "prône une érotique expansive dont le terme est le jaillissement de la vie" (230).

434 -----. "A Semiological Study of Guillaume de Lorris." Tr. Margaret Ann Leff. *Yale French Studies* 51 (1974):170-84.

An analysis of the "process of elaboration of the figures of speech" (170) in the first part of the *Rose*. The author gives the text a number of readings: literal (the narrative of an amorous quest); tropologic (the transposition of the courtly code of conduct, especially through didacticism); and anagogic ("a more general conception of the human experience" [170]). Especially in the last two readings, the author points out inconsistencies and shifts in the *actants*, both allegorical and symbolic, which reveal an evolution in the poet's thought. This semiological reading approaches a description of the process by which Guillaume de Lorris created his complex work: "he invents his figures of speech as his narration requires them" (180). The positing of an "existential semiology" (181) in the *Rose* leads Payen to warn that we cannot systematize our reading; the semiological ruptures in the text are the reflection of Guillaume's view of love as profoundly disruptive.

435 Peden, Alison M. "Macrobius and Mediaeval Dream Literature." *Medium aevum* 54 (1985):59-73.

A detailed analysis of the possible influence of general theorists of dreams, in particular of Macrobius, on writers of medieval dream and vision literature. The author outlines the growth and decline of interest in Macrobius based on codicological evidence and on references to his theory in medieval works, in the context of the widening of dream theory. The author argues that this is helpful background to interpreting the *Roman de la rose*, which established "the dream-vision form" (66). Peden questions Dahlberg's interpretation of the use of Macrobius in the *Rose* (see no. 203), in particular his approach to Nature's remarks on dreams. The article concludes with a discussion of Chaucer's possible familiarity with Macrobius's theory and of the influence of Nature's sermon on him.

436 Pelen, Marc M. *Latin Poetic Irony in the "Roman de la rose"*. Vinaver Studies in French 4. Liverpool: Francis Cairns, 1987. Pp. ix + 181.

An approach, through Ovid, Boethius, and other Latin writers, to the question of Jean de Meun's irony and how it may point us to the poetic unity of the continuation of the *Rose*, "an orthodox work of Christian irony" (40). After considering briefly

Guillaume de Lorris's "blend of academic seriousness and erotic comedy" (4), Pelen focuses on the search for "a systematic alternate meaning" (13) behind the ironic contradictions and inadequacies of the major speakers. As background to Jean's use of irony, Pelen explores "practical techniques of Latin poetic irony" (39) in poems written before the *Rose*. Ovid's poems are shown to establish ironic distance between poet and narrators in order to suggest a better world represented by the "better art of the poet himself" (47). Similar themes and techniques are described in the medieval Latin poem, "Carmen de Rosa"; the *Altercatio Phyllidis et Florae*; the *Metamorphosis Goliae*; and Alain de Lille's *De planctu Naturae*. These satiric works "assume the comic devices of Ovid, whereby a speaker's erotic interests become the ideal measure of all other human energy" (95), but they also use the irony for a Christian purpose. Pelen's discussion of the *Rose* shows how Jean uses Ovidian devices to create ironic inversions of Boethian themes and doctrines. Jean mocks the theses of "practical charity, friendship, chastity, freedom, natural generation and paradisal salvation" (163) propounded by his partisan authorities--Raison, l'Ami, the jealous husband, la Vieille, Nature, and Genius--in order to allude to a spiritual meaning, one allied with Augustinian charity, that is beyond their comprehension.

437 Pensom, Roger. "L'allégorie de Guillaume de Lorris." *Studi francesi* 78 [26.3] (1982):450-57.

A critique of Fleming's approach to the *Roman de la rose* (see no. 243) as methodologically untenable for several reasons, principally for treating the text and illustrations as if they were "deux codes parallèles" (450) which can be used to interpret each other, for using Jean de Meun to interpret Guillaume de Lorris, and for ignoring details of the text in favor of a thesis. Pensom's objections focus on three parts of Fleming's reading: the moral interpretation of the figures on the garden wall, the equation of Oiseuse with Luxuria, and the crystals in the Fountain of Narcissus with human vision. Rejecting Fleming's reductionist approach, Pensom argues that Guillaume's allegory should be read as a language where different paradigmatic elements interact syntagmatically to suggest a one-world view in which the sacred and profane are intertwined.

438   Pfeffer, Wendy. "Reflections of Narcissus." *Revue de l'Université d'Ottawa, University of Ottawa Quarterly* 55 (1985):15-22.

A study of how Guillaume de Lorris adapted the Ovidian version of the story of Narcissus for a medieval audience. After a summary of Ovid's version and of Vinge's analysis of it (see no. 536), Pfeffer points out the important changes that Guillaume made, such as removing both supernatural elements and physical transformations, setting the fountain in a lively rather than a lifeless environment, omitting any presentation of character, and including an explicit, and very medieval, moral. The author argues that such source studies are not only examples of medieval textuality but also means to understanding Guillaume's transformation of the dreamer into the lover.

439   Pickens, Rupert T. "*Somnium* and Interpretation in Guillaume de Lorris." *Symposium* 28 (1974):175-86.

An analysis of Guillaume's understanding of Macrobius's theory of the *somnium*, the type of dream in which "what will happen is veiled" (176) in allegories and ambiguities, an understanding which structures the first part of the *Rose*. The meaning of the dream is revealed through the interaction of its three layers: "the dream, its fulfillment, and the interpretation" (177). Pickens describes in detail how these three layers function and by what signs they reveal themselves in the poem. He argues, for example, that the narrator's generalizations about his experience belong not to the dream but to the interpretative layer, as do the "pre-history" (181) of Narcissus and of the conflict between Venus and Chasteté. The author concludes that the action of the first part is incomplete "because the narrator's comprehension of the *somnium* is imperfect" (184).

440 Piehler, Paul. *The Visionary Landscape: A Study in Medieval Allegory*. Montreal: McGill-Queen's UP, 1971 [first published London: Edward Arnold, 1971]. Pp. 170.

An approach to medieval vision allegories as "manifestations of a certain type of psychic experience in medieval literature" (1), that of a spiritual crisis, a vision involving a spiritual authority, the interpretation of that vision, and the resolution of the crisis. This conception of allegory sees it as the expression of mythic, pre-rational, intuitive elements related to the Jungian archetype. While concentrating on the visionary landscape in which the authority manifests itself, Piehler also discusses related elements such as the seminal image, the dialogue between the narrator and the authority, and symbols associated with the vision. The garden in the first part of the *Rose* is "a surrender to the wilderness in its deceptively benevolent aspect" (99), an idealized reflection of castle gardens of the period as symbols of "a private and limited morality" (101). Piehler points out Guillaume's power both to suggest great implications in seemingly casual descriptions and to express subtly "the process of succumbing to temptation" (103). In Jean's continuation, dialogue supplants landscape. While the authorities' discourses fit into their immediate setting, Jean ultimately fails to establish their hierarchical relationships. Includes discussions of Statius's *Thebaid*, Boethius's *De consolatione Philosophiae*, Servius's gloss on *Aeneid* I.314, the *Architrenius* of Jean de Hauville (which Piehler sees as having had a considerable influence on the *Rose*), and parodies of love, including André le Chapelain's *De amore*.

441 Planche, Alice. "L'odeur, le coeur et la clarté: sur un motif du *Roman de la rose*." *Romania* 105 (1984):359-67.

A survey of the occurrences and functions of the recurring motif of perfumes and related olfactory sensations in the *Rose*. Planche alludes to medieval attitudes toward smell and its importance as an intermediary between the material world and the immaterial and concludes that odor in the *Rose* "prête à la polysémie, mais aussi à l'équivoque" (366).

442 -----. "Les robes du ciel: autour d'une image de Jean de Meun."
　　　　Romania 98 (1977):349-66.

A three-part discussion that begins with the description of a storm and flood in the second part of the *Rose* (especially ll. 17889-996). Planche considers in turn Jean de Meun's poetic techniques of description, the three literary "courants qui alimentent" (354) this passage, and vestimentary images in later French poets. The detailed poetic analysis focuses on the poem's complex "va-et-vient" (353) between meteorological phenomena and the social systems of fashion and the expression of the sentiments. Planche concludes that Jean's esthetic used "la métamorphose comme motif et la métaphore comme moyen" (354) to suggest that the sensible and mental worlds are mutually referential. In the two following sections, the author establishes links between Jean's images of clouds and floods and similar images in three influential predecessors, Ovid, Boethius, Guillaume de Lorris (for the image of sewing one's sleeves) and in Jean's "successeurs" (366), including Charles d'Orléans, Ronsard, d'Aubigné, Victor Hugo, and Mallarmé. Her conclusion is that poets have seen the world as a unity in which the elements (in both senses) are in correlation.

443　Poirion, Daniel. "Alain de Lille et Jean de Meun." In *Alain de Lille, Gautier de Chatillon, Jakemart Gielée et leur temps*. Actes du Colloque de Lille, octobre 1978. Ed. H. Roussel et F. Suard. Publications de l'Université de Lille III. Lille: Presses Universitaires de Lille, 1980. 135-51.

A reexamination of the often-discussed question of Jean de Meun's debt to the twelfth-century Chartrian philosopher, Alain de Lille, in the context of a reflection on literary history and its methods. Three questions can be asked of the relationship between the two authors: did Alain influence Jean's theory of love; did he suggest to him a theory of nature; did Jean find in his predecessor's works a theory of God's relation to nature? Rather than clear-cut answers, Poirion suggests possible directions in which Jean may have been influenced in these areas and ways that he diverged from the earlier writer, as in his greater emphasis on a philosophical culture "plus ou moins indépendante de la théologie" (138). Since the *Rose* is poetry, Poirion also considers Jean's treatment of Alain's theory of the poetic integument, the truth under the cover of fiction. Furthermore, although Jean knew Boethius's work, he used principally Alain's poems to construct his "consolation."

444 -----. "De la signification selon Jean de Meun." In *Archéologie du signe*. Ed. Lucie Brind'Amour and Eugene Vance. Toronto: Pontifical Institute of Mediaeval Studies, 1983. 165-85.

A study of an important mutation that was taking place in French literature between the times of Guillaume de Lorris and Jean de Meun "au niveau de la langue, de l'idéologie, des formes mêmes de l'imaginaire" (166), and the ways the authors of the *Rose* reflected this "crise de la signification" (165). Jean de Meun turned away from the signifying system of courtly language, the fundamental source of meaning in the first part, to look for a more direct language that could express without euphemism both the nature of the world and of sexuality. Poirion analyzes Jean's conception of language primarily through Raison's stress on the arbitrariness of the sign, thereby undermining the power of symbols: "on n'a plus foi dans le symbole" (175). Revelation through symbolism is replaced by logical and discursive unveiling of meaning. Jean reuses generic sign systems from comedy, epic, *summa*, parable and myth in his search for the language of reason, a natural language. In this polyphonic romance, it is finally "la sensualité" which suggests a relation between "la signification et le sens" (185).

445 -----. "From Rhyme to Reason: Remarks on the Text of the *Romance of the Rose*." Tr. Kathy M. Krause. In *Rethinking* (no. 182). 65-77.

A study of variants in Guillaume's part and of his use of varying degrees of rich rhymes. The first part of the *Rose* is more difficult to establish in a critical edition because of the number of variants introduced by scribes familiar with Jean's part and perhaps by Jean himself. In an effort to understand Guillaume's language, Poirion discusses the effect of changes made by Langlois (see no. 6), Guillaume's "poetics of rhyme" and the "lyric intertextuality" (71) of some of the rhymes. He claims that the rhyme in -*ure* is "truly the signature of the allegorical poem" (72). Poirion concludes that we must not search for the rich rhyme so much as for the one "whose meaning agrees with what we know of the text as a whole, and of the signifying function of rhyme" (75).

446 -----. "Guillaume de Lorris, alchimiste et géomètre." *L'information littéraire* 36 (1984):6-11.

A dense introductory reading of the first part of the *Rose* for a non-specialist Francophone public (quotations from the text are given in translation, for example). The author discusses briefly allegorical, narrative, and lyrical works that may have influenced Guillaume de Lorris (including the prose *Lancelot* and courtly songs of Thibaut de Champagne); how the allegorical system changes over the course of the romance, as though the author were serving "un apprentissage de la manière d'écrire" (9); and Guillaume's temperament and imagination of a geometrist (as shown in the descriptions of the garden and the fortress) and an alchemist. Poirion's overall reading is favorable to the mystical itinerary outlined by Ribard (see no. 466), in which the "alchimie du verbe" (11) changes an Art of Love into a more sublime revery.

447 -----. "Jean de Meun et la querelle de l'Université de Paris: du libelle au livre." In *Traditions polémiques; Cahiers V. L. Saulnier 2*. Actes du Colloque du Centre V. L. Saulnier, 1984. Collection de l'Ecole Normale Supérieure de Jeunes Filles 27. Paris: Ecole Normale Supérieure de Jeunes Filles, 1985. 9-19.

A review of the major events in 1253-1257 and 1269-1277, that is, in the period of conflict over the mendicant orders at the

University of Paris. Poirion recognizes, along with many other scholars, that these events can help us to understand the second part of the *Rose*. The author places in this context the polemical works of Rutebeuf, from whom Jean de Meun took the idea of his character, Faux Semblant, as well as other elements of his allegory. Poirion then shows how Jean adapted the themes and techniques of the polemic to create an ironic portrait of hypocrisy and to suggest that the sophistry which runs through the poem is the other side of "cet esprit de vérité" (18) in which Jean believes.

448 -----. "Les mots et les choses selon Jean de Meun." *L'information littéraire* 26 (1974):7-11.

A study of the different conceptions of language which underlie the two parts of the *Rose*, especially as expressed in Raison's remarks on language and obscenity. The author argues that the conceptions reflect the different ideologies of courtly or clerical social groups. Raison's use of "le mot le plus trivial" (7) ("couilles," for testicles) is a consequence of Jean de Meun's "volonté de scandale," his "volonté de rupture" regarding both style and doctrine, and finally his "volonté de libération" from moral censure (8). Poirion also explores the thirteenth-century French nobility's conception of the sacred, even magical, power of words, which Jean de Meun attempts to undercut by cutting language off from reality. Thus Jean de Meun's "idéal de fécondité" replaces the courtly "idéal de pureté" (10).

449 -----. "Narcisse et Pygmalion dans *Le roman de la rose*." In *Essays in Honor of Louis Francis Solano*. Ed. Raymond J. Cormier and Urban T. Holmes. Studies in the Romance Languages and Literatures 92. Chapel Hill: U of North Carolina P, 1970. 153-65.

A comparison of the different roles played by the myth of Narcissus in the first part of the *Rose* and of Pygmalion in the second: reflections of the authors, elements of l'Amant's education, and expressions of a philosophy of life. Poirion sees

Narcissus as the sign of a temptation, the narcissism of the courtly lyric, while Pygmalion suggests creativity and fecundity. In the first case we witness a magical initiation, in the second "un enseignement progressif, critique, dialectique" (162). Pygmalion further suggests the alchemical transmutation which is intermediary between science and magic, symbolic of Jean's pansexualism. Thus these two myths reflect "l'évolution de la civilisation au XIIIe siècle" (164).

450 -----, ed. *Précis de littérature française du moyen âge.* Paris: Presses Universitaires de France, 1983. Pp. 405.

An overview of the *Rose* as part of a good introduction to allegorical literature in the Middle Ages. The discussion of the *Rose* by Armand Strubel focuses on the "procédés de l'écriture allégorique" (242), how levels of meaning are structured in allegorical poems. The *Rose* illustrates the complex process by which a narrative metaphor conveys at least three "ordres de signification" (259): the literal story, individual experience, and the general art of love. Guillaume succeeds in preserving "un univers de formes où le signifiant l'emporte encore sur le signifié" (260), while Jean's encyclopedic poem is characterized by exuberant amplification and commentary, and by irony on all levels of the text. Jean's continuation first destroys the illusions of courtly love, then celebrates the natural purpose of sexual desire--procreation. [See also no. 516.]

451 -----. *Le roman de la rose.* Connaissance des Lettres 64. Paris: Hatier, 1973. Pp. 223.

A good introduction to the *Roman de la rose.* Attention is divided equally between Guillaume de Lorris and Jean de Meun (three chapters for each); in addition there is a bibliography, a "Tableau chronologique du XIIIe siècle," and "Notes sur les auteurs et les oeuvres du moyen âge." Guillaume's complex use of allegory characterizes both the form and content of his work (his accomplishment was to have given "plus de cohérence à la technique et à la thématique de l'allégorie" [17]); the way in which a love story and a fantastic adventure are melded; and the underlying mythic structure of an initiation ritual or rite of passage. "Le schéma fondamental...est celui d'une purification, d'un raffinement que le jeune homme doit réaliser dans son corps et dans son âme" (87). Poirion's study of Jean de Meun's continuation, which includes textual analysis of the major personifications, describes the ways in which the love quest was amplified to become a cosmic affair. The techniques of enumeration, digression, concentric themes, and the use of exampla are aspects of Jean's amplification of the allegory. The last two chapters consider the question of irony and satire in the continuation and suggest that Genius, "le porte-parole de la divinité" (175), reveals the truth of the poem: "il faut assumer notre vie charnelle" (175).

452 Polak, Lucie. "Plato, Nature and Jean de Meun." *Reading Medieval Studies* 3 (1977):80-103.

An erudite analysis of the philosophical ideas in Nature's and Genius's discourses. Polak teases out the strands of Platonic, Neoplatonic, Chartrian, and Aristotelian influences. Nature's discussion of the creation of the world and of her role in God's plan shows that Jean was "fully conversant with Platonic commentaries and... his solution to the problems raised by them is strictly orthodox" (85). Furthermore, Jean's emphasis on Nature as generative force and as link to the divine source of all beauty and life follows twelfth-century commentators on Plato. As the *anima mundi,* Nature is given "a new cosmic grandeur" (87). But Nature's and Genius's ideas about man's sexual instinct make them parodies of Alain de Lille's message, a parody "made plausible by the Platonic framework of thought in which Nature had placed her discourse" (95). Finally, the author shows that Genius's sermon on procreation is a *reductio ad absurdum* of Neoplatonic ideas about nature: "That Genius is a burlesque figure of fun no longer needs to be demonstrated at length" (97).

453 Pompejano Natoli, Valeria. *Una "vie" inedita di Guillaume Colletet: Jean de Meung.* Biblioteca dei Quaderni del Seicento Francese 1. Fasano: Schena, 1985. Pp. 110.

An edition of a biographical study of Jean de Meun by the eighteenth-century academician. The editor's introduction and extensive notes help make the biography accessible today, but the text is of interest only as part of an historical study of the *Rose*'s reception in the Enlightenment. Colletet bases his thirty-page study on earlier authors, such as Honoré Bonnet (author of the *Apparition de Jean de Meung*), Claude Fauchet, and André Thévet, conscientiously repeating their speculations, errors, and apocryphal anecdotes. He reviews contemporary information of Jean's life, including the belief that the *Rose* was continued at the request of Philippe le Bel and that Jean died in 1316. The biography discusses more briefly the influence of the *Rose*, reproducing Jean Antoine de Baïf's sonnet which is a synopsis of the *Rose*, "pour le contentement de ceux qui sont bien aises de voir les grandes choses reduites en petit" (59).

454 Pucci, Robert Gregg. "The Metaphorical Rose: Mythology, Language, and Poetics in the *Roman de la rose*." Diss. Brown U, 1974.

455 Quicherat, Jules. "Jean de Meung et sa maison à Paris." *Bibliothèque de l'Ecole des chartes* 41 (1880):46-52.

A description of a notarized deed found by the author in the Archives Nationales which describes the donation to the Dominicans of the house in which Jean de Meun had lived. Quicherat argues that Jean de Meun did not own but rented the house; that he was dead by 1305; and that it is possible, through mention of a well, to locate the exact spot on which the house stood: 218 rue du Faubourg Saint-Jacques. [There is today a plaque on the building at that site commemorating Jean's writing of the *Rose*.] The complete text of the deed is also given.

456 Quilligan, Maureen. "Allegory, Allegoresis, and the Deallegorization of Language: The *Roman de la rose*, the *De planctu Naturae*, and the *Parlement of Foules*." In *Allegory, Myth, and Symbol*. Ed. Morton W. Bloomfield. Cambridge, Massachusetts: Harvard UP, 1981. 163-86.

A dense and suggestive discussion of two fundamental distinctions in relation to the works of the title: the critical distinction between allegoresis, "textual commentary or discursive interpretation," and allegory, "narrative peopled by personified abstractions moving about a reechoing landscape of language" (163); and the linguistico-sexual distinction between allegorical gloss and euphemism. Quilligan argues that Natura in the *De planctu Naturae* is more interested in language than in sexuality because she is primarily concerned about their relation within the divinely-ordered cosmos. Jean responds to the *De planctu* both in Raison's discussion of proper versus bawdy language and in the euphemistic pilgrim ending of the *Rose*, the effect of which should make us take "a more reasonable attitude toward sexual desire" (185). Chaucer takes the earlier presentations of these problems, "the conflict between euphemistic and natural-reasonable diction" (185), and deallegorizes them by means of an oral rather than a textual presentation in the *Parliament of Fowls*. He transforms "the silent, unvoiced textuality" of his sources into "a dramatic, mimetic fiction of audible, voiced sound" (164).

457 -----. *The Language of Allegory: Defining the Genre*. 1979; rpt. Cornell UP, 1992. Pp. 305.

A brief discussion of the continuation of the *Rose* as part of a study of allegorical narrative as a class or genre which puts a "very particular emphasis on language" (15) as its ultimate subject. As allegorical texts "address [the reader's] production of the texts' meaning" (21), Jean's text indicates "his concern with the reader's involvement in decoding the allegory" (243). Quilligan's discussion points to Jean's puns on cony-catching and the polite metaphors for sexual intercourse in the last section of the romance as indications that Jean is satirizing the dangers of Guillaume's courtly way of talking about love, a way which blinds us "to its real purpose, which is divinely ordained procreation" (85). [See no. 458 for a more extended discussion of this approach to allegory in the *Rose*.]

458 -----. "Words and Sex: The Language of Allegory in the *De planctu Naturae*, the *Roman de la rose*, and Book III of The Faerie Queene." *Allegorica* 1 (1977):195-216.

An analysis of how the three works juxtapose the theme of the "curious powers of language to corrupt or to clarify our conceptions of sexuality" (195). The author argues that Alain de Lille's subject is not sexuality but language, that is, the poet's dilemma faced with Venus's and Cupid's corruption of the rational function of language. Jean de Meun raises the same question in the "pivotal moment" (197) of the continuation, the debate between Raison and l'Amant over obscenity in which Raison argues that direct language is necessary for allegory. In both works, "the perversion of language *precedes* the rejection of reason" (202). Genius in both works is seen as attempting to describe the cosmic place of human sexuality, but Jean's Genius, like l'Amant, makes the mistake of taking allegorical language literally. In the *Rose*'s ending, Jean shows that the results of courtly language are "inherently obscene" (206), because euphemism makes it impossible to conceive of the larger purpose of sexuality. Quilligan also examines a number of episodes in Book III of *The Faerie Queene* to show how Spenser "completes the process of purification of the corrupted poetic language" (211) begun in the two previous works.

459 Ramsey, Susan. "Etat présent du *Roman de la rose*: 1891-1971." *Chimères* (Summer 1975):14-28.

A brief survey of important scholarship on the *Rose* beginning with Langlois's *Origines et sources du Roman de la rose* (no. 358). The author, while proceeding chronologically for the most part, attempts to point out the "préoccupations principales . . . de la critique" (16). [The list of four preoccupations on 16 is garbled, so the fourth one is not clear.] These critical questions include the nature and interpretation of the allegory, the cohesion of the two parts and the internal unity of the second, and the sources, traditions, and influences of the *Rose*. The author sees the presence of polemic in *Rose* criticism since the sixties as both beneficial and detrimental. She suggests future directions of research, in particular the need for textual studies (as opposed to historical ones, the utility of which she questions) to establish "la *sentencia* morale" (24) of the *Rose*.

460 Rand, E. K. "The Metamorphosis of Ovid in *Le roman de la rose*." In *Studies in the History of Culture*. Ed. Percy W. Long. 1942; rpt. Freeport, New York: Books for Libraries, 1969. 103-21.

A brief review, in the last six pages, of passages and characters in the *Rose* that Guillaume borrowed from Ovid, including the "very naughty" (120) *Ars amatoria*, the *Remedia amoris*, the *Metamorphoses*, and the *Amores*. Rand argues that Guillaume selects what suits his design, "but the design is already there" (120), and that Guillaume's Art of Love has purified the sentiment of love found in his Ovidian sources. The preceding pages discuss a number of topics, from the authors' education to the desirability of reprinting the internal summaries found in the manuscripts to the chief editions available before Langlois's (see no. 6).

461 Raynaud de Lage, G. "*Natura* et *Genius*, chez Jean de Meung et chez Jean Lemaire de Belges." *Le moyen âge* 58 (1952):125-43.

A comparison of the characteristics and roles of the two characters in Alain de Lille's *De planctu Naturae* with the *Rose* and (briefly) the late medieval "Temple de Vénus" by Lemaire de Belges. The author argues that the later works diminished the moral authority of Nature and increased the importance of Genius, making of him "le héraut de l'amour charnel" (142). In addition, in the *Rose* the two characters lose the independence they had in the *De planctu Naturae* and become voices of the author. Jean's Genius links natural and Christian morality, which are "conjointes plutôt que compénétrées l'une de l'autre" (133). The many digressions in the second part which, according to Raynaud de Lage, do not relate directly to a character's immediate point of view are also the words of Jean de Meun.

462 Redoli Morales, Ricardo. "En torno a la primera parte del *Roman de la rose*." *Analecta malacitana* 6 (1983):179-82.

An interpretation of the first part of the *Rose* which sees allegory both as "un refinamiento exagerado del *amour courtois*" (179) and a product of its creator's subconscious. The courtly elite learned to interpret the moral abstractions and affected symbolism of allegorical works through its experience with the romances in the Breton and Antiquity cycles. In the *Rose* the poet is "el protagonista de cada uno de sus personajes" (180), even perhaps of the Rose herself. The author, interpreting Danger as "Riesgo" (180), that is, the risk of the games of love, also suggests that the Rose may represent either "*el estado de ánimo de la mujer amada*" (181; author's emphasis) or, less likely, the woman lusting after a man.

463 Regalado, Nancy Freeman. "'Des Contraires Choses': La fonction poétique de la citation et des *exempla* dans le *Roman de la rose* de Jean de Meun." *Littérature* 41 (1981):62-81.

An important and wide-ranging essay on the meaning of the key phrase, "contraires choses" (Langlois l. 21573, Lecoy l. 21543), for Jean de Meun's use of exempla, references to and quotations from Latin *auctoritas*, and ultimately for his view of experience, sexuality, language, and the cosmos. Regalado begins with a discussion of the form and function of intertextuality in the second part of the *Rose*, in particular how Jean uses for literary effect citations and exempla, almost all of which are taken from Latin texts or ancient mythology and history. These citations and exempla are "contraires choses" in several senses, including the contrast of two languages and two cultures and of the irreducible "altérité" (71) of the exemplum in relation to the text of the *Rose*. The tension between the exemplum and the text--the gap between story and possible interpretation--leads the reader to reflect on the possible meanings of the exemplum. But the importance of "contraires choses" extends to Jean's conception of language and its ability to convey *proprement* the variety of human experience, in particular the experience of sexuality. It was through mythological stories such as those of Saturn and Jupiter, Mars and Venus, and Pygmalion that Jean could write properly about sexuality. Finally, the idea of "contraires choses" conveys Jean's remarkable project of expressing "la totalité de l'univers créé et les extrêmes limites de l'expérience humaine" (80), a world view which sees contraries not as oppositions but as complements.

464   Ribard, Jacques. "Calogrenant, Cahus et la rose." *PRIS-MA* 3 (1987):153-58.

A study of common elements in three medieval romances, *Le chevalier au lion (Yvain)* of Chrétien de Troyes, *Perlesvaus*, and Guillaume de Lorris's part of the *Rose*. These elements include the solitary quest, the aggressive "gardian du seuil" (155), and the perilous fountain. The correspondences among them suggest the esoteric pattern of "l'impossible aventure de la Connaissance de soi-même et de l'Autre" (157), a quest which the author pessimistically sees as leading to madness and death.

465   -----. "De Chrétien de Troyes à Guillaume de Lorris: ces quêtes qu'on dit inachevées." In *Voyage, quête, pèlerinage dans la littérature et la civilisation médiévales*. Actes du Colloque organisé par le Centre Universitaire d'Etudes et de Recherches Médiévales d'Aix-en-Provence, 5, 6, 7 mars 1976. Senefiance 2. Aix-en-Provence: CUER-MA, 1976. 313-21.

A short essay that outlines three levels of meaning in "certaines oeuvres maîtresses de notre Moyen Age" (315), including Chrétien de Troyes's *Chevalier de la charrete (Lancelot)* and *La queste del graal (Perceval)* and Guillaume de Lorris's part of the *Rose*. The sociological perspective sees the romance hero's quest as a transformation of feudal values, "une nouvelle éthique" (317) whose center is the beloved woman. A second reading proposes a psychological and didactic interpretation in which the quest becomes the young man's means to the "découverte fondamentale de soi-même" (318). Ribard also sees a third level in these works, that of a spiritual, even mystical, itinerary: in the *Rose* the lover passes through a series of obstacles, sustained by partial and mysterious revelations, until he reaches "la révélation ultime" (320)--the kiss of the rose. But the quest, a continuing interrogation, is necessarily interrupted because it cannot have an end.

466 -----. "Introduction à une étude polysémique du *Roman de la rose* de Guillaume de Lorris." In *Etudes de langue et littérature du moyen âge offertes à Félix Lecoy par ses collègues, ses élèves, et ses amis*. Paris: Honoré Champion, 1973. 519-28.

An interpretation of certain elements of the first part of the *Rose* as an allegory of mystical Christian experience similar to that of Jean Molinet in the sixteenth century. Superimposed on the quest for the Rose is a quest for Divine Love and for Knowledge. That is, instead of reading the *Rose* as an allegory of the fall from grace, Ribard interprets it as an attempt to return to paradise. In this reading the springtime motif, the vices painted on the wall of the garden, Oiseuse, the arrows of le Dieu d'Amour and le Dieu himself, Danger--even l'Ami--are given mystical meanings. [In many cases Ribard ignores elements that do not fit the mystical pattern, or, like l'Amant in his discussion of allegory with Raison, takes the allegory literally (see the literal reading of l. 2711, "precieus saintuaire" [526)]. In his conclusion, Ribard goes beyond arguing that many aspects of courtly love could have mystical resonances for medieval readers to assert that Guillaume de Lorris invites us to share the mystical experience of l'Amant.

467 Richards, Earl Jeffrey. "Poésie en tant que processus: la satire contre les ordres mendiants dans le *Couronnement de Renart, Renart le Bestourné* et la deuxième partie du *Roman de la rose*." Proceedings of the Third International Beast Epic, Fable and Fabliau Colloquium, Münster 1979. Ed. Jan Goosens and Timothy Sodmann. Cologne and Vienna: Böhlau, 1981. 312-29.

A study of satire of the mendicant orders in the two Renard poems (composed about 1260) and the second part of the *Rose*, not in terms of direct influence but "en termes poétologiques" (313). By presenting "une reprise originale de certains thèmes courtois" (313), each work suggests certain values and attitudes toward poetic creation, for the satire of the mendicants is as much a literary *topos* as a reflection of historical reality. After an analysis of the poet's relation to truth and to his public in the prologue to the *Couronnement de Renart*, Richards considers Jean de Meun's attitude toward his role as continuator: his act of continuing Guillaume's poem is "une valorisation poétologique de Guillaume" (320), Guillaume, and by extension his poem, symbolizing for Jean literary creation itself. Consequently, Richards asks what is Jean's dramatic motivation for bringing the non-courtly, anti-poetic Faux Semblant into the troops of le Dieu d'Amour. Thus the three works discussed take as point of departure the same system of literary values and are motivated by the "défense et illustration de la poésie du 12e siècle" (328).

468 -----. "Le problème du langage poétique dans les fabliaux et dans le *Roman de la rose*." In *Epopée animale, fable, fabliau*. Actes du IVe Colloque de la Société Internationale Renardienne, Evreux, 7-11 septembre 1981. Ed. Gabriel Bianciotto and Michel Salvat. Publications de l'Université de Rouen 83. Paris: Presses Universitaires de France, 1984. 469-80.

A brief consideration, in the context of a study of obscene language in the fabliaux, of Raison's discussion of explicit versus euphemistic language. By incorporating into a serious literary work such non-courtly, even obscene, language, Jean de Meun enlarged the linguistic dimensions of literature. According to Richards, both Jean de Meun and the authors of the fabliaux were drawing the reader's attention to "la fonction poétique des mots obscènes" (474), thereby putting into question lexical conventions. Ultimately obscenity in these works is seen as suggesting the "artificialité de toute convention lexicale en poésie" (477).

469 -----. "Reflections on Oiseuse's Mirror: Iconographic Tradition, Luxuria and the *Roman de la rose*." *Zeitschrift für romanische Philologie* 98 (1982):296-311.

A review and evaluation of the two principal approaches to the meaning of the character Oiseuse, who opens the garden gate to the lover. The patristic or Robertsonian interpretation (see no. 473) stresses the link between Oiseuse and medieval representations of the vice of Luxuria (lust); the "thematic" (296) approach sees her as an ambiguous figure for the poetic imagination. After reviewing the complex iconographic evidence, which Richards finds inadequate for either approach, he turns to a literary historical inquiry into the meaning of Old French *oiseuse* as a term for verbal folly or verbal frivolity and its use in Old French romances, especially those of Chrétien de Troyes. This connotation leads Richards to propose a connection between verbal frivolity and poetry and to see Oiseuse's connection with l'Amant as suggesting "a purely verbal involvement with the art of love" (311), one destined to end in failure.

470 -----. "The Tradition of 'otium litteratum' and Oiseuse in *Le roman de la rose*." *Studi francesi* 32 (1988):271-73.

A continuation of the discussion of Oiseuse's significance in the first part of the *Rose* (see no. 469), and in part a reply to Fleming's article on the character (no. 237). Richards argues that we need to take into account medieval readings of Seneca's and Cicero's concepts of *otium litteratum* (learned or literary leisure) as possible sources for Guillaume de Lorris's Oiseuse. Specifically, Richards points to John of Salisbury's prologue to the *Policraticus*, where remarks on "literary leisure, the truth of poetry and Scipio" (273) could have been Guillaume's model and source, rather than Ovid's line, "Otia si tollas..." from the *Remedia amoris*.

471 Rimlinger-Leconte, Colette. "L'expression métaphorique chez Jean de Meung: étude du discours de Raison dans le *Roman de la rose*." In *Etudes...Lanly* (no. 230). 301-11.

A study of the many "métaphores particulières" (301) in Raison's second discourse. In the formal structure of Raison's metaphors, Rimlinger-Leconte examines both those with one term and those with two or three. In the second part of the study she describes Jean's creative technique. His creativity is shown, for example, by using a common metaphor in an unexpected context (as when feudal ties of love become those of avarice). Certain "champs conceptuels" (309) are commonly found in Jean's creative use of metaphors: feudal life and custom, illness, religion. Often, one metaphor can suggest another, as when the image of the "chemin de vie" suggests the extended metaphor of the "maison" (307) of Youth or Old Age. The author concludes that Jean de Meun "utilise les motifs traditionnels d'une façon bien personnelle" (309).

472 Robertson, D. W., Jr. "The Doctrine of Charity in Mediaeval Literary Gardens: A Topical Approach Through Symbolism and Allegory." *Speculum* 26 (1951):24-49.

A discussion of the medieval Christian concepts of charity and cupidity as they were realized allegorically in descriptions of gardens and "garden materials" (25), such as trees, fountains, flowers, and birds. The author first describes typical allegorical gardens in medieval moral or theological works, then in literary works, including *Beowulf*, the *De amore* of André le Chapelain, *Cligés*, the *Roman de la rose*, and Chaucer's *Merchant's Tale*. By selecting analogous details in the religious and the creative works (shade-giving trees, for example, which he argues are an image of evil), Robertson asserts that "mediaeval literary authors frequently share the primary aim of Scripture, to promote Charity and to condemn its opposite, cupidity" (25). Thus in the *Rose*--"this plantation of heresy" (41)--Oiseuse represents sloth, Guillaume describes the fine ladies accompanying Deduit with "humorous irony" (41; no evidence given), the crystals in the Fountain of Narcissus are "the eyes of the flesh" (42), and le Dieu d'Amour is Satan. The poem as a whole is "a humorous and witty retelling of the story of the Fall" (43), an interpretation which Genius, speaking for Jean de Meun, confirms.

473 -----. *A Preface to Chaucer: Studies in Medieval Perspectives*. Princeton: Princeton UP, 1962. Pp. xvii + 519 + 118 plates.

A groundbreaking and controversial study of medieval literary and artistic principles which proposes that medieval aesthetics were based on patristic doctrine, and specifically on Augustine's thought, and that therefore they were fundamentally different from modern aesthetics--they were hierarchical rather than oppositional, "rigorously non-psychological" (34) and moral, and intellectual rather than emotional. The *Rose* is one of the major literary works which Robertson reinterprets according to these principles. The romance as a whole is seen as a portrayal of the three steps of succumbing to sin: "suggestion, delightful thought, and consent or passion" (84). In the first part of the *Rose*, such figures as Oiseuse (related to Luxuria or lust), Narcissus (an illustration of the danger of pleasurable thought), and the roses ("transient flowers of fleshly beauty" [95]), lead l'Amant along the path of concupiscence. In the second part, Jean elaborates the themes established by Guillaume: Raison, who speaks for Jean, is the word of God ("the *Verbum Dei*" [98]), and Pygmalion's story parallels Narcissus's as an exemplum of foolish desire. The end of the poem simply shows what happens to those who disobey Raison's counsels. Robertson's analysis of iconographical and stylistic elements argues that we should not be deceived by the first part's elegance or the second's realism into doubting their patristic basis. In addition to direct analysis of the *Rose*, the study includes brief references to the romance's influence on Chaucer.

474 Ronchi, Gabriella. "Il sogno di Guillaume de Lorris." *Medioevo romanzo* 13 (1988):409-19.

An interpretation which somewhat hesitantly maintains that Guillaume's *Rose* is not unfinished and that Jean de Meun is not a continuator but a systematic opposer. Assuming that Guillaume's *Rose* is an exemplary story of a love conquest, where success is a structural element (see the controversial lines 2749-3492), Ronchi argues that the poet is not obliged to unwind all the threads of the narration since a simple allusion will suffice. The episode of the kiss creates a caesura after which the poem continues with an increasingly realistic tone outside the *locus amoenus* where the entire *récit* had so far taken place. She compares the last section (ll. 3487-88 ff.) to the *lamento* and *tornada* of the Provençal lyric. As for the *senefiance*, Ronchi rejects the hypothesis of its identification with an art of love and sees it in the transformation which l'Amant undergoes after receiving le Dieu d'Amour's precepts. His metamorphosis into the *fin'amant* through the *gradus amoris* will lead him to the kiss "douz et savoré" (l. 3460). [MRB]

475 Roquet, Yves. "Philosophie et poésie de la transformation dans le *Roman de la rose* de Jean de Meun: recherches sur la signification de l'oeuvre." Diss. U of Paris, Sorbonne, 1984.

476 "*Rose* Scholarship, 1970-1973, *et al.*" *Encomia* 1 (1976):68-77.

A short bibliography which gives a fairly good selection of critical studies that appeared in 1970-1973, as well as some titles from 1962-1967 and 1974-1975 [this is apparently what is meant by "*et al.*"]. There are a few surprising omissions: Michael

Cherniss's 1975 article, "Jean de Meun's *Reson* and Boethius" is listed, while his "Irony and Authority: The Ending of the *Roman de la rose*," published the same year, is not. Included also are some editions, concordances, histories of French literature, reviews, bibliographies, and dissertations. Part of the list was compiled by Charles Dahlberg; part is based on "suggestions from Professors Dahlberg, Hicks, and Smith" (76). There are short comments on a few works. [The list was not carefully edited and has many errors. For example, Jean Batany's book should be *Approches*... Paris: Bordas, 1973--not *Approaches*... Tours: Bordas, 1972].

477 Rossi, Luciano. "Notula sul Re dei ribaldi." *Cultura neolatina* 33 (1973):217-21.

In this short reply following Contini's contribution on the *Fiore* (see no. 605), Rossi offers a detailed explanation of Langlois l. 10938 (Lecoy l. 10908), "Tu me seras reis des ribauz," translated by the poet of the *Fiore* with the expression "re de' barattier" (LXXXVII). Using Lucchese archival sources, Rossi proves it to be a technical expression indicating a police officer having jurisdiction over prostitution. [MRB]

478 Rossman, Vladimir R. "The Art of Contradiction in the *Romance of the Rose*." In *Beiträge zum romanischen Mittelalter*. Ed. Kurt Baldinger. Tubingen: Max Niemeyer, 1977. 270-81.

An interpretation that sees the conflict between religion and love in the *Rose* as the work's underlying structuring mechanism. This conflict, the "superposition of courtly and religious conceptions of love" (271), is, according to Rossman, the major source of irony in the *Rose*; it determines Raison and Nature's disagreement about the place of love in human life; it creates discrepancies between *allegoria* (the religious view of love) and *littera* (the earthly or courtly view of love). In support of this view, the author emphasizes the religious character of Raison, accepts Genius's criticism of Nature and of the garden of Deduit, and sees Oiseuse as simply a vice. The author thus sets up a hierarchy of Christian values which is read in the *Rose* through the mechanism of irony.

479 -----. *Perspectives of Irony in Medieval French Literature.* De proprietatibus litterarum, Series Maior 35. The Hague: Mouton, 1975. Pp. 198.

The same approach as in no. 478. Irony in the *Rose* results from the conflict between religious and courtly conceptions of love, that is, between incompatible views of natural love as sinful or virtuous. The author develops this thesis in three parts: a discussion of the oppositions between virtuous and sinful kinds of love in the romance; an analysis of the ironic conflict between Nature and Raison; an outline of ironic discrepancies between *littera* (love) and *allegoria* (religion). Raison's perspective is accepted as authoritative in order to establish the system of values with which to judge the *Rose*.

480 Rowe, Donald W. "Reson in Jean's *Roman de la rose*: Modes of Characterization and Dimensions of Meaning." *Mediaevalia* 10 (1984):97-126.

A perceptive, detailed study of the personification Raison in both parts of the *Rose,* but especially in the second. The author describes the characteristics of Raison, emphasizing her traditional association with *mesure* and with natural law and shows her relation to Boethian, Chartrian, and Old Testament sources. Jean's dramatic humanization of man's reason reveals its inadequacies, its incompatibility with man's postlapsarian nature. Thus the failure of Raison and l'Amant to understand each other is not simply the lover's fault. Ultimately, Jean's scrutiny of Raison suggests that "man's salvation, if it is to happen, is not to be accomplished solely by her" (119).

481 Roy, Bruno. "'Cristals est glace endurcie par molt d'ans'." In *Le nombre du temps*: *en hommage à Paul Zumthor.* Paris:

Honoré Champion, 1988. 255-61.

An article that first summarizes the medieval theory of the formation of crystals: water subjected to cold for a long time changes its nature and becomes mineral. The necessary components are water, cold, and time. Two principal, and beneficial, qualities were attributed to crystals in the Middle Ages: favoring lactation (also quenching thirst generally) and capturing sunlight. In the second part of the article, the author applies this view of crystals to the *Roman de la rose*, in particular to the puzzling crystals in the Fountain of Narcissus. In these crystals Roy reads only negative associations, those of illusion and death. He points to references to cold water and to chills in the *Rose* to support his argument, which, briefly presented, does not explore the consequences of this interpretation for the *Rose*.

482 Ruhe, Doris. *Le dieu d'amours avec son paradis*: *Untersuchungen zur Mythenbildung um Amor in Spätantike und Mittelalter*. Beiträge zur romanischen Philologie des Mittelalters 6. Munich: Wilhelm Fink, 1974. Pp. 188.

A broad study, based on the author's dissertation, of the medieval reception of the classical mythical figures, Cupid and Venus. Previous scholarship is shown to have neglected an overview of their development in medieval literature, especially in allegories of love, on which this study focuses. After chapters on the late Latin epithalamium, the medieval mythographers, and love allegories in Provençal and Latin, the author examines the high point of northern French love allegory, Guillaume de Lorris's *Rose*. Guillaume adapts the traditional attributes of le Dieu d'Amour to stress his power and to differentiate his effects (in the greater number of arrows, for example). Ruhe considers the difficult question of whether Guillaume's character is a personification or a mythical figure but feels that he incorporates elements of both. Finally she examines le Dieu d'Amour's relation to Christian elements but believes we cannot determine whether Guillaume was challenging churchly otherworldliness or simply expressing erotic wish fulfillment. In a briefer treatment of the second part of the *Rose,* Ruhe describes Jean's Dieu d'amour as a composite expression of various sources and a reflection of his encyclopedic goals. She argues that Jean increases Venus's importance in order to show his disregard for the courtly conception of love, which must be subordinate to natural sexuality.

483 Ruhe, Ernstpeter. *"In rosa venenum*: Das offene Ende des Romans von Guillaume de Lorris." In *Hommage à Jean-Charles Payen: farai chansoneta novele: essais sur la liberté créatrice au Moyen Age.* Caen: Centre de Publication de l'Université de Caen, 1989. 323-45.

A discussion of whether Guillaume's part can be considered a separate entity, which also gives a present state of research on the question. Until a short time ago, most studies of the composition of the *Rose* were based on Jean's statement, "quant Guillaumes cessera, Jehans le continuera" (ll. 10557-58), automatically assuming the incompleteness of the first part. But recently scholars have doubted Jean's utterance, trying to prove with different methods (elements of content or structure) whether the first part has its own unity. Ruhe comes to the conclusion that Guillaume's part, in his time, could very well have been considered complete and was actually so regarded by its readers. However, Jean de Meun brilliantly demonstrated a different version, the poem being completed only through his continuation. Thus, Ruhe suggests an acceptance of both interpretations. [ASK]

484 Rychner, Jean. "La flèche et l'anneau." *Revue des sciences humaines* 183 (1981):55-69.

A discussion of the narrative *dits* of the fourteenth-century poet and musician, Guillaume de Machaut, which compares their handling of poetic truth versus biographical reality to the way the *Roman de la rose* treats these themes. For Guillaume de Lorris, the dream is the figurative recounting of lived experience. Thus the arrow by which le Dieu d'Amour pierces l'Amant's heart is "une métaphore de sa souffrance, une façon de la dire dans un langage transposé" (58). Machaut, on the other hand, uses the image of the ring which the dreamer receives from the beloved (and brings to the real world on awakening), to make of the dream a biographical event, one which has important consequences for the poet's life. Further, in such works as the *Fonteinne amoureuse*, Machaut gives "de très beaux exemples de réel transformé par l'imagination" (60), that is, the supposedly real-life events that surround the dream become "une figure poétique du vécu" (62).

485 -----. "Le mythe de la Fontaine de Narcisse dans le *Roman de la rose* de Guillaume de Lorris." In *Le lieu et la formule: hommage à Marc Eigeldinger*. Neuchatel: A la Baconnière, 1978. 33-46.

A consideration first of the relation between l'Amant's dream and Guillaume's supposedly real experience of love: the relation stated by the text (everything that happened in the dream later came true) is reversed (Guillaume first experienced love, then translated his experience into the dream). Rychner alleges as evidence principally the narrator's remarks that feelings experienced in the dream continue to be real to him years later. The second part of the article applies the categories of dream and experience to an interpretation of the structural function of the myth of the Fountain of Narcissus. The crystals are interpreted as revealing "le mystère même de la naissance du désir" (42). It is through this myth of desire that time enters the metaphorical (atemporal) garden of Deduit. Thus the scene of le Dieu d'Amour stalking l'Amant becomes the pivot between the two allegorical means (myth and metaphor), a pivot which swings the romance from allegory to narrative and allows Guillaume to introduce his own experience of love into the garden.

486 Ryding, William W. "Faus Semblant: Hero or Hypocrite?" *Romanic Review* 60 (1969):163-67.

An attempt to understand Faux Semblant's relevance to the

Roman de la rose. Ryding divides the character's role into two parts, the religious hypocrite (as revealed in his confession) and the courtly lover who overcomes the slanderer, Male Bouche (as revealed by Faux Semblant's actions in the romance). The problem as Ryding sees it is that the second role is courtly while the first is not, and that Jean de Meun "cared little about the conventions and refinements of the game of *fin' amor*" (166). Therefore, Ryding concludes that Jean de Meun made only a "minimal effort to integrate the hypocrite into the action," being more concerned "to speak out against hypocrisy and sham" (167).

487 Sasaki, Shigemi. "Le jardin et son 'estre' dans *Le roman de la rose* et dans *Le dit dou lyon*." *Cahiers de l'Association internationale des etudes françaises* 34 (1982):25-37.

A summary of the characteristics of the gardens in the two romances. The author points out the importance of trees in Guillaume's garden ("un élément essentiel de ce séjour paradisiaque!" [27]), where the principal scenes take place in the shade of a tree. Both gardens--that of Guillaume de Lorris and of Guillaume de Machaut a century later--are enclosed in significant ways, to suggest theme and point of view. Jean de Meun transforms his predecessor's enclosed garden, without warning the reader, into an immense park. Thus a comparison of these gardens "nous donne une idée de l'ampleur des divergences de ton" (37) in this period of medieval literature.

488 ------. "Sur le personnage d'Oiseuse." *Etudes de langue et littérature françaises* [Tokyo] 32 (1978):1-24.

A somewhat disjointed article whose main point is that leisure is a value and a virtue "que Guillaume [de Lorris] intègre à bon escient dans l'éthique courtoise traditionnelle" (23). The argument rests both on a detailed analysis of Oiseuse's attributes and role in the first part of the *Rose* (in which Sasaki appears to accept unquestioningly the *Rose* narrator's admiring response to the personification) and on the connotations of *oiseuse* and related terms in French literature in the fourteenth, fifteenth, and even eighteenth centuries (as in Montesquieu). The author contrasts the positive value of the concept in the first part of the *Rose* with its negative value in the second, which is attributed to the expansion of capitalism. The article includes comments on other critical discussions of Oiseuse.

489 Scaglione, Aldo D. *Nature and Love in the Late Middle Ages*. Berkeley and Los Angeles: U of California P, 1963. Pp. x + 250.

A study of love's relationship to nature in selected medieval works, in particular in Boccaccio's *Decameron*, seen as an exemplary case. Love in the *Rose* is discussed briefly in the context of courtly love, which "contained the seed of much naturalism to follow" (16), and in the letters of Abelard and Heloise. The author stresses the influence of the school of Chartres, in particular that of Alain de Lille, whose works reflect the idea of the moral harmony of the cosmos. Raison in the second part of the *Rose* is juxtaposed to "an unabashed defense of sex" (36) in which Jean de Meun does not seriously attempt to reconcile Raison and l'Amant. A "brilliant master of paradox" (37), Jean's "biological approach marks the defeat of the sentimental tradition" (38). In addition to the discussion of reason and sexuality, Scaglione considers briefly attitudes toward marriage, freedom, and nobility in the *Rose* and summarizes the conflicting interpretations of the romance in the Querelle de la Rose.

490 Scheidegger, Jean R. "La peinture à l'or du *Roman de la rose*." In *L'or au moyen âge: monnaie, métal, objets, symbol*. Senefiance 12. Aix-en-Provence: CUER-MA, 1983. 397-414.

An analysis of occurrences of words for gold in the *Roman de la rose*. The author offers an essay on the words associated with gold, in particular the three "filons" (lodes; 397) of *pointure* (painting/writing), clothing, and love, all of which involve art and artifice and which are metaphors for each other. The discussion moves through a series of "jeu[x] du signifiant" (403), that is, homophonic associations (*l'art, l'arc, lard*) favored by manuscript variants. Three passages are shown to produce the richest veins of gold [author's pun]: the discovery of love (ll. 460-1100 approximately), the jealous husband's tirade, and the story of Pygmalion (who is shown to be the jealous husband's opposite). Thus the *Rose* is written in gold; its sexuality and writing (one a metaphor for the other) are gilded.

491 Schmid, Elisabeth. "Augenlust und Spiegelliebe: Der mittelalterliche Narziss." *Deutsche Vierteljahrsschrift für Literaturwissenschaft und Geistesgeschichte* 59 (1985):551-71.

492 Seward, Barbara. *The Symbolic Rose*. New York: Columbia UP, 1960. Pp. viii + 233.

A study of rose symbolism in modern British authors, in particular Yeats, Joyce, and Eliot. After a brief summary of the rose's literary and religious associations in Chapter 2, "The Medieval Heritage," the author describes the rose in the *Rose* as bringing "to culmination the whole secular side of love" (30), a reflection of a discord between courtly and Christian ideals. Guillaume's rose, when seen in the fountain, is the embodiment of l'Amant's private ideal but becomes, in the larger context of Deduit's garden, "a symbol of a highly developed courtly ideal" (31) [note that the lover sees rosebushes in the fountain, not the rosebud itself]. In describing Jean's rose, the author summarizes Gunn's approach (see no. 274).

493 Shoaf, R. A. "Medieval Studies after Derrida after Heidegger." In *Sign, Sentence, Discourse: Language in Medieval Thought and Literature*. Ed. Julian N. Wasserman and Lois Roney. Syracuse: Syracuse UP, 1989. 9-30.

A discussion of Jean de Meun's remarks on how contrary things gloss each other (ll. 21542-52) in the context of Derrida's theory of *différance*, of the same as other. Like other writers of the twelfth and thirteenth centuries, and like Derrida, Jean was concerned with the instability and finitude of language. This approach to Jean's view of language is part of the author's "method of juxtology," based on "the aleatory juxtapositions of minds or of sounds that produce the phenomena of meanings" (23). The article also offers a number of examples from Chaucer and Dante of a "Heideggerean understanding of language as 'the relation of all relations'" (13), in which the text must be broken up in order to find "the alien sense...and lift it out" (17).

494 Smith, Nathaniel B. "In Search of the Ideal Landscape: From 'Locus Amoenus' to 'Parc du Champ Joli' in the *Roman de la rose*." *Viator* 11 (1980):225-43.

A comparison of natural elements in the two parts of the *Rose*, based on Matthew of Vendome's seven-part paradigm (flowers, grass, trees, fruit, birds, water, and breezes). Smith's analysis of "any substantial development of one or usually several of the basic ingredients" (227) includes not only Deduit's garden, but le Dieu d'Amour's robe and, in the second part, Jupiter's ending of the Golden Age. Guillaume, who is "the first to set a psychomachic action in a *locus amoenus*" (227), depicts a calm and measured (i.e., courtly) nature. Jean greatly enlarges and varies the natural world to create "an entirely new assemblage of natural phenomena" (231), and he expresses, in Genius's Park of the Lamb, a more radical formulation of the harmony between man and nature, between "the natural and the Christian" (242).

495 -----. "Nature Comparisons and the Situation of Man in the *Roman de la rose*." *Res publica litterarum* 2 (1979):273-80.

A study of nature imagery that categorizes and counts comparisons (references to earth, air, water, fire, the heavens, light, time, plants, and animals) in both parts of the *Rose* and compares the poets' use of the theme of nature. Although the author finds the same average number of comparisons per line, there are significant differences in the types of comparisons. Jean, for example, often uses "anticourtly aqueous imagery" (275), and while Guillaume has--not surprisingly--"a very notable interest in the plant kingdom" (275), Jean prefers animal comparisons (his favorite animal is the wolf [also not surprising?]). On the hypothesis that such comparisons are a microcosm of the poets' vision of the natural world, Smith draws conclusions regarding the poets' ideology from these comparisons. While for Guillaume, "man belongs in the courtly garden" (279), for Jean, the cosmological optimist, all nature is basically good, despite "reminiscences of the fallen side of man" (279).

496 Smith, Thomas N. "The Garden Image in Medieval Literature." Diss. U of Connecticut, 1969.

497 Sneyders de Vogel, K. *De Rozeroman: Een Beeld uit het Middeleeuwsche Cultuurleven*. Bibliotheek voor weten en denken 26. The Hague: H. P. Leopolds Uitgevers Maatschappij, 1942. Pp. 95.

A general introduction for the Dutch reader to the basic issues of the *Roman de la rose*. Sneyders de Vogel characterizes the work of both Guillaume de Lorris and Jean de Meun before considering the Querelle de la Rose in a final chapter. The book stresses the exemplarity of the *Rose* as illustrative of French culture of the thirteenth century. [KB]

498 -----. "L'unité du *Roman de la rose*." *Neophilologus* 37 (1953):135-39.

A review of Gunn's *The Mirror of Love* (no. 274) which summarizes the main idea concerning the unity of the *Rose* and expresses some reservations: Gunn minimized the differences between the two parts; misinterpreted the verse "Ou l'art d'amours est toute enclose" (l. 38), which means simply that

Guillaume gives us a complete courtly code of love, not a work on all kinds of love; and failed to show that certain passages, such as Nature's description of optics, are anything but third- and fourth-degree digressions. [This passage on optics is today seen as relevant to a work that is a "mirror" of love.] The reviewer concludes by expressing admiration for a remarkable work by an "angliste" (139), a work of which even a Romance scholar would be proud.

499 Soyer, Jacques. "A propos de Jean de Meung: son véritable nom, la date exacte de sa mort, ce qu'il pensait de son langage et de son style." *Bulletin de la Société archéologique et historique de l'Orléanais* 24 (1942):325-29. Rpt. Orleans: R. Houze, 1945. Pp. 5.

An attempt to correct some factual errors that recurred in criticism of the period: Jean de Meun's family name was Chopinel, not Clopinel (and therefore he was not lame); the name Meun was bisyllabic and not spelled Meung until the fifteenth century; Jean died in 1305, not before. Soyer also quotes some verses from a prologue to a translation of Boethius's *De consolatione Philosophiae* in which the author (Jean de Meun?) excuses his Orleans dialect. [Soyer accepts the translation in verse and prose as Jean de Meun's, which Langlois has argued convincingly is not by Jean; see no. 118].

500 Spearing, Anthony Colin. *Medieval Dream-Poetry.* Cambridge England: Cambridge UP, 1976. Pp. vii + 236.

A good introduction to the *Rose* as a dream-vision, as part of an overview of the classical and medieval dream-visions which formed the literary tradition behind the dream-poem in English. Spearing shows how the *Rose* borrows its main characteristics from religious visions while adapting them to courtly and parodic ends. Within the dream it is Raison who establishes "a moral framework for the poem" (31). In the second part, the long speeches--the substance of the poem--reveal "an intricately interlinked structure of attitudes towards love and human nature" (31). The problem of which character may be speaking for the author is handled in a balanced way: Spearing argues that the absence of a center (i.e., Christian orthodoxy) makes possible the "incomparable vigour and fulness" of the characters (32-33). The discussion includes a further consideration of literary aspects of the *Rose* as dream-poem. A final section discusses a few important French dream-visions from the fourteenth century that were influenced by the *Rose*.

501 -----. "The Medieval Poet as Voyeur." In *The Olde Daunce: Love, Friendship, Sex, and Marriage in the Medieval World*. Ed. Robert R. Edwards and Stephen Spector. SUNY Series in Medieval Studies. Albany: State U of New York P, 1991. 57-86; notes 265-67.

An analysis of the voyeuristic tendencies of medieval literature, particularly in Béroul's *Tristan*, Chaucer's *Troilus and Criseyde* and the *Manciple's Tale*, Guillaume de Lorris's *Rose*, and Dunbar's *The Goldyn Targe*. Not only do specific characters show themselves to be voyeurs by watching private sexual encounters, but the author and the audience in medieval erotic literature are also placed in a voyeuristic position. Guillaume de Lorris goes beyond Béroul and Chaucer by making the narrator himself the voyeur, for Spearing places in a voyeuristic perspective the narrator's descriptions of enticing physical characteristics and erotic activities in the garden of Deduit (described as a fashionable discothèque). The author also analyzes briefly Guillaume's representation of the beloved "as an object, the rose, and as a collection of male personifications" (81). The final discussion, of Dunbar's dream-vision, suggests the Scottish poet's debt to Guillaume de Lorris.

502 Spencer, Richard. "The Treatment of Women in the *Roman de la rose*, the *Fabliaux* and the *Quinze joyes de mariage*." *Marche romane* 28 (1978):207-14.

An outline of Jean de Meun's views of love in marriage, and consequently of wives, based mainly on the comments of l'Ami, supplemented with Nature's and Genius's ideas on sex. L'Ami's remarks on maintaining the love relationship are applied to marriage and interpreted by Spencer as a form of feminism (although he does not use the word), for l'Ami is seen as arguing that men must check their despotism "and work benevolently to end feminine inequality" (208). The author then looks briefly at the *fabliaux* and the *Quinze joyes de mariage* in terms of their presentation of marriage, which is often similar to that in the *Rose*: sex is natural and women's wit in satisfying their natural appetites is admirable. All these works, preoccupied with the relationship of marriage to urban society, point "to the need for a change in male attitudes in marriage in the belief that the failure of marriage cannot be attributed exclusively to the woman" (214).

503 Stablein, Patricia Harris. "La femme-pharmakon: l'amour et le mariage dans les transgressions structurales du *Roman de la rose*." In *Amour, mariage et transgressions au moyen âge*. Université de Picardie, Centre d'Etudes Médiévales, Actes du colloque des 24, 25, 26 et 27 mars 1983. Eds. Danielle Buschinger and André Crépin. Goppingen: Kümmerle, 1984. 349-58.

An analysis that proposes Derrida's "réseau analytique" (349; from "La pharmacie de Platon") as the key to understanding the ambiguous but fundamental function of the woman in the *Rose*. The woman can be seen as incarnating each facet of the system, the woman as healer or poisoner, as beneficial or harmful drug, as doctor or witch, and as scapegoat.

504 Stakel, Susan [Lee]. *False Roses: Structures of Duality and Deceit in Jean de Meun's "Roman de la rose"*. Stanford French and Italian Studies 69. Saratoga and Stanford: Anma Libri and Department of French and Italian, Stanford University, 1991. Pp. 142.

An approach to meaning in the second part of the *Rose* based on the linguistic and thematic recurrence of deceit and related concepts. Using Greimas's and Courtès's semantic categories of true/false/secret/delusion, the conceptual field of deceit is shown to be "the primary *isotopie*" (31) of Jean's continuation (in contrast to the predominance of courtesy in the first part), with the consequence that other conceptual fields "become tainted" (34) by connotations of deceit. The paradigmatic embodiment of deceit is the character Faux Semblant, but other personifications are swept into the whirlpool of deceit and reveal similar deceptiveness: "Faux Semblant contaminates everything" (82). The theme of "the split of Appearance and Reality" (103) also underlies the *Rose*'s discussion of mirrors and its use of exempla. Finally, the "total disjunction characteristic of antithesis" (94) is expressed in the poem's use of irony and in its conception of allegorical language, which makes of the reader "the agent of the transmutation of falsity into truth" (121).

505 -----. "Faux Semblant: The Lexical, Thematic and Structural Implications of Deceit in Jean de Meun's *Roman de la rose*." Diss. U of Wisconsin, 1981.

506 Steinle, Eric M. "Anti-Narcissus: Guillaume de Lorris as a Reader of Ovid." *Classical and Modern Literature* 6.4 (1986):251-59.

A comparison of Guillaume's reading of the myth of Narcissus with Ovid's, which "he knew at first hand" (251). Guillaume consistently transforms Ovid's text in order to produce an anti-Narcissus and to transform the nature of the fountain to bring it into line with his "overall literary project" (251). Guillaume's reversals of the myth, Steinle argues, include the condemnation of Narcissus from without, by le Dieu d'Amour; the transformation of Echo into a courtly lady; and the turning of the fountain "out from itself, to the rest of the garden" (257).

507 -----. "Versions of Authority in the *Roman de la rose*: Remarks on the Use of Ovid's *Metamorphoses* by Guillaume de

Lorris and Jean de Meun." *Mediaevalia* 13 (1987):189-206.

An examination of the *Rose* authors' use of material from Ovid's *Metamorphoses* to reorient the meanings of the myths, to create in turn an Anti-Narcissus and an Anti-Orpheus. By having the Fountain of Narcissus reflect the entire garden in a way that leads the lover to the rosebud (thereby becoming the Fountain of Love), Guillaume reverses the Ovidian valences of the fountain. Guillaume's lover as Anti-Narcissus is renegotiated by Jean's reworking of two stories from Orpheus's book, *Metamorphoses* 10, those of Adonis and Pygmalion. Thus Jean creates an Anti-Orpheus who rejects sterile love in favor of procreation. Consequently the "constellation of values" (202) in the second part defines "a proper erotic discourse" (203), one which is expressed by "the voice of Nature and her rhapsode, Jean de Meun" (203).

508 Stone, Donald, Jr. "C. S. Lewis and Lorris' Lady." *Romance Notes* 6 (1964):196-99.

A series of speculations on the age and marital status of the young woman in the *Rose*. In *The Anatomy of Love*, C. S. Lewis suggests at one point that the character Jalousie could represent the lady's husband, at another point, her relatives. Stone reconsiders the textual evidence of the woman's marital status, which includes the poem's emphasis on youth (though a medieval wife could be very young), Jalousie's desire to protect the woman's chastity (though in the passage cited this term is applied satirically to monasteries), and the ways Bel Accueil represents the young woman's fear of separation from her family and her feelings of pity and shame (suggesting a woman "at the age of loving and giving but bewildered at the first assault of emotion" [197 n. 2]). The author concludes that "there is no justification for seeing the lady as married" (199).

509 -----. "Hierarchies and Meaning in the *Roman de la rose*." *French Forum* 6 (1981):5-12.

A short essay that supports, through selected lines from the second part of the *Rose*, John Fleming's patristic interpretation (see no. 243), in particular by reaffirming the superior position of Jean's Raison over both Nature and Guillaume's Raison. Since Nature's perspective is "theologically speaking, quite incomplete" (6), procreation cannot be a good in itself. The author further argues against the unity of the two parts by equating Guillaume's point of view with le Dieu d'Amour's representation of passionate love and by making of his garden wholly a creation of man's art (which Jean points out is inferior to nature). Thus Jean, through his character Raison, must be seen as condemning l'Amant's lustful desires.

510 -----. "Old and New Thoughts on Guillaume de Lorris." *Australian Journal of French Studies* 2 (1965):157-70.

Primarily a response to D. W. Robertson's patristic interpretation of the *Rose* (see no. 473) and an argument for reading the first part as an expression of the courtly vision. Stone examines the figures on the wall and inside the garden, the Fountain of Narcissus, le Dieu d'Amour's speech, and Raison's view of love, and in each case argues that a close reading of the text does not warrant a theological interpretation [Stone's approach does not distinguish between narrator and author]. Guillaume's Raison proposes a solution that is "esthetically impossible" (168) because it would introduce time and work into the garden. In the end Guillaume's poem becomes a balance of tensions that cannot be reduced "to a single idea or intention" (169), a balance that faithfully represents the "impasses and contradictions" (170) of his age.

511 Strohm, Paul. "Guillaume as Narrator and Lover in the *Roman de la rose*." *Romanic Review* 59 (1968):3-9.

An interpretation that tries to prove that Guillaume de Lorris's 4028 lines of the *Rose* stand alone as a complete work. A summary of opinion for and against this proposition is followed by the argument that Guillaume's separate but related identities as dreamer and narrator work together in such a way as to produce a finished literary piece. Strohm notes that the open ending is typical of a "lover's complaint" and sees "more finality than most readers have seen" (9). [KML]

512 Strubel, Armand. "L'allégorisation du verger courtois." In *Verger et jardins dans l'univers médiéval*. Senefiance 28. Aix-en-Provence: CUER-MA, 1990. 343-57.

A "rapide parcours" (355) of the metaphorical use of the garden and its components in medieval allegories of love and related works. Although the rhetorical richness of the garden *topos* and its affinities with courtly imagery predispose the garden to allegorical treatments, only the *Roman de la rose* attempts to use the garden "comme partie intégrante d'une fiction allégorique" (349). What is rhetorical ornament or reification of specific metaphors in other works becomes in the first *Rose* an allegorical space inhabited by the key concepts of courtliness. Jean de Meun's Park of the Lamb, on the other hand, is a commentary on his predecessor's garden through the juxtaposition of contrary images taken from the theological realm. The article concludes with a brief discussion of allegorical gardens in religious works and iconography. Struble's conclusion points to the "indigence de l'élaboration allégorique du verger, du moins au XIIIe siècle" (355).

513 -----. "Ecriture du songe et mise en oeuvre de la 'senefiance' dans le *Roman de la rose* de Guillaume de Lorris." In *Etudes. . . Lorris* (no. 231). 145-79.

An approach to the problem of the *senefiance* (meaning) that Guillaume de Lorris promises but apparently fails to reveal. Strubel restates the problem in terms of the structure of the dream itself. Rather than an alibi, an enigma, or the consequence of the lack of an ending, the apparent failure to provide an overt interpretation of the allegory in the first *Rose* is countered by the meaning revealed in the juxtaposition of the different levels of the dream. In a discussion of the significance of Macrobius's authority in the prologue, Strubel questions the possibility that the *Rose*'s meaning is simply the events of the poet's life and suggests instead that the poem's meaning must be found in "l'écriture du rêve" (157). Guillaume's three promises to explain the dream at the end--all found in the first half--suggest that the second half of the dream may be its own interpretation, for it is in the second half that l'Amant's experience is shown to be true both in terms of le Dieu d'Amour's predictions and of the narrator's subsequent experience (revealed by his comments on the dreamer's words). A long analysis of the linguistic elements in the narrator-dreamer relation, such as the verb tenses and the adverbs *puis* and *mar*, shows how the implementation ("mise en oeuvre" [169]) of the dream's meaning occurs through time. Ultimately Strubel sees the poem's *senefiance* as based on the interrelation of three levels: l'Amant's experience of love's suffering (predicted by le Dieu d'Amour), the perspective given by the personifications such as Raison, and the general relation of the "je écrivant" (174) to the dreamer.

514 -----. "La personnification allégorique, avatar du mythe: Fortune, Raison, Nature et Mort chez Jean de Meun." In *Pour une mythologie du Moyen Age*. Ed. Laurence Harf-Lancner and Dominique Boutet. Paris: Ecole Normale Supérieure de Jeunes Filles, 1988. 61-72.

A study of the relation of Jean de Meun's personifications, especially those of Fortune and Nature, to their sources in myth. Strubel discusses their meaning in Jean's time, their degree of abstraction, and their emblems, such Fortune's wheel and house and Nature's forge. There are references to other medieval works in which a certain "réseau métaphorique" (64), such as the house of Fortune, is found. The study of these personifications reveals the difficulty of integrating mythic elements into allegory, of fixing them in images.

515 -----. *Le Roman de la rose*. Etudes Littéraires 4. Paris: Presses Universitaires de France, 1984. Pp. 127.

An introduction for advanced students of the *Rose*; includes a discussion of the authors and the date; a brief outline; an overview of the literary and intellectual context and of models and sources of the romance. The largest part of the study is a detailed analysis of the major sections of the work which can serve as a good introduction for those who read a difficult level of linguistic and rhetorical French. Strubel focuses his analysis on the literary and stylistic techniques of the authors and on the ideological substratum. He argues that Guillaume's allegorical amplification of the lyric and romance models is countered by Jean's didactic and satiric gloss of his predecessor's poem. Thus the two authors represent the "dualité originelle de l'allégorie" (111), which is both a procedure for poetic creation (Guillaume) and an exegetical method of interpreting a pre-text (Jean). Jean reinterprets and critiques Guillaume's Art of Love (both the art of suffering love's pains and the art of cultivating physical, sentimental, and mental elegance), in order to return love to the "forces vives de la nature, une apologie de ses oeuvres" (93). After the literary analysis, a short chapter on the fortune of the *Rose* and an *explication de texte* of the images on the wall of the garden are followed by a short critical bibliography. [Note that "Hunt" on 125 should be "Hult"].

516 -----. *La rose, Renart et le graal: la littérature allégorique en France au XIIIe siècle*. Nouvelle Bibliothèque du Moyen Age 11. Paris: Honoré Champion, 1989. Pp. 336.

An exploration of allegorical literature in three parts: the language of allegory; allegorical poems, including the *Roman de la rose*; and allegorical readings of earlier narratives, in particular the Renard stories and the *La queste del saint graal*. Relying on the corpus of texts described in the *Grundriss der romanischen Literaturen des Mittelalters* (no. 318), the author's approach uses linguistic and formal analyses to describe the ways of producing the two-level meaning of allegory, such as metaphor and personification. Strubel's detailed analysis of the

Rose touches on nearly all major questions concerning its structure and language. In the first part of the *Rose* four "paliers définissent la frontière du monde allégorique" (201): the prologue, the I-narrator, the I-dreamer, and the I-protagonist. The generating metaphor, he observes, is not the rose but the quest, not the object but the actions and personifications that it provokes; this quest incorporates an art of love, a debate, and a siege. While Guillaume poetically unifies decor and action in a lyric mode, Jean introduces the moral and satiric tradition in order to gloss the first. Strubel argues that it is Raison who "donne le mode d'emploi du texte de Jean" (212): the dream ceases to be a mystery and becomes a text to decipher. While Strubel does not privilege one character's words over another as the key to the romance's meaning ("aucun discours ne peut être lu à la lettre" [219]), he does conclude by singling out Genius's utopic doctrine on procreation, and by inference on writing, as "deux chemins parallèles qui permettent de renouer avec la plénitude disparue" (224).

517 Tavera, Antoine. "Héritage sémantique, héritage moral: à propos des allégories du *Roman de la rose* de G. de Lorris." In *Actes du VIIIe Congrès international de linguistique et de philologie romanes, Université de Trèves (Trier) 1986.* Tubingen: Max Niemeyer, 1988. 323-43; discussion 343-44.

A study of parallels between most of the allegorical personifications in the first part of the *Rose* and abstract or general nouns in the poetry of the troubadours. Beginning with Guillaume IX d'Aquitaine, in whose poems Tavera finds twenty-three "substantifs abstraits importants, dénotant des notions essentiellement morales" (328), he points out similar abstract nouns in the *chansons* of the troubadours, such as Marcabru and Cercamon, and in a few trouvères, such as Thibaut de Champagne. Following this inventory of latent allegories, Tavera examines Guillaume de Lorris's allegories in order (except for le Dieu d'Amour and Oiseuse), to show their ties with other lyric and narrative works. Guillaume's Danger, for example, is related to the use of the word *dangier* in Chrétien de Troyes's *Chevalier au lion* and *Conte du graal*. In the discussion following the paper, Pierre Bec suggests the distinction between socio-poetic and psycho-poetic values in the works analyzed.

518 Taylor, Carol Margaret. "The Deceptive Paradise: The Garden as Image of Self and Society in Medieval Romance." Diss. Harvard U, 1982.

519 Thomas, Antoine. "La date de la mort de Jean de Meun." *Académie des Inscriptions et Belles-Lettres* (1916):138-40.

A report on Thomas's discovery of two references to the house "magistri Johanni de Magduno" (139) in the tax records of the Prévôté of Paris in 1299 and 1305. No historical record of Jean de Meun's existence had previously been found for those years [but see no. 465 for Quicherat's information on the date of Jean's death]. Thomas concludes that Jean de Meun died between May and November, 1305. The communication ends with an update on Ernest Langlois's edition, whose progress had been interrupted by World War I (see no. 6).

520 Thompson, Barbara. "The Paradoxes of Fortune in the *Romance of the Rose*." *Chimères* (Fall 1972):13-47.

A discussion of the theme and character of Fortune in the *Rose*. After a brief review of the Roman goddess Fortuna, the author examines the symbols of Fortune's wheel and her dwelling place, which suggest Fortune's inconstancy and paradoxical nature. The main section examines parallels between Fortune and Faux Semblant, Richesse, le Dieu d'Amour, and la Vieille, who also show themselves to be paradoxical, materialistic, duplicitous, and capricious. Following Fleming's argument that l'Amant regards love as a carnal thing (see no. 242), Thompson sees carnal love as one of the gifts of Fortune, and consequently, "Fortune and the Dieu d'Amour are involved in the same kind of undertaking" (26).

521 Thoss, Dagmar. *Studien zum locus amoenus im Mittelalter.* Wiener romanistische Arbeiten 10. Vienna and Stuttgart: Wilhelm Braumüller, 1972. Pp. 176.

A study of the *locus amoenus* motif which points to significant differences between Guillaume's text and his alleged model, Matthew of Vendome's *Ars versificatoria*. In a detailed comparison of the two texts, the author shows Guillaume's originality in his use of the *locus amoenus*: the description of the garden of love, far from recalling a mere topos, is an integral part of the narration and contributes to its coherence. Thus, Curtius's hypothesis of strong Latin influence is dismissed, and the author suggests that Guillaume was inspired rather by vernacular traditions. In a discussion of the second part of the *Rose*, Thoss shows how Jean de Meun, opposed to Guillaume's conception of love, systematically demolishes the garden's supportive function for the narrative. The *locus amoenus* appears then as a metaphysical space, combining elements of the Christian paradise and Ovid's description of the Golden Age, as well as of the bucolic tradition. [JSZ]

522 Thuasne, Louis. *Le roman de la rose.* Les Grands Evénements Littéraires. Paris: Société Française d'Editions Littéraires et Techniques, Edgar Malfère, 1929. Pp. 161.

An introduction in three parts: an overview of the sources of the *Rose* (relying on Langlois's study; see no. 358); a discussion of the influence of the *Rose*, including excerpts from Jean Gerson's treatise; a summary of the *Rose* with many excerpts. Thuasne sees the first part as a mystical reflection of André le Chapelain's didactic *De amore* and praises Guillaume's taste, clarity, and elegance. The second part, written in a completely different spirit, is an emancipating work which "réduit l'amour aux plaisirs des sens" (34). Jean's true successor was Rabelais: "Ce que Jean de Meun fut au XIIIe siècle, Rabelais le fut au XVIe" (76).

523 Thut, Martin. "Narcisse versus Pygmalion: une lecture du *Roman de la rose*." *Vox romanica* 41 (1982):104-32.

An interpretation of the *Rose*'s version of the Narcissus myth in order to find a "lecture unifiante" (106). The author shows how the myth has become a courtly tale (and suggests in passing that the two crystals in the Fountain are the green eyes of Narcissus himself). After looking in the fountain, the narrator takes on the unfortunate role of Narcissus: the Rose is "une image narcissique" (114), the projection of the narrator's desire. Thut suggests, through thematic and stylistic analysis of parallels, that the fundamental theme of mirrors and sight is played out in the way Narcissus is reflected in Pygmalion (whose story is told toward the end of the *Rose*) and in l'Amant himself, both of whom create objects of their narcissistic desire. Furthermore the theme of reflection is linked to deception and to the poetic work itself: the *Roman de la rose*, the greatest of deceiving mirrors, shows in the end "l'impuissance d'Art à atteindre Nature" (132).

524 Tillman, Mary Katherine. "Scholastic and Averroistic Influences on the *Roman de la rose*." *Annuale medievale* 11 (1970):89-106.

A survey of critical thinking on the influence of the university milieu and in particular of the Averroistic conflict in the late thirteenth century on Jean de Meun's language and ideas. While it is generally accepted that Jean de Meun reflects Scholastic thought and language, Tillman, relying heavily on Paré and Müller (see nos. 401 and 419), simplifies the complex ideas involved in the Condemnations of 1270 and 1277 and attributes the possible references to those ideas in the *Rose* to Jean de Meun, not to the narrator or the characters. Thus, "for Jean de Meun, Nature is absolute" (96), and he is an advocate of "free love" (97). [Useful only as an introduction to modern works on Averroism and the *Rose*.]

525 Topsfield, Leslie T. "The *Roman de la rose* of Guillaume de Lorris and the Love Lyric of the Early Troubadours."

Reading Medieval Studies 1 (1975):30-54.

A study by a specialist of troubadour poetry of "some aspects of the lyric tradition established by early troubadours" (31) that can be discerned in Guillaume's *Rose*. The personifications, especially Jalousie, are shown to have parallels in courtly lyric, and the thematic structure of the poem as a whole is seen as an initiation to *joi* and *fin'amors* followed by a conflict between desire and restraint (which Topsfield sees as the underlying theme of the work). The *Rose* is thus translated into troubadour language, in particular into the language of various kinds of erotic desire. Finally, Topsfield sees the most original part of Guillaume's work in the Lady's "delicate conflict between mind and feeling" (45) and in Guillaume's sympathetic understanding of her dilemma. Thus the medieval audience would have understood the levels of meaning--that Guillaume had composed both a work of imagination and an expression of his lived experience--suggested by his use of troubadour subject matter, themes, and expressions.

526 Toynbee, Paget. "Jean de Meun's Account of the Spots on the Moon: A Note on a Passage in the *Roman de la rose*." *Romania* 24 (1895):277-78.

A note which points out the similarity of Langlois ll. 18373-87 (Lecoy ll. 16851-64) of the *Roman de la rose* and a passage in Albertus Magnus's treatise, *De caelo et mundo*, which Langlois failed to identify (see no. 358). He shows that Jean de Meun's description of the dark patch on the moon matches that of Albertus Magnus and suggests that further study of the two authors would reveal other similar passages. [KML]

527 Tuve, Rosemond. *Allegorical Imagery: Some Mediaeval Books and Their Posterity.* 1966; rpt. Princeton, N. J: Princeton UP, 1974 and 1977. Pp. vii + 561.

A landmark work on kinds of medieval and Renaissance allegory and how to read them. Through detailed analysis of texts the author makes useful distinctions between moralization and allegory and between moral and metaphysical allegory. Tuve describes the dangers that readers face in reading allegory, in particular that of imposing a meaning, often religious, that the author did not intend. Using Jean Molinet's moralization of the *Rose* (first published 1500) as a guide to misreading, Tuve shows readers how to approach "the difficult and dangerous method of a Jean de Meun, a kind of weaving dance-like movement, a dialectic in which no figure is Auctor..." (49). Careful analyses of the major characters, in particular Faux Semblant, Nature, and Genius, show Jean's "extraordinary skill in using details and phrasings which bend all in one direction" (246). That direction is a moral one, for by showing a loveless world Jean draws a definition of love from the misdefined and misdirected love of his characters.

528 Uitti, Karl D. "'Cele [qui] doit estre Rose clamee' (*Rose*, vv. 40-44): Guillaume's Intentionality." In *Rethinking* (no. 182). 39-64.

A wide-ranging essay that asks how Guillaume's lover-protagonist assimilates the Narcissus story. Uitti first asks what Guillaume's "phallic, masculine sort of rose" (40) can tell us about his intentionality. To answer this question, the author discusses how scholars' intentionality shape their perceptions of the first author, how Guillaume's *Rose* presents the central issue of truth, how the Lady inspires the poet, and how the first *Rose* participates in medieval romance intertextuality, among other topics. The last section describes the process of growth through which the narrator matures, along with the rose, to bring about the "formation of the Couple that the poem celebrates" (56). In order to accomplish this, Guillaume's lover must see the Other in the Couple and move beyond rendering service to Love by rendering service to the Other.

529 -----. "From *Clerc* to *Poète*: The Relevance of the *Romance of the Rose* to Machaut's World." In *Machaut's World: Science and Art in the Fourteenth Century*. Ed. Madeleine

Pelner Cosman and Bruce Chandler. Annals of the New York Academy of Sciences 314. New York: New York Academy of Sciences, 1978. 209-16.

An essay on the *Rose* as a new conception of poetry. Relating only by implication to Machaut and the fourteenth century, the discussion analyzes Guillaume's prologue and le Dieu d'Amour's midpoint speech in Jean's part. According to Uitti, "The *Romance of the Rose* is, and was perceived to be, a defense and a renewal of poetry" (210), that is, a truly poetic *summa*, "an open-ended, marvelously ambiguous, and yet *total* discourse" (215). "Diction and love-experience" (211) are fused in the first part, as in the lyric, but the fusion takes place in the narrative context of the *translatio studii* (the passing on of learning from the ancients to the moderns, i.e., medieval *clercs*). In the second part, Guillaume, poet-lover in the first part, becomes simply the lover, and Jean de Meun, "never identified as a Lover" (213), becomes the poet who creates the idea of poetry that will be adopted by Machaut and later poets.

530 -----. "The Myth of Poetry in Twelfth- and Thirteenth-Century France." In *The Binding of Proteus*: *Perspectives on Myth and the Literary Process*. Collected Papers of the Bucknell University Program on Myth and Literature and the Bucknell-Susquehanna Colloquium on Myth in Literature Held at Bucknell and Susquehanna Universities 21 and 22 March 1974. Ed. Marjorie W. McCune et al. Lewisburg: Bucknell UP; London: Associated University Presses, 1980. 142-56.

A description of the *Rose*'s defense of poetry as presented in the prologue, in the context of a discussion of poetry's function as myth. Through poetry "the poet-narrator seizes his *own* truth, a poetry at once lyric *and* narrative" (152). Two kinds of truth are conjoined, for the narrator is "at once 'courtly lover' and 'wise and clerkly'" (153). Uitti further argues that the topos of the *translati studii* (the passing on of learning through the ages) underlies the relation between the two parts of the poem. Jean "has incorporated the myth of the *translatio studii*--the myth of poetry itself" (154) in his transformation of Guillaume's model. The author rejects the idea of poets either celebrating or negating a myth of courtly love and sees instead in the second part of the *Rose* a generic transformation of the first part typical of medieval literature.

531 -----. "Understanding Guillaume de Lorris: The Truth of the Couple in Guillaume's *Romance of the Rose*." In *Contemporary Readings of Medieval Literature*. Ed. Guy Mermier. Ann Arbor: Department of Romance Languages, University of Michigan, 1989. 51-70.

An approach that stresses the importance of the theme of truth in the *Rose*'s prologue and in particular of the truth of the protagonist's relationship with the real woman who "fully deserves to be proclaimed 'Rose'" (54). The "conjoined couple" (55) of the poet-protagonist and the rose will realize what has been latent in the dream. This and other truth-conventions in the *Rose*, such as naming, are shown to have parallels in other romances, in particular those of Chrétien de Troyes. The author further argues that the poet-protagonist's narrative mirrors that of Narcissus in that in the beginning he shows a self-obsession "focused merely on the 'shadow,' or self-projection, of a non-existent Other" (61). The poet-protagonist's growth, however, eventually reverses Narcissus's story by allowing him to form the couple, based on mutual love, which the poem celebrates.

532 Van den Boogaard, Nico. "*Le roman de la rose* de Guillaume de Lorris et l'art de mémoire." In *Jeux de mémoire: aspects de la mnémotechnie médiévale*. Ed. Bruno Roy and Paul Zumthor. Montreal: U of Montreal P; Paris: J. Vrin, 1985. 85-90.

A draft of a paper left incomplete because of the author's death. The *Rose* is studied for indications that Guillaume de Lorris was familiar with medieval mnemotechniques, in particular that of associating objects with places. The author decides that the opening promenade, though giving the impression of a moving camera, is not influenced by memory techniques. Rather he offers as examples of the memory technique of *loci* the order in which the images on the wall are described and the association of birds with particular places in ll. 641-56.

533 Van Dyke, Carolynn. *The Fiction of Truth: Structures of Meaning in Narrative and Dramatic Allegory*. Ithaca: Cornell UP, 1985. Pp. 315.

An analysis of representative allegories of the Middle Ages, including the *Rose*, in order to identify "a semiotic code that distinguishes allegorical works" (21). In a useful introduction to the history of critical theories of allegory, the author reviews and rejects previous definitions of allegory. Using the structuralists' concept of codes, Van Dyke proposes that allegorical works modify "the syntactic codes of narrative, or, less elegantly but more accurately, of the plot" (37) and that they are based on "the synthesis of deictic and nondeictic generic codes" (40). A chapter on the *Rose* examines in detail the ironic interplay of generic perspectives in both parts. In the first Guillaume incorporates the subjectivity of romance into an allegory of timeless abstractions. His allegory is multivalent and intermittent, "both genuinely untranslatable and amusingly incoherent" (80). Jean's ironic use of allegory broadens the issues suggested by the first part, each allegorical agent presenting a certain way of ordering reality. But Jean's subject becomes after the midpoint "the paradoxical status of the fiction of truth" (91), thereby undermining allegory and suggesting new categories of reality--experience and invention.

534 Verhuyck, Paul. "Guillaume de Lorris *ou* la multiplication des cadres." *Neophilologus* 58 (1974):283-93.

The first part of the *Rose* is described as a series of concentric frames of which the principal ones are the dream, the river, the garden, the dance, mirrors and optical mirages, the hedge, and--after the secondary level of discourse constituted by le

Dieu d'Amour's speech--the moat, castle, and tower that imprison Bel Accueil. Ultimately even the personifications and the rose are seen as frames for the constantly retreating object of the text, desire itself. This approach to the *Rose* sees every aspect of the work, including literary techniques and symbols, as layers covering the author's absent subject, "l'Eros platonique (l'âme qui tend vers le Beau)" (286). Since this desire is inherently inexpressible ("indicible" [286]), it was not possible for the author to finish his text. In a postscript Verhuyck suggests that if the subject of the *Rose* is seen as simply the love of a man for a woman, then, in a sociological perspective, Guillaume's "multiplication des cadres" (289) would be a sophisticated upper-class literary game.

535 Villeneuve, Anne-Marie. "Les images dans le *Roman de la rose*." Diss. U of Toulouse, 1985.

536 Vinge, Louise. *The Narcissus Theme in Western European Literature up to the Early 19th Century*. Tr. Robert Dewsnap et al. Lund: Gleerups, 1967. Pp. 448.

A summary and brief commentary on the Narcissus episode in the first part of the *Rose*, with critiques of previous interpretations, especially C. S. Lewis's and Erich Köhler's (see nos. 348 and 375). The *Rose*'s version is compared both to Ovid's and to the twelfth-century lay, *Narcisus*, with the conclusion that Guillaume de Lorris was influenced in several respects by the lay, but that Guillaume "readapted" (84) details to Ovid while making his own mark through significant cuttings. Vinge stays close to the meaning and function of the episode in the *Rose*, stressing its crime and punishment motif. Jean's allusions to the Narcissus theme are briefly discussed, as are later works that may have been influenced by the theme in either part of the *Rose*.

537 Vitz, Evelyn Birge. "Inside/Outside: First-Person Narrative in Guillaume de Lorris' *Roman de la rose*." *Yale French*

> *Studies* 58 (1979):148-64. Rpt. in *Medieval Narrative and Modern Narratology: Subjects and Objects of Desire*. New York: New York UP 1989. 64-95.

An analysis of the narrative Subject, in particular with regard to the concept of a "psychological interiority" (151) confronting an exterior object. The difficulties of this theoretical model become more pronounced when it is applied to a medieval work, such as Guillaume's *Rose*. Major differences with modern narrative include: the heart, not the mind, is the seat of interiority and is not accessible to verbal analysis; faculties are conceived of as supra-individual; and the inside is not the self but the desired place ("To love is to be outside..." [156]). After analyzing some of the religious metaphors of the *Rose*, Vitz proposes the model of mystical yearning for its concept of love. Finally, Vitz sees the medieval conception of the soul as radically different from that of the modern ego. Since the individual self is deficient, in medieval thinking, it must lose itself to a higher order: the inside must be filled by, or given over to, the outside.

538 -----. "The *I* of the *Roman de la rose*." Tr. Barbara DiStefano. *Genre* 6 (1973):49-75. Rpt. in *Medieval Narrative* (see no. 537). 38-63.

An analysis of the four identities in the *Rose*: the dreamer, the hero of the dream, the narrator, and the real-life hero, a configuration which constitutes a particularly complex manifestation of the "underlying tension" (49) in autobiography between *discours* and *histoire*, between the speaker's voice and the story of his life. A detailed study of the subtle relationship between the narrator and the dream hero, including a long discussion of the progressive change in use of verb tenses, shows that the minimal emotional distance between the voices is finally annulled and they "merge into a single voice" (64). The possibility is raised of a fifth voice, that of the implied author, from whom any irony in the romance would come. Vitz questions Fleming's ironic interpretation of the *Rose* (see no.

243) and concludes that the work "remains intensely harmonious and unified" (69).

539 Walters, Lori. "Chrétien de Troyes and the *Romance of the Rose*: Continuation and Narrative Tradition." Diss. Princeton U, 1986.

540 Walther, H. G. "Utopische Gesellschaftskritik oder satirische Ironie? Jean de Meun und die Lehre des Aquinaten über die Entstehung menschlicher Herrschaft." In *Miscellanea Mediaevalia* 12. Soziale Ordnungen im Selbstverständnis des Mittelalters. Berlin and New York: de Gruyter, 1979. 84-105.

541 Warren, F. M. "A Byzantine Source for Guillaume de Lorris's *Roman de la rose*." *PMLA* n. s. 24 [31] (1916):232-46.

An exploration of the possibility of a Byzantine narrative source for certain allegorical and mythological elements in the first part of the *Rose*, such as the figures on the park wall, the Fountain of Narcissus, the hunting of the hero by le Dieu d'Amour, and the rose maiden. After examining similar elements in a late twelfth-century Byzantine romance, *Hysmene and Hysmenias* by Eustathius Macrembolites, Warren concludes not that Guillaume knew Eustathius but that both followed an earlier model. This hypothetical source reached France "shortly after the middle of the twelfth century" (245) and subsequently influenced several romances, including *Eracle* and *Guillaume de Palerne*, but it was "Guillaume de Lorris who rescued the fading story from oblivion" (246).

542 -----. "On the Date and Composition of Guillaume de Lorris' *Roman de la rose*." *PMLA* n.s. 18 [23] (1908):269-84.

A discussion of various questions concerning the first part of the *Rose*. The author attributes Jean de Meun's knowledge of his predecessor to a manuscript of the first part of the *Rose* shown him by a friend or relative of Guillaume de Lorris and proposes that this was the only manuscript existing at the time [unfortunately he is writing before the publication of Langlois's study of the manuscript tradition]. He further suggests the dates of 1229 (or 1232) to 1236 for the composition of the first part, based on Jean's reference to Henry of Castile (ll. 6630-32). The relation of the first part to the *Roman de la poire* and to Gautier d'Arras's *Eracle* is also considered. Finally, the author describes Guillaume's art of composition as the ability to combine different kinds of allegory "into one continuous, consistent, romantic narrative" (277).

543 Warren, Glenda. "True and False Gestures in Jean de Meun's *Roman de la rose*." *Iris: Graduate Journal of French Critical Studies* 2.1 (1986):29-37.

A study that stresses the prevalence of false gestures, of hypocrisy, in the second part of the *Rose*, through a summary of the advice and behavior of Faux Semblant, l'Ami, and la Vieille. By deceiving and destroying Male Bouche, Faux Semblant shows how the lover can use deception to achieve his goal; he thus becomes "the archetype of the Lover's behavior" (32). The parallels between l'Amant and Faux Semblant even extend to their respective metaphorical pilgrimages. Furthermore, the two counselors on amorous behavior teach l'Amant and Bel Accueil how to manipulate the gestures of authentic love for their own self-interest.

544 Wetherbee, Winthrop. "The Literal and the Allegorical: Jean de Meun and the *De planctu Naturae*." *Mediaeval Studies* 33 (1971):264-91. [A shorter version was published in the author's *Platonism and Poetry* (Princeton: Princeton UP, 1972), 257-65.]

A rich and suggestive reading not only of Jean de Meun's dialogue with Alain de Lille through his reworking of Natura and Genius from the *De planctu Naturae* (a work that is "present as a more or less constant index to Jean's intention" [266]), but also of the underlying meaning of the second part of the *Rose*. Jean's Raison and Nature both reflect aspects of Alain's Natura, while Jean's Genius is a more complex and ambiguous reading of the earlier character. Wetherbee, in reply to Robertsonian scholars of the *Rose* (see nos. 202, 243 and 473), stresses Raison's theological limitations; Nature is shown to be largely a product of human artifice and perversion; Genius represents a higher power that attempts to control and channel man's sexuality, seen as "a symptom of the minimal survival of man's original dignity" (287). The author suggests that Jean's underlying theme is the relationship of man's fallen world to "the lost allegorical harmony" (290) that he still glimpses, especially through sexuality. The article concludes with a discussion of Jean's use of mythology, which links Genius and Vulcan, and of the *Canterbury Tales'* relation to the *Rose*.

545 -----, "The *Romance of the Rose* and Medieval Allegory." In *European Writers: The Middle Ages and the Renaissance*. Ed. W. T. H. Jackson. 2 vols. New York: Scribner's, 1983. 1:309-35.

A perceptive, erudite introduction to allegory in the *Rose* which concentrates on the first part. The author, who describes the poem as a classic example of "re-creative allegory" (309), reviews both the allegorical traditions which it reworked and its originality. While Guillaume created "a virtual archetype for the presentation of psychological experience," Jean's continuation opened the way for "major experiments in comic realism" (310). Through a psychological reading of the first part, Wetherbee suggests that the interplay between l'Amant's visionary or idealistic impulses and his sexual desire results in his demoralization after his intuition of the archetypal purity of the garden of Deduit, of "the plenitude of natural life" (326). Wetherbee's analysis of Danger and the castle of Jalousie are particularly perceptive. A brief review of Jean's continuation of the *Rose* pursues the question of the relationship between idealism and physical desire. A final section discusses the medieval influence of the *Rose*, including comments on Dante and Chaucer, whose *Canterbury Tales* refracted the "elements of the great allegory...into the fragmentary waking dream lives of ordinary human beings" (334). Includes selected, annotated bibliography.

546 -----. "The Theme of Imagination in Medieval Poetry and the Allegorical Figure 'Genius'." *Medievalia et Humanistica* 7 (1976):45-64.

A brief discussion of the *Rose* in the context of concepts of the imaginative faculty developed in medieval spiritual and scientific writings and expressed implicitly in the poetry of the twelfth and thirteenth centuries. Wetherbee distinguishes two views of imagination in twelfth-century thought: imagination as an expression of our natural bent toward harmonious participation in the natural order and the role of imagination in our intuitions of spiritual reality. Thus imagination was seen as related both to natural desire and to wisdom, but it was also potentially dangerous because it could contaminate reason. Wetherbee looks at the new love poetry's adaptation of these concepts to its own purposes, and Alain de Lille's Genius figure (in *De planctu Naturae*) as a positive synthesis of the various concepts: Genius points the way to "the reconstitution of the human psyche" (58). The implications of this view of imagination can be seen in Guillaume de Lorris's combination of "imaginative idealism and sexuality" (59) and in Jean de Meun's Genius, a visionary with limited vision who "appeals for the reassertion of Man's original dignity" (60).

547 Wilhelm, James J. *The Cruelest Month: Spring, Nature, and Love in Classical and Medieval Lyrics*. New Haven and London: Yale UP, 1965. Pp. 310.

A wide-ranging discussion of themes associated with springtime, youth, and courtly love in medieval poetry. A short discussion of the *Rose* does not deal with specific elements of the springtime complex but points to some Latin and Provençal prototypes of the first part of the romance and to the differences between the overall conception of the garden in the two parts. Wilhelm argues that Guillaume's "profeminism, social graces, and secular idealism" (239) eventually carried the day.

548 Wimsatt, James I. "Realism in *Troilus and Criseyde* and the *Roman de la rose*." See no. 778.

549 Wood, Chauncey. "La Vieille, Free Love, and Boethius in the *Roman de la rose*." *Revue de littérature comparée* 51 (1977):336-42.

An analysis of la Vieille's example of the caged bird in the *Rose*. The author proposes two ways to determine the ironic "tonality" (336) of the example as an argument for women's natural sexual freedom: a comparison of her version of the example with its source in Boethius's *De consolatione Philosophiae* and a comparison of the example with others that la Vieille uses. A review of critical opinion on this example precedes Wood's investigation of the "deliberate irony" (340) of la Vieille's use of the bird-in-the-cage image in a way diametrically opposed to that of Boethius. Her use of the examples of monks caught in their vows of chastity and of fish caught in a net further this ironic interpretation. While questioning whether such an allusion might have been beyond a non-learned audience, Wood argues that the medieval audience would have rejected la Vieille's argument nonetheless. Finally, Wood cites Jean de Meun's preface to his translation of the *De consolatione Philosophiae* to show that Jean de Meun also rejected her "facile sophistries" (341). [See also Economou, no. 616, which Wood seems not to have known.]

550 Wood, Mary Morton. *The Spirit of Protest in Old French Literature*. Columbia University Studies in Romance

Philology and Literature. 1917; rpt. New York: AMS Press, 1966. Pp. xii + 201.

Largely a collection of excerpts, with some interpretative comments, from French texts in the period 1150 to 1350 that express "the spirit of protest already astir" (1) against social, ecclesiastical, and political injustice and repression. Jean de Meun's part of the *Rose* is cited for its rationalistic ideas on royalty and nobility, on private property, asceticism, and marriage. Jean and his imitators reduced government and social hierarchy "to a successful combination of trickery and violence" (73). He is also seen as an uncompromising foe of asceticism and an Epicurean precursor of "Rabelais, Montaigne, La Fontaine and Molière" (155). Thus the *Rose*, "the clearest expression of the rationalizing temper in the thirteenth century" (158), saw marriage as a question of social economy rather than as a sacrament and was concerned with a better society on earth rather than with spiritual values.

551 Wright, Terrence, D. "Le cadre du rêve dans *Le roman de la rose*." *Chimères* 15.2 (Spring 1982):43-53.

A study that begins by discussing the romance's dream framework as a means of creating esthetic distance, but most of the remarks concern the growing realism, that is, the humanization of the characters, in the second part, in contrast to the unreal, that is, courtly allegorical characters of the first part. The clear conflict between good and evil in the first part (as embodied in the supporters and enemies of the lover) is attributed to the unreal nature of Guillaume's allegory. Wright in effect equates allegorical abstraction and courtly personifications with unreality and psychological complexity, and concrete characterization with reality [contrary to how the medieval mind conceived of the abstract and the concrete].

552 Zingarelli, Nicola. "L'allegoria del *Roman de la rose*." In *Studi dedicati a Francesco Torraca nel 36º anniversario della sua*

laurea. Naples: F. Perrella, 1912. 495-524.

A polemical study that takes a stand against Langlois's view of the poem as formed by two branches rather than two distinct parts. The author sees Jean de Meun's work as a parody of the first *Rose,* or at least an intentional contraposition. What binds the two poems is the affinity of the subject matter; henceforth "il Roman de la rose sarà sempre *le roman* e mai *les romans"* (497). Zingarelli compares Jean's *Rose* to a mountain which sends down from its peaks chilly gusts onto a pretty, much smaller hill (Guillaume's *Rose*); in fact, he believes that Jean transformed Guillaume's allegory of courtly love into an allegory of natural and social relationships. As the allegorical meaning is crucial to understanding the first *Rose*, Zingarelli stresses that the poet will explain in its true, universal significance what he had first presented as a personal experience. Benedetto's work supports his interpretation (see no. 581), while Langlois's diverges, especially since he narrows the role of allegory in the first *Rose* (see no. 358). A substantial part of the article is devoted to a detailed analysis of the characters and their allegorical meaning, the differences between the two parts being at the center of Zingarelli's attention. [MRB]

553 Zink, Michel. "The Allegorical Poem as Interior Memoir." Tr. Margaret Miner and Kevin Brownlee. *Yale French Studies* 70 (1986):100-126.

A slightly shortened version of a chapter in *La subjectivité littéraire* (no. 556, 127-70). [For an explanation of the enigmatic reference to the *Dit des quatre sièges* on 116, see 151-52 of *La subjectivité littéraire.*]

554 -----. "Bel-Accueil le travesti: du *Roman de la rose* de Guillaume de Lorris et Jean de Meun à 'Lucidor' de Hugo von Hofmannsthal." *Littérature* 47 (1982):31-40.

A description of a pattern involving a couple's go-between found both in the *Rose* (Bel Accueil) and "Lucidor"

(Lucidor/Lucile). The author does not intend to show influence (von Hofmannsthal had almost certainly not read the *Rose*) but to "interpréter les constantes de l'imaginaire" (31). These constants concern the sexually ambivalent role of the two characters, who originally represent the beloved but come to supplant her in the lover's feelings. Bel Accueil's ambivalence is indicated not only by the grammatical difficulties that his masculine gender causes the allegory, but also by the fact that he, as another male, can associate closely with the lover to the point of replacing the rose as the love object (the imprisoned flower thereby becomes the beloved's sex). Both Lucidor and Bel Accueil are symptoms of adolescent sexuality, fantasies of a male friend with female sexuality.

555 -----. "Die Liebe im *Rosenroman*." In *Das Schicksal der Liebe*. Ed. Dietmar Kamper and Christoph Wulf. Weinheim and Berlin: Quadriga, 1988. 130-49.

An examination of the complex interrelationship between the dream, the reality of the narrator, and the passage of time. The games with time exhibit the impossibility of capturing the present moment of love. The obvious obstacles which prevent the picking of the rose are the least serious ones for the realization of love. The poem represents, in fact, an effort to fulfill the present in the reminiscent illumination of a found-again past. However, love escapes the present and slips at the same time into the past and the future--into objective and subjective time. The season of love is May, but this month exists only in the subjective illusion of the dream. The age for love is the twentieth year, but at that age the narrator knew love only in the form of his dream and under the veil of allegory, and five years have since passed. The generalized objectivity of allegoric codes and the text in the present tense focus on a love whose representation is part of the past and whose realization is part of the future. This dream of love, this love without the other because it is only a dream, this love whose object is altered through the allegorical metaphor, can only finish badly, in non-completion (as with Guillaume de Lorris) or in awakening (as with Jean de Meun), which is just another death, the death of the dream and of love lived by the narrator. [ASK]

556 -----. *La subjectivité littéraire: autour du siècle de saint Louis.* Collection "Ecriture". Paris: Presses Universitaires de France, 1985. Pp. 267.

An analysis of the relation of allegory to subjectivity in the first *Roman de la rose*, which marks "l'aboutissement de la relation de plus en plus étroite entre l'allégorie et la subjectivité" (161), and in similar works, such as the allegorical poems of Watriquet de Couvin and Huon de Mery's *Tournoiement Antecrist*. Through the dream framework the poet was able to play with past time and with present reality, to explore the relation of the dreamer to his dream experience and of the narrator to his written recollection of it. This "jeu de l'intériorité et de l'extériorité" (159) is further manifested in the state of revery called "*dorveille*" (148), described in a number of medieval works as particularly conducive to allegorical visions, and in the two kinds of relationships that the dreamer can have with the allegorical argument--as observer or object. Zink's analysis, which includes discussions of Macrobius's theory of dreams and medieval theories of memory, argues that allegory is personal poetry, "le reflet d'une verité dans une conscience" (166).

557 Zschiegner, Christine. "Wortfeld Untersuchungen zum *Rosenroman*: Der Wortschatz der zwischenmenschlichen Beziehungen." Diss. U of Innsbruck, 1971.

558 Zumthor, Paul. "Autobiography in the Middle Ages?" Tr. Sherry Simon. *Genre* 6 (1973):29-48.

A linguistic and structuralist analysis of autobiographical forms in medieval French literature and the difficulty they pose for critical understanding. In this context, the author describes the first part of the *Rose* as one of the first romances to use the *I*-discourse. Zumthor links Guillaume's poem to the *grand chant courtois* and, more originally, to what he calls "songs of

Encounter" (34), such as the *pastourelle*: "The *I* of the *Roman de la Rose* is formally identical to the *I* of the *pastourelle*" (35), in which the lover recounts how he set out on a spring morning, saw a beautiful woman in an idyllic place, and attempted to seduce her.

559 -----. "De Guillaume de Lorris à Jean de Meung." In *Etudes de langue et littérature du moyen âge offertes à Félix Lecoy par ses collègues, ses élèves, et ses amis*. Paris: Honoré Champion, 1973. 609-20.

A linguistic study of a 270-line excerpt from the transitional section of the *Rose* (the last 109 verses of Guillaume de Lorris, the first 162 of Jean de Meun) in order to study "de manière microscopique" the marks of different "fonctionnalités" (610) in the two parts. The author analyzes phonetic, syntactic, and lexical elements, such as the number of verbs per sentence and their lexical categories (modals, verbs of affectivity, etc.), abstract or concrete nouns, and different kinds of adverbs. This linguistic study leads Zumthor to some sweeping, even enigmatic, conclusions: Guillaume's discourse constitutes "une réponse globale à quelque question informulée" (619), while Jean's play of open questions is founded on a reality which is "la totalité même du récit" (620); his allegory implies its own gloss which is constantly questioned.

560 -----. *Essai de poétique médiévale*. Paris: Editions du Seuil, 1972. Pp. 518.

A challenging semiotic introduction to the *Rose*. Guillaume's allegorical poem--a Meeting ("Rencontre," 371) set in a Dream--organizes the *actants* in three geographic paradigms: the wall, the garden, and the enclosure, and in three orders of meaning: the story ("le récit dans sa littérarité," 371), the subjective development of love, and the teaching about love. Thus the first part of the *Rose* creates an allegorical world like Prudentius's but oriented "dans le sens de l'histoire de l'imagination, non plus de celle du salut" (373). In Jean's continuation, which is "une immense glose interprétative additionnelle" (373-74), the form of the discourse changes, to become fundamentally "argumentative" (374). Finally Zumthor proposes a four-layer structure for allegory, based on the substance and the form of the literal level (the language or expression) and the figurative level (the content).

561 -----. "Narrative and Anti-Narrative: *Le roman de la rose*." Tr. Frank Yeomans. *Yale French Studies* 51 (1974):185-204.

Same article as no. 562 with a few small changes [not indicated whether made by author or not]. The French version is often clearer. Lacks the "Works Cited" given in the French version.

562 -----. "Récit et anti-récit: *Le roman de la rose*." *Medioevo romanzo* 1 (1974):5-24. Rpt. in *Langue, texte, énigme*. Paris: Editions du Seuil, 1975. 249-67.

A treatment of the broad topic of the production of meaning in the *Rose* and how the two parts create meaning in different ways. The difference is largely a result of "la diversité de statut des figures signifiantes, et l'ambiguïté fonctionnelle de l'allégorie poétique" (249). The discussion of the figures distinguishes between an emblem (the Rose) and a symbol (the Fountain of Narcissus--the only symbol in the first part); between a "symbole-objet" (the Fountain) and a "symbole-récit" (251) (the story of Pygmalion). Also discussed is the special significance of Nature for generating meaning in the second part: "sa puissance embrasse toute action narrée, sous-tend et justifie la glose" (252). Next, the allegory of the *Rose* is described in terms of its three functions: didactic or explicative; deictic (making perceptible an illusive reality); and narrative. In the first part these functions are treated linearly, while the discourse of the second part oscillates from one level to another. In particular, the first part moves from the quest model--"histoire"--to the lyric model--"discours" (259). Jean de Meun takes up Guillaume's allegorical figures and actions but derives a different meaning from them: the text and significance of the first part become the text for a second-level significance in the second part, and the quest becomes one for meaning itself ("La quête n'est plus que celle d'un sens..." [263]. Finally, Zumthor suggests that the relation of the two parts is homologous to that of the rewriting of Chrétien de Troyes's romances by the prose romances of the thirteenth century.

563 -----. "Roman de la rose." In *Le moyen âge*. Vol. 1 of *Dictionnaire des lettres françaises*. Ed. Paul Bossuat, Louis Pichard, and Guy Raynaud de Lage. Paris: Arthème Fayard, 1964. 654-55.

An overview of the *Rose* that sees both the disparities between the two parts and their coherence as significant of the evolving mentality of the thirteenth century: "les dissonances et les contradictions mêmes concourent à donner l'image vivante et complexe d'une époque tournante" (654). While Guillaume created the crowning expression of the troubadour conception of love, Jean's work reflects "une scolastique hédoniste...une entreprise de démystification" (655). The article focuses on questions of allegory--the tradition of medieval allegorical works, the differences between the allegorical foundations of the two parts, the *Rose*'s overwhelming influence which led to "le triomphe définitif de l'allégorie" (655) in subsequent European literature.

CHAPTER FOUR

THE INFLUENCE OF THE *ROMAN DE LA ROSE*

564 Adler, Alfred. "The Topos *Quinque Lineae Sunt Amoris* Used by Ronsard in *Amours* (1552), CXXXVI." *Bibliothèque d'humanisme et renaissance* 15 (1953):220-25.

An analysis of Ronsard's sonnet in which the poet speaks in the voice of l'Amant in the *Rose* ("Ha, Belacueil, que ta doulce parolle..."). The final verse refers to the *cinq pas* or stages of love described in medieval discussions of erotic desire. Adler believes that Ronsard is not following the *Rose*'s glorification of love's folly but instead attempts to create a balance "between the dissonance of the content and the harmony of the form" (223), the five steps of the dance at the end of the sonnet functioning as a pause between dissonance and harmony. Specifically it is between "moral (mediaeval) dissonance and (Renaissance) harmony" (225) that Ronsard effects a conciliation.

565 Allen, Mark and John H. Fisher. *The Essential Chaucer: An Annotated Bibliography of Major Modern Studies.* Boston: G. K. Hall, 1987. Pp. xiii + 243.

A bibliographical guide to twentieth-century studies of Chaucer. Several dozen entries, including some not included here, explore the relationship of Chaucer's works to the *Rose*. The short annotations are clear and precise.

566 Ames, Ruth M. "The Feminist Connections of Chaucer's *Legend of Good Women*." In *Chaucer in the Eighties*. Ed. Julian N. Wasserman and Robert J. Blanch. Syracuse: Syracuse UP, 1986. 57-74.

A perceptive analysis that uses the fourteenth-century controversy over women and the *Rose* to interpret the *Legend*'s meaning and in particular Chaucer's conception of women's virtue. The controversy sheds light on the references to the *Rose* in the prologue to the *Legend*, on "the words of the narrator to the God of Love, and on the techniques of the villains in the legends" (58). Ames's review of the arguments in the controversy, which she sees as a direct influence on the *Legend*, shows that Christine de Pizan "wanted to keep the garden of romance but to domesticate the God of Love" (64). In the *Legend of Good Women*, however, Chaucer demonstrates "the failure of the feminist compromise with romance" (71): "As the *Rose* shows love as a trap for men, the legends show it as a trap for women" (72).

567 Arnoldo, Moroldo. "L'emprunt dans le *Fiore*: pour un essai d'attribution de l'oeuvre." Diss. U of Nice, 1987.

568 Arrathoon, Leigh A. "'For craft is al, whose that do it kan': The Genre of the *Merchant's Tale*." In *Chaucer and the Craft of Fiction*. Ed. Leigh A. Arrathoon. Rochester, Mich.: Solaris Press, 1986. 241-328.

A lengthy study of the *Merchant's Tale* that argues that "both Jean de Meun and Geoffrey Chaucer were satiric apologists" (241-42) and that "Chaucer translated *The Romance of the Rose* in his *Merchant's Tale*" (245). Arrathoon points out echoes of the *Rose* in the *Merchant's Tale*, including the theme of the mirror as image of the mind or of lust, and the satire of prudish language. More generally, the author adopts Fleming's concept of the "intertext" (244; see also no. 241) in order to maintain that in both works allusions to other texts--Biblical and patristic--provide a "heavily charged oversense," which serves as "the corrective to a deceptive tale surface" (242).

569   Babcock, R. W. "The Mediaeval Setting of Chaucer's *Monk's Tale*." *PMLA* 46 (1931):205-13.

A discussion of the questions of how representative was the *Monk's Tale* of a medieval type of tale and what were the possible sources of its concepts of tragedy and fortune. After considering works which Babcock groups into three categories, the Roman tradition, the medieval clerical tradition, and the medieval non-clerical tradition, he concludes that "the idea of the *Monk's Tale* grew out of the *Roman de la Rose*" (211) and that the tale owed little to Boccaccio.

570   Badel, Pierre-Yves. "Alchemical Readings of the *Romance of the Rose*." In *Rethinking* (no. 182). 262-85.

A good history of the principal readings of the *Rose* based on alchemical concepts or vocabulary. Badel begins with a review of the many alchemical works that have been attributed to Jean de Meun over the centuries because of a short passage in his continuation [the list of these works reveals that they were continually transmuting like the metals they describe]. The author is careful to distinguish the medieval definition of alchemy as a physical process from the more modern spiritual understanding, a crucial distinction largely ignored by earlier literary historians. The most important alchemical reading of the *Rose* was the influential one of Jacques Gohory (sixteenth century), which is analyzed in some detail by Badel; contemporary alchemists "still exploit Gohory's ideas" (276). The last section discusses briefly but perceptively two modern alchemical readings of the first part by Méla and Poirion (see nos. 389 and 446), which are shown to be unsatisfying. Ultimately they pose cogently "the problem of valid interpretation" (280) of the *Rose*.

571 -----. "Pierre d'Ailly auteur du *Jardin amoureux*." *Romania* 97 (1976):369-81.

A discussion of the *Jardin amoureux*, a short devotional treatise from the period of the Querelle de la Rose which incorporates elements from the *Rose* in a religious context. From textual evidence, such as identical phrases in the *Jardin* and in one of Pierre d'Ailly's sermons, Badel argues strongly that the author is not Jean Gerson, as has usually been assumed, but Pierre d'Ailly. Furthermore, he suggests that Pierre was the recipient of Jean de Montreuil's Letter 103, *Cum ut dant*, and that the treatise may have been written either after May 14, 1402, or in July or August 1401. The study shows to what extent imagery from the *Rose* was incorporated even into sermons in the late Middle Ages.

572 -----. *Le roman de la rose au XIVe siècle: étude de la réception de l'oeuvre*. Publications Romanes et Françaises 153. Geneva: Droz, 1980. Pp. xii + 534.

A wide-ranging but detailed investigation, based on the author's dissertation, of how readers read the *Rose* in the fourteenth century, including a chapter on the Querelle de la Rose. After a review of criticism on the *Rose* and an examination of Genius's sermon on procreation (one of the "maîtres mots" [115] of Jean de Meun), Badel explores the many facets of public response to the *Rose* in three ways: how specific authors were influenced by the romance, how readers generally perceived the work and its authors, and how the Querelle defined opposing theories of literature by means of the *Rose*. The evidence shows that the *Rose* was soon seen as a literary work in the modern sense; that Jean de Meun, to whom many readers attributed the entire poem, was the first author to be taken as a personality and as an authority; that while very few readers before the Querelle explicitly questioned the unity of the *Rose*, readers saw it in effect as a collection of speeches, sayings, and instruction on various topics. The topics most often referred to are eroticism, women, and clerics, to each of which Badel devotes a chapter. He also studies the perception of the *Rose* as un "'miroir de vie humaine'" (263), which suggested to medieval authors the philosophical and moral possibilities of a vernacular poetic work. The *Rose* was the first vernacular work to reach the status of a classic, to be quoted and studied as an authority. Badel touches on questions of literary form in his description of how later poems varied the elements of the dream framework--the dream itself, first person narration, and personifications. A chapter on the Querelle focuses on how the adversaries defined their conception of literature through their response to the *Rose*. The author concludes with a review of readers' responses to the *Rose* in the Renaissance. Among the many authors and works discussed in this ambitious study are Gui de Mori, Guillaume de Machaut, Eustache Deschamps, the *Echecs d'amour* and its prose commentary, Guillaume de Deguileville, and Nicole de Margival.

573 Baird, Joseph L. "Pierre Col and the *Querelle de la Rose*." *Philological Quarterly* 60 (1982):273-86.

A re-examination of Pierre Col's part in the Querelle de la Rose. According to Baird, critical theories have led scholars, in particular D. W. Robertson and his followers, to misinterpret the documents in the Querelle de la Rose. Pierre Col has been represented as expressing "the properly medieval view of the poem" (274), but Baird offers evidence that Col may have been much less serious in his defense of the *Rose* than previously believed. His replies to the *Rose*'s critics contain many examples of his sense of comic absurdity, of his "light, playful attitude" (277). Baird concludes that Col was no more serious than Jean de Meun himself, of whom Col considered himself the especial disciple. Thus Baird argues that modern scholarship has handled Pierre Col's contribution to the debate too heavy-handedly.

574 Baird, Joseph L. and John R. Kane. "*La Querelle de la Rose*: In Defense of the Opponents." *French Review* 48 (1974):298-307.

A study of the Querelle de la Rose which attempts to counter what the authors see as mistaken evaluations of the outcome of the debate on the *Rose*. Baird and Kane make a strong case for the opponents of the romance, in particular for Christine de Pizan, who offered serious but witty criticism of the *Rose*. In contrast, the work's defenders are shown to resort to *ad hominem* arguments and to "strained moral pleading" (303). This article is incorporated into the introduction to the authors' translation of the documents in the Querelle (see no. 575 below), with the quotations translated.

575 -----, eds. and trs. *La Querelle de la Rose: Letters and Documents*. North Carolina Studies in the Romance Languages and Literatures 199. Chapel Hill: University of North Carolina Department of Romance Languages, 1978. Pp. 170.

A translation of twenty-two documents in the Querelle de la Rose; excerpts from Christine de Pizan's related work, *L'Epistre au Dieu d'Amours* (see no. 590), are also included. The translations are carefully prepared from manuscripts and other editions and are clear and readable while striving to retain the irony and wit of the originals. In addition to a brief introduction to each document, the translators' introduction summarizes the development of the *débat*, proposes a chronology, reviews modern critical response to the discussion, especially to Christine's role in it, and offers a thoughtful, balanced appreciation of the opponents and their arguments.

576 Baker, Denise N. "The Priesthood of Genius: A Study of the Medieval Tradition." *Speculum* 51 (1976):277-91.

A reexamination of the major medieval works in which Genius appears, especially Bernard Silvestre's *De mundi universitate*, Alain de Lille's *De planctu Naturae*, and Jean de Meun's part of the *Rose*, in order to clarify the apparent contradictions in the character of Genius in Gower's *Confessio Amantis*, who is both god of procreation and tutelary spirit. Because of the mode of comic irony in which he was working, Jean divided the moral and procreative roles of Nature and Genius, thereby making his Genius the false priest of natural concupiscence. Gower, by restoring Genius's role as priest both of the laws of *kinde* and of *reson*, corrects Jean de Meun: his Genius is "a complex and sophisticated assimilation of his two precursors in the literary tradition" (291), that is, in the *De planctu Naturae* and the *Roman de la rose*.

577 Barron, W. R. J. "Luf-Daungere." In *Medieval Miscellany Presented to Eugène Vinaver by Pupils, Colleagues and Friends*. Ed. F. Whitehead et al. Manchester: Manchester UP; New York: Barnes and Noble, 1965. 1-18.

An attempt to clarify the connotations of the two appearances of the word *daunger* in the late fourteenth-century *Pearl* (see ll. 9-12 and 249-50). The author reviews the "complex semantic history of [Old French] *dangier*" (2), including its uses in the *Roman de la rose*, where Danger is both a common noun and an important character. The overtones of meanings associated with Old French *dangier*, from Latin *dominus* through *dominiarium*, include resistance, fickleness, disdain, and frustration (that is, the lover's feelings caused by the lady's resistance, fickleness, or disdain). It is the latter meaning, "frustration," which Barron suggests as appropriate for the occurrences in *Pearl*. Since the influence of the *Roman de la rose* is evident elsewhere in *Pearl*, it is not surprising that the English poet "should also have borrowed something of the structure of emotional relationships with which the terms were associated there" (14).

578 Batany, Jean. "Jean de Meun et Rabelais." *Bulletin de l'Association des amis de Rabelais et de la Devinière* 4.5 (1986):161-62.

A short article that argues that Jean de Meun was an important predecessor of Rabelais. As evidence Batany outlines a comparison between what he calls "la personnalité" (161) of the two authors: both were "'intellectuels bavards'" (161) who used personification, parody, and crude language in similar ways. Furthermore, Jean de Meun and Rabelais shared similar ideas on nature, women, social classes, and religious hypocrisy. He sees them as members of the same family.

579 Beck, Friedrich. *Les épistres sur le "Roman de la rose" von Christine de Pizan nach drei Pariser Handschriften bearbeitet und zum ersten Male veröffentlicht.* Neuberg: Griessmayersche Buchdruckerei, 1888. Pp. x + 25.

The first modern edition of the dossier of documents relating to the Querelle de la Rose assembled by Christine de Pizan in 1402. It is based on one manuscript, Paris B. N. fr. 604, but has many mistakes and omissions. The editor did not know about Gontier Col's brother, Pierre, and so would not accept references to him as authentic.

580 Becker, Ph. Aug. "Clément Marot und der *Rosenroman*." *Germanisch-romanische Monatsschrift* 4 (1912):684-87.

A series of arguments against attributing the 1526 modernization of the *Rose* to Marot. Becker argues that Pasquier's attribution in *Recherches de la France* (Book 7, Chap. 3) is not certain and that both internal and external evidence goes against the attribution.

581 Benedetto, Luigi Foscolo. *"Il Roman de la Rose" e la letteratura italiana.* Beiheft zur Zeitschrift für romanische Philologie 21. Halle: Max Niemeyer, 1910. Pp. 259.

A survey of Italian works influenced by the *Rose*. The author begins with the recognition of the intellectual affinities between Guillaume and Jean but soon turns to examining the stages of Jean's emancipation from the poetics of the first *Rose*. While maintaining that the "storia allegorica delle vicissitudini d'un amante" (25) constitutes the backbone of the entire poem and guarantees its fundamental unity, Benedetto is critical of Jean's role as a continuator. Working with his "cervello e non col cuore" (84), Jean deeply modifies the spirit of the poem and as a result "vien meno l'omogeneità; sparisce la grazia e la misura" (84). From this lack of harmony comes not a work of art but "un tutto mostruoso" (85). Benedetto's preoccupation with true poetry was fostered by neo-Hegelian ideas (see Benedetto Croce's *Estetica*); therefore, his bias against those authors whose intellectual passion prevailed over poetic inspiration is not surprising. In his treatment of Brunetto Latini's *Tesoretto* he not only denies that Brunetto introduced the *Rose* to the Italian public but also accuses him of "imitazione malaccorta" (100) and lack of a quick and noble mind. Benedetto conscientiously examines all Italian works which present a possible descent from the *Rose* and tries to establish their lineage. Among many poets whom Benedetto presents, Sor Durante, the poet of the *Fiore*, is especially praised (his closeness to the spirit of Guillaume's *Rose* is noted), and Dino Frescobaldi's use of allegory in a "stilnovo" manner is the object of an interesting examination. [MRB]

582 Bernardo, Aldo S. "Sex and Salvation in the Middle Ages: From the *Romance of the Rose* to the *Divine Comedy*." *Italica* 67 (1990):305-18.

A general comparison of the *Rose* and the *Divine Comedy*, especially in regard to the poets' opposing conceptions of love. The author first shows how the *Fiore* rewrites the *Rose in malo* (negatively) by stripping lust and carnality of non-essential elements; then how the *Divina commedia* constitutes an "antidote" to "the lecherous and carnal lovers" (309) of the preceding works. More specifically, many elements of the *Rose*, such as flowers and the rose itself, are given spiritual meaning by Dante's poem, which is "a total deconstruction and reconstruction of the undisputed French masterpiece of erotic allegory" (311).

583 Biagi, Vincenzo. *Opere anonime e di dubbia autenticità nella letteratura italiana; I predanteschi: "Il fiore," "Il detto*

d'amore," "L'intelligenza". Florence: Bemporad, 1921. Pp. 86.

A collection of essays which includes a discussion of the relation of the *Fiore* and the *Detto* to the *Rose*. Contrary to what other scholars believe, for Biagi it is Jean de Meun who uses the *Fiore* as one of his sources. One of his arguments is that Guillaume's part has few literal correspondences in the *Fiore* and is synthesized in just thirty-two sonnets, while Jean's text is faithfully translated and, furthermore, presents obscurities which can be easily explained by Jean's imperfect understanding of the Italian text: if the poet of the *Fiore* (and of the *Detto*) had known the *Rose* in its entirety, his treatment of it would not have presented the disparities described above. Biagi is convinced that the first part of the *Rose* became known in Italy before Jean's continuation was written and was in fact the source which inspired the "elegantissima concezione" (79) of the Anonimo and became in turn the scaffolding for Jean's "enorme edificio" (79). The author identifies the Anonimo of the *Detto* and later of the *Fiore* with Rustico di Filippo whose poetic personality and friendship with Brunetto Latini make him a plausible candidate. [MRB]

584 Blanchard, Joël. "L'effet autobiographique dans la tradition: le *Livre du cuer d'amours espris* de René d'Anjou." In *Courtly Literature: Culture and Context*. Selected Papers of the Fifth Triennial Congress of the International Courtly Literature Society, Dalfsen, The Netherlands, 9-16 August 1986. Ed. Keith Busby and Erik Kooper. Amsterdam: John Benjamins, 1990. 11-21.

An analysis of the autobiographical structure and the "inventaire des représentations (emblèmes, reflets, fragments)" (11) found in the *Livre du cuer d'amours espris*, an allegorical work which reshapes elements of two great traditional models, the *Roman de la rose* and the *Queste del saint graal*. René d'Anjou's allegorical figures, unlike those of the *Rose*, no longer have a "fonction catégorielle" (15); they have become powerless representations, a necessary anachronism, "un mécanisme qui tourne à vide" (17). The poet's "fétichisme littéraire" (18), his holding onto and detachment from his models, reveals both "une crise des signes" (19) and a need for self-definition which is the real subject of his text.

585 Bouché, Thérèse. "L'*Histoire comique de Francion* de Charles Sorel et le *Roman de la rose*." In *Mélanges offerts au Professeur Maurice Descotes*. Ed. Yves-Alain Favre and Christian Manso. Pau: Université de Pau et des Pays de l'Adour, Faculté des Lettres, Langues et Sciences Humaines, 1988. 13-35.

An evaluation of the influence of the *Rose* on Sorel's novel that sees this influence as going beyond a recognition of the dramatic qualities of the second part, especially of the antifeminist jealous husband and la Vieille. Sorel knew the romance so well that the *Histoire comique* can be considered "la réécriture proprement romanesque et exclusivement 'comique'" (15) of the *Rose*. This rewriting focuses on l'Ami and la Vieille in order to show the limits of "une philosophie de la jouissance" (15). Thus Sorel's novel constitutes the "commentaire continu" (16) missing from medieval readings. Bouché studies Sorel's novelistic development of the old woman in Agathe, a powerful character who undermines the philosophical bases on which Francion has built his youth. Agathe clarifies the deeper meaning of the novel by demystifying "un art de vivre fondé exclusivement sur la recherche du plaisir" (21). The author suggests that Sorel, through the counterpoint of Agathe and Francion, has his hero accomplish in reverse l'Amant's progress in the *Rose*; he discovers not pleasure for itself but the necessity of the ideal and the exaltation of the individual.

586 Bourdillon, F. W. "*Le jaloux qui bat sa femme* (Extract from the *Roman de la rose*)." *Romania* 36 (1907):444.

An examination of the historical context of the 144-line excerpt from the *Rose* that was printed separately in the sixteenth century. Bourdillon points out that it was drawn from an edition of Clément Marot's recension, probably the one of 1526, and that therefore the "undated little book" (444) was probably printed about 1527 or 1528. [This would appear to be evidence of sixteenth-century interest in the character of the jealous husband. See Montaiglon, no. 784, for the text of the excerpt.]

587 Braddy, Haldeen. "The French Influence on Chaucer." In *Companion to Chaucer Studies*. Ed. Beryl Rowland. 1968; rpt. New York: Oxford UP, 1979. 123-38.

An introductory survey of criticism on the influence of French writers on Chaucer's works, beginning with the four love-visions and continuing through the minor pieces and the *Canterbury Tales*. Although Braddy emphasizes Chaucer's familiarity with many French authors, in particularly with Machaut, Froissart, and Deschamps, he recognizes that the *Roman* is "ubiquitous" (129) in Chaucer's works: "In many details and special usages of style, the *Roman* served as a quenchless reservoir..." (132). The *Rose*'s influence is singled out in the *General Prologue*'s sketches of the Squire, the Wife of Bath, and the Pardoner, and in the prologues and tales of the Physician, the Monk, and the Pardoner.

588 Brown, Emerson, Jr. "What is Chaucer Doing with the Physician and His Tale?" *Philological Quarterly* 60 (1982):129-49.

A detailed discussion of Chaucer's retelling of the story of Virginia and Virginius which includes a brief comparison of the Physician's version with those of Livy and Jean de Meun (as told by Raison, ll. 5559-628). The Physician's version confuses the causes of Virginia's death and weakens the moral meaning of the example, both of which are clearly expressed in Jean de Meun's version [although he also leaves out the detail given by Livy of Virginius's attempted use of friends to thwart the evil judge]. Brown argues from his source study that Chaucer may have been casting doubt on the Physician's competence at diagnosing the causes of illness, and that the "curious morality"

(130) of the tale has its place between the Franklin's and the Pardoner's tales, which see evil differently. Thus Chaucer makes "a mediocre story told rather poorly by an incompetent narrator 'work'" (143).

589 Brown, Peter. "The Prison of Theseus and the Castle of Jalousie." *The Chaucer Review* 26 (1991):147-52.

A comment on the symbolic meanings (Fortune, the *prison amoureuse*, and the prison of life) of Theseus's prison tower in the *Knight's Tale* as suggested earlier by V. A. Kolve in *Chaucer and the Imagery of Narrative*. Brown expands the symbolic meaning of Chaucer's castle by adding the castle of Jalousie in the *Rose* as a possible model. While the situation of Chaucer's two suitors is the reverse of that of Guillaume's lover, nonetheless "Chaucer's version may be read as an ironic account of a model which he knew from the *Rose*" (150). Brown points to passages in the tale in which jealousy is an issue and concludes that the "representation of jealousy as an imprisoning castle tower is an important factor in this complex process of allusion" (152).

590 Brownlee, Kevin. "Discourses of the Self: Christine de Pizan and the *Rose*." *Romanic Review* 79 (1988):199-221. Rpt. as "Discourses of the Self: Christine de Pizan and the *Romance of the Rose*" in *Rethinking* (no. 182). 234-61.

An exploration of the development of Christine de Pizan's identity as a courtly and clerkly woman writer through detailed analyses of three of her works which are responses to the *Roman de la rose*: the *Epistre au dieu d'amours* (1399), the *Dit de la rose* (1402), and the *Epistres sur le débat* (1401-1402). In the *Epistre au dieu d'amours*, Christine creates a corrected version of Cupid who reprimands both courtly and clerkly writers for their deception and defamation of women. Through Cupid, Christine critiques clerkly authority from the outside (i.e., from the perspective of experience) and uses clerkly discourse to disprove the misogynistic position, thereby implicitly establishing herself as female clerk. The *Dit de la rose* redefines the central metaphor, the rose itself, which becomes the sign of the "proper relation between speech practice and intentionality" (245), between courtly speech and behavior. In the second part of the *Dit*, Christine as a first-person protagonist incorporates her identity as courtly poet and professional writer into the *Dit*. The third stage of the development of her authorial identity is her arrangement of the documents in the *Epistres sur le débat* and her self-presentation in that dossier, which thereby completes her female authorial identity; even her opponents in the *Débat* are made "to bear witness to her public identity as a new kind of clerkly speaking subject" (256).

591 -----. "Machaut's Motet 15 and the *Roman de la rose*: The Literary Context of *Amours qui a le pouoir/Faus Samblant m'a deceü/Vidi dominum.*" *Early Music History* 10 (1991):1-14.

A summary of the author's earlier study of the character Faux Semblant and his dialogue with le Dieu d'Amours (see no. 180), a study used here to interpret references to both characters in Guillaume de Machaut's motet 15. In Jean's text Faux Semblant emerges as "a kind of emblem of multi-voicedness" (10); both his and le Dieu d'Amour's utterances express multiple viewpoints whose meaning is a function of "a temporally evolving speech situation which alone confers meaning upon the characters' discourse" (11). Similarly the motet places the two characters' language in "the fallen linguistic world of appearances, of seeming" (12), which characterizes courtly discourse. Finally the author suggests that Machaut "implicitly opposes this fallen linguistic world...to God's transcendent Word" (13).

592 -----. *Poetic Identity in Guillaume de Machaut*. Madison: U of Wisconsin P, 1984. Pp. x + 268.

A revised version of the author's dissertation, which studies the development of Machaut's concept of poetic identity in his narrative poems or *dits*. Brownlee refers several times to the central position of the *Rose* in that development and proposes that elements of the first part, in particular, were incorporated and radically transformed, often through inversion, in Machaut's poems. The texts analyzed include the *Dit dou vergier*, the *Remede de Fortune*, and the *Voir-dit*. The author concludes that in the *Fontaine amoureuse*, as in many of Machaut's other poems, the *Roman de la rose* is "an almost omnipresent subtext" (198).

593 Brumble, Herbert David III. "Genius and Other Related Allegorical Figures in the *De planctu Naturae*, the *Roman de la rose*, the *Confessio Amantis*, and the *Faerie Queene*." Diss. U of Nebraska, 1970.

594 Brüning, Detlef. *Clement Marots Bearbeitung des Rosenromans (1526): Studien zur Rezeption des Rosenromans im frühen sechzehnten Jahrhundert*. Berlin: E. Schmidt, 1972. Pp. 200.

595 Bryan, W. F. and Germaine Dempster, ed. *Sources and Analogues of Chaucer's "Canterbury Tales"*. 1941; rpt. New York: Humanities Press, 1958. Pp. xvi + 765.

A collection of source studies of the framework, the twenty-four tales, and two of the prologues, compiled as "a collaborative undertaking by members of the Chaucer Group of the Modern Language Association of America" (vii). Several chapters discuss the *Roman de la rose* and give excerpts of varying length and in Old French (from Langlois's edition), principally in relation to the Wife of Bath's prologue and tale, the tales of the Physician, the Monk, and the Manciple, and the Pardoner's prologue. Brief references are made to other tales and works by Chaucer.

596 Bullock-Kimball, Beatrice Susanne. "The European Heritage of Rose Symbolism and Rose Metaphors in View of Rilke's Epitaph Rose." Diss. U of California, San Diego, 1986.

597 Calabrese, Michael A. "May Devoid of All Delight: January, the *Merchant's Tale* and the *Romance of the Rose*." *Studies in Philology* 87 (1990):261-84.

An approach to the meaning of the *Merchant's Tale* and its connection to the Merchant. Calabrese uses Raison's sermon on money and avarice in the second part of the *Rose* as the paradigm. Because Chaucer had the *Rose* in mind in composing the *Merchant's Tale*, Calabrese sees important parallels between the two works. He argues that l'Amant and January are not simply foolish lovers. Rather, both are "in a very profound sense 'merchants'" (263) in their avaricious lust for a woman. Relying mainly on articles by Paul Olson, Calabrese stresses the negative mercantile aspects of January's love, for January--l'Amant grown old--"has merged lust and avarice" (277). For this reason the tale also reflects on the teller, the Merchant who is unknowingly speaking of his own spiritual state, not about wives and marriage.

598 Calin, William. "Problèmes de technique narrative au Moyen-Age: le *Roman de la rose* et Guillaume de Machaut." In *Mélanges de langue et littérature françaises du Moyen-Age offerts à Pierre Jonin*. Senefiance 7. Aix-en-Provence: CUER-MA, 1979. 127-38.

A study that traces the development of Chaucer's "narrateur comique, naïf et maladroit" (127) back through Guillaume de Machaut to the *Roman de la rose*. An analysis of technical problems with narrative voice in the first *Rose* shows the complex use of the narrator and his relation to l'Amant who experiences the dream, which is at once confession, sublimation, consolation, and seduction. Jean de Meun undermines the privileged voice of the first-person narrator and establishes a distance between this narrator and himself as author. Jean's

Roman is thus "un exemple précoce de polymodalité" (130), which forces the reader to judge each character for himself. In three works of Machaut, the *Dit dou vergier*, the *Jugement dou roy de Behaigne*, and the *Voir dit*, Calin works through the poet's creation of various types of complex narrators, a process which ends in the creation of a new literary type, "le narrateur inepte et maladroit" (137). Thus Machaut must be considered a pioneer in the development of a more refined literary technique.

599 Chamard, Henri. *Les origines de la poésie française de la Renaissance*. Paris: E. de Boccard, 1920. Pp. viii + 307.

A review of favorable appreciations of the *Roman de la rose* throughout the sixteenth century in France, including that of Ronsard, who read it in his youth, followed by a brief plot summary and suggested reasons, general and specific, for the continued popularity of the *Rose*. In general, Chamard claims that although the bipartite work lacks artistic merit, it embodied "cet esprit gaulois [Jean de Meun] et cet esprit courtois" [Guillaume de Lorris] (98) which make up the French spirit. More specifically, Renaissance authors appreciated the *Rose* for its use of allegory and for Jean de Meun's erudition and naturalism, both of which the Renaissance saw as links with the classical past.

600 Child, F. J. "The *Roman de la rose*." *The Athenaeum* 2249 (December 3, 1870):721.

A short note, in reply to Marsh and Ten Brink, pointing out the lines in the *Rose* that are the source of the passage concerning true nobility in the *Romaunt*. Although many other works present the same idea, the "best things, and best said, are in the 'Roman de la Rose'" (721). The author also doubts that the English translation is by Chaucer.

601 Cipriani, Lisi. "Studies in the Influence of the *Romance of the Rose* upon Chaucer." *PMLA* 22 (1907):552-95.

An investigation into the *Rose*'s influence on Chaucer through a comparison of passages from the *Rose* with analogous ones from five works, the *Book of the Duchess*, the *Parliament of Fowls*, *Troilus and Criseyde*, the *House of Fame*, and, briefly, the *Legend of Good Women*. The similarities may be only "verbal reminiscences" (554) or "verbal coincidences" (586) [concepts which Cipriani does not define or analyze], or they may indicate larger congruences in the authors' conception of love or of ethical and religious ideas. Of the works discussed, the influence of the *Roman* appears "nowhere more distinctly than it does in the *Troylus*" (575). Although the author believes it dangerous to reach "any absolute conclusion" (554), the evidence offered supports the impression of the *Roman*'s primordial influence on Chaucer.

602 Clark, George. "Chauntecleer and Deduit." *English Language Notes* 2 (1965):168-71.

A discussion of the *Nun's Priest's Tale* which argues that Chauntecleer and his *amie* Pertelote are not likened simply to "an abstracted notion of courtly lovers" (168) but to two of the idealized inhabitants of the garden in the *Roman de la rose*, Mirth and Gladness [Deduit and Leesse]. In addition to the evidence of "general parallelism of scene and situation," the author offers the "specific echo" (170) of the ages of the two heroines: seven years for Leesse, seven days for the hen. These parallels between the *Rose* and the tale of barnyard fowl would have increased Chaucer's audience's appreciation of the comedy of his tale.

603 Cocito, Luciana. "La 'Fontanne de Benimor' e la 'Fontaine d'amour'." *Convivium* 35 (1967):227-30.

An examination of ll. 32-37 of the *Rime* written by the Anonymous Genoese between the end of the thirteenth and the beginning of the fourteenth century, lines which contain a reference to the "fontanne de Benimor." When collated with ll. 1535-45 of the *Rose*, we see that the author, a well-read poet, had as a model Guillaume's description of the Fountain of Love. Its hermeneutics, however, is missing in the Genoese *Rime*. [MRB]

604 Combes, André. *Jean de Montreuil et le chancelier Gerson: contribution à l'histoire des rapports de l'humanisme et de la théologie en France au début du XVe siècle*. Etudes de Philosophie Médiévale 32. Paris: J. Vrin, 1942. Pp. 665.

A detailed examination of the alleged letters of Jean de Montreuil to Jean Gerson relating to the Querelle de la Rose. Combes subjects previous studies, especially those of Alfred Coville (see no. 606) and Antoine Thomas, to an unsparing critique. He also examines all the letters and documents relating to the supposed correspondence and concludes that we have no evidence of such an exchange. Furthermore he proposes revising earlier evaluations of the two men's opposing views of the *Rose*, an evaluation which saw Gerson as the conservative theologian and Jean de Montreuil as the progressive humanist: Gerson was also a humanist, and Jean, far from fearing or opposing him, admired him.

605 Contini, Gianfranco. "Un nodo della cultura medievale: la serie *Roman de la rose--Fiore--Divina commedia*." *Lettere italiane* 25 (1973):162-89.

An essay focusing on the reception of the *Rose*, where Contini attempts to explain its lack of popularity in modern times. The *Rose*'s "quotazione di borsa" (162) was high until the Pléiade poets; after that time Contini sees a dramatic shift in terms of literary taste and sensibility best represented by the Romantic generations who invented romance philology. The new discipline was not capable of receiving so exquisitely and merely literary a work as the *Rose*. Contini therefore does not find it surprising that scholars such as Francesco Novati or Joseph Bédier should take an openly dismissing position towards Jean's

Rose. Such positions are a reflection of the "scissione postromantica tra naturalismo e verismo da una parte...e dall'altra il versante simbolistico..." (166). After tracing this perspective on the *Rose* literature, Contini explores the issue of Dante's reception of the *Rose*. At stake is the attitude of the poet as author of the *Commedia* which, with a pun, he defines as "un'anti-parodia della *Rose*" (172). For Contini, Dante saw it as a work of uninterrupted linearity while his own *Commedia* can be conceived as an upward spiral. A comparison between Dante's *terzina* (ABA, BCB, etc.) and Guillaume's and Jean's metrical choice (AA, BB, etc.) gives substance to the interpretation. [MRB]

606 Coville, Alfred. *Gontier et Pierre Col et l'humanisme en France au temps de Charles VI*. 1934; rpt. Geneva: Slatkine Reprints, 1977. Pp. 256.

An essay that evokes "quelques esprits très cultivés, en avance...sur leur temps" (5), in particular a small group of early humanists that centered around Gontier and Pierre Col and Jean de Montreuil. Coville describes the life, character, and humanistic interests of the members, high-placed clerics and royal officers who tried to draw from classical authors "leur morale et leur esthétique" (103), to the point of neglecting Christian literature. The chapter on the Querelle de la Rose reviews the contributions of the humanists in support of the *Rose*, and to a lesser extent the arguments of their opponents. Coville stresses that Jean de Meun had the humanistic qualities that would please these scholars, qualities such as his poem's encyclopedic nature and its bold moral thought, and especially his knowledge and personal interpretation of classical authors. Through the admiration of these humanists "le débat sur le *Roman de la Rose* se rattache à l'histoire du premier humanisme français" (226). [For a critique of Coville's ideas, see no. 604.]

607 Cunningham, J. V. "The Literary Form of the Prologue to the *Canterbury Tales*." *Modern Philology* 49 (1952): 172-81.

In contradiction to the general critical belief that there is no literary tradition for the Prologue to the *Canterbury Tales*, Cunningham argues that analogues to the scheme of the Prologue are to be found in the *Roman de la rose*--the first place to look "for the source of anything in Chaucer" (174)--and associated French and English poems. The underlying scheme of the dream-vision prologue not only describes Chaucer's early works (Cunningham discusses the *Book of the Duchess*, the *House of Fame*, the *Legend of Good Women*, and the *Parliament of Fowls*), but also the General Prologue and the A Fragment of the tales. Furthermore, Cunningham shows that "the technical features of the portraits in the Canterbury Prologue have exact analogues in the portraits of the *Romance*" (181). Thus Chaucer was "original and traditional at the same time" (181).

608 David, Alfred. "How Marcia Lost Her Skin: A Note on Chaucer's Mythology." In *The Learned and the Lewed: Studies in Chaucer and Medieval Literature*. Ed. Larry D. Benson. Harvard English Studies 5. Cambridge: Harvard UP, 1974. 19-29.

An investigation first into Chaucer's source for his reference to "Marcia that loste her skyn" in the *House of Fame* (ll. 1229-32), then a suggestion concerning Chaucer's use of mythology. The author argues that Chaucer's source for his knowledge of Marcia and his reason for transforming the male satyr Marsyas into a woman was not Ovid, Dante, or Boccaccio, but an interpolation in a group of *Rose* manuscripts in which the sex change seems to have occurred. From this "small fact" (19) David draws several important conclusions: that practically everything in Chaucer's works can be traced not to Latin writers but to the *Rose* or another French work; that "learned Christian exegesis of classical mythology" (27), when applied to Chaucer or Jean de Meun, misses "the quality of humor" (28). The pagan gods, "substantial beings in an imaginary world," are "a storehouse of homely and humorous examples" (28) for Chaucer and Jean de Meun.

609 Dean, James. "Gather Ye Rosebuds: Gower's Comic Reply to Jean de Meun." In *John Gower: Recent Readings*. Papers presented at the meetings of the John Gower Society at the International Congress on Medieval Studies, Western Michigan University, 1983-1988. Ed. R. F. Yeager. Studies in Medieval Culture 26. Kalamazoo, Michigan: Medieval Institute Publications, Western Michigan University, 1989. 21-37.

An analysis of what Gower's brief comic voice at the end of *Confessio Amantis* owes to Jean de Meun's conclusion to the *Rose* and how Gower's moral comedy moves away from Jean's coarseness. Dean focuses on the questions of the two authors' views of love and sexuality, and their use of language. Also studied is Gower's courtly and humorous "Frenchifying" (26), both in terms of language and ambience, of l'Amant's complaint. Finally, Dean notes in Gower's "mingling of mirth and pathos" a "subtle, yet comic, portrayal of Amans's plight--*la condition humaine*" (33). [Note that Dean occasionally attributes Guillaume de Lorris's lines to Jean de Meun.]

610 Dean, James M. "Mars the Exegete in Chaucer's *Complaint of Mars*." *Comparative Literature* 41 (1989):128-40.

A discussion of the *Complaint* that suggests that critics have missed the "darker aspect of the poem" (128). Dean points to la Vieille's retelling of the myth of Venus and Mars caught in Vulcan's net (see ll. 13817-14156) as the hitherto unrecognized source for the complaint section of the poem. After reviewing how Chaucer altered his other possible sources (*Ars amatoria* and the fourteenth-century *Ovide moralisé*), an exploration of the relationship of Chaucer's version to la Vieille's suggests that Mars as the exegete of his own situation "utterly misreads his text" (135).

611 Dembowski, Peter F. "Le faux semblant et la problématique des masques et déguisements." In *Masques et déguisements dans la littérature médiévale*. Ed. Marie-Louise Ollier.

Montreal: Presses de l'Université de Montreal; Paris: J. Vrin, 1988. 43-53.

A study of religious hypocrisy as portrayed in the fourteenth-century *Roman de Fauvel*, which was influenced by the *Roman de la rose*. Earlier popular and literary examples of "le 'genre Faux Semblant'" (43), such as John of Salisbury's *Policraticus*, are indicated, but it is Jean de Meun who gave "une place prépondérante" (46) to religious hypocrisy: his presentation of Faux Semblant underlies the ideological conception of the *Roman de Fauvel*. An analysis of the *Fauvel* concludes that despite the romance's description of the triumph of evil, it remains a Christian work which never doubts the existence of divine justice.

612 Diekstra, F. N. M. "Chaucer and *The Romance of the Rose*." *English Studies* 69 (1988):12-26.

An "attempt to read the *Romance* through the eyes of Chaucer" by emphasizing "modes of thinking and techniques of writing" (12), in particular the ironic mode, "the dominant mode of the *Romance*" (26). The ironic techniques discussed include the juxtaposition of incongruous elements, inconsistent characterization, ironical digressions, innuendo or insinuation, and the exposure of hypocritical or fallacious reasoning; examples of similar techniques from Chaucer's works are given. As Jean de Meun uses the same ironical techniques when he addresses the reader in his own voice as when he speaks through characters, the ultimate effect is to draw the focus of interest to the author's manipulations: "our attention becomes author-directed" (19).

613 Dragonetti, Roger. "Specchi d'amore: *Il romanzo della rosa* e *Il fiore*." *Paragone* 81 (1981):3-22. Rpt. in *La musique et les lettres* (no. 215). 399-418.

An analysis that begins with a discussion of the traditional view that the *Rose* was written by two authors. Dragonetti argues that this interpretation is based on a rhetorical scenery built by the poet, whose too-definite assertions ought not to be taken at face value. Jean de Meun is ultimately driven by his love for language itself: he devises all kinds of means to explore the sentence, the word, the letter, in all their potential. The *Rose* is indeed an adventure within the word's world: the poet takes the meaning into account only as "un primo gradino di quella scala tortuosa che conduce verso l'intimità della lingua" (399). Arguing that the opposition of *"falsi contrari"* (401) is the pivot of the realistic deception, Dragonetti analyzes the anagrammatic relations of words such as *rose, eros, rosée, rosignox* which form what he calls a "rete consonantica che produce senso" (404). He then focuses on the figure of the flower and its influence on the structure of the *Rose* to conclude that if Guillaume's courtly and oneiric discourse includes an almost physical description of the rose, while Jean's realistic discourse implies anticipation and therefore imagination, in the end they both merge into a purely oneiric reality. In his conclusion, Dragonetti turns to the *Fiore*, observing that the poet, Durante, seems to have understood the *malizia* of the author of the *Rose*. The strategy of the *Rose* lies entirely in the process of enshrouding while feigning to display or demonstrate. Of course Durante will create his own *malizia*, his flower will be a frozen one and the reader "entra nello specchio del poema senza accorgersene, soddisfatto di aver riconosciuto il modello originale, un po' come l'amante crederà di baciare il fiore senza poter distinguere però nell'obscurità e nel gelo della notte invernale, la superficie liscia dello specchio, dal vetro naturale del gelo" (414). [MRB]

614 Dupire, Noël. *Jean Molinet: la vie--les oeuvres*. Paris: E. Droz, 1932. Pp. vi + 368.

A study of the life and works of the late medieval poet and chronicler in which Dupire devotes a chapter to a literary history of Molinet's prose translation and religious allegorization of the *Roman de la rose*. Dupire argues strongly for 1500 (given in the colophon of Molinet's version) as the date of composition, despite Bourdillon's widely accepted hypothesis of 1483 (see no. 49). He further argues that Molinet's undertaking was based on a long medieval tradition of prose reworkings and moralizations. After discussing Molinet's source manuscripts, the chapter concludes with an overview of some of the ways that Molinet Christianized the *Rose*, including parallels between characters in the romance and Biblical figures. Although Dupire recognizes some qualities in Molinet's allegorization, such as his allusions to contemporary events and his lively retelling of anecdotes, he admits that Molinet does not avoid "la pure extravagance" (99).

615 Eckhardt, Caroline D. "The Art of Translation in *The Romaunt of the Rose*." *Studies in the Age of Chaucer* 6 (1984):41-63.

An analysis of language in the *Romaunt*. After reviewing critical opinion on the attribution of the *Romaunt* to Chaucer, the author offers this study to help remedy the lack of a "detailed assessment of the quality of the A fragment as a literary translation" (44). She evaluates "its very high degree of literal reproduction of its source" (46), in which Chaucer finds the right balance between familiarity and distance. There is, nonetheless, a "slight but pervasive alteration in tone" (51), in the direction of a more personal, more visual, and more emotional rendering. Thus by viewing favorably both faithfulness to and changes in the original, Eckhardt emphasizes Chaucer's literary skill.

616 Economou, George D. "Chaucer's Use of the Bird in the Cage Image in the *Canterbury Tales*." *Philological Quarterly* 54 (1976):679-84.

A discussion of the bird in the cage image, found three times in the *Canterbury Tales*, and also occurring in two of Chaucer's "favorite books" (679), Boethius's *De consolatione Philosophiae* and Jean de Meun's part of the *Rose*. Economou shows how the image is used to support a particular argument in each work: Boethius uses it to illustrate Nature's laws, but Jean's old woman makes it serve as an argument for women's sexual freedom. Chaucer follows Jean in suggesting, through the bird in the cage, women's sexual unfaithfulness.

617 -----. "Januarie's Sin against Nature: The *Merchant's Tale* and the *Roman de la rose.*" *Comparative Literature* 17 (1965):251-57.

A study of Nature's remarks on mirrors in the second part of the *Rose* (Langlois ll. 17875-18298; see Lecoy ll. 17983-18256), seen as the primary source for ll. 1577-87 of the *Merchant's Tale*. The author suggests that the "influence of the *Roman de la Rose* is so great that its acknowledgment is essential to our understanding of the poem" (252). Januarie's use of the simile of the mirror in his fantasies about young women recalls Nature's description of mirrors which distort perception and foster self-deception. Thus, Economou concludes, Januarie's selfish first steps in love lead him "down the wrong path into the Garden of Mirth [Deduit], a place where selfish and deceitful love is fruitless and deceived" (257).

618 Edelman, Nathan. *Attitudes of Seventeenth-Century France toward the Middle Ages*. New York: King's Crown Press, 1946. Pp. xv + 459.

An impressive, erudite survey of scholarly and lay tastes, inclinations, opinions, and judgments concerning the Middle Ages and medieval literature in the seventeenth century. The author has assembled comments both derogatory and laudatory on the *Roman de la rose*, "the medieval work which had the most interesting history in seventeenth-century France" (383). The laudatory views, especially those of scholars, dominate: Fauchet, Pasquier, le Père Bouhours, Mlle de Scudéry, and many lesser-known writers praise it as the outstanding work of the Middle Ages (Deimier even praised its versification). Edelman suggests briefly the possible influence of the *Rose* on some authors, such as Sorel, and concludes that it was a familiar work in the period.

619 Elliott, R. W. V. "Chaucer's Reading." In *Chaucer's Mind and Art*. Ed. A. C. Cawley. Edinburgh and London: Oliver and

Boyd, 1969. 46-68.

An examination not only of what Chaucer read or may have read, but how his reading affected his poetic creation. Particular emphasis is put on Chaucer's interest in and use of dreams, including the *Roman de la rose* (mentioned only a few times). Jean de Meun's scholarship, his wide-ranging interests, and "his critical, often satirical, attitudes can be traced...throughout Chaucer's poetry," while to the first part of the *Rose* Chaucer "owed his initiation into the garden of love entered through the curtain of sleep" (54).

620 Eusebi, M. "Saggio sulle edizioni cinquecentesche del 'Roman de la rose' attribuite a Clement Marot." In *Rendiconti dell' Istituto lombardo accademia di scienze e lettere; classe di lettere e scienze morali e storiche* 92 (1958): 527-57.

A study of the techniques of the author of the 1526 *Rose* modernization. Eusebi asks if there is a stylistic concern behind his use of old and new language. Should it be considered the expression of a rich and multifaceted personality, as in Rabelais, for example? Eusebi's answer is no; the revision of the *Rose* follows the principles familiar to the *dérimeurs*. Its lack of attention for the essential structures of the poetic text shows how the author works "au petit bonheur, sans grand effort intellectuel" (556). The author's declared intention is the "rajeunissement" of the language "pour l'intelligence des lecteurs" (555) and the correction of the versification which he finds "imparfaite" (555). The number of innovations, however, significantly declines after the first 1,000 verses. As for their character, Eusebi maintains that the modernizer's only rule is easiness, which leads him to preserve words no longer understood and to innovate where no difficulties are present. This very negligence and lack of uniformity constitute the strongest argument against the attribution of the 1526 version to Clément Marot, who has proved himself such an "editore amoroso e discreto" (556) of Villon's poetry. [MRB]

621 Fansler, Dean Spruill. "Chaucer and the *Roman de la rose*." Diss. Columbia U, 1913.

622 -----. *Chaucer and the "Roman de la rose"*. New York: Columbia UP, 1914. Pp. 269.

Principally a discussion of lines in the *Rose* that Chaucer may have used. Fansler both evaluates other scholars' suggested parallels and adds a few new ones. The categories of comparison are historical, legendary, and mythological allusions; elements of Chaucer's style, situations and descriptions; proverbs and proverbial expressions; and philosophical discussions. Although Fansler is often skeptical of others' parallels, he recognizes the importance of the *Rose* in Chaucer's art and thought without diminishing his originality. Guillaume de Lorris influenced Chaucer most in the *Book of the Duchess* and *Troilus and Criseyde*, while Jean de Meun, in addition to influencing every aspect of Chaucer's works, "furnished him with a list of authorities worthy of study" (23). The book includes a table of line numbers in the editions of Méon, Michel, and Marteau, (see nos. 4, 5, and 37); a table of line numbers in Ellis's translation of the *Rose* (no. 26) and the *Romaunt of the Rose*; and an index of Chaucerian passages referred to in the study.

623 Fenley, G. Ward. "Faus-Semblant, Fauvel, and Renart le Contrefait: A Study in Kinship." *Romanic Review* 23 (1932):323-31.

A study of the "close kinship" (323) between the three characters, who are nearly contemporaneous types of hypocrisy. Jean de Meun's Faux Semblant is the earliest and evidently the model for the others. After a short summary of their literary roles, Fenley describes the characters' family resemblance, which includes their association with religious hypocrisy, sin, and deceit, and their changeability and ubiquitousness. A mention of later writers influenced by these three characters concludes the article.

624 Fenzi, Enrico. "Boezio e Jean de Meun, filosofia e ragione nelle *Rime allegoriche* di Dante." *Studi di filologia e letteratura* 2-3 (1976):9-69.

A study of Dante's philosophy and philosophical background. Despite the title, Fenzi only briefly expounds the influence of the *Rose* on the Florentine poet. After establishing that both Guillaume de Lorris and Jean de Meun interpreted Boethius's philosophy as "la ragione umana...nel suo grado estremo di perfezione" (41), going beyond the Christianized version of the Carolingian commentators, Fenzi argues that for Dante too the voice of Philosophy carries the echoes of Cicero and Boethius and that rather than to console she comes to propose an alternative ideal of life. But if the lovers of the *Rose* and of the *Fiore* reject the offer of Raison, such a solution is inconceivable for Dante who, Fenzi argues, following Contini's authoritative position (see no. 605), intended to refute the positions expressed by the poets of the *Rose*. [MRB]

625 Ferster, Judith Ilana. "Chaucer and *L'art véritable*: The Epistemology of Art in Two Early Dream Visions and Two of the French Sources." Diss. Brown U, 1974.

626 Finlayson, John. "Chaucer's Prioress and *Amor Vincit Omnia*." *Studia neophilologica* 60 (1988):171-74.

A study that argues that the second part of the *Rose* was almost certainly the direct source not only for the Prioress's table manners but also for the phrase, *Amor Vincit Omnia*, "which provocatively ends the description" (171) of her courtliness. Further, since both of these passages from the *Rose* are linked with cupidinous love, Finlayson suggests that they help confirm the impression of a "deliberate tension directed between the ideal of spiritual courtesy and the Prioress's penchant for the manifestations of secular and social courtesy" (173).

627 -----. "The *Roman de la rose* and Chaucer's Narrators." *The Chaucer Review* 24 (1989/1990):187-210.

A close reading of the narrator's functions in the *Book of the Duchess*, the *House of Fame*, and the *Parliament of Fowls* as they compare to the narrative voices in the *Rose*. In the first part of the *Rose*, Finlayson examines the "complications surrounding the use of the pronoun 'I'" (189), which include the functions of "naïf Lover, biographer, retrospective commentator, and mere recorder by turns" (192), in accord with the narrator's varying interests. In the second part, Jean de Meun multiplies the narrative voices while deprivileging the narrator-protagonist as part of his "expanding and contextual allegoric purposes" (194), rather than as part of the development of character. Applying this approach to Chaucer, Finlayson shows through a detailed analysis of three narrators that we must distinguish levels of personalization: narrative voices vary as much and as frequently in Chaucer as in the *Rose*; they function as "localized rhetorical instruments, more as a *way* of presenting the matter than as the matter itself" (205). Thus the author warns that both New Criticism and structuralism may have imposed realistic and ironic meanings on the medieval narrator which were not intended.

628 Fleming, John V. "Chaucer's Squire, the 'Roman de la rose,' and the 'Romaunt'." *Notes and Queries* n. s. 14 [212] (1967):48-49.

A note that points to le Dieu d'Amour's commandments as the source for three lines describing the Squire's skills, thus putting praise of the Squire "in an ironical light" (49). Fleming further suggests that four lines introduced by the translator of Fragment B of the *Romaunt* are not from a *Rose* manuscript but are suggested by the description of the Squire in the General Prologue.

629 -----. "Hoccleve's 'Letter of Cupid' and the 'Quarrel' over the *Roman de la rose*." *Medium aevum* 40 (1971):21-40.

Both an appraisal of the relation of Hoccleve's "Letter of Cupid"

(1402) to its source, Christine de Pizan's *Epistre au dieu d'amours*, and an assessment of the English poet's interest in the Querelle de la Rose. Fleming maintains that neither the deletions nor the additions in the "Letter of Cupid" change the tone of the *Epistre*, and therefore Hoccleve is not guilty of antifeminism. But Fleming argues that Hoccleve differs from Christine de Pizan in his positive valuation of Jean de Meun's part of the *Rose*. After reviewing the Querelle and reiterating the arguments of the *Rose*'s supporters (Gerson and Christine de Pizan's views are dismissed as "squeamish inhibition" [36]), Fleming concludes that Hoccleve's "subtle but telling interpolations" (39) were intended to teach us how to read the *Rose*.

630 -----. "The Moral Reputation of the *Roman de la rose* before 1400." *Romance Philology* 18 (1964/1965):430-35.

An essay that attempts to expose "a modern myth about the *Roman*" (430) which posits adverse moral and theological responses to the *Rose* before the Querelle de la Rose in 1400. The two major pieces of evidence--the condemnation of radical Aristotelian propositions in Paris in 1277, and critical remarks in the Deguileville's *Pèlerinage de vie humaine*--do not support the contention that the *Rose* was criticized early. Fleming offers counter evidence that "moral traditionalists found it pleasing" (434) and attributes the criticism of the *Rose* in 1400 to (quoting D. W. Robertson) "a change in taste" (435; see also 473, 364).

631 -----. "Smoky Reyn: From Jean de Meun to Geoffrey Chaucer." In *Chaucer and the Craft of Fiction*. Ed. Leigh A. Arrathoon. Rochester, Michigan: Solaris Press, 1986. 1-21.

A discussion of Chaucer's remarkable phrase, "smoky reyn" (the rain that helps bring together the lovers in *Troilus and Criseyde*; see 3:628). To understand the phrase we need to see how Chaucer "'translated'" elements of Jean de Meun's *Rose*, in particular Genius's sermon on procreation. This limited question takes Fleming through a discussion of many broader topics, including correspondences in the careers of the two poets, their conceptions of modes of translation, and Chaucer's handling of the *Filostrato*. By tracing parallels between Chaucer's images of rain, smoke, and candles to passages in the *Rose*, Virgil, Alain de Lille, and others, Fleming delineates "a muted cacophony of textual associations Latin and vernacular alike" (18), associations of which Pandarus/Genius seems to be the key. Thus Chaucer's complex image of "smoky reyn" alludes less to a meteorological phenomenon than to "that amatory fume rising from Genius' candle" (20).

632 Flügel, Ewald. "Über einige Stellen aus dem Amalgestum Cl. Ptolemei bei Chaucer und im *Rosenroman*." *Anglia* 18 (1895/1896):133-40.

A comparison of Chaucer's citations of the *Almagest* with those of Jean de Meun and a discussion of the problem of their sources. The author argues that both writers relied directly on a copy of Ptolemy's text and not on glosses or Arabic translations (as suggested by Langlois). [The problem of the availability of good manuscripts seems to play an important role in the author's criticism of other scholars.] [JSZ]

633 Françon, Marcel. "Jean de Meun et les origines du naturalisme de la Renaissance." *PMLA* 59 (1944):624-45.

An essay that traces aspects of Jean de Meun's conception of naturalism (the sovereignty of nature) in late-medieval and Renaissance French literature: how elements of Catholic ceremony are used in "un esprit tout païen" (627), and how man and his works are glorified. After a short resumé of the roles of Nature and Genius in the *De planctu Naturae* of Alain de Lille and in the *Rose*, Françon discusses the works of Martin Le Franc, Jean Molinet, Clément Marot, Maurice Scève, Montaigne, Rabelais, and especially Jean Lemaire des Belges. He concludes that the Renaissance and later centuries are "étroitement reliés" (643) to the Middle Ages in terms of the humanistic and naturalistic ideas found in the *Rose*.

634 -----. "The *Roman de la rose* and Vauquelin de la Fresnaie." *Modern Language Notes* 68 (1953):410-11.

A note that points out several references to characters in the *Rose* (Faux Semblant, Bel Accueil, the Rose) in the works of the sixteenth-century writer, Vauquelin de la Fresnaie, who seems to have known the *Rose* better than did Marot and Ronsard, according to Françon.

635 -----. "Ronsard et la poésie populaire." *Modern Language Notes* 65 (1950):55-57.

A brief discussion of references to popular songs in Ronsard's poetry (the Pléiade poets usually rejected such sources), including the sonnet in the *Amours* of 1552 which recalls the *Rose* "en mettant en scène des personnages allégoriques comparables à ceux que ce poème a rendus célèbres" (56). The sonnet also contains an allusion to the *incipit* of a popular song mentioned by Molinet.

636 Furr, Grover Carr III. "The Quarrel of the *Roman de la rose* and Fourteenth-Century Humanism." Diss. Princeton U, 1979.

637 Galpin, Stanley L. "*Les eschez amoureux*: A Complete Synopsis, with Unpublished Extracts." *Romanic Review* 11 (1920):283-307.

A summary of the anonymous fourteenth-century imitation of the *Rose* (based on the Dresden ms.), which includes excerpts of passages on the wonderful city of Paris and its university, Fortune's wheel, the music of the spheres, and the five ways of becoming rich. *Les eschez* uses many of the characters, the setting, and plot elements of the *Rose* to tell the story of a chess game between the poet and a beautiful maiden (love is seen as a chess game). Most of the manuscript consists of a long discourse by Pallas which describes in great detail good political and domestic economy, including advice on how to choose a wetnurse.

638 Geissman, Erwin William. "The Style and Technique of Chaucer's Translations from French." Diss. Yale U, 1952.

639 Gill, R. "A Study of Traditional Elements in Middle High German Literature, with Special Reference to the *Tristan* of Gottfried von Strassburg and its Similarities with the *Roman de la rose* of Guillaume de Lorris." Diss. London, Univ. College, 1958-1959.

640 Glidden, Hope H. "Regeneration and Writing in the *Roman de la rose* and *Gargantua and Pantagruel*." In *Contending Kingdoms: Historical, Psychological, and Feminist Approaches to the Literature of Sixteenth-Century England and France*. Ed. Marie-Rose Logan and Peter L. Rudnytsky. Detroit: Wayne State UP, 1991. 69-89.

A comparison of the themes of procreation and language in the *Rose*, especially the second part, and in Rabelais's giant chronicles. After describing the "discursive strategies" (71) of the *Rose*, the author focuses on Rabelais's refiguration of Jean de Meun's allegory "by reconceiving the relation between reason, nature, and language in the comic play" (75) between Pantagruel and Panurge. Rabelais's double view of language as plain speech or duplicity leads Glidden to suggest the association of Panurge with l'Amant of the *Rose*, narcissism, and misguided interpretations of sign systems, while Pantagruel is linked with reason, community, and plain speaking. Thus both Jean de Meun and Rabelais are seen as proponents of plain speaking, for language "falsifies the natural procreative instincts by glossing them" (81), and these instincts are an expression of the divine principle governing rational sexuality.

641 Green, Richard Firth. "Chaucer's Victimized Women." *Studies in the Age of Chaucer* 10 (1988):3-21.

An examination of a group of victimized Chaucerian heroines--Dido and "several of her fellow martyrs (Medea, Hypsipyle, Ariadne, and Phyllis), Anelida, and Canacee's Falcon" (3)--to better understand Chaucer's attitude toward the courtly double standard, which did not see the seduction and betrayal of women as immoral. Chaucer's treatment of these characters is compared to Jean de Meun's versions in the second part of the *Rose*, in particular to his account of Dido. Green argues that, unlike Jean de Meun, Chaucer recognized and was disturbed by the current assumption that the sworn word in affairs of the heart "became merely an expedient device to gain one's end" (18).

642 Guy, Henry. "Les sources françaises de Ronsard." *Revue d'histoire littéraire de la France* 9 (1902):217-56.

A survey of Ronsard's works that looks for what the poet "a fatalement conservé des habitudes littéraires du moyen âge et de la première partie du XVIe siècle" (217). In addition to sections on medieval epics and romances and on Clément Marot, Guy devotes nine pages to the possible influence of the *Roman de la rose* on Ronsard. The *Rose* resurfaces both in details, such as le Dieu d'Amour's arrows, the natural equality of human beings, and the avarice of women, to more extended parallels in several poems. In particular Guy discusses a *chanson* which presents the antithetical definition of love found in the *Rose* (and other works), the *Discours d'un amoureux désespéré*, which derives "tout droit du *Roman de la Rose*" (241), and an ode about the combat of the Flesh and the Spirit. While Guy is cautious about positing a conscious imitation in all cases, he believes that the *Rose*'s importance for Ronsard is undeniable.

643 Hall, Ellen Wood. "A Study of Rabelais' Thought in the Context of Jean de Meung's *Roman de la rose*." Diss. Bryn Mawr College, 1973.

644 Harbison, Sherrill. "Medieval Aspects of Narcissism in Sigrid Undset's Modern Novels." *Scandinavian Studies* 63 (1991):464-75.

A study of the theme of narcissism in Undset's novels and its possible literary sources. On the hypothesis that Undset's use of the theme can be better understood in the context of medieval literature rather than modern psychology, Harbison sketches the development of the Narcissus theme in courtly poetry, then examines it in more detail in the *Rose*. Some of Undset's heroines are then examined "in light of Guillaume's vision" (467). The last part of the study defines Jean de Meun's strategies for "domesticating love" (469) and shows how Undset's characters, wittingly or unwittingly, "follow de Meun's curriculum" (470). For both authors "procreation and the beauties of nature were inextricably connected" (471). [The article contains the surprising and unsubstantiated assertion that Guillaume de Lorris died in 1237.]

645 Harrison, Robert Pogue. "The Bare Essential: The Landscape of *Il Fiore*." In *Rethinking* (no. 182). 289-303 [given as 290 in table of contents].

An analysis of the anonymous Italian sonnet translation of the *Rose* that is concerned with "the discrete poetic gestures by which the poem reappropriates its own minimalist originality" (291). After a discussion of the implications of scholars' continuing quest for the author of the *Fiore* (Dante has been suggested), Harrison examines instead "those features that set it off from the *Rose*" (293). The Italian poem reveals a "narrative essentialism" (293) in its omission of the digressions and descriptions of the original, thus preserving the essential narrative. An analysis of the opening sonnet, of sonnet 33 (which contains the scene of a boat on high seas), of the winter setting, and of other passages, reveals a "poverty of resource" (296) which constitutes the poem's originality.

646 Heuer, Hermann. *Studien zur syntaktischen und stilistischen Funktion des Adverbs bei Chaucer und im "Rosenroman"*. Anglistische Forschungen 75. Heidelberg: Carl Winter, 1932. Pp. vii + 168.

647 Hicks, Eric, ed. and tr. *Le débat sur "Le roman de la rose": Christine de Pisan, Jean Gerson, Jean de Montreuil, Gontier et Pierre Col*. Bibliothèque du XVe Siècle 43. Paris: Honoré Champion, 1977. Pp. xcix + 236.

The best modern edition of the documents in the Querelle de la Rose. Hick's introduction describes the almost mythical thinking about the debate and its participants by modern scholars and reconstructs the possible origin and course of the debate, its probable chronology, and the relationships of the participants. The manuscripts are described in detail, as is the plan of the edition, which includes two sets of the documents (the one assembled by Christine de Pizan in 1402, the other by Pierre Col), selected letters by Jean de Montreuil and Jean Gerson (in Latin with facing translation in modern French), and other related works, such as an excerpt from the *Cité des dames* in which Christine de Pizan discusses the debate. Includes variants and critical notes.

648 -----. "De l'histoire littéraire comme cosmogonie: la Querelle du *Roman de la rose*." *Critique* 32 (1976):511-19.

A summary of early scholarship on the Querelle de la Rose and a description of how certain simplistic or erroneous ideas became incorporated into standard criticism on the topic. The debate early came to be seen in mythic, cosmogonic terms: the first humanist (Jean de Meun) confronting the first feminist (Christine de Pizan) and the representative of the old scholastic order (Jean Gerson). This view, however, is not based on sound knowledge of the documents. Furthermore, Hicks puts the debate in the larger context of a climate of controversy that involved many more participants than the principal players. The existence of these other partisans, though not manifested textually, should not be ignored by those studying "la première querelle *écrite* des lettres françaises" (519).

649 -----. "The 'Querelle de la Rose' in the *Roman de la rose*." *Les bonnes feuilles* 3 (1974):152-69.

In part an attempt to reconstruct the arguments in favor of the *Rose* in Jean de Montreuil's lost treatise, by working from Christine de Pizan's reply. The treatise argued that what seems offensive, including language, is not really so, and that the immoral characters or teachings are negative examples to be avoided. The supporters of the *Rose* found many of their arguments already stated in the romance itself. The first conflict is between the two authors: Guillaume wrote a romance of initiation, Jean a warring chaos of "antipathetical forces" (156). In addition, Hicks takes on the difficult question of rhetorical distance, of whether we can attribute the opinions of any of these conflicting forces to the author. Though the question of Jean's "personal engagement remains an open one" (160), Hicks feels that Jean's romance rests on "the essential goodness of the sexual act and its consequences" (162).

650 Hicks, Eric and Ezio Ornato. "Jean de Montreuil et le débat sur le *Roman de la rose*." *Romania* 98 (1977):34-64 and 186-219.

An introduction to a detailed analysis of the documents relating to Jean de Montreuil's role in the Querelle de la Rose: the Provost of Lille, Jean de Montreuil, provoked the debate on the *Rose* by his discussions with Christine de Pizan and by his now-lost treatise in favor of the poem, a copy of which he sent her. The authors review earlier publications on the debate, describe the collections of Jean de Montreuil's letters, and summarize the events in the debate. Most of the first half of the article attempts to determine both from external evidence, such as the travels of the interested parties during the period in question, and internal evidence, such as the reference to a liturgical text, the date of Letter 103, which accompanied the treatise. The evidence suggests that the debate began in April-May 1401. The second part examines the content, dates, and recipients of five other letters and concludes with a summary of the three phases in the evolution of Jean de Montreuil's attitude toward the debate. The authors give a detailed Tableau Chronologique Récapitulatif (215-19) of the documents in the debate, the letters that accompanied the sending of the documents, and other events or documents relating to the debate.

651 Hieatt, Constance B. *The Realism of Dream Visions: The Poetic Exploitation of the Dream-Experience in Chaucer and his Contemporaries.* De Proprietatibus Litterarum, Series Practica 2. The Hague: Mouton, 1967. Pp. 120.

A study of Middle English dream visions in the context of medieval and modern theories of dreams to see how poetic visions used the elements of real dreams, such as blending and double-meaning. The first part of the *Rose* is discussed briefly as "a sort of prototype" (15) offering almost all of the dream elements which became part of the tradition, including the natural setting, birds, and flowers. The study also explores the affinity of the dream with allegory and symbolism.

652 Hilder, Gisela. "Der Streit um den Rosenroman: Eine kritische Auseinandersetzung mit P. Potansky." *Zeitschrift für romanische Philologie* 91 (1975):79-94.

653 Hill, Jillian M. L. *The Medieval Debate on Jean de Meung's "Roman de la rose": Morality Versus Art.* Studies in Mediaeval Literature 4. Lewiston, New York: Edwin Mellen, 1991. Pp. xiii + 269.

A study of the Querelle de la Rose which, in addition to reviewing the arguments, also reviews responses to the *Rose* before the debate and the participants' possible motivations for their view of the romance. In opposition to Badel's interpretation of Jean de Meun's meaning (see no. 575), Hill sees the second *Rose* as a conventionally moral work and believes that most readers before the debate also saw it that way. The only criticisms (mistaken, according to Hill) before the debate pointed to Jean's misogyny and anticlericalism. Before reviewing the debate itself, Hill examines the personal motivations and professional responsibilities of the future participants in order to suggest reasons for their choosing one position or another. The debate itself is presented as a conflict between a moral approach to literature (Christine de Pizan and Jean Gerson) and a literary one (the royal secretaries). The conclusion describes the *Rose*'s reputation in subsequent works, which most often saw it as one of many works attacking women. Hill also points out that the general issues raised by the debate are still with us, in trials of literary works, for example, such as Flaubert's *Madame Bovary* and Baudelaire's *Fleurs du mal*.

654 Hult, David F. "Gui de Mori, lecteur médiéval." *Incidences* n. s. 5 (1981):53-70.

An approach to Gui de Mori's thirteenth-century revision of the *Rose* through the question of the complicated relationship of medieval scribe to author. A preliminary discussion of the interrelated concepts of scribe and author introduces a review of the manuscript sources of Gui de Mori's version and of the work of Langlois and Jung (see nos. 682 and 666) and reproduces a crucial central passage by the revisor. The rest of the analysis raises the question, "Gui de Mori n'est-il vraiment qu'un copiste?" (61). The answer is that Gui saw himself fully as an author who created a new work from an older one in order to make the *Rose* both more understandable and more "délitables" (56) for the reader (in effect the role of every medieval scribe).

655 Huot, Sylvia. "Authors, Scribes, Remanieurs: A Note on the Textual History of the *Romance of the Rose*." In *Rethinking* (no. 182). 203-33.

A detailed analysis of important revisions of the *Rose* by Gui de

Mori and by an anonymous reviser whose changes are found in some of the *B* family manuscripts (see Langlois, no. 66). Huot describes Gui's many interpolations and deletions, which reflect his desire to make the *Rose* more unified, orthodox, and decorous. While the *B* version agrees with Gui's changes in many cases, the reviser's primary goal was to recast Jean de Meun in the image of Guillaume de Lorris, to preserve "the integrity of Guillaume's *Rose*" (227) (while deleting Guillaume's name, as well as Jean de Meun's). The article concludes with a discussion of how modern scholarly response to these two revisions has differed and of the evolution of medieval *Rose* reception.

656 -----. "'Ci parle l'aucteur': The Rubrication of Voice and Authorship in *Roman de la rose* Manuscripts." *SubStance* 56 [17.2] (1988):42-48.

A description of the three types of rubrics in *Rose* manuscripts and an analysis of the function of types two and three: the rubrics that comment on the two authors and those that identify the characters speaking in the dialogues. The rubrics are "simultaneously a clarification of the text, and an imposition on it" (44). By making known the change of author, from Guillaume to Jean, at the point at which it actually occurs (before the text itself makes the change known), and by choosing to identify the speaker either as *l'Amant* or *l'Aucteur*, the rubricator creates "a meta-narrative account of the dynamics of the poem's narrative voice and its joint authorship" (45). Additionally, the study of rubrication in *Rose* manuscripts points to the innovative nature of the romance both as book and as poem.

657 -----. "From *Roman de la rose* to *Roman de la poire*: The Ovidian Tradition and the Poetics of Courtly Literature." *Medievalia et Humanistica* n. s. 13 (1985):95-111.

A discussion of the two romances that predicates a close relationship between them, seeing the *Poire* as an early response to Guillaume de Lorris, thus predating Jean de Meun. In her perceptive analysis of the *Poire* as "a response to the particular crystallization of poetic elements offered by the *Rose*" (96), the author focuses on the garden setting (in particular the figures on the wall and the courtly inhabitants) and on the *Rose*'s retelling of the story of Narcissus. The "dialectic between textuality and experience" (108) creates a new synthesis in which the *Poire*'s author, Tibaut, substitutes the central myth of Pyramus and Thisbe for that of Narcissus, which is in some ways its mirror image. Going beyond source study emphasis on similarity of allegorical personifications and verbal echoes, Huot shows how Tibaut reworks poetic and structural elements in the earlier work to give his own vision of the poles between which medieval literature moved: "lyric and narrative, text and performance, vernacular and Latin" (108).

658 -----. "Medieval Readers of the *Roman de la rose*: The Evidence of Marginal Notations." *Romance Philology* 43 (1990):400-20.

A study of marginal *Nota* signs in twenty-five fourteenth- and fifteenth-century manuscripts, signs seen as "precious traces of that all but mythical figure, the medieval reader" (401). The analysis looks at three kinds of evidence: notations of traditional maxims and proverbs (or to verses in the *Rose* which became proverbs); specific themes which readers appear to have singled out, such as the theme of discretion in speech or mercantilism and love; other passages frequently noted (an appendix lists passages annotated in at least five manuscripts). In addition to suggesting the conflicting diversity of medieval readings of the *Rose*, the manuscript evidence points to "a creative tension between continuous and discontinuous modes of reading of medieval texts" (402).

659 -----. "The Medusa Interpolation in the *Romance of the Rose*: Mythographic Program and Ovidian Intertext." *Speculum* 62 (1987):865-77.

An examination of a fifty-two-line interpolation from the late thirteenth or early fourteenth century which compares the female image at which Venus shoots her arrow near the end of the *Rose* to the head of Medusa [the article does not give the interpolation *in toto*; see the Langlois edition [n. 6], note to ll. 20810-11]. This Medusa passage provides evidence for a medieval reading of the poem, in particular for our understanding of three important Ovidian exempla. The anonymous redactor of the Medusa passage appears to respond to the myths, recounted earlier in the *Roman*, of Narcissus, Deucalion and Pyrrha, and Pygmalion. The "network of imagery" (870) involving petrification or its opposite suggests that the redactor was responding both to Ovid and to the *Rose* in the interpolation, thereby expanding the "mythographic program" of the *Rose* (877). The Medusa passage further suggests that l'Amant's lady will reciprocate his desire and grant him the rose. As Genius argues in his sermon (according to Huot, the key to the poem's love doctrine), l'Amant becomes "a corrected image of Narcissus" (873) by participating in procreative love and thus countering Narcissus's stony fate.

660 -----. *The "Romance of the Rose" and Its Medieval Readers: Interpretation, Reception, Manuscript Transmission*. Cambridge Studies in Medieval Literature 16. Cambridge, England: Cambridge UP, 1993.

A study of the reception of the *Rose*, mainly through the manuscript tradition and readers' annotations. Includes chapters on Guillaume de Machaut, Guillaume Deguilleville, and iconography. [I did not receive this book in time to do a more complete annotation.]

661 -----. "The Scribe as Editor: Rubrication as Critical Apparatus in Two Manuscripts of the *Roman de la rose*." *L'esprit créateur* 27.1 (1987):67-78.

An examination of evidence of two different readings of the *Rose* in fourteenth-century manuscripts, one clerkly or moralistic, the other courtly. Through rubrics, miniatures, and glosses, the scribes interpreted the *Rose* according to a thematics of condemnation of love's folly or celebration of its courtly qualities and connection to life and durability. Huot's conclusion suggests that we can learn as much "from these early editors and critics of the *Rose* as we do from those of our own time" (77).

662 -----. "Seduction and Sublimation: Christine de Pizan, Jean de Meun, and Dante." *Romance Notes* 25 (1985):361-73.

A reconsideration of the "issue of Christine de Pizan's feminism" (361) in which Huot relates Christine's position on the "woman question" to "her ideas about literary language and its role in society" (363). After a brief summary of Christine's arguments concerning the *Roman de la rose*, the analysis contrasts the central poetic metaphor of the *Rose* (poetic and sexual begetting) with Christine's metaphors of pregnancy and birth, as developed in the prologue to the *Mutacion de Fortune*, *Lavision-Christine*, and the prologue to the *Cité des dames*. While rejecting Jean de Meun's phallic poetics, Christine found that Dante's *Commedia* offered poetic and linguistic models that could help her "valorize feminine creativity" (372).

663 -----. "Vignettes marginales comme glose marginale dans un manuscrit du *Roman de la rose* au quatorzieme siècle (B.N. fr. 25526)." In *La présentation du livre.* Actes du colloque de Paris X-Nanterre (4, 5, 6 décembre 1985). Ed. Emmanuèle Baumgartner and Nicole Boulestreau. Litterales: Cahiers du Département de Français 2. Nanterre: Centre de Recherches du Département de Français, 1987. 173-86.

An analysis of the numerous and varied marginal drawings in this manuscript of the *Rose* which are, according to the author, an important visual commentary on the text. First, the scenes from the lives of Christ and Saint Marguerite and the erotic drawings accompanying la Vieille's discourse are shown to point both to the spiritual limitations of Raison and to la Vieille's illicit erotic role. Second, Huot deciphers the unusual way in which the book was made through the use of bifolios (double pages that were later folded). She argues that through this method, the "disposition emboîtée des marginalia correspond au procédé d'emboîtement thématique" (185) of the romance; further, the concentric structure of the pages corresponds to the form of the Rose itself.

664 Huppé, Bernard. F. "The Translation of Technical Terms in the Middle English *Romaunt of the Rose*." *Journal of English and Germanic Philology* 47 (1948):334-42.

A study which presents "preliminary and tentative" (342) evidence of difficulties in translating scholastic terms encountered in the *Romaunt* based on eight examples of translation of Jean de Meun's scholastic terminology in the Middle English Glasgow ms. (Hunterian Museum V.3.7). Huppé's findings include the difficulty of exact translation of technical terms from French to Middle English, translatorial resistance to direct borrowing from the French, and the carelessness of translators who had "seemingly little concern to establish a technical English vocabulary" (342). A good example of the terms examined in this study is the use of *letter* and *sentence* as technical opposites. These two terms are made clear in the scholastic figure of bark and pith or rind and core. In the English translation of Jean's lines, Langlois ll. 11858-60 (ll. 11828-30), Huppé notes a "careless, perhaps inaccurate, translation of 'dou sen l'escorce'" (337) into "menyng of the bark and rynde." He feels that a reversal of the nouns would make the translation more accurate. [KML]

665 Jager, Eric. "Croesus and Chauntecleer: The Royal Road of Dreams." *Modern Language Quarterly* 49 (1988):3-18.

An analysis of how Chaucer's Monk "selectively edits the legend of Croesus in his source, Jean de Meun's *Roman de la rose*" (3), in order to show the king's powerlessness before his fate, and how the Nun's Priest's Tale about Chauntecleer's dream and its consequences is a reply to and a rectification of the Monk's deficient view of Fortune. Jager points to many parallels between the cock and the Lydian king and to some significant differences: Chauntecleer is "the victim of his own rationalization" (10) rather than of his literalist reading of the warning dream. Through his revision of the Monk's tale, the Priest dramatizes the idea that "the fulfillment of dreams is not inevitable but rather contingent upon the dreamer's response" (16).

666 Jung, Marc-René. "Gui de Mori et Guillaume de Lorris." *Vox romanica* 27 (1968):106-37.

A discussion of how the cleric Gui de Mori reworked the *Roman de la rose* in the thirteenth century, adding long sections, omitting verses, and making many smaller changes. After describing the texts in which this revision is found, Jung points out some of the ideas and poetic tendencies of the reviser, especially in the first part of the *Rose*, such as his tendency to make moral qualities independent of social qualities and to spell out in a more pedantic way some of the implications of the first part. The article includes long excerpts from the revision's additions, in particular additions to the story of Narcissus and a lecture by le Dieu d'Amour on the rewards he gives his followers (related to the medieval concept of the stages of love).

667 Kaluza, Max. *Chaucer und der Rosenroman: Eine litterargeschichtliche Studie*. Berlin: Emil Felber, 1893. Pp. vi + 253.

A discussion of Kaluza's work on the Glasgow manuscripts of the *Romaunt*. He concludes that the *Romaunt* is made up of three fragments, the first two of which are by Chaucer.

668 -----. "The *Romaunt of the Rose* from the unique Glasgow MS." *English Studies* 18 (1893):106-11.

The introduction to Kaluza's parallel text edition of the *Romaunt of the Rose* described in chapter 1 (see no. 19).

669 Kaske, Carol V. "Getting Around the *Parson's Tale*: An Alternative to Allegory and Irony." In *Chaucer at Albany*. Ed. Rossell Hope Robbins. New York: Burt Franklin, 1975. 147-77.

An approach to the *Parson's Tale* through the broad question, "Is the *Parson's Tale*--is Christianity itself--relevant for the secular tales, and if so, how?" (147). The author suggests that the Parson's tale, like the rest of the *Canterbury Tales*, should be seen in a limited perspective, as part of a debate, rather than as "the ironic or allegorical moral of everything in the work" (148). Kaske considers the question of limited perspective in relation to two topics, destiny versus free will, and marriage, and the dichotomy they pose between authority and experience. Evidence for this perspective comes from Chaucer's sources, including the *Roman de la rose*, in which, Kaske argues, no speaker is the authority and in which "the norm can only be found between the lines and in self-betraying asides" (153). Therefore experience, like reason, "has a degree of validity independent of revelation" (154).

670 Kaufman, Janice Horner. "Original Borrowings from the French in Chaucer's Translation of *Le roman de la rose*." *MIFLC [Mountain Interstate Foreign Language Conference] Review* 1 (1991):58-67.

A reevaluation of Chaucer's borrowings from French in Fragment A of the *Romaunt* by concentrating on "words relating to fashion, a domain where France holds sway to this day" (60). Disagreeing with Merete Smith's conservative estimate (see no. 746), Kaufman estimates that "close to 25% of the OFr. loanwords in Fragment A are either new to English or used with a new English meaning" (59). After discussing some of the words relating to clothes and appearance, the author lists direct borrowings of French words in Fragment A, according to four sources: Joseph Mersand's

Chaucer's Romance Vocabulary, Smith, and her own studies, all of which are compared to the "Original French" (63, column heading), by which the author evidently means the text of Sutherland's edition (see no. 20). [The table is not fully explained; why for example does Kaufman also list some of Smith's words but not others?]

671   Kee, Kenneth. "Two Chaucerian Gardens." *Mediaeval Studies* 23 (1961):154-62.

A brief discussion of the major traditions, Biblical and classical, in medieval literary gardens. The garden of the twelfth century Latin poem, *De Phyllide et Flora*, "can be said to represent the inception of a new topos in later medieval literature which we may call the *paradis d'amour*" (157), while the garden of the *Roman de la rose* is "the finest flowering" of this topos (157). Kee also points out the similarities and differences in Chaucer's use of garden conventions in the Merchant's and the Franklin's tales.

672   Kelly, F. Douglas. "Reflections on the Role of Christine de Pisan as a Feminist Writer." *SubStance* 2 (Winter 1972):63-71.

An evaluation of Christine de Pizan's ideas about women and men in the light of medieval conceptions of women's irrationality. Kelly argues that Jean de Meun's jealous husband reveals through his irrational anger and his lack of control over his wife that reason no longer dominates, thus reproducing the "figurative pattern for sin" (64) found in Eden. Furthermore, the submissive courtly lover in medieval literature was simply the other side of the rapist of the pastourelle. Thus Christine's role was to "encourage men to live up to their own standards" (67). Through her attempts to define good and bad love and to encourage "the maintenance of honorable love as it had been known in the past" (69), Christine, who was essentially conservative, appealed "to the restoration of reason in the relations between men and women" (71).

673 Kelly, Joan. "Early Feminist Theory and the *Querelle des Femmes*, 1400-1789." *Signs* 8 (1982):4-28.

A discussion of the Querelle de la Rose which places it in the context both of the "renewed belittlement of women as a sex" (8) that accompanied the rise of the new secular and humanistic culture of the modern European state, and of a "400-year-old tradition of women thinking about women and sexual politics" (5) begun by Christine de Pizan. When Christine wrote *L'épître au dieu d'amours* in 1399 in response to Jean de Meun's part of the *Roman de la rose* (the classic statement of "mockery of women and chivalric love" [10]), she became the first woman to counter, in the name of women, the "misogynist voice of literate opinion on women's inferiority" (11).

674 Kittredge, George Lyman. "The Authorship of the English *Romaunt of the Rose*." *Studies and Notes in Philology and Literature* 1 (1892):1-65.

A lengthy refutation of the authorship theories espoused in an article by Lounsbury found in the second volume of his *Studies in Chaucer*. Lounsbury concluded that a fragmentary English version of the *Roman de la rose* was a translation at the hand of Chaucer. Kittredge systematically proves or disproves each of Lounsbury's arguments, ranging from those of dialect to those of content. Some twenty-nine pages list parallel passages between the *Rose* and attributed Chaucerian texts. Kittredge comments on the 126 parallels that Lounsbury treats and then offers thirty-four parallel passages not noted by Lounsbury, commenting that "parallel passages do not imply identity of authorship" (61). Finally, Kittredge allows that one must "believe that the *Romaunt* is not Chaucer's, with the possible exception of the first seventeen hundred lines" (65). [KML]

675 Knopp, Sherron. "Chaucer and Jean de Meun as Self-Conscious Narrators: The Prologue to the Legend of Good Women

and the *Roman de la rose* 10307-680." *Comitatus: A Journal of Medieval and Renaissance Studies* 4 (1974):25-39.

A study of Chaucer's prologue which places it in the context of late-medieval French sources, such as works by Machaut, Froissart, and Deschamps, and especially the *Rose*: Knopp asserts the primary importance for "the distinctive character and temper of Chaucer's Prologue" (27) of Jean de Meun's *Rose*, in particular the mid-point speech by the Dieu d'Amour (Langlois 10307-680). In contrast to Jean's "gloriously comic egotism" (31) when dealing with love, Chaucer in the prologue makes himself a caricature of l'Amant through his gullibility, ineptness, and "niceness." However, although Chaucer seems to dissociate himself with Jean through le Dieu d'Amour's angry accusation of heresy, in effect the dissociation is only superficial: "their basic goals and beliefs are strikingly similar" (37). Both authors "insist on viewing love in its broadest dimensions, unlimited by a restricting code," and it is the "self-conscious narrative voice" (37) which is the focal point and creates the comedy in both works.

676 Knowlton, E[dgar] C. "The Genii of Spenser." *Studies in Philology* 25 (1928):439-56.

An examination of the allegorical figure Genius by which Knowlton intended to supplement his previous examinations (see no. 342) and specifically to refer to use of the figure by Spenser. Jean de Meun is mentioned on 440 as evidence that the figure was notable in French literature of the thirteenth century. [KML]

677 -----. "Genius as an Allegorical Figure." *Modern Language Notes* 39 (1924):89-95.

A continuation of the analysis in no. 342, "The Allegorical Figure Genius," which the author summarizes. Jean de Meun's Genius is seen as "a half-grotesque, vigorous demigod" (89), a semi-diabolic degenerate form of Alain de Lille's moral guide in the *De planctu Naturae*. Knowlton traces the evolution of the character through a number of late medieval and Renaissance works, including Gower's *Confessio Amantis*, whose Genius is related to Jean's "sceptical figure" (90); Martin Le Franc's *Champion des dames*; Jean Lemaire de Belges's *Concorde des deux langages* (a tribute to the *Rose* and to Jean de Meun); and Clément Marot's *Temple de Cupido*. Knowlton concludes that after the establishment of Genius "on a lofty plane by Alan of Lille, Genius steadily altered for the worse" (95).

678 Koeppel, E. "Jehan de Meung." *Anglia* 14 (1891/1892):238-67.

A juxtaposition of lines from Chaucer's works with similar lines in the *Roman de la rose* and Jean's *Testament*. Koeppel focuses on sections of the *Rose* not included in the *Romaunt of the Rose* fragments and offers his survey as a supplement to earlier ones, such as Skeat's. In addition to the *Canterbury Tales*, ten poems are surveyed, including the *Book of the Duchess*, *Troilus and Criseyde*, and the *Parliament of Fowls*. [Article in German.]

679 Köhler, Erich. "Lea, Matelda und Oiseuse." *Zeitschrift für romanische Philologie* 78 (1962):464-69.

A discussion of Dante's *Divina commedia* which focuses on two characters from the end of *Purgatorio*: Leah, who appears briefly with her sister Rachel in a dream in Canto 27, and Matelda, who leads Dante to Beatrice in Canto 31. Although aspects of their function and attributes can be found in other sources, such as Ovid, Köhler suggests that both characters may have been influenced by Guillaume de Lorris's Oiseuse. A number of parallels among the three women are pointed out: the mirror in a woman's hand, for example, cannot be found in the Bible or Ovid or the love poets, and Oiseuse, like Leah, appears as a beautiful, flower-bedecked woman in an earthly paradise. Köhler interprets the parallels between the *Rose* and *Purgatorio* as evidence of Dante's ability to combine and rework elements from many different traditions.

680 Kooijman, Jacques. "Envoi de fleurs: à propos des échanges littéraires entre la France et l'Angleterre sous la Guerre de Cent Ans." In *Etudes...Lanly* (no. 230). 173-83.

A discussion of the epistolary relations of Eustache Deschamps and Chaucer about 1377-1380 that includes brief remarks on the cultural significance of Chaucer's translation of the first part of the *Rose*, described as "le trophée" (182) of England's victories over France during the Hundred Years' War. Kooijman proposes a reading of Deschamps's famous ballad which refers to Chaucer's translation of the *Rose* "En bon anglès" (175) (the refrain of the ballad is "Grant translateur noble Geffroy Chaucier").

681 Kuhl, E. P. "Chaucer and the Red Rose." *Philological Quarterly* 24 (1945):33-38.

An inquiry into Chaucer's references to roses, especially to red ones, one of which is an intercalated line in the *Romaunt of the Rose* (l. 1680). Other rose references include the Prologue to the *Legend of Good Women* and the *House of Fame*. Kuhl concentrates on the possible political and courtly symbolism of Chaucer's roses and argues for the poet's political involvement in his country's difficulties. Since Kuhl sees both the translation and the original as "in part a civic document of the day" (37), he urges an exhaustive study of the translation on the grounds that it might help us understand Chaucer's idealisms and his sources of inspiration and "may even lead us to modify our conceptions of Chaucer's whole philosophy of composition" (37).

682 Langlois, Ernest. "Gui de Mori et le *Roman de la rose*." *Bibliothèque de l'Ecole des Chartes* 68 (1907):249-71.

A description of the reworking of the *Rose* (c. 1290) by the cleric Gui de Mori. After summarizing what we can learn about the reviser and his work from an intercalated passage in the Tersan manuscript (based on Méon's edition of it), Langlois describes and analyzes the other thirteenth-century manuscript of the revision, the Tournai manuscript. He reproduces several passages of interest, including the midpoint speech in which the authors are named (Gui adds himself to the other two), the four stages of love in which the beloved's body is envisaged as mountainous topography, and the system of diacritical marks which indicate the changes Gui made. Langlois concludes that the Tournai manuscript was the second edition of Gui's work.

683 -----. "Le traité de Gerson contre le *Roman de la rose*." *Romania* 45 (1918/1919):23-48.

The first edition in the original French of the allegorical judgement of the *Rose* by the rector of the University of Paris, one of the documents in the early fifteenth-century Querelle de la Rose (Ward had printed the Latin translation, which was not made by Gerson; see no. 770). Langlois discusses briefly the Latin version and describes the manuscripts in which the French text is found. The text, based on Paris, BN fr. 1797 (anc. 7848), is accompanied by variants from two other manuscripts and a few notes.

684 Lanly, André. "Villon, le *Roman de la rose* et le *Testament* de Jean de Meun." In *Hommage à Jean Séguy*. Via domitia 14. 2 vols. Toulouse: Université de Toulouse-Le Mirail, 1978. 1: 237-51.

An appreciation of Villon's debt to the *Rose*. That Villon knew the *Rose* is proved by the reference to it in the *Testament* (stanza XV), but how much his poetry owes to the earlier poem is disputed by scholars. Lanly, who translated both Villon and the *Rose*, attempts to show that Villon was influenced not only by the *Rose* but by the *Testament* attributed to Jean de Meun. He does this through what he calls "réminiscences" (238), similarities of theme (satire of the mendicant orders, for example, or of women), literary procedure (contradictory propositions, famous examples), and reminiscences of details (expressions, images, words). For example, the famous image from Villon's *Testament*, "plus noir que meure" (stanza XXIII) echoes *Rose*, l. 8511. Lanly concludes that Jean de Meun was for Villon "son grand homme" (250), the principal source of his poetry (251).

685 Larmat, Jean. *Le moyen âge dans le "Gargantua" de Rabelais.* Publications de la Faculté des Lettres et Sciences Humaines de Nice 12. Paris: "Les Belles Lettres," 1973. Pp. 583.

A study of the medieval roots of Rabelais's thought in *Gargantua* which includes a discussion of parallels with Jean de Meun, in particular regarding the two authors' ideas on political theory and religion. Larmat believes that he can only suggest a possible influence of Jean de Meun on Rabelais, but the *Rose* was still widely known and read in the early Renaissance, and a number of similarities in *Gargantua* and the second part of the *Rose* exist: the satire of women and monks, the belief in reason, nature, and free will (Larmat accepts the interpretations of Jean de Meun's thought by Gorce and Paré, see nos. 265 and 419), and the use of an earlier work as a mask for subversive ideas. Above all the author points to the authors' shared optimism and *joie de vivre*.

686 Lecoy, Félix. "Une mention du *Roman de la rose* au XVIe siècle." *Romania* 87 (1966):119-20.

A note on the farce entitled *Le vendeur de livres* (c. 1515-1520), in which two women customers ask the merchant if he has a copy of the *Roman de la rose*; he replies that he does but it will take him a while to dig it out. Lecoy interprets the passage as indicating that the poem, though not much in demand, still had a faithful public in the early sixteenth century, a few years before Marot's revision.

687 Le Duc, Alma. "Gontier Col and the French Pre-Renaissance; Part Second: Literary Antipathies and Personal Sympathies." *Romanic Review* 8 (1917):145-65.

A concise discussion of the Querelle de la Rose in a three-part article on the life and works of the early Humanist, Contier Col (Parts One and Three are in Volumes 7 and 9). The author suggests various reasons for the warm support of Jean de Meun by Col and his associates, including the fact that they were "intellectual pioneers on certain lines, just as he was" (152). Their interest in classical literature was certainly also a factor. Le Duc sees the Humanists' dismissal of the *Rose*'s misogyny as a forerunner of the "'querelle des femmes' which belongs to the history of the literary development of the Greater Renaissance" (153). The second part of the article discusses Col's membership in the Cour Amoureuse of Charles VI.

688 Leonard, Frances McNeely. *Laughter in the Courts of Love: Comedy in Allegory, from Chaucer to Spenser.* Norman, Oklahoma: Pilgrim Books, 1981. Pp. x + 184.

An analysis of comic aspects of medieval and Renaissance allegories ("how jest and earnest can coexist and cooperate within a single work" [25]) that includes references to the *Rose*'s influence. The author sees Jean's continuation especially as having shaped Chaucer's comic vision in a number of ways, among which he points to the reworking of certain characters such as la Vieille and Faux Semblant, the poetic use of anticlerical sentiment, the technique of "unconscious self-revelation" (31) and the related device of the obtuse narrator, and the dream-vision framework. Through parody, satire, and farce, Jean portrays a comic lover whose self-delusion cannot hide the destructiveness of his triumph. Thus Jean's "subtle and skillful blending of comedy and allegory into one mode of knowing" (33) created a model for Chaucer and later writers.

689 Levey, David. "'Courtly love' and the Middle English *Romaunt of the Rose*." *Unisa English Studies* 25.2 (1987):1-6.

An analysis of courtly love in the first two fragments of the *Romaunt*. Levey first reviews scholarly arguments concerning the term (scholars discussed include C. S. Lewis, D. W. Robertson, and Joan Ferrante [see nos. 375, 473, and 234]) and summarizes briefly Chaucer's presentation of courtly love as "both valuable of itself and treacherous" (2). Levey's discussion of narrative and descriptive passages in the *Romaunt* sees the narrator as "self-consciously distanced from the scene he describes" (4) and the protagonist as almost admirably naive. Throughout the analysis Levey argues that irony and ambiguity expose courtly love in the *Romaunt* as "a stylized game, which is entertaining but not to be taken too seriously" (5). This interpretation of the *Romaunt* shows that in regard to a specific work the concept of courtly love can be of some value.

690   Longo, John Duane. "Literary Appropriation as *Translatio* in Chaucer and the *Roman de la rose*." Diss. Princeton U, 1982.

691   Lord, Carla. "Tintoretto and the *Roman de la rose*." *Journal of the Warburg and Courtauld Institutes* 33 (1970):315-17.

An analysis of a painting, now in the Alte Pinakothek, Munich, in which jealous Vulcan attempts to discover Venus and Mars in adultery. Tintoretto placed in the painting a mirror that could have served as an alarm system for the lovers. This original detail, Lord suggests, was an allusion to the passage in the *Rose* in which Nature discusses how Mars and Venus might have used a mirror to become forewarned of Vulcan's approach (ll. 18031-18074) [their discussion turns, however, on how the mirror could have revealed Vulcan's net] and to take evasive action, such as hiding Mars under the bed, where he is found in Tintoretto's painting. The painting thus reflects the continued popularity of the *Rose* at least until about 1538 "when printed production...stopped for almost two centuries" (317).

692   Luquiens, Frederick Bliss. "The *Roman de la rose* and Medieval Castilian Literature." *Romanische Forschungen* 20 (1905):284-320.

A study based on the author's dissertation which traces the possible influence of the *Rose* on Castilian literature of the fourteenth and fifteenth centuries, in particular on the poets represented in the *Cancionero de Baena*. The author's conclusions are largely negative--he finds few "sure traces of influence" (293), that is, few clear echoes of images or ideas in the *Libro de buen amor*, the allegorical poems, or the cancioneros, and the approximate similarities can be explained by the influence of other medieval poems or of a common source, such as Boethius. However, Luquiens does distinguish three poems whose nature descriptions are similar enough to the *Rose* to indicate sure evidence of influence. The authors of these poems, Francisco Imperial and Diego de Valencia, influenced in turn other Castilian poets' use of nature description.

693 Luria, Maxwell. "A Sixteenth-Century Gloss on the *Roman de la rose*." *Mediaeval Studies* 44 (1982):333-70.

The first printing of the over 200 marginal inscriptions found in the fifteenth-century Collins manuscript of the *Roman* in the Philadelphia Museum of Art. These comments, added early in the sixteenth century, were probably written by a "learned, humanistic, sometimes eloquent glossator, of rather conservative and orthodox disposition" (341). The gloss is thoroughly Christian "in spirit and letter" (341) and interprets what l'Amant feels as "délit charnel" (342), as an example of "voluptuosite charnelle" (343). The glossator apparently treats the two parts as a unity. Luria argues that this approach to the *Rose* is more authentic than the imposed allegory of the glossator's contemporaries, Molinet and Marot.

694 Magoun, F. P., Jr. "Chaucer and the *Roman de la rose*, vv. 16096-105." *Romanic Review* 17 (1926):69-70.

A note to H. B. Hinckley's observation that the same examples concerning unknown causes (glass from fern ashes, or thunder and natural phenomena) are found in the *Rose* as in Chaucer's *Squire's Tale*. Magoun reprints the passage in question from the *Rose* and observes that while Chaucer's version is not a literal translation, "he is consciously or unconsciously drawing definitely and directly on the French poem which he knew so well" (70).

695 -----. "Chaucer's Sir Gawain and the OFr. *Roman de la rose*." *Modern Language Notes* 67 (1952):183-85.

A note that questions B. J. Whiting's suggestion that Chaucer's reference to Gawain and his courtesy in the *Squire's Tale* was inspired by *Sir Gawain and the Green Knight*. Magoun points instead to the reference to Gawain in the *Rose* (Langlois ll. 2209-10 [ll. 2081-82]): "Tant con Gauvains, li bien apris, / par sa cortoisie ot de pris." In effect the *Rose* may have been more accessible to Chaucer than the English romance.

696 Margolis, Nadia. "Elegant Closures: The Use of the Diminutive in Christine de Pizan and Jean de Meun." In *Reinterpreting Christine de Pizan* (no. 736). 111-23.

A study of Christine de Pizan's diminutives, in particular those referring to women (i.e., *pucellette, fillette, femmelette*, etc.). Margolis gives examples of three major ways of using diminutives: as a conventional image, as a noticeable departure from tradition, or as an inventive, bivocal, and oppositional juxtaposition of "the dominant male terminology with that of the minority female" (112). After looking at the use of diminutives in the Querelle de la Rose, Margolis summarizes in two pages the use of diminutives in the *Rose*, suggesting that Jean de Meun's diminutives "mock their traditional background" (120).

697 Mathew, Gervase. "Ideals of Friendship." In *Patterns of Love and Courtesy: Essays in Memory of C. S. Lewis*. Ed. John Lawlor. London: Edward Arnold; Evanston, Illinois: Northwestern UP, 1966. 45-53.

An overview of characteristics of "the ideal of romantic friendship" (45) in medieval works, especially in *Amis and Amiloun*. The author mentions some of the classical and patristic ideas that influenced medieval thinking on the subject. The "quality of friendliness, as distinct from the habit of friendship" (50) is seen in the personifications of Franchise and

Bel Accueil as presented in the *Romaunt of the Rose*; Raison's remarks on friendship are also briefly discussed.

698 McLeod, Enid. *The Order of the Rose: The Life and Ideas of Christine de Pizan.* Totowa, New Jersey: Rowman and Littlefield, 1976. Pp. 185.

A summary of Christine's part in the Querelle de la Rose, in which she was a main protagonist and perhaps the source. McLeod stresses Christine's courage and restraint in the face of the arrogant and insulting letters she received from the Col brothers. Rather than a review of the arguments concerning the *Rose*, the study explores Christine's personal response to her opponents.

699 Mead, William E. "The *Prologue of the Wife of Bath's Tale*." *PMLA* n.s. 9 [16] (1901):388-404.

An analysis of the Wife of Bath that links her, not with the character of la Vieille in the *Rose*, with whom she has been compared, but with the jealous husband. After describing the characteristics of Chaucer's "witty and frisky shrew" (395) and Jean's wornout old woman, Mead suggests that the Wife puts the jealous husband's antimatrimonial ravings in the mouth of her own husbands, while taking the same attitude toward them that the jealous husband does toward his wife. The author suggests further that Chaucer's "first acquaintance with the railing accusations that Theophrastus brings against women" (401) he got from the *Rose*. The reversal effected by turning the jealous husband into the Wife of Bath would have strongly appealed to Chaucer's "peculiar type of humor" (403). Finally, Mead notes that the Wife glories in doing the very things for which the jealous husband scolds his wife.

700 Meyer, Paul. "Un extrait du *Roman de la rose*." *Romania* 6 (1877):449.

A note identifying a short Renaissance play about a jealous husband as an excerpt from the *Rose*. [See nos. 586 and 784.]

701 Miguet, Thierry. "L'ésotérisme de Villon." In *Etudes...Lanly* (no. 230). 239-62.

A study which offers a number of alchemical and astrological parallels for terms found in the second part of the *Rose* and in Villon's poems, in particular the ballad to Marie d'Orléans. The terms discussed are common ones, such as *fountaine, rubie*, and *Saturne* [the author's parallels may seem tenuous to many readers]. Miguet believes that Villon's esoterism can be explained by reference to Jean de Meun: "Villon, lecteur 'intérieur' de Jean de Meun, est imprégné de l'ésotérisme, simultanément alchimique et chrétien, de son devancier" (248).

702 Miller, Robert P., ed. *Chaucer: Sources and Backgrounds*. New York: Oxford UP, 1977. Pp. xv + 507.

An anthology of excerpts from a variety of Biblical, classical, and medieval titles that are essential for the study of Chaucer's works. The excerpts from the *Rose* come from the speeches of Faux Semblant, the jealous husband, and la Vieille [taken from Dahlberg's translation; see no. 24]. Notes to other selections include references to relevant passages in the *Rose*.

703 -----. "The Epicurean Homily on Marriage by Chaucer's Franklin." *Mediaevalia* 6 (1980):151-86.

An interpretation of the Franklin's marriage advice which shows how closely he follows the counsel, supposedly based on Epicurean principles, of two characters in the *Rose*, l'Ami and la Vieille. All three characters argue that love and marriage can be a source of pleasure if mankind's fallen nature is indulged.

Miller judges this Epicurean view by Christian standards and finds it to be "really neither humble nor wise" (152).

704 Moody, Helen Fletcher. "The Debate of the Rose: The Querelle des Femmes as Court Poetry." Diss. U of California, Berkeley, 1981.

705 Morawski, J. "Parodie d'un passage du *Roman de la rose* dans un *sermon joyeux*." *Romania* 52 (1926):159-60.

A note pointing to a speech that ridicules jealousy in the *Sermon joyeux des foulx* (c. 1543). This speech "apparaît comme une parodie triviale d'un passage analogue du *Roman de la Rose*" (160), a parody in which the metaphor of a hole in the wall is substituted for the more noble one of a candle's flame (both metaphors for a woman's favors).

706 Morgan, Gerald. "The Self-Revealing Tendencies of Chaucer's Pardoner." *Modern Language Review* 71 (1976):241-55.

An approach to the question of the appropriateness of psychological approaches to medieval texts, based on a comparison of the *Romaunt of the Rose* and on the *Pardoner's Tale*. Medieval literature assumes a "unity between action and intention" (244) that makes a psychological approach based on individual motivation misleading. Instead of the psychological and subjective view, Morgan argues that medieval poets were concerned about the moral and objective view, with a general rather than particular significance. Thus the *Rose* should be read not, as C. S. Lewis argued, as a psychological study, but as a moral poem dealing with adulterous love. Similarly, Chaucer's Pardoner can best be understood if, like Faux Semblant in the *Rose*, he is seen as embodying the disunity between action and intention. Using "the same self-revealing techniques by which Jean de Meun exhibits the nature of Fals-Semblant" (251), Chaucer shows how "the moral scheme of the sermon is related to the moral degeneracy of the man that delivers it" (254).

707 Morpurgo, S[alomone]. "*Detto d'amore*: antiche rime imitate dal *Roman de la rose*." *Il propugnatore* n.s. 1 (1888):18-31.

A description and analysis of the *Detto d'amore* found in four small folios in the Codex Laurenziano-Ashburnham 1234 which, as Morpurgo saw from the paleographical evidence, used to belong to the unique codex of the *Fiore*, found in Montpellier. Both works are inspired by the same allegorical material of which the *Rose* is largely composed and, although Morpurgo in the end seems uneasy attributing both works to the same author, in the 480 lines of the *Detto* many literal concordances with the *Rose* (not surprisingly) and with the *Fiore* are found. The fragment edited here contains, in the first three folios, the beginning and the core of the *Detto*, where we find praise of the courtly God and characters obviously inspired by the *Rose* such as Ragione, Folle-Larghezza, Povertà, and Cuor-Fallito. In the last folio we have instead "*gastigamenti*" (19), or admonishments, concerning love. The *Detto*, which uses a seven-syllable line, is extraordinarily rich in rhymes containing double meanings (*rime equivoche*), an exercise comparable to the Old Provençal *trobar clus*. [MRB]

708 Morris, Lynn King. *Chaucer Source and Analogue Criticism: A Cross-Referenced Guide*. Foreword by Donald K. Fry. Garland Reference Library of the Humanities 454. New York: Garland Publishing, 1985. Pp. xvii + 584.

A bibliographical list of 1,477 source studies of Chaucer's works, including many that refer to the *Rose*. Morris also gives four indexes: by Chaucer's works, by authors of sources or analogues, by genre or origin of source (that is, the document which contains a source or analogue), and by title of source or analogue. Brief annotations are included with a few entries, and an asterisk indicates works of particular importance. In addition to the major studies of Chaucer and the *Rose* also found in the present bibliography, Morris's list includes a number of articles, not listed here, that refer to the *Rose* tangentially. [Note that article no. 959 discusses not the *Roman de la rose* but the *Roman de Renart*.]

709 Muscatine, Charles. *Chaucer and the French Tradition.* Berkeley: U of California P, 1957. Pp. 282.

A seminal attempt to understand "conventional traits of style" (4) in medieval literature, in particular as Chaucer incorporated them. The study includes a section on the courtly tradition in Guillaume's part of the *Rose* and one on the bourgeois tradition in Jean's. Muscatine argues that these roughly-defined styles were tools developed in concert with certain attitudes and meanings. The author examines courtly conventions, of which the most refined expression is Guillaume's *Rose*, in romance descriptions, settings, and, in particular, speech. The precision and finesse with which Guillaume explores the invisible world of the emotions "show us literary convention at its best" (36). In Jean's continuation, for the first time "the battle lines are clearly drawn" (71) between the courtly and bourgeois or realistic styles. Muscatine analyzes three characters as representing the "main loci of satiric realism in the poem" (73): the jealous husband imagined by l'Ami, la Vieille, and Faux Semblant. The first two reflect the "increasing valuation of direct experience" and "the conversion of comic realism to the ends of more respectable art" (77), while the third suffers from the "incomplete dramatization" (92) resulting from direct didacticism. The remaining chapters analyze Chaucer's more complex reworking of the courtly and bourgeois styles in his early poems, *Troilus and Criseyde*, and the *Canterbury Tales*.

710 Neilson, William Allan. *The Origins and Sources of the "Court of Love".* Harvard University Studies and Notes in Philology and Literature 6. 1899; rpt. New York: Russell and Russell, 1967. Pp. vi + 284.

A study of the literary conventions concerning le Dieu d'Amour and Venus that preceded the pseudo-Chaucerian work, *The Court of Love* (dated by Neilson as c. 1525). The author describes five characteristic features in medieval works portraying a court of love, which are, briefly, a court, statutes of love, a guide and interpreter, birds, and parody of church services. The *Rose* was the source of many of these elements in medieval literature. In his review of a large number of English, Provençal, French, Italian, Latin, and German works, the author also discusses related topics, such as Cupid's arrows. Although *The Court of Love* does not show all five major characteristics, it does clearly show the influence of the *Rose* in other elements, such as the May morning and the personifications at the court. However, since the author presumes that the influence of the *Rose* was as pervasive in the late Middle Ages as the Bible, he does not discuss in detail the relations of *The Court of Love* to the *Rose*.

711 Nichols, Stephen G., Jr. "Marot, Villon and the *Roman de la rose*: A Study in the Language of Creation and Re-Creation." *Studies in Philology* 63 (1966):135-43; 64 (1967):25-43.

A discussion of the theory and practice of translation as a form of poetic invention in the early French Renaissance. In the first part Nichols reviews the opinions of Sébillet, Geoffroy Tory, and especially Clément Marot, who believed in translating medieval works "to illustrate the poetic resources of the vernacular" (140). Marot's translation of Villon is briefly examined. The second part analyzes the approach adopted in the translation of the *Rose* attributed to Marot: the translator felt free to change syntax but kept archaic vocabulary, since vocabulary was seen as the essence of language. Nichols generally approves of Marot's adaptation of the *Rose* to the point of calling some of his lines "poetically superior" (33) to the original. The final section points to Marot's use of polemics and satiric monologues as comparable to Jean de Meun's but argues that Marot transforms what he draws from the *Rose* to create an original work.

712 Nordahl, Helge. "*Ars fidi interpretis* (un aspect rhétorique de l'art de Chaucer dans sa traduction du *Roman de la rose*)." *Archivum linguisticum* n. s. 9 (1978):24-31.

A linguistic study of how Chaucer translated the many

"tautologies binaires" in the *Rose*, which involve the formal coordination of two or more related terms for stylistic emphasis (for example, "de mautalant et de corroz," *Rose*, l. 322; "For angre and for maltalent," *Romaunt*, l. 330). The author found that Chaucer used six approaches to the problem: conservation of the original tautology, "transcatégorisation grammaticale" (24), amplification, emphatic or non-emphatic reduction, and obliteration. Many examples are given, with brief linguistic commentaries. The author concludes that Chaucer shows himself "un traducteur excellent" (31) in the way he conscientiously works to recreate the *Rose*'s tautologies.

713 Ord, Hubert William. *Chaucer and the Rival Poet in Shakespeare's Sonnets.* 1921; rpt. New York: AMS Press, 1973. Pp. 63.

An essay on two aspects of the relation of Shakespeare's sonnets to the *Roman de la rose*: the possible influence of Chaucer's translation of the *Rose* on the language, themes, and philosophy of the sonnets, and the likelihood that Chaucer himself is the rival poet to whom the later poet attributes an important influence on his work. The discussion of thematic and linguistic similarities includes references to reason, roses, and Cupid or the god of love in the sonnets, while Ord's discussion of Chaucer's influence broaches the possibility that Shakespeare refers derogatorily to Speght's second edition of the *Romaunt* in the sonnets. Ord believes that this evidence of the *Rose*'s importance to Shakespeare supports the theory "of the more general and varied outlook of the Sonnets as contrasted with the personal theory" (33).

714 Ortego, Philip Darraugh. "A Bibliography of Chaucer's French Sources." *Bulletin of Bibliography* 27 (1970):72-76.

A list of critical studies which discuss the relation of Chaucer's works to a variety of possible French sources, including the *Roman de la rose* and Jean de Meun's translation of Boethius's *De consolatione Philosophiae*. About twenty titles are listed for these two works. Some entries are accompanied by short summaries.

715 Oulmont, Charles. *Le verger, le temple et la cellule: essai sur la sensualité dans les oeuvres de mystique religieuse.* Paris: Hachette, 1912. Pp. 335.

A wide-ranging essay on elements in medieval mystical works that appealed "à la sensibilité et à l'imagination du lecteur" (13). In these works "l'amour mystique et l'amour humain tendent à se confondre" (14). Oulmont defines three degrees of mystical sensuality by means of the three places of the title: the garden, the temple, and the monastic cell. Although the section on the profane garden does not discuss the *Rose*, a later discussion of the Querelle de la Rose analyzes briefly allegorical works by or attributed to Jean Gerson which incorporate or respond to the *Rose*. [For a discussion of the attribution of the *Jardin amoureux*, see no. 571]. Oulmont argues that the *Rose* had a wide-spread but unfortunate influence on fifteenth-century mystical writings by encouraging didactic and sentimental allegories.

716 Owen, Dorothy L. *"Piers Plowman": A Comparison with Some Earlier and Contemporary French Allegories.* 1912; rpt. Folcroft, Pa.: Folcroft Library Editions, 1971. Pp. 173.

A comparison of allegorical elements in nine French works, including the *Rose*, to "points of resemblance" (3) in *Piers Plowman*. The second part of the *Rose* is of much greater significance for the English allegory than the first: they are compared in terms of their purpose, the setting of the allegory, and the three elements of personification, allegorical action, and allegorical devices. The author concludes that although there "are no similarities so striking as to justify the conclusion that the English writer must certainly be here borrowing from the French" (127), the author or authors of *Piers Plowman* almost certainly knew and remembered the *Rose*. An appendix summarizes the major allegories discussed, though not the *Rose*.

717 Palmer, R. Barton. "The Metafictional Machaut: Self-Reflexivity and Self-Mediation in the Two Judgment Poems." *Studies in the Literary Imagination* 20 (1987):23-39.

An analysis of Guillaume de Machaut's *Jugement dou Roy de Behaigne* and *Jugement dou Roy de Navarre*, both of which are to different degrees metafictional poetry, "poems about the artistic/social fact of composing poetry" (26). The author points to the *Roman de la rose* as a major influence on Machaut's poems. Although Machaut did not produce a slavish imitation of the *Rose*, nonetheless, "the reader is being challenged to read Machaut's work in reference to its illustrious predecessor" (28).

718 Patterson, Lee. "'For the Wyves love of Bathe': Feminine Rhetoric and Poetic Resolution in the *Roman de la Rose* and the *Canterbury Tales*." *Speculum* 58 (1983):656-95. Rev. version in author's *Chaucer and the Subject of History* (Madison: U of Wisconsin P, 1991), 280-32. Rev. further as "Feminine Rhetoric and the Politics of Subjectivity: La Vieille and the Wife of Bath," in *Rethinking* (no. 182), 316-58.

An ambitious interpretation of the Wife of Bath's performance "as an act of deliberate self-fashioning" by means of which Chaucer "sought to establish the construction of subjectivity--the representation of character--as itself a topic worthy of serious literary practice" (319). In other words, through the Wife of Bath, Chaucer attempted to define and defend his own poetics. In the course of his analysis of femininity, textuality, and subjectivity, Patterson discusses other texts involving old women as precedents or parallels to the Wife, including Jean Lefèvre's *La vieille*, Roger de Collerye's *Sermon pour une nopce*, and the *Roman de la rose*. After suggesting that Guillaume de Lorris abandoned the first part as "a graceful submission to the inevitability of history" (325), Patterson examines how Jean's old woman introduces "the ambivalences of *temporality* into the poem in a fully human form" (327). She does this largely through the structure of her autobiographical sermon, a structure described as *dilatio*, or a process of delay and fulfillment which matches the rose's dilation. This structure of dilation is not only a function of sermon technique but also of female eroticism. La Vieille's discourse is also significant for providing the model for Nature's speech, thereby making it possible to align "the Lover's amorous obsessions with the poem's larger, more severe perspectives" (330). The discussion of la Vieille is a prelude to the complex analysis of the Wife's "dilated discourse" (335) which both masks and discloses the subjectivity at its heart. Finally, the author argues that the "'joly body' of the Wife's text is thus a paradigm for the *Canterbury Tales* as a whole" (347).

719 Payen, Jean-Charles. "Diderot et le Moyen Age: recherches complémentaires." *La licorne* 6 (1982):239-52; discussion, 253-54.

In the context of a continuing investigation into the possible influence of medieval works in the eighteenth century (see for instance nos. 433 and 720 by the same author), Payen here looks at two works by Diderot which he believes may refer indirectly to the *Roman de la rose*, in particular to Raison's remarks on euphemism and linguistic directness, and to Jean de Meun's ideas on the origins of property and power (which Rousseau also may have known). The texts of Diderot considered here are a passage from *Jacques le fataliste*, where the author denounces the paradox of linguistic propriety, and the *Suite du dialogue*, which refers to an idyllic society existing before the introduction of the concept of private property. Payen reiterates his hypothesis that Jean was a "précurseur lointain des philosophes" (244), although he points out that Diderot could not and would not have recognized his debt to the *Rose*.

720 -----. "Jean-Jacques Rousseau et le *Roman de la rose*." *Revue philosophique de la France et de l'étranger* 168 (1978):351-56.

A discussion of Rousseau that suggests that the probable impact of Jean de Meun's part of the *Roman de la rose* on Rousseau's thought is a topic that should be investigated by specialists of eighteenth-century literature. To point out possible lines of investigation, Payen gives an overview of certain ideas in the *Rose* that have parallels in Rousseau's work, in particular the recurring theme of a Golden Age and the collaboration between prince and *clerc* in an enlightened government.

721 Peck, Russell A. *Chaucer's "Romaunt of the Rose" and "Boece," "Treatise on the Astrolabe," "Equatorie of the Planetis," Lost Works, and Chaucerian Apocrypha: An Annotated Bibliography 1900 to 1985*. The Chaucer Bibliographies. Toronto: U of Toronto P, 1988. Pp. xviii + 402.

An excellent introduction to and annotated bibliography of the Middle English translation of the *Rose*, part or all of which has been attributed to Chaucer. The introduction summarizes the long critical battle over Chaucer's possible authorship of the translation, concluding that "Chaucer's authorship of at least part--certainly the best part--remains a defensible possibility" (9). Twelve editions and sixty critical studies of the *Romaunt* are annotated, often at some length, as well as ninety-five critical works on the *Rose* or on its influence on Chaucer.

722 Pézard, André. "Lune et fortune chez Jean de Meung et chez Dante." In *Studi in onore di Italo Siciliano*. 2 vols. Florence: Leo S. Olschki, 1966. 2:985-95. Rpt. in *Dans le sillage de Dante*. Paris: Société d'Etudes Italiennes, 1975. 463-73.

A discussion of the themes of the moon and Fortune in the second part of the *Rose* and in the *Divina commedia*. The pilgrim--the friend of Beatrice but not of Fortune--describes the island of Purgatory in terms that echo details in Jean de Meun's description of the house of Fortune. Other passages cited include the association of Florence with Fortune and the juxtaposition of Nature's digression on the physical structure of the moon with Beatrice's theological explanation. Pézard argues that Dante was directly inspired by the *Rose*, and that he gave "une signification continue, pressante et une" (470) to what was fragmentary and insignificant in Jean de Meun's poem.

723 Piaget, Arthur. "Chronologie des *Epistres sur le 'Roman de la rose'*." In *Etudes romanes dédiées à Gaston Paris par ses élèves français et ses élèves étrangers des pays de langue française*. Paris: Emile Bouillon, 1891. 113-20.

A revision of the date--from 1407 to 1401--that early scholars of the Querelle de la Rose placed on Christine de Pizan's act of sending some of the letters in the debate to the queen of France and the provost of Paris. Piaget also suggests a chronology for the writing of those letters and a few other documents in the debate.

724 Picone, Michelangelo. "Dante e il mito di Narciso: dal *Roman de la rose* alla *Commedia*." *Romanische Forschungen* 89 (1977):382-97.

A reconstruction of the development of the myth of Narcissus starting with Guillaume de Lorris's and Jean de Meun's interpretations of it and illustrating Dante's solution. The focus is on the Fountain: for Guillaume the negative model, represented by Narcissus's indulging in the contemplation of the self reflected on the water's surface, is superseded by l'Amant's vision of the two magical crystals which allow him to see the final object of his quest, the rose, the Domina. For Jean, instead, love is a power totally inscribable within man's possibilities, with him we observe a "declassamento ideologico di questo sentimento" (392). The two crystals become a trifaceted carbuncle (the Trinity) and the Fountain of Narcissus, the Fountain of Life. Dante goes back to Guillaume's approach to the myth, but, like Jean, he cannot be satisfied by his solution: his Donna is Guillaume's, but the *queste* cannot end with her. She is the bridge and her eyes (the two crystals) make access to divine perfection possible. [MRB]

725 -----. *"Vita nuova" e tradizione romanza.* Padua: Liviana, 1979. Pp. vii + 203.

A study of the *Vita nuova* in the context of the romance tradition. For Dante the highest poetic testimony of *fin' amor* is Arnaut Daniel's (see *Purgatory* XXVI), but it is to the *Rose*, "summa perfetta della cultura medievale" (40), that he turned for a systematic illustration of amorous principles. Picone, who, needless to say, accepts Contini's attribution of the *Fiore* and the *Detto d'amore* to Dante (see no. 605), views the *Rose* as a dramatic text with two opposite theses: Guillaume's is courtly and positive, and Jean's, bourgeois and negative. The adjectives positive and negative refer to love's role: in the first *Rose*, *amor* indicates a superior morality, aristocratic and elitist, while in the second, Jean wants to unveil the errancy of *fin'amor* and elaborate a theory of love which will allow for the realization of man's earthly mission. Nature of course will be the center of it. Picone's interpretation is well sustained by his analysis of the role of the fountain(s) of Love (see no. 724) and of the final metaphor which sees the *peregrinus amoris* finally conclude his quest. [MRB]

726 Polizzi, Gilles. "Le devenir du jardin médiéval? Du verger de la Rose à Cythère." In *Vergers et jardins dans l'univers médiéval.* Senefiance 28. Aix-en-Provence: CUER-MA, 1990. 267-88.

A comparison of the gardens in the *Rose* with those in the *Songe de Poliphile* (the 1546 French translation of the late fifteenth-century *Hypnerotomachia Poliphili*) of Francesco Colonna, a work which is "un catalogue peut-être exhaustif, des motifs qui construisent le jardin de la Renaissance" (267). After discussing briefly the direct or indirect influence of the *Rose* on the *Poliphile*, Polizzi considers the evolution of allegorical elements such as the visual notations (Guillaume's descriptions are controlled by temporality, while Colonna's reflect an idealized geometry); the garden shapes; and the topography of buildings, such as Guillaume's castle. While Colonna's gardens are seen as sharing the emblematic character and allegorical dimension of the garden of Deduit, Polizzi argues that the Italian author's gardens are closer to Jean de Meun's Park of the Lamb as "lieu du sacré et instrument d'une 'révélation'" (280). Thus, for the first readers of the *Poliphile*, the gardens of Cythera must have appeared as a variation on familiar medieval models. Includes twelve figures from the *Poliphile*.

727 Post, Chandler Rathfon. *Mediaeval Spanish Allegory*. Harvard Studies in Comparative Literature 4. Cambridge: Harvard UP, 1915. Pp. xii + 331.

A study that traces the development of Castilian allegory from the thirteenth to the fifteenth century. A chapter on French influence surveys a variety of Spanish literary genres that show familiarity with French works. Post points to the influence of the *Rose*, particularly in the fifteenth-century works of Francisco Imperial (whose *Decir de la siete virtudes* includes an allegorical lady in a garden with bow and arrows), Ruy Páez de Ribera, the Marquis of Santillana, and Juan de Mena.

728 Potansky, Peter. *Der Streit um den "Rosenroman"*. Münchener romanistische Arbeiten 33. Munich: Wilhelm Fink, 1972. Pp. 240.

729 Ragen, Brian Abel. "Chaucer, Jean de Meun, and Proverbs 30:20." *Notes and Queries* n.s. 35 [233] (1988):295-96.

A detail from a passage in Proverbs--that the adulteress wipes her mouth--is offered as the "ultimate source" (296) for the advice of la Vieille in the *Rose* and for Chaucer's portrait of the Prioress. [The author's argument that "La Vieille is, after all, describing the ways of the adulteress" (296) does not fit with the text (la Vieille is giving advice to all women who have or want to have sexual relations), nor is she a champion of "courtly love" (296)]. Ragen also argues for a parallel, following Fleming (see no. 241), between Raison and the Sapientia of Proverbs 7. According to Ragen, in the cases of the Prioress and la Vieille, the allusion to Proverbs is used to undercut Ovidian sources.

730   Ralph, Dorothy Marie. "Jean de Meun, the Voltaire of the Middle Ages." Diss. U of Illinois, 1940.

731   Reid, T. B. W. "Chaucer's 'Ferthing of Grece'." *Notes and Queries* n.s. 11 [209] (1964):373-74.

A reexamination of the question of whether Chaucer's use of "ferthing" (farthing) in his description of the Prioress's table manners was a mistranslation of "mailletes" ("little spots," *Rose* l. 13401). A work "roughly contemporary" (373) to the *Rose*, the *Clef d'amors*, however, renders the passage in terms of coinage, in what is perhaps a pun or a metaphor. Thus it is possible that Chaucer derived his expression, "ferthing of grece," from the *Clef d'amors*.

732   Rice, Winthrop Huntington. *The European Ancestry of Villon's Satirical Testaments*. Syracuse University Monographs 1. New York: The Corporate Press, 1941. Pp. 244.

A brief discussion of the possible influence on Villon of the *Testament* attributed to Jean de Meun. Chapter 5 points to the striking development of literary testaments in late medieval France. It is in Jean's *Testament* and *Codicile*, however, that we find "the first seriously possible prototype for the testaments of Villon" (149). Villon himself paraphrases several lines from the *Testament* in his poem, but he inaccurately attributes the lines to the *Rose*. Rice describes the subjects and form of Jean's testament and gives a few excerpts from satirical passages. He believes that the *Testament* contains, "in the germ, almost all the elements which will later go to make up the two wills of Villon" (157), just as the *Rose* contained the germ so much of medieval literature.

733 Richards, Earl Jeffrey. "Christine de Pizan, the Conventions of Courtly Diction, and Italian Humanism." In *Reinterpreting Christine de Pizan* (no. 736). 250-71.

An interpretation of Christine de Pizan's works as moving away from courtly conventions and toward "later Renaissance humanist criticisms of medieval courtly romance" (257). Richards suggests that her opposition to the *Rose* was in part based on this courtly/humanist opposition (and not simply on prudery). Christine rejected the *Rose*'s "essentially formalist paradigm of literary composition" (255) in her "attempt to shift attention away from the overemphasis on the purely formal and contrived" (256). Scholars have recognized the importance of Dante for Christine's search for a new paradigm, but Richards argues that Petrarch's influence was also crucial: "her critique of the *Rose* continues Petrarch's" (261). The article concludes with a discussion of Christine's political ideas and their relation to humanism.

734 -----. *Dante and the "Roman de la rose": An Investigation into the Vernacular Narrative Context of the "Commedia"*. Beiheft zur Zeitschrift für romanische Philologie 184. Tubingen: Max Niemeyer, 1981. Pp. viii + 116.

A study of Dante's possible relation to the *Rose* and to Old French vernacular narrative. Richards first reconstructs the literary climate of thirteenth- and early fourteenth-century Italy with regard to Italian writers' contact with Old French and Provençal literature and their concerns for a vernacular national literature. In this context he reconsiders the attribution of the *Fiore* to Dante, and although deciding against such an attribution, he argues that the *Fiore*, as a translation of sorts of the *Rose*, may have played a "possible mediating role between the O. F. [Old French] canon and Dante" (32). The second chapter explores the *translatio studii* topos (see definition, 20) which is expressed with a striking affinity in the *Inferno* and the midpoint of the *Rose*. Chapter 3 reviews medieval and modern opinions comparing the *Commedia* and the *Rose*, including those of Christine de Pizan, Laurent de Premierfait, Jean

Lemaire de Belges, and Gianfranco Contini (see no. 605). Richards then proposes five "significant textual reminiscences" (85) between the *Rose* and the *Commedia*, including their conceptions of paradise, moonspots, and fountains. Richards concludes that Dante "clearly seems to be 'continuing' the *Rose* in the *Commedia*" (104), a continuation which is "highly complex and somewhat ambiguous" (105).

735 -----. "The *Fiore* and the *Roman de la rose*." In *Medieval Translators and Their Craft*. Ed. Jeanette Beer. Studies in Medieval Culture 25. Kalamazoo, Michigan: Western Michigan University, 1989. 265-83.

An analysis of the ways in which the poet of the *Fiore*, a medieval Italian adaptation of the *Rose* in sonnets, "radically recast" (265) the *Rose*. The Italian poet made a number of changes in narrative structure and characterization, generally compressing, condensing, and increasing lyrical intensity. The dream format has been eliminated, perhaps to increase the apparent truthfulness of the adaptation (Richards discusses briefly how medieval translators, such as Benoît de Sainte-Maure and Gottfried von Strassburg, saw the truth function of their works). Through a comparison of two sonnets with corresponding passages in the *Rose*, Richards brings out both changes in narrative emphasis and stylistic peculiarities which may be seen as (which may be seen as innovative or artificial) of the Italian text.

736 Richards, Earl Jeffrey, ed., with Joan Williamson, Nadia Margolis, and Christine Reno. *Reinterpreting Christine de Pizan*. Athens: U of Georgia P, 1992. Pp. x + 310.

A collection of articles, many of which refer in passing to Jean de Meun and the *Rose*. The two articles which treat the *Rose* in some detail are those by Margolis (no. 696) and Richards (no. 733).

737 Robertson, D. W., Jr. "The Physician's Comic Tale." *The Chaucer Review* 23 (1988):129-39.

An analysis of the humorous elements in Chaucer's Physician. Robertson compares the Physician's tale of Virginius and his daughter to the work from which it is "clearly derived" (129), Jean de Meun's continuation of the *Rose*. The Physician deliberately distorts Jean's theological version (and both distort Livy) in a number of ways, such as by shifting the attention from Appius to Virginia and by distorting the moral. Chaucer's Physician unintentionally reveals himself as "a kind of Appius himself" (137), a "striking exemplar of medical fraud" (137) devoid of justice and charity.

738 -----. *A Preface to Chaucer: Studies in Medieval Perspectives*. See no. 473.

739 -----. "The Wife of Bath and Midas." *Studies in the Age of Chaucer* 6 (1984):1-20.

A discussion of the Wife of Bath's "mistelling" (5) of the story of Midas, which is seen as a key to her progress and which echoes in the *Tale* itself. Furthermore, parallels between the Wife and the characters of l'Ami and la Vieille, in terms of what these parallels reveal of the Wife's sinful nature, indicate that the *Roman de la rose* can "enhance our appreciation for the wider significance of the story of Midas" (2). Through the tale of Midas, the Wife shows herself to be an exemplar both of "disobedient flesh or sensuality in terms of both scriptural and classical imagery" (5) and of what women really want -- sovereignty. Robertson suggests finally that the Wife represents the general deterioration of morals in England, where persons of all ranks "had very clearly been pursuing wealth or Epicurean satisfactions, or both together, for some time" (16).

740 Schibanoff, Susan. "Taking the Gold Out of Egypt: The Art of Reading as a Woman." In *Gender and Reading: Essays on*

Readers, Texts, and Contexts. Ed. Elizabeth A. Flynn and Patrocinio P. Schweickart. Baltimore: The Johns Hopkins UP, 1986. 83-106.

A study of the Wife of Bath in the context of a discussion of ways of reading medieval misogynistic texts. Schibanoff compares the Wife of Bath's methods of reading, which resemble those of oral tradition, with Christine de Pizan's evolution from the methods of patristic exegesis to reading as a woman in the *Book of the City of Women* (*La cité des dames*). Christine's part in the Querelle de la Rose, in which she expressed her views on misogynistic texts through her critique of Jean de Meun's part of the *Rose*, "transformed her from being the immasculated reader who composed the *Othea* into the woman reader, one who claimed her right to reread texts according to her own experiences and knowledge" (97).

741 Schueler, Donald G. "Gower's Characterization of Genius in the *Confessio Amantis*." *Modern Language Quarterly* 33 (1972):240-56.

An examination of Genius's perspective on love and nature in order to counter modern misconceptions of Gower's apparent inconsistencies in the *Confessio Amantis*. Like the Genius of Alain de Lille and Jean de Meun, Gower's Genius is allied both with Nature and Venus, but whereas he has been generally seen as the priest of courtly love by earlier scholars, Schueler argues that Genius is the spokesman of Nature and as such serves both God and love. Schueler shows that Genius consistently subordinates love, both natural and courtly, to the "rational modifications" (254) which man must apply to it. Thus Genius must be seen as charting a careful course between the blind force of Venus and the ordered cosmos of Nature.

742 Shoaf, R. A. "'Mutatio Amoris': 'Penitentia' and the Form of *The Book of the Duchess*." *Genre* 14 (1981):163-89.

An interpretation of the *Book of the Duchess* that places it in the context of medieval confessional and dream models. Shoaf stresses the Black Knight's early resistance to change through repentance. In his loyalty to courtly love and its rhetoric, the Knight "insists on following his greatest model in *fin' amor* literalism--namely, *Amans* in the *Roman de la Rose*" (165). Chaucer revises Jean de Meun's image of "confession sanz repentence" (l. 6890) to suggest that the Knight's proper response is to "translate the past for a meaningful present" (166).

743 Sichi, Edward, Jr. "Milton and the *Roman de la rose*: Adam and Eve at the Fountain of Narcissus." In *Milton and the Middle Ages*. Ed. and intro. John Mulryan. Lewisburg: Bucknell UP; London: Associated University Presses, 1982. 153-82.

An essay that suggests parallels between the *Rose* and *Paradise Lost*, principally in the theme of illusionary love, the pattern of the Fall, and the fountain scenes (the Fountain of Narcissus and Eve's contemplation of her reflection). [The parallels, which adhere to a strict Robertsonian approach (see no. 473), may seem strained, as when Eve is compared both to the lover and the rose, or when the moral of Narcissus's story in the first part of the *Rose* is interpreted as blaming the Lady for "man's fall from grace and reason" (164).] Sichi concludes that both works were meant to be the means by which the reader could turn from sin and find salvation.

744 -----. "'These two imparadis't': A Comparative Study of the Gardens in *Paradise Lost* and the *Roman de la rose*." Diss. Duquesne U, 1977.

745 Siciliano, Italo. *François Villon et les thèmes poétiques du moyen âge*. 1934; rpt. Paris: Nizet, 1967. Pp. xviii + 592.

An overview of medieval literature and an accumulation of references to and citations from four centuries of medieval works, grouped according to poetic themes that are also found in Villon's poetry: Death, Fortune, Woman, "l'amant martyr et la dame sans merci" (313). The author frequently refers to Jean de Meun's part of the *Rose* and to the *Testament* and *Codicile* attributed to him but concludes that Villon knew Jean "plus vaguement qu'on ne le croit" (435). It is the Middle Ages, in particular its commonplaces and clichés, that are the source of Villon's images and themes, not a particular author or group of authors. Siciliano's conclusion is based on the assumption that the Middle Ages was a homogeneous, unchanging period, characterized by little literary originality (see for example his remarks on allegory: "Les songes et les allégories sont innombrables, mais, aussi, inaltérablement creux et vides" [157]).

746 Smith, Merete. "Literary Loanwords from Old French in *The Romaunt of the Rose*: A Note." *The Chaucer Review* 17 (1982):89-93.

A study of Middle English lexical borrowing. Smith argues that the common assumption that many Old French loanwords found in Middle English were the result of literary borrowings cannot be proven through examination of those loanwords appearing in the *Romaunt of the Rose*. Admittedly, the words studied in this article--"words designating articles of dress and fabrics used for dress" (89)--are a restricted group, and Smith notes that further investigation would be useful. (See also no. 670.) [KML]

747 Smith, Roland M. "Chaucer's 'Castle in Spain' (*HF* 1117)." *Modern Language Notes* 60 (1945):39-40.

A note on the reference to a castle in Spain in the *House of Fame*, which previous editors and even Fansler in *Chaucer and the Roman de la rose* (no. 622) had failed to see as a possible allusion to Guillaume de Lorris's line, "Lors feras chastiaus en Espaigne" (Langlois l. 2442 [l. 2430]): "The *Roman de la Rose* thus affords not only the earliest extant instance of the proverbial phrase 'castles in Spain,' but an excellent 'working definition' as well" (40). While recognizing with earlier scholars that Guillaume may have been using a phrase that was already proverbial, Smith suggests further investigation.

748   Sneyders de Vogel, K. "'Le cercle dont le centre est partout, la circonférence nulle part' et le *Roman de la rose*." *Neophilologus* 16 (1931):246-50.

An inquiry into the sources of this famous description of God that is also found in the work of Marguerite de Navarre and Rabelais. In opposition to Abel Lefranc's suggestion that the former found the formula in the work of Saint Bonaventure, Vincent de Beauvais, or Symphorion Champier, the author points to the passage in the *Rose* which includes a similar phrase and which Marguerite almost certainly knew (ll. 19099-108). As for Jean de Meun's source, Sneyders de Vogel sees no way of deciding between Saint Bonaventure or Vincent de Beauvais, but in a postscript he points out the presence of the expression in the work of Alain de Lille.

749   -----. "Encore une fois 'Le cercle dont le centre est partout, la circonférence nulle part'." *Neophilologus* 17 (1932):211-12.

A follow-up to the preceding article, suggesting that Rabelais's source for this phrase in the *Tiers livre*, based on his reference to Hermes Trismegistus, is the thirteenth-century Bartholomaeus Anglicus's *De proprietatibus rerum*, who in turn probably found the expression in an Arab work.

750   -----. "Marot et *Le roman de la rose*." *Neophilologus* 17 (1932):269-71.

A summary of Becker's arguments against Marot's authorship of a 1526 revision of the *Rose* (see no. 580). The author reaffirms the hypothesis of Marot's authorship based both on weaknesses in Becker's evidence and on the positive evidence provided by Pasquier's remarks in *Les recherches de la France*.

751 Stuip, R. E. V. and T. J. van Tuijn. "Interférences entre *La châtelaine de Vergy* et *Le roman de la rose*." *Neophilologus* 70 (1986):469-71.

A comparison of a sixteenth-century adaptation of *La châtelaine de Vergy* to the thirteenth-century original. The authors describe a twenty-five line fragment of the *Rose* imbedded in the 1540 version of the *Châtelaine*, a fragment taken from Genius's portrayal of a wife's attempts to wheedle her husband's secret out of him (ll. 16408-38 and 16479-80). Not only may this borrowing help us to determine the author of the adaptation, but it also gives information about sixteenth-century attitudes toward the *Rose* and its use by contemporary authors.

752 Sullivan, Karen. "The Limit of Feminist Theory: An Architectonics of the *Querelle de la Rose*." *Exemplaria* 3 (1991):435-66.

An audacious translation into architectural images of the attitudes of participants in the fifteenth-century debate on the *Rose* in order to reevaluate Christine de Pizan's relation to feminist ideas. Jean de Montreuil's attitudes to his famous predecessor, Jean de Meun, are seen as placing Jean de Meun in a crypt lodged within Jean de Montreuil himself, a "crypt whose haunting effect permeates the letters as a whole" (444). Two other architectural images emerge in Sullivan's analysis of Christine de Pizan's letters: her authority is based on her relation to the silent order of women, viewed both as a *secretum* (secret place) and as a castle. Since Christine must leave the female "castle" (459) in order to defend women against misogynistic attackers, it is the "instability of her location as a woman" (466) that makes Christine profoundly feminist.

753 Sutherland, Ronald. "The *Romaunt of the Rose* and Source Manuscripts." *PMLA* 74 (1959):178-83.

A comparison of the Middle English *Romaunt of the Rose* both with manuscripts of the *Roman de la rose*, as categorized by Langlois (see no. 66), and with Langlois's reconstructed edition of the *Rose* [called the "standard" text (179)], in order to determine both the possible family of mss. which the translator(s) used and the likelihood that the *Romaunt* fragments were translated by the same person. Sutherland makes the case that the manuscript family for Fragment A "is established" (180) as a ms. from the H family. The source mss. of the other fragments is less clear, and in addition, they were reworked and tampered with. Nonetheless, Sutherland argues that these fragments were based on mss. from groups different from each other and from A's. Therefore, if Fragment A is the work of Chaucer, as Sutherland strongly argues, then Fragments B and C must be by someone else.

754 Thompson, Nesta M. "A Further Study of Chaucer and the *Romance of the Rose*." Diss. Stanford U, 1927.

755 Thuasne, Louis. *Villon et Rabelais: notes et commentaires*. 1911; rpt. Geneva: Slatkine Reprints, 1969. Pp. vi + 466.

A collection of studies, all but two of which were published previously. Chapter 1 discusses Villon and Jean de Meun, Chapter 3 Rabelais and the *Roman de la rose*. Thuasne believes that both Villon and Rabelais were very familiar with the *Rose* and intensely shaped by it in both the form and content of their works. Villon in particular "avait lu et relu le *Roman de la Rose*, et en savait par coeur des passages entiers" (98) as well as other works by Jean de Meun, including his translations. However, Villon's "immense supériorité" (47) refined the crude ore of the *Rose* into pure gold. The study distinguishes similarities both of general theme and of detail, which are illustrated by the juxtaposition of passages from each work. While the later writers rarely reproduce the exact terms or images of the *Rose*,

Thuasne points out a number of similar themes and ideas. He also recognizes that a particular correlation may be "fortuite et amenée par l'analogie des idées" (21), and that other works, such as Renaut de Louhans' translation of the *De consolatione Philosophiae*, may have influenced the later writers.

756 Took, John. "Dante and the *Roman de la rose*." *Italian Studies* 37 (1982):1-25.

A review of evidence for Dante's selective but persistent reading of the *Rose*, in particular of Jean de Meun's views as expressed by Raison and Nature. A clear and balanced summary of the two distinctive conceptions of love in the *Rose*, rationalistic and naturalistic, is followed by an analysis of parallel themes and ideas in the *Vita nuova*, the *Convivio*, and the *Commedia*. Dante's reading of Raison's spiritual solution to the problems of love in his earlier works is expanded in the *Commedia* by his response to Nature's cosmological view of man's relation to the macrocosm. Took concludes that the most appropriate way of defining Dante's relationship to the *Rose* is as a "redistribution of emphasis" (24), a foregrounding of one in particular of Jean's interlocutors, Raison. The *Rose* thus furnished a precedent and authorization for Dante's own undertaking.

757 -----. "Towards an Interpretation of the *Fiore*." *Speculum* 54 (1979):500-27.

A study of the *Fiore* that argues, after a review of critical opinion on the naturalism or orthodoxy of the *Rose*, that the *Fiore*, an allegorical fourteenth-century sonnet sequence attributed to Dante, can best be understood if read according to the moral interpretation of the *Rose* proposed by Fleming and Robertson (see nos. 243 and 473). Rather than works of comic realism, both the *Rose* and the *Fiore* are a meditation "on the spiritual predicament of the lover" (511), whose love is shown to be irrational, sensual, and hypocritical. The author compares the discourses of le Dieu d'Amour, Raison, l'Ami, Faux Semblant, and la Vieille in the *Fiore* to their partners in the *Rose*; parallels are also pointed out between the *Fiore* and other works of Dante.

758 Torres-Alcalá, Antonio. "El *Libro de buen amor* y el *Roman de la rose*: algunas analogías." *Anuario medieval* 2 (1990):172-83.

A comparative study that suggests that there exist not direct influences but some "analogías comunes" (173 n. 4) between the two works. Beyond superficial similarities of subject (arts of love), allegory, and polysemic meaning, the author outlines themes centered in the works' "transfondo filosófico-teológico-cultural" (174), in particular the conflict of necessity and free will in relation to love. While Jean de Meun's character Genius treats as a theoretical moralist the Aristotelian subject of man's entelechy realizing itself in procreation, the hero of *El libro de buen amor* approaches the problem in a more personal and practical manner; for him the question of the inevitability of sin is more important than for Jean. The article concludes with a brief discussion of the importance of this conflict in medieval thought, which explains in part the open-ended nature of both works.

759 Uitti, Karl D. "From *Clerc* to *Poète*: The Relevance of the *Romance of the Rose* to Machaut's World." See no. 529.

760 Vallone, A. "Personificazione, simbolo e allegoria del Medio Evo dinanzi a Dante." *Filologie e Letteratura* 10 (1964): 189-224.

761 Van der Poel, Dieuwke E. "A Romance of a Rose and Florentine: The Flemish Adaptation of the *Romance of the Rose*." In *Rethinking* (no. 182). 304-15.

A description of the principal modifications in the allegorical structure of the Flemish adaptation of the *Rose*. After describing both Middle Dutch adaptations, the author concentrates on two significant changes made by the Flemish poet--the new framework for the allegorical story, and the presence of a real lady, Florentine, who doubles and at times even replaces the allegorical figures such as the rose and Bel Accueil. The author observes that changes in the characters' discourses are less radical than those in the narrative, indicating that they were the most important part, and that the Middle Dutch poet desired to convey not only general lessons about love "but also a working knowledge" (312) of it.

762   Van der Poel, Dieuwke [E]. "The *Romance of the Rose* and *I*: Narrative Perspective in the *Roman de la Rose* and its Two Middle Dutch Adaptations." In *Courtly Literature: Culture and Context*. Selected Papers of the 5th Triennial Congress of the International Courtly Literature Society, Dalfsen, The Netherlands, 9-16 August 1986. Ed. Keith Busby and Erik Kooper. Amsterdam: John Benjamins, 1990. 573-83.

An analysis first of the complex figure of the first-person voice (Dreamer, Lover, or Narrator) in Guillaume's *Rose*, then of the ways the two Middle Dutch translations from about 1300 dealt with this figure. The Brabantine translation, which of the two remains more faithful to the text, shifts between the protagonist as *I* and as the lover, suggesting that the translator felt uncomfortable with the "new narrative style" (578) of internal viewpoint and slipped back into the external viewpoint. The freer Flemish adaptation, on the other hand, uncomfortable with the allegorical status of the romance, simplified the narrative structure. Further, the Flemish adaptor did not interpret the *Rose* as ironic but instead expected the public to identify with and approve of the character, Joyous Lover. Thus these translations give us "a glimpse of a contemporary reaction to the narrative technique of the *Roman de la Rose*" (581).

763   -----. *De Vlaamse "Rose" en "Die Rose" van Heinric: Onderzoekingen over twee Middelnederlandse bewerkingen*

van de *"Roman de la rose"*. Middeleeuwse Studies en Bronnen 13. Hilversum: Verloren, 1989. Pp. 259.

A comparative description of the two Middle Dutch versions of the *Rose*, one from about 1290, anonymous, in Flemish, and existing in fragments from two manuscripts; the other written in Brabantine between 1278 and 1325 by "Heinric," who may have been Heinric van Aken. Heinric follows the *Rose* closely while abridging it, but the anonymous version makes more radical changes, such as eliminating the dream framework. It is primarily with this text that the study is concerned. A chapter on the possible source manuscripts suggests that the translators used manuscripts from different groups. A comparison of the techniques of adaptation finds that the translators often clarify the French poem. Chapter 6 discusses the narrative perspective and the use of allegory, which has been profoundly changed in the Flemish version: the dream has become the love story of two characters encountered by the narrator. Van der Poel concludes that Heinric wanted to make the content of the *Rose* more accessible, while the Flemish adapter wanted his public to identify with new protagonists, Jolijs and Florentine. [Includes a resume in French (227-33) on which this entry is based.]

764 Vanossi, Luigi. *Dante e il "Roman de la rose": saggio sul "Fiore"*. Biblioteca dell'Archivum Romanicum I, 144. Florence: Leo S. Olschki, 1979. Pp. 373.

A systematic analysis of Dante's perusal of the *Rose* which investigates and compares the structures of the *Fiore* and the *Rose*. The *Fiore* contributes to an understanding of the project undertaken by Dante: aware of the ideological and stylistic divide which separates Guillaume and Jean, Dante proceeds to select from the *Rose* those themes which respond to his "logica inflessibile" (40). Vanossi, who has elegantly mastered the literature on the *Rose* and on Dante, shows us the significance of Guillaume's *visio* and Jean's *imago mundi* and their relevance to Dante's own *summa*. In fact, not only the *Fiore*, but the entire corpus of Dante's works is in various ways affected by the *Rose* which, to Vanossi, is "la fonte volgare di gran lunga più importante per la *Commedia*" (349), its influence being comparable only to the Latin sources. [MRB]

765 Vantuono, William. "*Cleanness* and *Le roman de la rose*." *English Language Notes* 26.2 (1988):1-6.

A review of the critical disagreement between Oliver F. Emerson and later editors of *Cleanness* about which part of the *Rose* served as the source for ll. 1057-64. By juxtaposing the two proposed passages from the *Rose* with the one in the English work, Vantuono suggests that "de Lorris' verses are the ones the poet [of *Cleanness*] had in mind when he composed his own religious allegory" (5).

766 Vyvyan, John. *Shakespeare and the Rose of Love: A Study of the Early Plays in Relation to the Medieval Philosophy of Love*. London: Chatto and Windus, 1960. Pp. 200.

An analysis of the *Rose*'s influence, especially the first part, on Shakespeare's conception of love as a redeeming power and of the heroine as the symbol of that power. Shakespeare probably knew the *Rose* partly through the *Romaunt*, "a pervasive presence in Shakespeare's early love-plays" (40), partly through early editions. Vyvyan integrates elements of courtly love into a larger pattern of conflict between a life-intrigue and a death-intrigue in the plays, a conflict which unfolds according to a "Terentian construction" (16). For Shakespeare, love is the mystical, idealized "star by which his characters must set their course" (32). Vyvyan suggests that the crystals in the Fountain of Narcissus are the lady's eyes, which represent the baptismal font initiating the lover into a new life. He argues that Shakespeare took to heart certain conflicts elaborated in the second part of the *Rose*, such as love and friendship or love and justice, and attempted to synthesize the unreconciled opposites. Chapter 3 gives a summary of and commentary on the *Rose*.

767 Wallace, David. "Chaucer and the European *Rose*." *Studies in the Age of Chaucer* 1 (1984):61-67.

An overview of five generations of Italian poets who "defined their individual enterprise against the constant standard of the *Rose*" (61) and of Chaucer, who concentrated their efforts into a single lifetime. Discussed briefly are Latini's *Tesoretto*, whose Latin learning, urbane manner, and occasional sarcastic wit anticipate Jean de Meun; the *Intelligenza*, which elaborates on themes and images from the *Rose*; the *Fiore*, which Wallace believes was likely written by Dante; Dante's *Commedia*; Boccaccio's *Filocolo*, especially Book 4, and his *Amorosa visione*; and Petrarch's *Trionfi*. Wallace points out Chaucer's debt to the *Rose* and its Italian successors in the *House of Fame* and *Troilus and Criseyde*, and suggests a curious parallel among Chaucer, Boccaccio, Dante, and Jean de Meun in that each sees himself as the sixth in a succession of six authors.

768 Walter, J. H. "*Astrophel and Stella* and *The Romaunt of the Rose*." *Review of English Studies* 15 (1939):265-73.

An analysis based on the thesis that Sidney's *Astrophel and Stella* was modeled on the English *Romaunt of the Rose* ("there is no hint that Sidney used the French version" [273]). This argument is supported by points of resemblance in the outline of the story, including the point at which both works break off (the end of Guillaume de Lorris's section) and by similarities of theme and idea, such as those of wealth and reason. Walter argues that the authors' allegorical methods are different, however.

769 Walters, Lori. "Illuminating the *Rose*: Gui de Mori and the Illustrations of MS 101 of the Municipal Library, Tournai." In *Rethinking* (no. 182). 167-200.

A description of the Tournai manuscript of Gui de Mori's extensive revision of the *Rose* and an analysis of the relation of the text to the illustration of the manuscript. The conceptualizer or planner of the manuscript actualized Gui's understanding of the *Rose* as expressing both human and divine love. Furthermore, the planner places Gui's authorial persona "within the Christianizing frame of the manuscript" (168). The study includes a description of the manuscript and of Gui's revisions, a comparison of the medieval poem *Floris et Lyriope* to Guillaume's Narcissus episode, and an interpretation of Gui's complex persona and the conflicts that a clerkly author would experience when writing about sexual love. Finally, the author discusses the possibility that the manuscript was prepared for a marriage. [Includes five reproductions from *Rose* manuscripts.]

770 Ward, Charles Frederick. *The Epistles on the "Romance of the Rose" and Other Documents in the Debate.* Chicago: U of Chicago P, 1911. Pp. 117.

An edition based on ms. 647 Paris, B. N. fr. 835. According to Hicks (see no. 647, xciii), whose edition has replaced both this one and Beck's (see no. 579), the transcription of Christine de Pizan's letters is generally correct, but Pierre Col's are unreadable. In addition Ward does not give an authentic text of Jean Gerson's treatise.

771 Webster, C. M. "Chaucer's Turkish Bows." *Modern Language Notes* 47 (1932):260.

A note on two passages in Chaucer's works, the *Knight's Tale* and Fragment A of the *Romaunt of the Rose*, which refer to Turkish bows. Guillaume de Lorris, and Chaucer following him, make the mistake of describing the Turkish bow, a very effective weapon, as wooden; it was instead "a reflexed bow, skillfully fashioned of layers of horn, wood, and sinew" (260).

772 Weinberg, Bernard. *Critical Prefaces of the French Renaissance.* Evanston, Illinois: Northwestern UP, 1950. Pp. ix + 290.

An edition of prefaces dating from 1525-1611, with

bibliographical information, variants, and notes. The edition is intended "for those concerned with the critical ideas of the sixteenth century" (vii). Weinberg reproduces the preface to the 1526 version of the *Rose* usually attributed to Clément Marot (see no. 36) (Weinberg disputes that attribution). In the preface the reviser explains the reasons for modernizing the *Rose*, which he says was requested by the bookseller Galiot du Pré, and proposes a Christian reading of the rose symbolism to show us the possible "sens allegoric et moral" (61) that underlies the sensual love story: the rose may be interpreted as wisdom, grace, the glorious Virgin Mary, or "la gloire d'eternelle beatitude" (62).

773 -----. "Guillaume Michel, dit de Tours, the Editor of the 1526 *Roman de la rose*." *Bibliothèque d'humanisme et renaissance* 11 (1949):72-85.

A review of evidence for the hypothesis that Guillaume Michel de Tours, not Clément Marot, was responsible for the 1526 modernized version of the *Rose*. After a review of Michel's works, including his translations, Weinberg offers two types of arguments for adding the translation of the *Rose* to the list: relations between the 1526 version of the *Rose* and certain editors and printers were similar to Michel's relations to his editors and printers; stylistic qualities in the preface to the modernized *Rose* are similar to Michel's style in known works by him. This "textual evidence" (79) includes similar phrasings, ecclesiastical passages, and unusual words or phrases (which Weinberg calls "Michelisms" [84]). Although not conclusive, the textual evidence gives "a kind of statistical impression" (85) which leads to Weinberg's hypothesis of Michel's authorship of the revised *Rose*. [But see Baridon's preface to his edition of the *Rose*, no. 36.]

774 Wetherbee, Winthrop. *Chaucer and the Poets: An Essay on "Troilus and Criseyde"*. Ithaca: Cornell UP, 1984. Pp. 249.

An assessment of Chaucer's debt in the *Troilus* to classical and medieval works, including the *Roman de la rose*. Chapter 2 focuses on how Chaucer's love psychology remakes the paradigmatic love experience expressed in the *Rose* while also reworking Boccaccio's *Filostrato*. Wetherbee argues that Jean de Meun is as much a presence in the *Troilus* as Guillaume de Lorris, that a tension between the practical and the ideal, the material and the spiritual, underlies Pandarus's and Troilus's conflicting conceptions of love. This conflict is also reflected in the characters' "conflicting tendencies of the imagination" (84), the appetitive vs. the aesthetic or idealizing. While Troilus incorporates many aspects of l'Amant in the *Rose*, his idealism and innocence go beyond the model. Ultimately Troilus's vision of love can only sense the divine harmony that Criseyde's beauty suggests, while finding "no resolution of the perennial conflict of imagination and desire, love and lust" (83).

775 Willard, Charity Cannon. *Christine de Pizan: Her Life and Works*. New York: Persea Books, 1984. Pp. 266.

A sympathetic approach to Christine's role in the "first recorded literary quarrel in France" (73) that places Christine's arguments in the context of her literary development. Her participation in the Querelle, in which she took the unusual position of protesting against Jean de Meun's unfair portrayal of women, marked a shift in her activities from court circles to broader contacts. Willard summarizes the *Rose* and reviews the events in the Querelle, which had begun in the late spring of 1401, before turning to Christine's arguments. The author sees Christine as concerned that Jean's ideas would contribute "to the low estate of public morality" (81) evident around her and to the unjust slander of women. Perhaps Christine's greatest achievement in the debate was to remove discussion of women from clerical circles and to make it possible "for a layperson, and a woman at that, to take part" (86). In this way she was a forerunner of ideas that became popular more than a century later, in, for example, Baldissare Castiglione's *Book of the Courtier*.

776 Wimsatt, J[ames] I. "Chaucer and French Poetry." In *Geoffrey Chaucer*. Ed. Derek Brewer. Writers and Their Background. Athens: Ohio UP, 1975. 109-36.

A good introduction to Chaucer's "immersion in the French tradition of poetry" (110). Wimsatt argues that even when Chaucer was working with Latin and Italian originals, "he usually found versions in French to assist his composition" (111). Basic were the romances of two poets of the *Rose* and Guillaume de Machaut, each of whom Wimsatt discusses in some detail. Guillaume de Lorris's influence can be seen in the appearances in Chaucer's work of personifications from the *Rose*, in his analysis of the process of love, and in such "appurtenances" (114) as the figure of the narrator-lover, garden descriptions, and details of the dreams. But Wimsatt recognizes that Jean de Meun had an "impressive and unique influence on the English poet" (130). While pointing out that the performances of Jean's personifications provide inspiration for Chaucer's characterizations and models for his dialogues, Wimsatt sees Jean's most important influence on Chaucer's development "in his immense widening of the range of the love poet" (131), which showed Chaucer how to diversify his love poetry.

777 -----. *Chaucer and the French Love Poets: The Literary Background of the "Book of the Duchess"*. University of North Carolina Studies in Comparative Literature 43. 1968; rpt. New York: Johnson Reprints, 1972. Pp. ix + 186.

A study of the influence of French love poetry on Chaucer's *Book of the Duchess*. Wimsatt discusses elements in Guillaume de Lorris's part of the *Rose* that he considers to be either the immediate or the ultimate influence on Chaucer's work. While recognizing significant differences in the two poems, Wimsatt stresses such common elements as the birds and other natural details in the two gardens, and the process of withdrawing into the world of the vision. Similar elements in French *dits amoureux* written between the *Rose* and Chaucer are pointed out. The conclusion argues that the first part of the *Rose* "provides the most direct source for several matters of narrative, detail, and structure of the *Book of the Duchess*" (27).

778 -----. "Realism in *Troilus and Criseyde* and the *Roman de la rose*." In *Essays on Troilus and Criseyde*. Ed. Mary Salu. Chaucer Studies 3. Cambridge, England: D. W. Brewer; Totowa, New Jersey: Rowman and Littlefield, 1979. 43-56; notes 130-33.

A study stressing the importance of generic frame of reference in interpreting the two works. Wimsatt argues that two realistic frames must be taken into account--Arts of Love and Platonic cosmic fables. Both types approach love in a realistic manner, the Arts of Love by their "close connection with the world of fact and of practical action" (48), the cosmic fables by their stress on the place of sexuality in the natural order. The author discusses the role of the go-between as an example of the realism of the Arts of Love and suggests that Pandarus in *Troilus and Criseyde* is a go-between modeled on the *Pamphilus* (which was "an essential influence" [46] on the *Rose*) and the *Libro de buen amor*. Pandarus is also allied to le Dieu d'Amour and l'Ami in the *Rose*.

779 Wood, Chauncey. "Speech, the Principle of Contraries, and Chaucer's Tales of the Manciple and the Parson." *Mediaevalia* 6 (1980):209-29.

A review of medieval theories of the principle of contraries and an analysis of l'Amant's discussion of the doctrine in the *Rose* (ll. 21543-44) in the context of an analysis of proper and improper speech in two of the *Canterbury Tales*. Wood further suggests that Jean de Meun's amusing use of the doctrine toward the end of the *Rose* "was in Chaucer's mind when he caused Pandarus to mention the concept" (212).

780 Work, James A. "The Manciple's Tale." In *Sources and Analogues of Chaucer's "Canterbury Tales"*. Ed. W. F.

Bryan and Germaine Dempster. 1941; rpt. New York: Humanities Press, 1958. 699-722.

A selection of passages from classical and medieval works which resemble the narrative or non-narrative material of the *Manciple's Tale*. Four passages from Jean de Meun's *Rose* offer similar ideas on the impossibility of restraining nature and on the need to restrain one's tongue. However, none of the works compared to Chaucer's tale offer "general or verbal parallels that point undeniably to his use of any of these texts" (700).

781   Wright, Steven [Alan]. "Deguileville's *Pèlerinage de vie humaine* as 'Contrepartie Edifiante' of the *Roman de la rose*." *Philological Quarterly* 68 (1989):399-422.

A review of the relationship of Deguileville's work to its source. While the primordial influence of the *Rose* on the *Pèlerinage* has been noted, the author believes that this influence is "both more formal and more generative" (399) than borrowed details of content. Wright examines this influence in some detail to show that the later poem reworks the *Rose* in its thematic structure as well as in particular allusions to images and characters. Deguileville recast the *Rose*'s major images, such as the garden and the fountain, "in a form that would cut them off from their secular setting in the romance" (404). Furthermore the *Pèlerinage* incorporates three times the romance's pattern of enclosure, porter, company of personifications, hunter. Even when Deguileville drew on characters and ideas from Jean's continuation, he used them "to develop scenes conceived around the action of Guillaume's part of the poem" (411).

782   -----. "Literary Influence in Medieval Literature: Chaucer and the *Roman de la rose*." Diss. Indiana U, 1986.

783   Zink, Michel. "La tristesse du coeur dans *Le livre du cuer d'amours espris* de René d'Anjou." In *Le récit amoureux*. Ed. Didier Coste and Michel Zeraffa. Paris: Editions du

Champ Vallon, 1984. 22-38.

An analysis that proposes the *Rose* as the model for the *Livre du cuer d'amours espris*, a late medieval allegorical dream vision of a love quest. In addition to an explicit reference to "Le tres bel Romant de la Rose" (23), the later romance offers many characters borrowed from the *Rose*, the most curious of which is Pitié, who suddenly becomes la Vieille. But René d'Anjou's poem borrows from the *Rose* not only in details of plot and allegory, but in "ce supplément de tristesse" (24) which gives his romance its meaning. Zink explores this self-mocking sadness and disenchantment in the *Livre du cuer* and argues further that it is an inevitable feature of the genre and a characteristic of late-medieval courtly literature.

CHAPTER FIVE

MISCELLANEOUS

784 Anon. "Le Jaloux qui bat sa femme." In *Recueil de poésies françoises des XVe et XVIe siècles, morales, facétieuses, historiques*. Ed. Anatole de Montaiglon. 13 vols. Paris: P. Jannet, 1856. 3:162-67.

A 144-line play from about 1527, which is simply an excerpt from the monologue of the jealous husband in the *Rose* and the succeeding discussion between l'Ami and l'Amant. The editor does not indicate that it is a section of the *Roman de la rose* and seems to find much of it in deplorable condition and unintelligible. (See Bourdillon, no. 586, and Meyer, no. 700).

785 Berkeley, Michael. *The Romance of the Rose: Theme and Variations*. Oxford: Oxford U P, Music Department, 1985. Pp. 28.

A work for amateur orchestra commissioned by the St. Paul's Schools' Chamber Orchestra and first performed at St. John's Smith Square, London, on November 1982, conducted by Jonathan Varcoe. The music is based on the composer's incidental music for the BBC radio production of the *Rose*.

786 Guiffrey, Jules [Marie Joseph]. *Histoire de la tapisserie depuis le moyen âge jusqu'à nos jours.* Tours: Alfred Mame et fils, 1886. Pp. viii + 535 + illus.

A survey of French tapestries that includes several references to the *Rose* as a subject. Records show that the romance was portrayed in richly-made tapestries from the fourteenth to the sixteenth centuries. One such tapestry worth 1000 francs was given in 1387 by the Duke of Burgundy, Philippe le Hardi, to his brother, the Duke of Berry (who was "fort sensible aux cadeaux" [39]), along with tapestries portraying religious subjects. [The author does not indicate whether any of the *Rose* tapestries still exist.]

787 Hugo, Victor. "La Préface de Cromwell." In *La Préface de Cromwell: introduction, texte et notes.* Ed. and intro. Maurice Souriau. Paris: Boivin, n. d. Pp. xviii + 330.

A reference to the lines in the *Rose* describing "une cérémonie auguste, l'élection d'un roi" (209) at the dawn of civilization, a ceremony in which a big, raw-boned peasant is chosen to be king (see ll. 9579-80). Hugo, citing probably from memory (the lines are in modern French), points to this passage as an example of "l'avènement et la marche du grotesque dans l'ère moderne" (208).

788 Jaroslawiecka-Gasiorowska, Maria. *Trzy francuskie rekopisy iluminowane w Zbiorach Czartoryskich w Krakowie.* Krakow: Muzeum Narodowe w Krakowie, 1953. Pp. 26 + 53 pp. plates.

A reproduction of illuminations in a manuscript belonging to the Czartoryski collection in Krakow. Includes the *Roman de la rose*, the *Livre des tournois* by René I, King of Naples and Jerusalem, and the *Traité de la charité chrestienne* by Nicolas Houel. [I have not been able to see this.]

789 *The Romance of the Rose.* Oxford: Bodleian Library, n.d. 35mm color filmstrip, roll 157A.

A photographic reproduction of 128 miniatures from a *Rose* ms., Bodleian Douce 195 (French, end of the fifteenth century). The manuscript was probably executed for Charles d'Orléans, and the illuminations have been attributed to Robinet Testard. The filmstrip is accompanied by a four-page guide which gives folio number and a brief description of the scene in each frame. Other, shorter filmstrips are also available from the Bodleian, including Roll 180H, 61 slides of ms. Astor A, 12. [Indexed in *Illuminated Manuscripts: An Index to Selected Bodleian Library Color Reproductions*, compiled and ed. by Thomas H. Ohlgren.]

790 *Le roman de la rose.* Brian Merrilees, intro. and commentary. Media Centre and Centre for Medieval Studies. Toronto: U of Toronto P, 1981. One color filmstrip.

An introduction to and summary of the *Rose* through selected miniatures. The French version runs 37 minutes, the English version 32 minutes.

791 *Le roman de la rose.* Bruno Roy, producer. Montreal: Audio-Visual Center, University of Montreal, 1980. One color videocassette.

Selected readings from the *Rose*, illustrated with miniatures from a fifteenth-century manuscript and accompanied by medieval music (30 minutes).

792 *The Romaunt of the Rose.* Hudson, Quebec: Golden Clarion Literary Services, 1962. One soundcassette.

The Robinson edition of the *Romaunt* read in Middle English by Paul Piehler (89 minutes).

793 Steuben Glass, inc. *The Romance of the Rose.* New York: Steuben Glass, 1977. Pp. 29 + ill.

A special commemorative edition of photographs of a unique five-petaled crystal rose "unfolding to expose a core of ruby pistils surrounded by diamond stamens--their green-yellow filaments set in yellow gold" (12). On the petals five scenes from the *Rose* are engraved: Oiseuse opening the gate (this petal swings aside), the dance in the garden, le Dieu d'Amour shooting the dreamer, l'Amant peering at his face in the fountain, and l'Amant kissing the rose. Includes brief excerpts from a manuscript in the Pierpont Morgan library.

794 Viollet-le-Duc, Eugène-Emmanuel. *Dictionnaire raisonné de l'architecture francaise, du XIe au XVIe siècle.* 10 vols. Paris: B. Bance (A. Morel from vol. 7), 1859-68. 3:122-28.

A discussion of the castle of Jalousie in the *Rose* by the eminent architectural historian, who argues that the castle that Guillaume de Lorris describes (ll. 3779-892) is the Louvre of Philippe Auguste. [The excavated foundations of this chateau can be seen today on the lower level of the Louvre museum].

INDEX

Numbers refer to entries in the bibliography. Authors of works annotated in the bibliography are indexed only when referred to by another author. Most proper names are included, as well as important topics.

Abelard, Peter, 304, 384
Abelard and Heloise (*See also* Jean de Meun, *Les épistres*), 93, 160, 489
"*Abstractum agens,*" 319
Adaptations (*See also* Van Aken), Dutch, 30, 45, 346, 347, 761, 762, 763
Adonis, 155, 179, 507
Aelred of Rievaulx, *De amicitia spirituali*, 201, 236, 241, 252
Alain Chartier, 345
Alain de Lille, 199, 202, 256, 323, 347, 358, 379, 414, 418, 443, 456, 489, 631, 748
   Anticlaudianus, 315, 421
   De planctu Naturae, 315, 436, 458; Genius in, 190, 224, 342, 407, 461, 544, 546, 576, 593, 633, 677, 741; Natura in, 225, 233, 298, 343, 345, 421, 452, 456, 461, 544, 633; Raison and, 544
Albertus Magnus, 401, 418
   De caelo et mundo, 526
Albigensian heresy, 272
Albumazar, *Introductorium in astronomian*, 293, 353, 380
Alchemy, 257, 389, 394, 395, 424, 446, 570, 701
Alphonse de Poitiers, 313
Altercatio Phyllidis et Florae, 436, 671
Amis and Amiloun, 697

Ampère, J.-J., 37, 326
"*Amplificatio,*" 274, 414
André le Chapelain, 141, 209, 334, 426, 440, 472, 522
Anelida, 641
Anticlericalism (*See also* Mendicant orders, Satire), 372, 384, 572, 653, 688
Apocalypse, 227, 228, 371
Apocalypse of Golias, 201, 228
Apollinaire, 376
Aristocracy, 219, 263, 300, 448
Aristotle, 167, 225, 309, 355, 360, 373, 401, 418, 452, 758
Armament (*See also* Arrows), 321, 771
Arnaut Daniel, 321, 725
Arnulf of Orleans, 341
Arrows, 202, 278, 318, 426, 466, 484, 642, 710
Art, *See* Personifications
Arthur (King), 317
Astrology, 286, 293, 331, 701
Attis, 280
Aucassin et Nicolette, 428
Augustine (Saint), 201, 202, 236, 241, 292, 309, 381, 401, 436, 473
Autobiography (genre), 558
Averroism, 221, 355, 396, 401, 524
Avicenna, 167

Badel, Pierre-Yves, 415, 653
Baïf, Jean Antoine de, 453
Bakhtine, Mikhail, 171
Bale, John, *Scriptorium illustrium majoris Britanniae catalogus*, 249
Bartholomaeus Anglicus, *De proprietatibus rerum*, 749
Batany, Jean, 413, 476
Baudelaire, Charles, *Les fleurs du mal*, 653
Baudoin de Condé, 308
Beatrice (in the *Divina commedia*), 678, 722
Bec, Pierre, 517
Beck, Friedrich, 770
Becker, Ph. A., 750
Bédier, Joseph, 605
Benedetto, Luigi Foscolo, 326
Benoît de Sainte-Maure, 735

Beowulf, 472
Bergson, Henri, 187
Bernard de Ventadour, 426
Bernard Silvestre, 156, 233, 323, 342, 343, 379, 407, 576
Bernois (Abbot), 370
Béroul, *Tristan*, 501
Berry, Duke of, 786
Bibliographies, 207, 212, 326, 376, 459, 476, 565, 721
Birds, 284, 363, 390, 409, 532, 549, 616, 651, 710, 777
Boccaccio, Giovanni, *Amorosa visione*, 767
    Decameron, 489, 569, 608
    Filocolo, 767
    Filostrato, 631, 774
Boethius, *De consolatione Philosophiae*, 199, 239, 241, 324, 358, 388, 414, 440, 443, 624, 692
    caged bird in, 549, 616
    Fortune in, 256
    imagery in, 442
    irony in, 436
    Jean de Meun's translation of, 86, 87, 92, 101-121, 499
    Raison and, 194, 480
Boiardo, Matteo Maria, 341
Bonaventure (Saint), 282, 748
Bonnet, Honoré, *L'apparition de Jean de Meung*, 453
Botticelli, Sandro, 376
Bouhours (Père), Dominiquez, 618
Bourdillon, F. W., 614
Bradley, Ritamary, 238
Brownlee, Kevin, 299

Canacee, 641
Cancionero de Baena, 692
Carbuncle, 394, 724
"Carmen de Rosa" (poem), 426, 436
Carmina burana, 251
Carte de Tendre, 320
Carthage, 236, 415
Castiglione, Baldissare, *Book of the Courtier*, 775
Castilian literature, 692, 727
Castle of Jalousie, 191, 334, 402, 534, 545, 589, 726, 791

Celibacy, 26
Céline, Louis-Ferdinand, 408
Cercamon, 517
Chalcidius, 225
Champier, Symphorion, 748
Charlemagne, 399
Charles V of France, 9
Charles VI of France, 687
Charles d'Anjou, 222
Charles d'Orléans, 442
Châtelaine de Vergy, 68, 751
Chaucer, Geoffrey (*See also* Romaunt of the Rose), 5, 204, 292, 375, 473, 612, 619, 621, 622, 625, 667, 678, 702, 754, 782; bibliographies of, 565, 708, 714; comic vision of, 688; French influence on, 587, 709, 776; Heidegger and, 493; language in, 646; Macrobius and, 435; roses in, 681; Shakespeare and, 713
   Boèce, 8-13
   Book of the Duchess, 601, 607, 622, 627, 678, 742, 777
   Canterbury Tales, 544, 545, 587, 595, 616, 669, 678, 709, 719; General Prologue, 587, 607, 675; Franklin, 588, 671, 703; Knight, 589, 771; Manciple, 501, 779, 780; Merchant, 472, 568, 598, 617, 671; Monk, 569, 587, 665; Pardoner, 587, 588, 706; Parson, 669, 779; Physician, 587, 588, 737; Prioress, 626, 729, 731; Squire, 587, 628, 694; Wife of Bath, 199, 587, 699, 718, 739, 740
   Complaint of Mars, 610
   House of Fame, 601, 607, 608, 627, 681, 747, 767
   Legend of Good Women, 566, 601, 607, 680
   Parliament of Fowls, 456, 601, 607, 627, 678
   Troilus and Criseyde, 501, 548, 601, 622, 631, 678, 709, 767, 774, 778
Cherniss, Michael, 476
Chess, 240, 637
Chrétien de Troyes, 237, 246, 270, 345, 408, 469, 531, 539, 562
   Le chevalier au lion (Yvain), 464, 517
   Le chevalier de la charette (Lancelot), 159, 176, 465
   Cligés, 472
   Le conte du graal (Perceval), 248, 465, 517
Christ, 152, 663
Christine de Pizan (*See also* Querelle de la Rose), 210, 243, 566, 574, 647, 649, 650, 653, 662, 672, 696, 723, 733, 734, 736, 752, 775
   La cité des dames, 647, 740

Le dit de la rose, 590
L'épistre Othéa, 740
L'épistre au Dieu d'Amours, 575, 590, 629, 673
Les épistres sur le débat, 579, 590, 770
Lavision-Christine, 662
Le livre des fais d'armes et de chevalerie, 128, 133
La mutacion de fortune, 662
Cicero, 201, 236, 241, 252, 324, 343, 470, 624
Claudian, *Second Panegyric on the Consulship of Stilicho*, 342
Cleanness, 765
Clef d'amours, 731
Clothes, 186, 198, 217, 357, 410, 413, 442, 490, 746
Col, Gontier (*See also* Querelle de la Rose), 94, 579, 606, 687, 698
Col, Pierre (*See also* Querelle de la Rose), 573, 579, 606, 647, 698, 770
Colletet, Guillaume, 453
Colonna, Francesco, *Le songe de Poliphile*, 726
Compagnon, Antoine, 302
Concordances, 46, 50, 51
Condemnations of 1270 and 1277 (*See also* Tempier), 524, 630
Confessions (literary), 329, 742
Conradin Hohenstaufen, 222
Contini, Gianfranco, 266, 477, 624, 725, 734
Cour amoureuse, *See* Charles VI
Courcelle, Pierre, 104
Court of Love, 710
Courtès, Joseph, 504
Coville, Alfred, 604
Croce, Benedetto, *Estetica*, 581
Croesus, 312, 665
Croissandeau, Jules, *See* Marteau, Pierre
Crystal(s) (*See also* Fountain of Narcissus), 247, 268, 297, 301, 337, 348, 389, 437, 472, 481, 485, 523, 724
Cupid, 225, 315, 458, 482, 490, 713
Curtius, Ernst Robert, 521

Dahlberg, Charles, 435, 476
Dante Alighieri, 207, 493, 545, 582, 605, 608, 624, 645, 724, 756, 760, 764, 767
  Convivio, 756
  Divina commedia, 388, 662, 678, 722, 725, 733, 734, 764

Vita nuova, 315, 725
D'Aubigné, Agrippa, 442
De Collerye, Roger, *Sermon pour une nopce*, 718
Decorum (literary), 290
Deguilleville, Guillaume de, *Pèlerinage de vie humaine*, 572, 630, 660, 781
Demeter, 271
Derrida, Jacques, 493, 503
Deschamps, Eustache, 341, 572, 587, 679
Desprez, Nicolas, 60, 61
Detto d'amore, 583, 707, 725
Deucalion and Pyrrha, 659
Diderot, Denis, 360, 719
Dido, 641
Diego de Valencia, 692
Dit (genre), 270, 333, 484, 592, 777
Dit des quatre sièges, 553
Djabar al Koufi, *See* Geber
Dominicans, *See* Mendicant orders
Dreams (*See also* Macrobius), 161, 167, 306, 333, 350, 378, 416, 500, 555, 572, 651, 688
Dream of Scipio (*See also* Macrobius), 306
Dufournet, Jean, 415
Dunbar, William, *The Goldyn Targe*, 501
Durante, *Il Fiore*, 477, 567, 581, 582, 583, 605, 613, 645, 725, 734, 735, 757, 764, 767

Echecs amoureux, 637
Echecs d'amour, 572
Echo, 281, 341, 506
Eden, *See* Garden imagery
Elegiac comedy, 163
Ellis, F. S., 622
Emerson, Oliver F., 765
Enlightenment, the, 290, 360, 372, 427
Epicurus, 550, 703, 739
Epithalamium (genre), 315, 482
Ethelred of Rievaulx, *See* Aelred of Rievaulx
Eustathius Macrembolites, *Hysmeme and Hysmenias*, 541

Fableau du Dieu d'Amours, 358
Fabliaux, 163, 171, 425, 468, 502
Fansler, Dean, 747
Faral, Edmond, 326
Fatrasie (genre), 245
Fauchet, Claude, 453, 618
Fauvel, Roman de, 611, 623
Ferrante, Joan, 689
Filmstrip (of *Rose*), 789, 790
Flaubert, Gustave, *Madame Bovary*, 653
Fleming, John, 24, 184, 221, 226, 250, 326, 415, 437, 470, 509, 520, 538, 568, 729, 757
Floris et Lyriope, 769
Fontaine d'amour, *See* Fountain of Narcissus
Fortune (deity), 240, 381, 423, 514, 520, 589, 722, 745
    Wheel of, 256, 514, 637
Fountain of Narcissus (*See also* Crystal[s], Narcissus), 15, 159, 217, 264, 280, 348, 369, 408, 485, 510
    alchemy and, 389
    Byzantine source, 541
    Dante and, 724
    deception and, 238
    love and, 247, 297, 507
    Milton and, 743
    moral of, 209, 438
    Ovid and, 506
    poetic invention and, 161, 248, 301
    symbolism of, 282, 284, 312, 328, 472, 481, 523, 562
Frame of reference (*See also* Dreams), 311, 534, 548, 551, 556, 742, 778
Françon, Marcel, 326
Frappier, Jean, 212, 297, 326, 348
Freeman, Michèle, 336
Free will, 154, 379, 401, 669, 685, 758
Frescobaldi, Dino, 581
Freud, Sigmund, 269
Friedman, Lionel B., 188
Friendship, 236, 241, 697, 766
Froissart, Jean, 308, 335, 341, 587

Garden imagery (*See also* Deduit under Personifications; Garden of
  Deduit), 161, 189, 192, 261, 390, 408, 409, 440, 472, 487, 494,
  496, 512, 518, 521, 547, 671, 715, 726
  Garden of Eden, 238, 312, 417, 672, 743
  Garden of Deduit (*See also* Garden imagery), 35, 159, 246, 261, 363,
    409, 413, 416, 430, 492, 545
  André le Chapelain and, 209
  Genius's critique of, 178, 193, 298, 478, 494
  Songe de Poliphile and, 726
  voyeurism in, 501

Gautier d'Arras, *Eracle*, 345, 541, 542
Gautier de Coinci, *Miracles de Notre-Dame*, 363
Geber (Djabar al Koufi), 257
Genette, Gérard, 302
German literature, medieval, 349, 639
Gerson, Jean (*See also* Querelle de la Rose), 243, 406, 522, 571, 604,
  647, 653, 683, 715, 770
Girart de Biaulieu, 91
God of Love, *See* Dieu d'Amour under Personifications
Godefroy de Lagny, 176
Gohory, Jacques, 570
Gold, 490
Golden Age, 166, 260, 261, 295, 325, 381, 396, 425, 433, 494, 521, 720
Golden Chain, 379
Golden Legend, 26
Goldin, Frederick, 238
Goliardism, 398, 425, 426, 428, 432
Gorce, M.-M., 207, 326, 685
Gottfried von Strassburg, *Tristan*, 639, 735
Gower, John, *Confessio Amantis*, 224, 281, 342, 375, 388, 407, 576, 593,
  609, 741
"*Gradus amoris,*" 199, 251, 474, 564, 667, 682
Grandes Chroniques de France, 208
Greimas, A. J., 158, 504, 560
Gui de Mori, 62, 572, 654, 655, 666, 682, 769
Guillaume de Lorris, identification of, 213, 272, 313, 314, 370
Guillaume de Palerme, 541
Guillaume de Saint-Amour, *De periculis...*, 164, 180, 220, 373, 414
Guillaume IX d'Aquitaine, 517

Guillaume Rebrachien, 213
Guillon, Félix, 313, 314
Gunn, Alan M. F., 140, 146, 207, 221, 238, 326, 359, 387, 414, 492, 498
Guy Fabi, 213

Hatzfeld, Helmut, 326
Hell, 258
Heloise (*See also* Abelard and Heloise), 160
Henry of Castile, 542
Henry of Septimello, *Elegia*, 240
Hermaphroditus, 280
Hermas, *Pasteur*, 371
Hermes Trismegistus, 749
Hicks, Eric, 476, 770
Hinckley, H. B., 694
Hoccleve, Thomas, *Letter of Cupid*, 249, 629
Homosexuality (*See also* Sexuality), 280, 425
Horace, 251
Houel, Nicolas, *Traité de la charité chrestienne*, 788
Hugo, Victor, 442, 787
Huizinga, Johan, *The Waning of the Middle Ages*, 347
Hult, David F., 238, 299, 415, 515
Hundred Years' War, 680
Huon de Mery, *Tournoiement Antecrist*, 315, 316, 323, 363, 556
Huot, Paul, 37
Hypnerotomachia Poliphili, 726
Hypsipyle, 641

Iconography, study of, 191, 250, 350, 391, 469, 473, 512
Image du monde, 345
Imperial, Francisco, *Decir de la siete virtudes*, 692, 727
Intelligenza, 767
Ipomedon, 188
Italy, 222, 240

"Le jaloux qui bat sa femme" (play), 586, 700, 784
Jarry, Louis, 272
Jauss, Hans Robert, 206, 326, 348
Jean de Condé, 308
Jean de Hauville, *Architrenius*, 440

Jean de Meun, life of, 37, 222, 249, 267, 273, 318, 354, 424, 453, 455, 499, 519; alchemical works, 2, 3, 4, 6, 16
  L'art de chevalerie, editions, 88, 89; studies of, 92, 97, 118, 122-133
  Codicile, 2, 4, 732, 745
  Consolation de Philosophie, editions, 86, 87; studies of, 92, 93, 101-121, 714
  Les épîtres d'Abélard et Héloïse, editions, 78-85; studies of, 92-100
  Testament (*See also* Villon), editions, 2, 4, 90, 91; studies of, 93, 112, 134, 135, 164, 678, 684, 732, 745
Jean de Montreuil (*See also* Querelle de la Rose), 243, 571, 604, 607, 647, 649, 650, 752
Jean de Vignay, 122, 123, 128
Jean Perréal, 139
Jean Priorat, 89
Jean Pucelle, 385
Jean Renart, *Guillaume de Dole (Le roman de la rose)*, 216
Jean Robertet, 345
Jehan du Pré, 44
Jerome, "Epistle to Eustochium," 186
Joachim de Fiore, *Introduction à l'Evangile éternel*, 164, 180
Johannes Scotus Eriugena, 347
John of Garland, 341
John of Salisbury, *Metalogicon*, 248
  Policraticus, 470, 611
Jung, Carl, 189, 440
Jung, Marc-René, 654
Jupiter (deity), 254, 331, 463, 494
Juvenal, 166

Knuvelder, G. P. M., 339
Köhler, Erich, 297, 536
Kolve, V. A., 589
Kuhn, Alfred, 385, 391

Lactantius, 241
La Fontaine, Jean de, 550
Lancelot in prose, 64, 159, 446
Langlois, Ernest, 13, 14, 15, 147, 175, 207, 239, 277, 326, 354, 366, 383, 385, 445, 459, 460, 499, 519, 522, 526, 542, 552, 595, 632, 654, 655, 753

Language (*See also* Raison under Personifications), 124, 229, 285, 309, 351, 410, 444, 457, 458, 493, 504, 513, 516, 559
    adverbs, 646
    diminutives, 696
    metaphors, 457, 471
    obscenity, 304, 448, 456, 468, 719
    of manuscripts, 8, 277
    pronouns, 351, 383
    rhymes, 445
    syntax, 259
    vocabulary, 294, 517
Lanson, Gustave, 326, 396
Lantin de Damerey, 267
Latin literature (*See also* individual authors, works), 239, 322, 337, 343, 345, 358, 423, 436, 547
Latini, Brunetto, *Il tesoretto*, 164, 315, 581, 767
Laurent de Premierfait, 734
Leah (Old Testament), 678
Lecoy, Félix, 6, 7, 326
Lefèvre, Jean, *La vieille*, 718
Le Franc, Abel, 748
Le Franc, Martin, *Champion des dames*, 633, 677
Lejeune, Rita, 140, 272, 393
Lemaire des Belges, Jean, *Concorde des deux langages*, 677
    "Temple de Vénus," 337, 461, 633, 734
Lenglet Dufresnoy, 3, 4, 5, 267
Lewis, C. S., 238, 244, 297, 326, 508, 536, 689, 706
Libro de buen amor, 548, 692, 758, 778
Light imagery, 246
Livre de Boece de Consolacion, 106, 108
Livy, *See* Titus Livius
"*Locus amoenus*," *See* Garden imagery
Louis, René, 35
Lounsbury, T. R., 674
Louvre Museum, 794
Lovejoy, A. O., *Great Chain of Being*, 274
Lucretia, 160
Lydgate, John, *Disguising at London*, 423
Lyric poetry, 5, 159, 308, 319, 336, 369, 393, 449, 474, 517, 525, 529, 547, 558, 562

"Trobar clus," 245, 707

Machaut, Guillaume de, 188, 308, 335, 424, 484, 487, 529, 572, 587, 591, 592, 598, 660, 675, 717, 776
Macrobius, 167, 203, 225, 306, 350, 379, 435, 439, 513, 556
Mallarmé, Stéphane, 159, 442
Manfred Hohenstaufen, 222
Manuscripts, descriptions of, 8, 9, 43, 52-59, 62, 63, 66-75, 77, 308, 402, 422, 660
    rubrics in, 308, 656, 661
    miniatures, 64, 174, 186, 226, 242, 243, 308, 350, 352, 385, 391, 404, 661, 769, 788
    marginalia, 658, 660, 663, 693
Marcabru, 517
Marguerite de Navarre, 748
Marguerite (Saint), 663
Marie d'Orléans, 701
Marot, Clément, *Le roman de la rose* (adaptation attributed to), 36, 207, 307, 422, 580, 586, 594, 620, 633, 634, 642, 686, 711, 750; preface to, 2, 5, 693, 750, 772, 773
    Temple de Cupido, 677
Mars (deity) (*See also* Venus, Vulcan), 296, 340, 463, 610, 691
Marsyas (satyr), 608
Marteau, Pierre, 26, 622
Martianus Capella, 323
Massieu, Guillaume, 267
Matelda (in the *Divina commedia*), 678
Matthew of Vendome, *Ars versificatoria*, 494, 521
Medea, 641
Medusa, 659
Méla, Charles 570
Memory technique, 532, 556
Mena, Juan de, 727
Mendicant orders, 180, 211, 220, 227, 365, 387, 447, 455, 467, 684
Méon, Dominique Martin, 2-5, 622, 682
Mersand, Joseph, 670
Metamorphosis Goliae, 436
Michel, Francisque, 11, 19, 622
Michel, Guillaume, 773
Midas, 739

Milan, Paul B., 381
Milton, John, 341, 743, 744
Mirrors (*See also* Fountain of Narcissus, Oiseuse under Personifications, Optics), 143, 156, 214, 238, 247, 250, 504, 523, 534, 568, 617, 691
Misogyny (*See also* Women), 160, 163, 187, 198, 234, 253, 307, 361, 362, 372, 376, 384, 400, 411, 590, 653, 673, 687, 740, 752, 775
Molière, Jean-Baptiste Poquelin, 361, 550
  Tartuffe, 307, 372, 406
Molinet, Jean, 307, 422, 466, 527, 614, 633, 635, 693
Montaigne, Michel de, 361, 550, 633
Montesquieu, Baron de, 360, 488
Moon, John, 249
Moon (heavenly body), 722, 734
Morris, William, 26
Müller, F. W., 154, 326, 396, 524
Musical score (of *Rose*), 785
Mysticism, 282, 328, 363, 371, 389, 394, 446, 465, 466, 537, 715

Narcissus (*See also* Fountain of Narcissus), 155, 165, 247, 264, 274, 301, 305, 336, 341, 348, 439, 449, 473, 491, 523, 528, 531, 536, 657, 659
  contrast with Pygmalion, 165, 214, 295, 308, 449
  Dante and, 724, 769
  Echo and, 281
  Gui de Mori and, 666
  narcissism and, 269, 449, 644
  Ovid and, 179, 248, 280, 341, 386, 438, 506, 507, 536
  Sigrid Undset's novels and, 644
Narcisus (lay), 264, 281, 536
Naturalism, 7, 34, 326, 355, 362, 418, 489, 599, 605, 633, 757
Navarre (country), 191
Neoplatonism, 401, 452
New Criticism, 627
Nicole de Margival, 572
Norman soldiers, 206
Novati, Francesco, 605
Nykrog, Per, 415

Obscenity, *See* Language, Raison under Personifications

Odor, 441
Old Age, 392, 471
Old Testament, 480, 678
    Book of Proverbs, 729
Olson, Paul, 598
Optics, 150, 217, 223, 498
Orpheus, 179, 507
Ott, Karl August, 157, 398
Ovid (*See also* Fountain of Narcissus, Narcissus, Pygmalion), 166, 239, 266, 280, 351, 358, 368, 414, 436, 442, 460, 659, 679, 729; Golden Age in, 260, 521
    Amores, 185, 460
    Ars amatoria, 141, 142, 146, 172, 340, 460, 608, 610
    Metamorphoses, 179, 185, 198, 205, 281, 341, 460, 507
    Remedia amoris, 143, 460, 470
Ovide moralisé, 264, 341, 610

Pallas, 637
Pamphilus, 548, 778
Paré, Gérard Marie, 326, 379, 524, 685
Paris, Gaston, 207, 326, 354
Paris, Paulin, 37, 354
Paris (city), 299, 416, 637
Paris, University of, 91, 180, 220, 227, 265, 355, 373, 401, 418, 447, 637, 683
Park of the Lamb [Park of the Good Shepherd] (*See also* Genius under Personifications), 193, 245, 261, 268, 298, 318, 394, 512, 726
Pasquier, Etienne, 36, 207, 580, 618, 750
Pastourelle (genre), 188, 558, 672
Payen, Jean-Charles, 398
Pearl, 388, 577
Perlesvaus, 464
Personification (general), 155, 206, 244, 288, 301, 311, 403, 431
Personifications in *Rose*, 15, 35
    l'Amant, 155, 234, 297, 302, 324, 328, 405, 410, 433, 484, 513, 520, 545, 627, 718, 762, 790; alchemy and, 389; Apocalypse and, 227; courtly love and, 334, 373, 474, 492; Croesus and, 312; Danger and, 577; ekphrasis and, 404; Faux Semblant and, 227, 543; homosexuality and, 280; immorality of, 190, 200, 201, 202, 233,

243, 284, 509; lament of, 176, 194; Narcissus and, 247, 248, 264, 280, 336, 523; procreation and, 295; Raison and, 236, 241, 304, 309, 415, 458, 466, 480

l'Ami, 158, 166, 184, 351, 411, 422, 436, 466, 543; Charles Sorel and, 585; Chaucer's works and, 703, 739, 778; the *Fiore* and, 757; Golden Age and, 260, 325, 396; humor in, 187; misogyny and, 253, 502

Art, 179, 218, 523

Bel Accueil, 162, 184, 206, 278, 328, 508, 534, 543, 554, 564, 634, 697, 761

Chasteté, 158, 439

Courtoisie, 328, 375, 410

Danger, 175, 200, 255, 278, 328, 335, 433, 462, 517, 545, 577

Deduit, 335, 375, 409; companions of, 158, 472; coat of arms, 272; Chaucer and, 602, 617; robe of, 494

Dieu d'Amour, 170, 191, 201, 221, 268, 276, 368, 375, 410, 482, 485, 520, 710, 790; cupidity and, 202, 509; courtly love and, 190, 297, 315, 334; Christine de Pizan and, 566; divine love and, 328, 466; Faux Semblant and, 467, 591; the *Fiore* and, 757; Genius and, 224; lecture on love, 388, 413, 513, 534, 666; Male Bouche and, 332; midpoint speech of, 216, 217, 268, 331, 510, 675; Pandarus and, 778; Raison and, 378; Satan and, 472; sleeves and, 186

Doux Regard, 278

Faux Semblant, 156, 180, 332, 351, 360, 387, 406, 486, 504, 505, 527, 543, 591, 702; Apocalypse and, 222; arguments of, 184, 201, 433; Chaucer and, 706; the *Fiore* and, 757; *Renart le Contrefait* and, 623; *Roman de Fauvel* and, 611, 623; satire and, 372, 467, 688, 709; Vauquelin de la Fresnaie and, 634

Franchise, 184, 697

Genius (*See also* Alain de Lille), 145, 245, 274, 307, 315, 318, 342, 367, 407, 411, 461, 527, 546, 593, 676, 677; carbuncle and, 268, 394; critique of first part, 178, 193, 298, 478, 494; Golden Age and, 260, 331, 381, 396; goliardism of, 428; Gower and, 576, 741; irony in, 190, 201, 436, 472; language and, 458; misogyny and, 751; parody and, 152, 171, 452; procreation and, 26, 184, 224, 225, 264, 308, 351, 425, 451, 502, 516, 544, 572, 631, 659, 758; Renaissance and, 633

Jalousie (*See also* Castle of), 35, 170, 177, 278, 334, 335, 369, 508, 525

Jealous Husband, 160, 166, 171, 253, 436, 490, 585, 586, 672, 699, 702,

709
Leesse, 602
Male Bouche, 171, 177, 328, 332, 486, 543
Nature (*See also* Alain de Lille), 69, 168, 178, 184, 219, 225, 274, 275, 276, 298, 307, 315, 337, 343, 344, 345, 361, 411, 418, 419, 421, 422, 452, 461, 489, 507, 514, 527, 544, 562, 616; Art and, 179, 218, 523; Dante and, 756; dreams and, 435; Genius and, 224, 576, 741; God and, 264, 394; Golden Chain and, 379; irony and, 436; optics and, 217, 223, 340, 617, 691; Raison and, 478, 479; Saturn and, 254, 381; sexuality and, 372, 425, 429, 433, 502; la Vieille and, 718
Oiseuse, 143, 157, 237, 250, 335, 349, 363, 376, 437, 466, 469, 470, 472, 473, 478, 488, 517, 678, 790
Pitié, 184, 783
Raison, 149, 234, 240, 241, 405, 411, 418, 480, 510, 513, 663; as Jean's spokesperson, 184, 201, 241, 378, 500, 509, 516; Boethius and, 194; Chaucer and, 588, 597; Croesus and, 312; Dante and, 624, 756; the *Fiore* and, 757; Fortune and, 423; God and, 201, 243, 473, 729; Golden Age and, 260, 331, 381, 396; humor and, 187, 372; irony and, 436; Nature and, 225, 233, 276, 478, 544; on friendship, 236, 252, 697; on language, 215, 304, 309, 324, 444, 448, 456, 458, 468, 471, 719; sexuality and 433, 489
Rose, 318, 411, 528, 531, 613, 718; ambiguity of, 335, 410; identification of, 213; marital status of, 508; Middle Dutch versions, 761; psychology of, 234, 426, 462, 501; sources of, 426, 541; Vauquelin de la Fresnaie and, 634
Richesse, 416, 520
Venus (*See also* Mars, Vulcan), 315, 331, 334, 458, 482, 710; arrow of, 26, 191, 659; Genius and, 152, 224, 741; in *Tournoiement Antecrist* 317; Mars and, 296, 340, 463, 610, 691; mirror of, 250; Nature and, 225; sexuality and, 295, 425, 433, 439; torch of, 143 La Vieille, 162, 206, 411, 420, 543, 585, 663, 702; arguments of, 184, 276, 436, 520, 703, 729; characterization of, 163, 709; the *Fiore* and, 757; free love and, 424, 433, 549, 616; Golden Age and, 260, 396; humor and, 171, 187, 688; Mars and Venus and, 296, 610; misogyny and, 253 Ovid and, 172; René d'Anjou and, 783; Wife of Bath and, 699, 718, 739
Pervigilium Veneris, 339
Petrarch, Francesco, 733
Secretum, 241

Trionfi, 402, 767
Philippe Auguste (king), 213, 794
Philippe le Bel (king), 273, 372
Philippe le Hardi (duke), 786
Phoenix (myth), 282, 379
Phyllis, 641
Pierre d'Ailly, *Le jardin amoureux de l'âme dévote*, 265, 571, 715
Pierre de Blois, 202
Pierre Vidal, 272
Piers Plowman, 716
Plato, 225, 233, 254, 343, 360, 397, 426, 431, 452, 534, 548, 778
Plenitude, philosophy of, 189, 221, 274
Pliny the Elder, 343
Plotinus, 225
Poirion, Daniel, 309, 570
Portraits (on wall of garden), 335, 363, 391, 392, 404, 437, 466, 510, 532, 541, 657
Potansky, Peter, 652
Provençal poetry, *See* Lyric poetry
Proverbial expressions, 289, 364, 399, 622, 658, 747
Prudentius, *Psychomachia*, 315, 316, 318, 319, 323, 391, 403, 560
Ptolemy, *Almagest*, 632
Pygmalion, 155, 191, 198, 214, 217, 274, 324, 358, 400, 430, 473, 490, 562, 659
    contrasted with Narcissus, 165, 295, 308, 341, 449, 523
    humor and, 171
    Ovid and, 179, 185, 198, 205, 507
    sexuality and, 295, 463
Pyramus and Thisbé, 657
Querelle de la Rose, 7, 168, 210, 212, 267, 300, 304, 422, 489, 497, 571-575, 579, 604, 606, 629, 630, 636, 647-650, 652, 653, 673, 683, 687, 696, 697, 704, 715, 723, 728, 740, 752, 770, 775
Queste del saint graal, 246, 516, 584
"Quinque lineae," See "Gradus amoris"
Quinze joyes de mariage, 502

Rabelais, François, 36, 189, 361, 520, 522, 550, 578, 640, 643, 755; definition of God, 748, 749
    Gargantua, 685
    Pantagruel, 640, 685

Le tiers livre, 749
Rachel (Old Testament), 678
Rand, E. K., 172
Raoul de Houdenc, *Le songe d'enfer*, 316, 317
Recordings (of *Rose*), 789
Renard tales, 516
    Couronnement de Renart, 183, 467
    Renart le Bestourné, 467
    Renart le Contrefait, 623
    Renart le Nouvel, 183
Renaut de Louhans, 755
Renclus de Moiliens, *Roman de Miserere*, 317
René d'Anjou, *Livre du cuer d'amours espris*, 335, 584, 783
    Livre des tournois, 788
Ribard, Jacques, 446
Ribera, Ruy Pez de, 727
Richards, Earl Jeffrey, 237
Robert d'Artois, 164
Robert Grosseteste, *Château d'amour*, 223, 317
Robertson, D. W., 143, 203, 250, 284, 290, 297, 312, 417, 469, 510, 544, 573, 630, 689, 743, 757
Romance (genre), 270, 311, 333, 403
Roman de la poire, See Tibaut
Roman de la rose, anonymous conclusion, 13
    audience, 181
    date of second part, 11, 365, 542
    differences between parts, 43, 162, 278, 294, 347, 358, 359, 361, 362, 367, 375, 417, 420, 509, 515, 522, 552, 562, 563, 613, 650, 777
    early editions, 2, 44, 49, 53, 60, 61
    methods of composition, 166
    narrative structure, 140, 159, 274, 325, 369, 382, 393, 411, 414, 451, 516, 663; as *Bildungsroman*, 330; quest, 159, 263, 434, 464, 465, 562
    prologue, 306, 529, 530, 531
    unfinished (first part), 140, 305, 308, 474, 483, 511
Romaunt of the Rose, 11, 15, 186, 377, 600, 615, 622, 638, 664, 674, 680, 689, 712, 721, 746, 753
    Astrophel and Stella and, 768
    Fragment A, 15, 17, 18, 20, 357, 615, 670, 771
    Fragment B, 628
    Recording of, 792

Thynne edition, 17, 19, 20
Ronsard, Pierre de, 442, 564, 599, 634, 635, 642
Rose *(See also* Personifications)
   history of, 322, 596
   symbolism of, 15, 33, 271, 274, 284, 322, 323, 328, 339, 346, 363, 376, 492, 523, 562, 596
Rousseau, Jean-Jacques, 360, 719, 720
Rustico di Filippo, 583
Rutebeuf, 183, 211, 220, 447

Santillana, Marquis of, 727
Satan, 472
Satire, 372, 377, 392, 515, 516, 568, 684, 685
Saturn (deity), 254, 295, 304, 331, 381, 463, 701
Scève, Maurice, 633
Scholasticism, 154, 265, 294, 401, 418, 419, 524, 563, 648
School of Chartres, 315, 319, 375, 452, 480, 489
Scudéry, Mlle de, 618
Sébillet, Thomas, 711
Seneca, 223, 343, 381, 470
Sept sages de Rome, 59
Sermon joyeux des foulx, 705
Servius, 440
Sexuality *(See also* Homosexuality), 154, 239, 241, 243, 250, 260, 284, 295, 296, 334, 346, 367, 376, 411, 425, 426, 427, 432, 433, 449, 450, 456, 457, 458, 463, 482, 489, 501, 502, 544 546, 548, 554, 572, 609, 640, 650, 718, 778
Shakespeare, William, 199, 239, 321, 713, 765
Sidney, Sir Philip, *Astrophel and Stella*, 768
Simond de Freine, 345
Sir Gawain and the Green Knight, 695
Skeat, W. W., 17, 357
Smith, Merete, 670
Songe du vieil pèlerin, 148
Sorel, Charles, *L'histoire comique de Francion*, 585, 618
Speech act theory, 290
Spenser, Edmund, *The Faerie Queene*, 341, 375, 458, 593, 676
Starobinski, Jean, 134
Statius, *Thebaid*, 440
Steuben Glass, Inc., 790

Strubel, Armand, 414
Structuralism, 533, 558, 627
Sutherland, Ronald, 670

Tapestries, 402, 786
Tempier (Bishop) (*See also* Condemnations of 1270 and 1277), 199, 378
Ten Brink, Bernhard, 600
Theophrastus, 698
Thévet, André, 2, 4, 37, 453
Thibaut de Champagne, 446, 517
Thomas, Antoine, 604
Thomas Aquinas (Saint), 91, 381, 401, 418, 540
Tibaut, *Roman de la poire*, 542, 657
Tibullus, 376
Tintoretto, 691
Titus Livius (Livy), 160, 588, 737
Tory, Geoffroy, 711
Translations, Dutch, *(See also* Adaptations, Van Aken)
    German, 27, 28, 33, 39
    Italian, 22, 25
    Japanese, 42
    Spanish, 21, 40
Troubadours, *See* Lyric poetry
Trouvères, *See* Lyric poetry
Tyrwhitt, Thomas, 11

Ugliness, 235
Undset, Sigrid, 644
Utley, F. L., 689

Valerius, 166
Van Aken, Heinric, 30, 45, 74, 763
Vauquelin de la Fresnaie, 634
Vegetius (*See also* Jean de Meun), 133
Vendeur de livres (farce), 686, 700
Videocassette (of *Rose*), 791
Villon, François, 36, 208, 620, 684, 701, 711, 732, 745, 755
Vincent de Beauvais, 59, 748
Vinge, Louise, 438

Virgil, *Aeneid*, 199, 239, 241, 260, 351, 376, 404, 631
Virgin Mary, 152, 265, 363
Virginia and Virginius, 588, 737
Voltaire, François Marie Arouet de, 189, 198, 361, 421, 730
Von Hoffmannsthal, Hugo, "Lucidor," 554
Vulcan (*see also* Mars, Venus), 296, 340, 544, 610, 691

Walton, John, 116
Ward, Charles Frederick, 683
Watriquet de Couvin, 556
Weinrich, Harald, 302
Whiting, B. J., 695
William of Aragon, 104, 108
Women (*See also* Misogyny), 273, 502, 503, 572, 672, 673
  in Chaucer, 566, 641
Wycliffite Bible, 102